D1482770

PROVENCE AND POUND

❀❀❀❀❀❀❀❀❀❀

PROVENCE AND POUND

✿✿✿✿✿✿✿✿✿

Peter Makin

UNIVERSITY OF CALIFORNIA PRESS
Berkeley   Los Angeles   London

University of California Press
Berkeley and Los Angeles, California

University of California Press, Ltd.
London, England

Copyright © 1978 by The Regents of the University of California
ISBN: 0-520-03488
Library of Congress Catalog Card Number: 77-76186

Printed in the United States of America

To Stella

Ben com' aos que van per mar
a estrela guia

—Alfonso X el Sabio

CONTENTS

✤✤✤✤✤✤✤✤✤

ACKNOWLEDGEMENTS

Eric Mottram, Reader in American Literature at King's College, London, first inspired this book. He gave me the confidence to think I could do it, and challenged me on with his rigorous demands for connections between scholarship and human culture in general. Mary Hackett, formerly Reader in Romance Philology at King's College, London, set standards of linguistic competence, and did a great deal of self-sacrificing work in helping me try to live up to them. Hugh Kenner, Professor of English at Johns Hopkins University, read the book at various later stages, and pointed unerringly to the excrescences that must be cut—though I am afraid that I may since have allowed new redundancies to grow. I also owe him a considerable debt for support at critical points. David L. Mansell's formidable range of culture and expertise gave me access to many sources I would not otherwise have found. Bill Scobie many years ago, in my personal Wabash, stimulated my juvenile interest in the arts and in Provençal. I owe a longer-term intellectual debt to my father. To my mother I owe my ambitions.

This book also owes its existence to three people who gave me material help when I needed it. Barney Broadbent employed me when I had no academic means of support; I look back to Holland Park Avenue with nostalgia. Robert Walshaw let my wife and me live and work in his beautiful Collow Abbey. I owe my stay in Paris to the quiet generosity of the late Dick Cornwallis.

My wife gave me whatever sensitivity and understanding the book contains.

The excerpt from *Briggflatts* by Basil Bunting, copyright © 1968, 1970, 1978 by Basil Bunting, is reprinted by permission of the author and Oxford University Press as publishers of the revised edition (1978) of his *Collected Poems*.

Ezra Pound's copyrights have been assigned. Except where other names are given all copyrights are in the name of the Trustees of the Ezra Pound Literary Property Trust. For reasons of convenience this

INTERVIEW WITH EDITH HAMILTON, quoted in Eustace Mullins, *This Difficult Individual, Ezra Pound,* New York, 1961. — Copyright by TTEPLPT. All Rights Reserved.

'PREFACE: *DISCRETE SERIES* BY GEORGE OPPEN', in George Oppen, *Discrete Series,* New York, 1934, reprinted in *Stony Brook,* 3-4 (1969). — Copyright 1934; © 1969 by TTEPLPT. All Rights Reserved.

'ON "NEAR PERIGORD"', in *Poetry,* VII.3 (Dec. 1915). — Copyright 1915 by TTEPLPT. All Rights Reserved.

'HOW I BEGAN', in *T. P.'s Weekly,* XXI.552 (6 June 1913). — Copyright 1913; © 1965 by TTEPLPT. All Rights Reserved.

'VORTEX. POUND', in *Blast,* I (20 June 1914). — Copyright 1914 by TTEPLPT. All Rights Reserved.

'POSTSCRIPT', in Remy de Gourmont, *The Natural Philosophy of Love,* Ezra Pound, trans., London, 1957. — Copyright 1922; © 1957 by TTEPLPT. All Rights Reserved.

INTERVIEW, in Kay Dick, ed., *Writers at Work: The Paris Review Interviews,* Harmondsworth, Middx., 1972. — Copyright © 1972 by TTEPLPT. All Rights Reserved.

'INTERESTING FRENCH PUBLICATIONS', in *Philadelphia Book News Monthly,* XXV.1 (Sept. 1906). — Copyright 1906 by TTEPLPT. All Rights Reserved.

LETTER TO PATRICIA HUTCHINS in Patricia Hutchins, *Ezra Pound's Kensington: An Exploration, 1885-1913,* London, 1965. — Copyright © 1965 by TTEPLPT. All Rights Reserved.

'MEDIAEVAL MUSIC AND YVES TINAYRE', in *The Listener,* XVI.395 (22 July 1936). — Copyright 1936 by TTEPLPT. All Rights Reserved.

'PROVINCIALISM THE ENEMY. III', in *New Age,* XXI.13 (26 July 1917). — Copyright 1917 by TTEPLPT. All Rights Reserved.

Permission to quote from the above works by Ezra Pound has been granted by New Directions Publishing Corporation, New York, and Faber and Faber Ltd., London, with the following exceptions:

U.S.A. and Canada permission to quote from *Confucius: The Great Digest, The Unwobbling Pivot, The Analects,* and *The Spirit of Romance,* by Ezra Pound, has been granted by New Directions Publishing Corporation, New York; British and Commonwealth (excluding Canada) permission to quote from *Confucius: The*

Unwobbling Pivot and the Great Digest, Confucius: The Analects, and *The Spirit of Romance,* by Ezra Pound, published by Peter Owen, London, has been granted by Peter Owen, London; permission to quote from *Confucius to Cummings,* by Ezra Pound and Marcella Spann, has been granted by New Directions Publishing Corporation, New York; permission to quote from *Impact,* by Ezra Pound, has been granted by Gateway Editions, Ltd., South Bend, Indiana.

A NOTE ON TEXTS

❖❖❖❖❖❖❖❖❖

I break passages in Pound's verse thus: [. . .]; but in all other quotations by ellipses without brackets. In the notes, many titles of works are given in abbreviated form, and works by Pound are always cited without the author's name. Full information on all books and articles will be found in the Bibliography. Cross-references to the main text are in the style of the following example: 'see Chapter 5, text before n. 12' (meaning the part of the text in Chapter 5 immediately preceding note-marker 12).

In Chapter 4, nn. 14 ff., the reader will find a discussion of some textual sources of Pound's Provençal material; also see Introduction, n. 17. Elsewhere, I quote from and refer to the best recent text of any Provencal material, except where the text Pound used (if it is ascertainable) either may throw light on the origin of some point that matters in his product or significantly fails to account for such a point. Translations, from whatever language, are mine unless otherwise indicated; they are intended as literal cribs, even keeping where possible to the line-breaks of the original verse to help future students of Provencal, except in certain instances that are clearly indicated. As there is no canonical spelling of Provencal names, I have not laboured for consistency in this particular, but have taken care that no confusions are possible.

For Pound's own works, I cite the original publication in the case of certain important pieces or where the original text may illuminate the matter in hand. In these cases I often cite in parentheses a currently available publication, if there is one, but I do not use its text unless otherwise stated. For all other Pound material I cite a currently available text. However, individual short poems are cited without source. The source is always the *Selected Poems,* edited by Eliot, in the edition of 1959, except for the following, which are quoted according to the text of first publication:

'Dompna pois de me no'us cal' (originally *A Translation
from the Provençal of En Bertrans de Born*)
Near Perigord

and the following, which are quoted according to the text given in
Collected Early Poems, edited by King:

> *In Durance*
> *Na Audiart*
> *Sestina: Altaforte*
> *The Alchemist*
> *Guillaume de Lorris Belated: A Vision of Italy*
> *Planh for the Young English King*
> *Piere Vidal Old*
> *Donzella Beata*

Cantos are cited in the manner devised by Hugh Kenner for *The
Pound Era,* thus: *Cantos,* 20/89:93 = Canto XX, which is on p. 89
of the 'Revised Collected' edition (Cantos 1-117), published by
Faber & Faber in 1975 (pagination as New Directions, 1970), and p.
93 of the 'New Collected' edition (Cantos 1-109), published by Faber
& Faber in 1964. For Cantos not included in this latter edition, I
refer to the 'Revised Collected' and the Faber *Drafts and Fragments,*
thus: *Cantos,* 110/777:7. Where there are differences, citations are
always according to the Faber text.

INTRODUCTION

Provencal poetry was born 'in Poitou and in Limousin' at some time around 1100, and had effectively died out everywhere by about 1260. Ezra Pound was born in Hailey, Idaho, in 1885, and died in Italy in 1972.

The Provencal poets[1] — the troubadours — were princes, ex-monks, poor knights, bakers' sons and beggarly plagiarists. Some wandered and sang for a living, some could count on an appreciative, tied audience. They developed to a great refinement a short lyric, the *canso,* which was about love: the 'courtly love' which set before its audience a new image of the relations between man and woman, in which moral well-being was entirely in the hands of the lady.[2] The *canso* was surrounded by its offspring, the *sirventes* (verse diatribe), the *tenson* (verse disputation), and other forms. It was, as Dante said of the canzone, the form into which all the poet's skill could be put, and it originated most of the tunes, metrical schemes, and refinements that were imitated in these other forms.[3]

The troubadours had networks of communication whose nature we can only guess at. We know of their existence from the way that mutual borrowings were refined and assimilated almost instantly, eventually to become components of masterpieces in the hands of those craftsmen who possessed something more than craft.[4] The troubadours also had social status, some of which came from the rank that a considerable number of them possessed. The first and one of the greatest troubadours was a great territorial magnate; others were lesser barons; and some were poor knights who clung to their independence and tried to reinforce their standing with propaganda disseminated in their verse.[5] Great lords who had not the talent themselves took the trouble to support singers of humble origin, who often had no means of livelihood but their songs.[6] The songs themselves were so valuable that one singer might beg songs from another, to live by.[7] Singing seems to have been the path to success as courtiers for Sordello and for Raimbaut de Vaqueiras,

1

and William IX of Aquitaine seems to have chosen his friends by their talent for singing.[8] In this fierce competition for livelihood and reputation the troubadours often tried to enhance their own standing as independent poets by attacking others', through their own poems — accusing them for example of being *jongleurs,* mere singers of other men's songs; while the *sirventes* was a recognised political and personal weapon, occasionally being banned by law.[9] Provençal song was not a minor and dispensable ornament on the surface of society.

When the framework of the society that had supported them was wrecked by the Albigensian Crusade, in the years following 1209, many troubadours fled. Their art found soil in foreign lands that was fertile for brief periods only. But in Italy they were courted, and listened to, and imitated; they set the standards by which the native art raised itself into the flowering of Cino da Pistoia, Cavalcanti, and Dante. Their songs were copied from scraps of paper or memory into the luxurious volumes that survive today, illuminated with minute portraits of their authors.[10] Native *raconteurs* set themselves to make this courtly art more circumstantially interesting, with prose amplifications and embellishments of the songs' contents, and thus created the *vidas* ('lives' of the troubadours) and the *razos* ('explanations'). This art in turn was dead by the early fourteenth century, and songs and *vidas* gathered dust in the libraries of princes, to be pored over from time to time by a romancer like Nostredame in search of stories to re-embellish, or by a scholar like the Este librarian studying the history of the culture.[11] The philological interest continued to motivate various unrelated labours on the Provencal manuscripts through the late Renaissance and up to the beginning of the nineteenth century, when at last it led Raynouard to compile a dictionary on which to base his theory of Romance linguistics. With this, modern Provencal scholarship was under way.

'Provence' was both a dead, mysterious culture and a subjugated, 'lost' land and tongue; Romanticism could seize upon it as a cause, and it was Goethe who put the young Diez onto the trail of the Provençal lyrics and thus helped to erect one of the first pillars of genuine Provençal scholarship, as it has come to be regarded. Romantic currents have always been behind the more public side of interest in Provençal culture — the literary interest (Mistral, the Pre-Raphaelite period), the local interest (the crushed heretics of Languedoc, language revival, and separatism), and the historical-romance interest. A Romantic current was also, as Hugh Kenner has argued,[12] behind the belief in language as an organically mutable expression of cultural 'spirit' that led Raynouard, Diez, and their contemporaries to search into the development of Provençal as one of the Romance family of tongues. But from its beginnings, Provençal scholarship has had a strong current of positivist scepticism, a belief that only the provable should be taken into account. The content of the poem was too 'subjective' for satisfactory discussion—unless one could prove that it had some simple behaviourist base, like greed, or fraud; and creative translations, or attempts to show forth the virtues of the original song, were even more so. A great proportion of the scholarly energy has gone into preparing editions of authoritative readings based on tangible and mathematically computable manuscript variations; into discussing chronologies, itineraries, and the like; and into demonstrating the untrustworthiness of commentator and copyist.[13] All of this tended and tends to produce a shelf of impeccable Provencal texts and a public very sceptical as to their value as reading matter.

Into this arena strode Pound, in about 1905. His technical incompetence in Provencal was considerable, as we shall see. He was not incapable; in his final dealings with Arnaut Daniel, for example, he showed that armed with a crib in one foreign language he was quite capable of resolving the very intricate difficulties in another.[14] But he was unwilling. The task he had set himself was to discover the best in all surviving poetry from all parts of the world, and he must very soon have realised that if he involved himself in the detail of proving correct interpretations, the mere consumption of time would make his target impossible to reach. So he declared his scorn for 'the slough of philology'[15] and proceeded with his task, armed with an extraordinary ability to discern life (or the absence of it) in obscure texts. He would, however, take guidance from those whose works themselves showed signs of life: it was impossible for him to wade through the 2,542 surviving Provençal poems,[16] and so he followed Dante's hints from the beginning, finding confirmation of Dante's sound judgement as he continued.[17]

Pound had a strong leaning towards the paradisal or untrammelled-beauty aspects of life, strong in Provencal poetry, and this was acceptable when he and his audience were Pre-Raphaelite in

sensibility; but when both grew 'modern', and required a broader
base in actuality, it was a great struggle for Pound to justify his
interest in the subject of Provençal. It seemed so tainted (in the eyes
of a Cocteau, for example) with mediaevalism; so unworldly; and so
much, in its previous renderings, wrapped in the old language that
a Bridges could admire. But Pound persisted and, as I shall try to
show, brought Provençal culture not only into the modern world
but also into the heights of his personal late-achieved Paradise.

In this book I wish to present the Provencal culture to those who
know Pound, and Pound to those who know Provençal culture; and
both, if possible, to those who know neither. The subject of Pound
in 'Provence' has been touched upon many times, but writers have
skimmed through the anthologies and general histories for just
enough references to keep the anxious Pound-reader quiet, or have
cited a few points only as illustration of the new Pound 'education'.[18]
It is assumed that Pound has no interest for the Provençal expert.
This assumption is easily confirmed by the beginner in Provençal,
who confronts Pound with the *dicta* of the experts and finds them
talking at right angles; or by the expert himself, who observes that
Pound makes what are known as 'howlers'.[19] But the significance of
'Provence' was not settled by Mosaic diktat in 1905, and does not
depend on syntactical accuracies alone. Pound allowed himself
great economies by ignoring all detail except that which struck him,
and instead sniffing for the 'breath' that animates the cultural product. He was therefore automatically a revisionist in every subject he
undertook.[20] Neither this book nor any other amassing of detail can
prove that Pound's sense of smell was right or wrong, but it may supply the material which our own self-understanding and knowledge
of the world can evaluate. But Pound had an exceptionally clear
reaction to art, and he developed it by a rigorous self-training in
cultural comparison. Given the ultimate impossibility for the modern reader of knowing all the cultural *données* that were familiar to
the Provençal audience, and given the fact that we exercise a degree
of 'intuitive' extrapolation in all our reading (since it all contains
elements unknown to us), it is possible that the element of *jen* or
humanitas that Pound possessed in such abundance may more than
make up for the scholarly apparatus that he lacked. Though this
book attempts to introduce rather than to prove, it does suggest that
some standard critical ideas in Provençal letters should be revised in

Pound's direction; that more than once the essential grasp of human situation, without which any data are miscompiled, has been lacking. Provencal studies are not yet free, for example, from that approach which unites a Jeanroy to the modern Marxists: the supposedly scientific spirit which makes the troubadour a unit of singing-power moved only by his own greed and that of his patron, so that poetry rises and dies spontaneously as hacks 'pullulate'[21] around the biggest spender.

Pound's own *humanitas,* to judge by his efforts of research and creation in Provençal, seems to have been strongest in the 1910s and 1920s. In that period he was past his Pre-Raphaelite emotionalism and not yet deeply bitten by that bug of analysing evil which made his world (including the past) one huge conspiracy. These movements in his psyche are all visible in his successive views of 'Provence', as we shall see. We should try to preserve the best of them, since Pound had an ability to decide, and a freedom from the covert building of defensive or aggressive positions — both stemming from his extraordinary self-confidence — that allowed him to bring genuine new inspiration to this field.

Provence and Pound takes advantage of the very full available discussions of the way Pound used Provencal material in his early verse and in the metamorphosis-Cantos by ignoring these matters as far as possible. Once we realise that, as I shall show, the *vidas* and *razos* behind this work were imaginative efforts as much as the Provençal poems they accompanied, or the poems that Pound made from them, there is little that a wider knowledge of Provençal culture can add to the subject.[22]

Instead of starting with an essay on the nature of the Provençal culture, I shall start roughly where Pound started: with Bertran de Born. This will give some perspective, since Bertran kept Pound's interest from Pound's most Romantic period until he began to make some application of poetry

> to relation of the state
> To the individual[23]

To Pound, Bertran stood, first, for Provençal vigour (Latin, and un-Puritan); then for anti-usurious honesty; and finally for a certain limited, but still honest charm.

PART ONE

1. GLAMOUR AND POLITICS

❊❊❊❊❊❊❊❊❊❊

Pound first needed the troubadours for the same reasons as Americans like Ida Farnell and Justin H. Smith, preceding him into 'Provence', had needed them: for 'drama'. Nineteenth-century America hungered after vicarious glory and the glamorous deed as after a substitute for its own life, so successfully repressed in the name of wealth. Europe, and especially dark, irrational, mediaeval Catholic Europe could provide such substitutes; Poe borrowed them straight and Hawthorne laboured hard to convince his readers that his American transposition was as exciting. Twain laughed at the credulity of the provincial audiences and was disgusted by their humility when it came to anything from wonderful Europe, but was not averse to using an Italian count or two himself, well glamorised. The American lecture tour was an important means of satisfying this demand, and the style of the American popularisations of troubadours shows that they were aimed at a thrillable audience — an aim which has its advantages, as readers of Farnell and Smith will find. Pound first aimed at this kind of audience with his articles on mediaeval Europe in provincial American magazines. He learned how to get the 'personal' and 'dramatic' angle from writers like Smith, who had related one troubadour story like this:

This viscountess had not been mistaken: it was Guillem de Sain Leidier. Covered with a mantle of black silk, he wore a long dagger sheathed in his belt; and a coat of mail, clinking softly beneath it, showed that he, too, understood the peril of his enterprise. But no hint of that appeared in his face, and lightly throwing back the pointed hood of his mantle he advanced with eyes cast down, and fell on one knee before the viscountess.[1]

Thus Pound, on location, reconstructing the *Poema del Cid* for the readers of the *Philadelphia Book News Monthly:*

The only one of all Burgos that dared tell these tidings to the Cid was a little maid of nine; and there are yet in Burgos window and balcony from

9

which she might have leaned, with her black eyes wonder wide, and held
parlance with the stern-bearded Campeador, saying:

   Aie Campeador, in good hour girt ye on your sword....[2]

But the culture-heroes for the European glamour were Wilde, Yeats,
and the *Yellow Book* men, and their example showed that sex must
be a part of this resurrected emotional life. Following this model was
what had Pound thrown out of his job teaching college in Indiana:
not only had he to wear *outré* clothes, but he must frequent *risqué*
company—painters and stranded burlesque actresses[3]—and that
was too much for the locals. Throughout his earlier years there was
a running battle between Pound, his American colleagues, and
their common American audience, with the latter two parties
always in some way wanting superior sophistication but thinking
that 'this time' the Europeanised artist (Pound) had gone too far:
from William Carlos Williams hinting at 'poetic anarchy' in 1908,[4]
to Harriet Monroe considering Pound's *Langue d'Oc* and *Moeurs
Contemporaines* in 1918:

She accepted neither series, considering both 'unprintable.' Her notes on
several of the poems are instructive. Of 'Vergier': 'lovely, but—frank!' Of
'Mr. Styrax': 'Impossibly frank—*virgo*.' Of 'Ritratto': 'Amusing—about
Lowell—but "stomped into my bedroom." '[5]

   To Pound in 1907, stuck in the depths of the Mid-West at Wabash
College, Crawfordsville, Indiana, the troubadour Bertran de Born
could supply both drama and sensuality. He wrote *In Durance* here:

I am homesick
After mine own kind that know, and feel
And have some breath for beauty and the arts.

He also wrote *Na Audiart,* taken (as he noted) from

the tale of Bertran of Born and My Lady Maent of Montaignac, and . . . the
song he made when she would none of him, the song wherein he, seeking to
find or make her equal, begs of each preëminent lady of Langue d'Oc some
trait or some fair semblance. . . . And all this to make 'Una dompna soiseu-
buda' a borrowed lady or as the Italians translated it 'Una donna ideale.'[6]

In his song, Bertran says that he will take some part from all the women, to make up his substitute lady; he wants something even from the Lady (*Na*) Audiart, 'though she wishes me ill', *si be·m vol mal.*[7] (Pound emends this and quotes it at the end of his poem as *Que be-m vols mal,* 'Though you wish me ill'.) There is nothing but this line in all Bertran's seven-and-a-half stanzas to give Pound the idea of rejection by Audiart; but he takes this 'germ'[8] to make it the underlying theme of his whole *Na Audiart*. It is true that in this line Bertran's lady acquires more life than do many troubadours' ladies in a great acreage of verse: there has been (for once) a reaction from her. Pound also picks up something that the Provençal-speaking audience might not even have been conscious of: the *be* part of *si be* ('although') means 'well', so that Pound can get out of it both antithesis and alliteration:

> Though thou well dost wish me ill

Pound's singer says that his lady rejects him. Now, the beauties of her body give her what seems like the privilege to do as she pleases; but one day, and in particular the day when she is 'reincarnated' as an old woman, her pride will be broken, she will regret her arrogance. The expression of perfect beauty in this poem owes much to Platonism. Other things in Pound also did in those early days. The rejected *Guillaume de Lorris Belated: A Vision of Italy*[9] conceives of the cities of Italy as Platonic forms that 'accidentally' inhabit the material cities, but forms that are with equal truth 'a maid I knew on earth', 'a lotus-flower', and so on. In that poem material things are

> yet so fine and delicate a haze
> It did impede the eyes no whit

just as in the (also rejected) *Donzella Beata* the girl's soul is

> Caught in the rose-hued mesh
> Of o'er fair earthly flesh

In *Na Audiart,* the lady's beauty is the perfect marriage of soul with body, spirit with matter, form with 'accident': the placing of a beautiful soul in a body that fits it like a well-made dress.

This theme comes from the interstices of the same few lines in Bertran. The woman in Pound's poem is one with her well-fitting dress, or her body is as right in its casing as a fifties leg in its fishnet stocking:

> Where thy bodice laces start
> As ivy fingers clutching thru
> Its crevices

and again:

> Having praised thy girdle's scope,
> How the stays ply back from it

The germ for this in Bertran is in the conjunction of lines that literally mean:

> I want her to give me some of her shapes,
> because clothes go well on her,
> and because she is whole,
> for her love never broke
> or twisted awry

In the word *faissos*, 'shapes', there are curves, and a hint of 'fashion'. In *liazos*, 'clothes', there is the Romance root meaning 'bind' that is in 'lien', the French *lier,* and so on. All the sensuous dress in Pound's version comes from these two words. For the tight fit there are the other three lines, which also gave rise to this idea of the lady's body as a perfect piece of craftsmanship. Pound has it:

> 'Cause never a flaw was there
> Where thy torse and limbs are met

He probably took *entieira*, 'whole', as a kind of Shakespearian 'entire', referring (like the previous lines) to her body. After the *entieira* Bertran shifts the meaning from the anatomical range to 'her love', but his sentence colours this with the anatomical feeling of the earlier lines; Pound simply took them as anatomical. So the lines

>   her love never broke
>   or twisted awry

are the imaginative germ for the flawless body, even though in his later translation of the original Pound rendered them literally.[10] We shall see later that this picking up of stimuli from semantic triviali-ties and misreadings to augment the imaginative part of a re-crea-tion is exactly what was done by the authors of the Provencal *vidas* and *razos* that Pound used in turn.[11]

In *Na Audiart* Pound's Bertran intimates that since the lady is using her bodily privileges with arrogance, she will come to a sticky transmigration. At the moment when she is speaking, she 'fits' her Platonic form perfectly. According to the Pythagorean doctrine of the transmigration of souls, the shape in which one will be reincar-nated depends on how one behaves in the present incarnation. The lady will be

>   Broken of ancient pride

born into a shapeless shape, a body that fulfils no Platonic 'form', and in fact her 'old soul' will be as ill-at-ease with itself as it will be with her new body:

>   Thy loveliness is here writ till,
>   Audiart,
>   Oh, till thou come again.**
>   And being bent and wrinkled, in a form
>   That hath no perfect limning, when the warm
>   Youth dew is cold
>   Upon thy hands, and thy old soul
>   Scorning a new, wry'd casement
>   Churlish at seemed misplacement
>   Finds the earth as bitter
>   As now seems it sweet,
>   Being so young and fair
>   As then only in dreams,
>   Being then young and wry'd,
>   Broken of ancient pride,
>   Thou shalt then soften
>   Knowing I know not how,
>   Thou wert once she

> Audiart, Audiart
> For whose fairness one forgave
>   Audiart, Audiart,
>   Que be-m vols mal.

>   **reincarnate.*

The footnote 'reincarnate' is Pound's; this theme is not in Bertran's poem. Pythagorean ideas of the soul were on Pound's mind: Pythagoras is praised for the visions in *Guillaume de Lorris Belated,* and *Donzella Beata* suggests to the damozel in question that she has 'stooped' from aetherial spheres to be caught in the prison of human flesh and 'bear' it (like a cross) for the poet's sake. It is no wonder that Pound's Kensington girls (as in *The Garden*),[12] fed for years on this sort of stuff, seemed to be on the brink of evaporating. The idea of reincarnation, a little better fleshed out, stayed with Pound: certain types of soul recur in the Cantos' view of history, and Pound's myth of the justice of the universal order shows states of mind enduring beyond death.[13] A fairly profound Platonism is the centre of Pound's later religious cult: woman is the manifestation of Wisdom. But neither Platonism nor Pythagoreanism is in *Na Audiart* except as nicely weighed flavours to add a touch of 'seriousness' to the poem, and to distance it from the direct sensuality that Pound thought he was looking for but for which he was in fact by no means ready. He came after all from an extremely desensualised background, and always retained leanings towards the idea of chastity; and nineties mediaevalism did not necessarily help, as we may see from his later autobiographical-sounding remark that Gourmont's *Songe d'une Femme* 'is untranslatable into English, but should be used before thirty by young men who have been during their undergraduate days too deeply inebriated with the *Vita Nuova.*'[14] The tones of *Donzella Beata,* apparently addressed to Hilda Doolittle, show that he was one such young man:

> Soul,
> Caught in the rose-hued mesh
> Of o'er fair earthly flesh,
> Stooped you this thing to bear
> Again for me? And be
> Rare light to me, gold-white
> In the shadowy path I tread?[15]

Pound in fact had a long way to go to catch up with the sensuality of his original for *Na Audiart* — Bertran de Born — who would not have survived for one minute at Wabash. We shall see this by looking at Bertran's poem of the 'borrowed lady' itself.

This is a literal translation:

> Lady, since you are not interested in me
> and have sent me away
> without any reason,
> I don't know where to look. . . .
>
> Since I can find no lady equal to you,
> who should be as beautiful or excellent,
> or her fine person so happy,
> with such beautiful clothes,
> so gay,
> or her fine worth so true,
> I shall go everywhere begging
> a beautiful appearance from each lady,
> to make a borrowed lady
> until I get you back.
>
> I take your fresh unfaked colour
> from you, Beautiful-Cembeli,
> and your sweet loving look,
> and I act with great presumption
> in leaving anything behind,
> because you never lacked anything good;
> from milady Helis I ask
> her clever witty talk,
> to help my lady,
> then she won't be stale or dumb. . . .
>
> I want Audiart, though she wishes me ill,
> to give me some of her shapes,
> because clothes go well on her,
> and because she is whole,
> for her love never broke
> or twisted awry;
> of my better-than-Good I ask
> her upright, fresh and valued body —
> from what one sees
> it would be fine to hold her naked. . . .

Beautiful-Lord, I ask of you nothing other
than that I should be as covetous
of this [borrowed] lady as I am of you;
since a greedy
love is springing up
with which my body is so avid
that I prefer asking you
to kissing another woman;
so why does 'milord' refuse me
when she knows I have wanted her so much?

This is the Provençal of the stanza to Audiart and 'Better-than-Good' that Pound started from:

N'Audiartz, si be·m vol mal,
vuolh que·m don de sas faissos,
que·lh estai gen liazos,
    e car es entieira,
        c'anc no·is frais
s'amors ni·s vols en biais.
a mon Mielhs-de-ben deman
son adreich nou cors prezan,
de que par a la veguda,
la fassa bon tener nuda.

Bertran's tone is definite. He has a regular, almost a jogging metric, except in the quick half-lines in the middle. He flattens out to a detached anticlimax with the feminine rhymes at the end:

de que par a la veguda,
la fassa bon tener nuda.

The tone runs as definitely as if Bertran were concocting a menu from his favourite dishes, and in the last stanza it turns into sensual greed when the short lines dwell on the hisses and slurps of *lechadieira, nais, lechais:*

c'una lechadieira
amors nais
don mos cors es tant lechais

where the key-words have primary meanings of gluttony:

since a greedy
love is springing up
with which my body is so avid

Bertran's poem is the poem of a man who, being no longer star-
struck with sex and women, can compare and savour, and find them
a delight and a pleasure. Pound's poem comes from a different age,
culturally and personally:

Tho thou well dost wish me ill
                    Audiart, Audiart,
Where thy bodice laces start
As ivy fingers clutching thru
Its crevices,
                    Audiart, Audiart,
Stately, tall and lovely tender
Who shall render
                    Audiart, Audiart
Praises meet unto thy fashion?
Here a word kiss!
                    Pass I on
Unto Lady 'Miels-de-Ben,'
Having praised thy girdle's scope,
How the stays ply back from it;
I breathe no hope
That thou shouldst. . . .
                    Nay no whit
Bespeak thyself for anything.
Just a word in thy praise, girl,
Just for the swirl
Thy satins make upon the stair,
'Cause never a flaw was there
Where thy torse and limbs are met:
Tho thou hate me, read it set
In rose and gold.

He has developed a lilting and surging music, with a sophisticated
combination of Bertran's sudden rhymed half-lines, a subtle varying
of the speed by sequences of light stresses:

Just a word in thy praise, girl,
Just for the swirl
Thy satins make upon the stair

and the chanting of 'Audiart, Audiart' in the background. He is elaborating an aesthetic 'moment', something to do with the meeting of clothes and skin —

> Having praised thy girdle's scope,
> How the stays ply back from it

into a prolonged breathless flight. The original has not been idealised or 'platonised' in the popular sense of being moved away from sex; Pound's product is as sexual as may be, but it is an early Yeatsian sex-in-the-head, or permanent state of unconsummated excitement. Sex has been used to produce not the Platonic, but the debased, Romantic idea of 'ecstasy' — meaning roughly any heightened emotional state that we can get away with calling 'spiritual'. In the same way another Provencal-based poem of this early period, *Piere Vidal Old* (of 1909), uses the device of a love-madness to give a spiritual surface to a standard post-Romantic search for heightened emotions — in this case based on sex and sadomasochism.[16] Pound's Provençal-based verse of this period went along with the 'artistic' costume that he wore: he was not at this time a budding neo-Platonist, but a late Romantic. At least *Na Audiart* has finish and consistency, something in the same way that Burne-Jones's *Beggar Maid* has.

'NEAR PERIGORD'

Bertran de Born's *Dompna, puois de mi no·us cal* kept Pound's interest for a long time. *Na Audiart* was written some time before Pound went to Venice and published *A Lume Spento*, his first collection of poems, in 1908; he gave special praise to the original in 1910, translated it in 1914, used it as the source for a major reconstruction in 1915, and praised it again in 1917.[17] The reconstruction was *Near Perigord* (by which title Pound means 'near Périgueux', Périgueux being the chief town of the counts of Périgord). With a far less emotional and far more reasoned method than *Na Audiart*, this poem tries to present a situation that could 'explain' Bertran's strange song.

Leaving aside for the moment the relations between Pound's

starting-points and history as it can be determined, this is the situation Pound imagines. Bertran de Born, enemy of the Count of Périgord and of his brother-in-law Tairiran who holds the castle of Montaignac, addresses a song (the *Dompna puois*) to 'Beautiful-Lord', who is Maent, châtelaine of Montaignac. In this song he says that he will make a 'borrowed lady' from the finest attributes of all the region's beauties; and he speaks to each of them in turn, asking permission. Pound has noticed that the castles inhabited by these ladies (Chalais, Rochechouart, Malemort, and Montfort) effectively encircle Bertran's enemy, the Count of Périgord. Working on his side these castles would make the perfect anti-Périgord strategy; but Maent's Montaignac is the kingpin, since it both covers the approaches to Périgueux and flanks Bertran's own Hautefort:

> And all his net-like thought of new alliance?
> Chalais is high, a-level with the poplars.
> Its lowest stones just meet the valley tips
> Where the low Dronne is filled with water-lilies.
> And Rochecouart can match it, stronger yet,
> The very spur's end, built on sheerest cliff,
> And Malemort keeps its close hold on Brive,
> While Born his own close purse, his rabbit warren,
> His subterranean chamber with a dozen doors,
> A-bristle with antennae to feel roads,
> To sniff the traffic into Perigord.
> And that hard phalanx, that unbroken line,
> The good ten miles from thence to Maent's castle,
> All of his flank — how could he do without her?

Near Perigord asks a series of questions: with his poem, was Bertran trying to convert Montaignac, the key to his strategy, by making the other women jealous of Maent, and giving her 'pride in them'? But was Bertran in love with her? And then, extrapolating the guesses, was the song an attempt at alliance with all these castles, using the compliments to cover up communications with them? Betrayed, perhaps, by the astute Sir Arrimon; with the result that Bertran was thrown out of his castle by Richard Lionheart?

A discussion between Arnaut Daniel and Richard, imagined by Pound, leaves these questions open. Pound then makes his main suggestion. He sets a love-scene on the banks of the Auvézère (which runs near Bertran's castle, Hautefort) where the lady seems to lament her instability:

> 'Why do you love me? Will you always love me?
> But I am like the grass, I can not love you.'
> Or, 'Love, and I love and love you,
> And hate your mind, not *you*, your soul, your hands.'

Pound's observer speaks of an estrangement, perhaps after the break between Bertran and the lords of Périgord, and finally Maent is a prisoner in the castle of her lover's enemy:

> There shut up in his castle, Tairiran's,
> She who had nor ears nor tongue save in her hands,
> Gone — ah, gone — untouched, unreachable!
> She who could never live save through one person,
> She who could never speak save to one person,
> And all the rest of her a shifting change,
> A broken bundle of mirrors . . . !

So that the poem seems to leave another question: was Bertran's intriguing quite separate from his love for Maent, which was of the very particular kind described in these last few lines of the poem? If so, the first strophes of Bertran's poem could be, instead of a complicated piece of political manoeuvring, a large-scale metaphor for this special personality — as Hugh Kenner has said. Bertran wanted to use the poetic lines of communication to the castles inhabited by the other ladies, but he also wanted to use fragments of these ladies for a picture of the lost and havering soul of the beautiful Maent,

> A broken bundle of mirrors . . . ![18]

The most striking thing about Pound's poem is the pervasive question-marks; the way questions are half-elaborated and then cut short by other questions:

> 'Papiol,
> Go forthright singing — Anhes, Cembelins.
> There is a throat; ah, there are two white hands;
> There is a trellis full of early roses,
> And all my heart is bound about with love.

> Where am I come with compound flatteries—
> What doors are open to fine compliment?'
> And every one half jealous of Maent?
> He wrote the catch to pit their jealousies
> Against her, give her pride in them?
>
> Take his own speech, make what you will of it—
> And still the knot, the first knot, of Maent?
>
> Is it a love poem? Did he sing of war?
> Is it an intrigue to run subtly out

The effect of all this is to make the reader very conscious of his own function as part-arbiter of the kind of reality being presented; of how the re-creation of the past depends as much on him, as receiving intelligence, as on the poet; or even, since we see Arnaut Daniel and Richard Lionheart unable to decide on any facts, as on contemporary audiences and protagonists. Browning's kind of reality and non-reality is very effectively created. Hereby Pound tried to make the past real and hard, with the psychological clarity of an analysis of character in which we must participate; yet at the same time he could force the reader to realise that such situations are based on nothing more 'real' than his own experience, with its uncertainties and shifts of emphasis. And the poem is also another attempt to remedy the age-long defect in the Western 'split' sensibility that had eventually thrown up the pale 'idealism' of Pound's youth, by connecting a sensual love with something as down-to-earth as politics.

But *Near Perigord* was a blind alley, the end of which Pound later reached with the first three draft Cantos. In these draft Cantos, Pound took the Browning psychological relativism to another extreme of complication, by addressing Browning, the addresser of questions to half-resurrected ghosts, as another ghost, with more questions about the ghosts he (Browning) had half-resurrected:

> Ghosts move about me patched with histories.
> You had your business: to set out so much thought,
> So much emotion, and call the lot 'Sordello.'
> Worth the evasion, the setting figures up
> And breathing life upon them.
> Has it a place in music? And your: 'Appear Verona!'?[19]

Though these draft Cantos review this method and find it unable to get back to the real men,[20] Pound's rejection of it is not to be found here, since in them he continued to use Browning's 'meditative, semi-dramatic' tone, and his detached observer, presenting, commenting, addressing:

> Ha! Sir Blancatz,
> Sordello would have your heart up, give it to all the princes[21]

just as in *Near Perigord* everything was discussed in a public tone of voice, masculine and hearty, with a 'Cino' whom Pound claimed to be fictional but who coincides with a Cino in Browning's *Sordello*.[22] Pound finally rejected this relativism in the final-version Canto II, by stating that his own Sordello was the real one, the Sordello of the contemporary texts:

> Hang it all, Robert Browning,
>   there can be but the one 'Sordello'.
> But Sordello, and my Sordello?
> Lo Sordels si fo di Mantovana.[23]

When the sensibility is working as one whole, when the intelligence is seen simply as an extension, not as a contradiction of the sensual faculties, then one can 'know' the reality or otherwise of a presented character by the same means as one knows the truth of a painting or a piece of music: by exercise of the eyes, ears, and skin, by instinctive assessment of the non-rationalisable factors, like images, rhythms, and voice-tones. So Pound later contrasted one of the Confucian Odes with the Browning *persona* or mask: 'There is no "progress" from this form. Here the actual author speaks; in Browning's *Personae* the speaker is an imagined character.'[24] The implication is that Browning's added complexity adds nothing.

So Pound's other aim in *Near Perigord*, to put back a little sensual reality into an etiolated culture, failed: you cannot create strong emotion with mere ideas,[25] or if you do, they must be large operatic ideas, as adolescent as what you are trying to replace. The central idea of *Near Perigord*, the warrior-troubadour mixing his poetic passion with intrigue and strategy, is no more than a grand gesture suitable for some historical romance.

Pound had come to the Browning method partly because it

seemed to offer a great psychological depth, and perhaps also partly because the academic elements in his audience had begun to give him worries about the historical accuracy of his sources; worries that relativism could bypass. But he could not abandon the belief that his Provençal stories were historical. He jumped hard — too hard to convince — on those who might doubt the reality of his scene where Bertran confronts the ageing Henry II; and part of his criticism of Browning in the first-draft Cantos was that Browning got his facts wrong.[26] When at last he ditched Browning along with the whole discursive approach of *Near Perigord* and the first-draft Cantos, he concentrated instead on getting into the historical and artistic remains of his subject so deeply that he felt he intuitively 'knew' character and situation; and finally created in the Cantos a William IX, an Eleanor of Aquitaine, a Sordello, and a Cunizza who are more than just 'ideas'. This step, I believe, is representative of Pound's main contribution to the twentieth-century renaissance.

HISTORY AND 'NEAR PERIGORD'

Pound admitted that 'as to the possibility of a political intrigue behind the apparent love poem we have no evidence save that offered by my own observations of the geography of Perigord and Limoges. . . .'[27] He had a fairly intimate knowledge of this geography, and a lasting love for it. The sense of its layout is quite strong in *Near Perigord,* though Smith's *The Troubadours at Home* may have helped both to inspire it and to present it verbally.[28] *Provincia Deserta* is the record of Pound's meditations there in 1912; later he took Eliot through the region on foot, and said that the 'world's best' architecture 'afoot from Poitiers, from Brives, from Périgord or Limoges' should be part of the new education. That is why 'the roads of France' are still alive in the *Pisan Cantos.*[29] But these are not exact indications; almost everything exact in *Near Perigord* is wrong.

Pound figured a situation where Bertran de Born was threatened by the power-greed of the lords of Périgord:

> Tairiran held hall in Montaignac,
> His brother-in-law was all there was of power

> In Perigord, and this good union
> Gobbled all the land and held it later for some hundreds years

The most accurate dating it is possible to give to the poem that this is all about, Bertran's *Dompna puois,* places it before 1182, that is to say, before Bertran was involved with the sons of Henry II Plantagenet.[30] *Dompna puois* would have preceded the interference from Richard Lionheart that Pound's poem speaks of:

> Sir Arrimon counts on his fingers [. . .]
>   guesses beneath, sends word to Coeur de Lion:
>
> The compact, de Born smoked out, trees felled
> About his castle, cattle driven out!

Richard, indeed, did not take Bertran's castle until 6 July 1183, a date specified by Geoffrey of Vigeois.[31] Now Bertran's songs against the barons, including the house of Périgord, did not begin until 1183, being occasioned by the treachery of these lords in leaving him at the mercy of Richard.[32] It is true that Clédat, whose work Pound could have read (but probably did not), placed much earlier the song that Pound quotes under his title.[33] But not only had Clédat misinterpreted this song as dealing with the fall of Périgueux (it only mentions the siege there by Richard's Poitevins), but Pound misinterprets the same strophe as implying that Périgueux was in the enemy's camp, that is, Richard's. Talairan of Périgord in fact had always been, with the other barons of the region, hostile to Richard, and until the *brouille* of 1183 had been allied with Bertran, like all the other tardy lords urged on in the same poem. So the object of the strategic exercise that *Near Perigord* sees behind Bertran's *Dompna puois* — the encirclement of the house of Périgord — was necessarily absent at the time.[34]

There are other conflicts of detail, mostly taken from the accounts given by the *razos,* the late Provencal prose commentaries on troubadour songs. Tairiran in *Near Perigord* is the chatelain of Montaignac and brother-in-law to the Count of Périgord. The *razo*-writer speaks of 'milady Maeut of Montagnac, wife of Sir Talairan, who was brother to the Count of Périgord; and she was the daughter of the Viscount of Turenne and sister of milady Maria de Ventadour and milady Hélis de Montfort.' He also speaks of 'Sir Talairan, lord of Montagnac'.[35] Pound must have considered that the lady would not necessarily be born 'de Turenne' and married 'de Montagnac' if her husband's brother were Count of Périgord; so he made the gentlemen brothers-in-law. He may also have realised that the forms the *razo* manuscripts give for Maent's toponymic would all give rise to a modern 'Montagnac', which is etymologically incompatible with the modern place-name 'Montignac'. If so, he avoided the questions this seems to raise by using the spelling 'Montaignac'. These compromises show how little he understood of what actually happened.

Bertran de Born's supposed heroine was in fact invented by the *razo* writer, and he did it by the same kind of hopeful compromise that Pound used to sort out inconsistencies. The real heroine of the *Dompna puois* is unidentifiable; Maeut (Pound's 'Maent') is not to be found in Bertran's poems, and only exists in the *razos,* written many years later.[36] This is how Stronski reconstructed the *razo* writer's method:

He learned that in the time of Bertran de Born a lady of Turenne brought to the house of the Counts of Périgord the castellany in which was situate the important town of Montagnac. Not knowing the name of this lady, he called her Maeut, probably because the wife of Raimon I [of Turenne] had borne this name at the beginning of the twelfth century, and a memory of this traditional name had reached him. Then, not having any exact information on the house of the Counts of Périgord, he made her the wife of a brother of the Count of Périgord, perhaps because people remembered at Montagnac that this town still belonged at the beginning of the 13th century to an appanage that was only incorporated into the Counts' lands after the death of Archambaut de Ribérac in 1211.[37]

In fact this lady was not sister to the famous beauties of Turenne, but came from another branch of that house; she did not marry the Count of Périgord's brother, but the Count himself, who alone could carry the surname 'Talairan'; and she did not bring in her dowry Montignac (this is not the mistake of the *razo* writer, but that of modern historians), but Ménesterol-Montignac, known as Montagnac at least in the 13th century.[38]

Pound and the *razo* writer between them constructed a situation unknown to Bertran de Born. Bertran's ally Talairan of Périgord became, as 'Perigord', Bertran's chief enemy, and as 'Tairiran', his

own brother-in-law, a possible ally for Bertran against himself (as
'Perigord') if his fictitious wife Maent could be influenced by Bertran's poem to make him support Bertran with the castle 'Montaignac', which is supposed to outflank Bertran but whose historical
prototype was some 66 kilometres the other side of Périgueux.[39]

Pound then added further fictions. In *Near Perigord:*

> We come to Ventadour

where:

> In the mid love court, he sings out the canzon

This is presumably because Maria de Ventadorn, wife of Eble V,
was sister to the two beauties of Turenne who are mentioned in Bertran's poem: Hélis de Montfort and (if she was in fact the other one)
'Beautiful-Lord', the real addressee of the poem who has been given
the name 'Maent'. But Maria was not to marry Eble de Ventadorn
until several years later.[40] Then Pound mentions Bertran's domestic
troubles:

> The four round towers, four brothers — mostly fools

The *razos* and Provençal scholarship know of only two other brothers: Constantine, whose struggles with Bertran we shall come back
to, and Itier.[41] But Pound misread the poem in which Bertran
wished on himself all sorts of trouble if he really had been untrue to
his lady:

> Let me be lord of a co-owned castle,
> and let us be four equals in the keep,
> and let us never be able to like one another (. . .)
> if I ever wished to love another lady.[42]

Pound was sufficiently struck by the 'four towers' (parallels to the
four towers of Wagadu) that he found in these lines, to bring them
back in *Thrones* in an anecdote about a wealthy Jew who had
bought Hautefort.[43] And lastly there is the line in *Near Perigord:*

> Or take his 'magnet' singer setting out

This is a misreading of the envoi or *tornada* that Pound omits from his translation of *Dompna puois*. Papiol is Bertran's *joglar*, his *jongleur* or singer-deputy, and Bertran says to him,

> Papiol,
> you will go and tell my magnet, singing,
> that love is snubbed
> here, and has fallen from high to low.[44]

So the situation in Pound's *Near Perigord* was pretty well unknown to Bertran. Pound's method of fabulation was very like that of the *razo* writers: each took a situation that was suggestive to him and, not understanding all the points and not knowing many referents, squared off inconsistencies — the *razo* writer starting from Bertran's songs plus remembered, probably oral history, and Pound starting from Bertran's songs and the works of the *razo*ist. So the *razo*ist had the lady marry the Count's brother, and Pound had her marry the Count's brother-in-law. But Pound claimed that 'mythological expression' 'permits an expression of intuition without denting the edges or shaving off the nose and ears of a verity.'[45] *Near Perigord* is mythopoeic, since it sets out to go beyond the known facts; but it tramples all over these facts in the process. Of what use is it?

Pound's mythopoeia is simply attempts to point out governing processes in the universe, generally on two scales: as applicable to a particular historical problem, thought of as 'recurrent', and as applicable to 'permanent' aspects of nature.[46] *Near Perigord* looks for a governing process on the local or 'recurrent' scale. It proposes the question, which scholars have not touched on for lack of information, of the relation between the love-affairs and the political aims of such a poet as Bertran de Born, known to have engaged in both. May not the one have served the other, and if so, how? Bertran is an apt example of this possibility, since a large number of his songs are half love, half war, first the one and then the other. One might guess that the love half served to gain entry to the courts of Poitou and Limousin, ruled by their 'salon-queens', from which the propaganda of the war half might effectively spread. If a *joglar* gained entrance or attention more easily by announcing that he had a song about the lady of the house, the troubadour could very well

insert a mention of her, just so as to have his man welcomed at that
particular castle. And so, if we look on the map and find that the
traceable ladies in a particular song form a neat circle around the
troubadour's potential enemy, as despite all Pound's mistakes they
do in *Dompna puois,* may we not suspect some kind of political
intrigue?

But all this can only be as valuable as the resulting poem is good.
For its value as usable information it depends on communicated
insights into human states of being; without a sense of real flesh and
real bones in the situation, we will take no more notice of it as a
statement about human behaviour than the assertion that 'gentlemen prefer blondes'. If it fails as a poem, the conjectures in *Near
Perigord* are of no more and no less value than those in a (badly re-
searched) historical monograph, whether we call it myth, history, or
poetry.

Pound made exactly the same kind of mistake as some of the *razo*
writers in interpreting the songs which were a chief source of information for them both — Pound, for instance, ruled a song out of the
Arnaut Daniel canon because of a misreading, the same misreading
that was probably the basis of a whole *razo* about Arnaut.[47] Not all
these mistakes were equally fruitful, either with the *razo*ists or with
Pound. Some of the most powerful and completely felt myths that
Pound makes from Provencal culture are based on the slightest
'germs', issuing from the interstices of misunderstood Provençal
phrases. The *romerya,* 'wandering', of Gausbert de Poicebot in
Canto V:

> Came lust of travel upon him, of *romerya*

— the centre of Pound's rendering of the story, changing the atmosphere from Provencal sunlight to grey — is an addition by Pound,
who borrowed a misread phrase from another *vida* because it had
struck him. There are many other examples, like the 'put glamour
upon her' of the same Canto.[48] A slight shift of focus that came from
a misreading of Arnaut Daniel later produced a whole string of bril-
liancies.[49] But there is no inverse law of scholarship and insight. We
shall see that some of Pound's greatest solidities are constructed
from mixtures of these three elements: 'germ'-phrases; poetic equivalents that catch the exact tones of particular Provencal songs, or

even legal documents; and quotation from obscure documents whose use by Pound shows a great deal of historical understanding — this latter being so far unrecognised. The strength of mythopoeia depends on the poet's understanding of his 'subject', whatever it be, and not on any other 'reasons'. Blanket justification for fable-making and blanket condemnation of unscholarliness are both easy ways out.

BERTRAN AS MALE PRINCIPLE

In 1909, a year after he had published *Na Audiart* and well before he attempted the difficult speculations of *Near Perigord,* Pound had brought out another piece based on Bertran de Born: *Sestina: Altaforte.*[50] It offers another clue to the affinities between Pound and Bertran. Pound may have been looking for Latin 'drama' in general, but he took up Bertran in particular — chiefly because of Bertran's aggressive vigour. This trait was an important one in Pound's own character, and had a strong connection with the myth-world of Provence that he built.

Sestina: Altaforte is not taken directly from any one of Bertran's songs. It is an attempt to show forth the troubadour himself as a set of living and powerful emotions, as Pound's note says:

> Dante Alighieri put this man in hell for that he was
> a stirrer-up of strife.
> Eccovi!
> Judge ye!
> Have I dug him up again?

It is a pugnacious poem, starting:

> Damn it all! all this our South stinks peace

but alternating that tone with one of ecstasy:

> Then howl I my heart nigh mad with rejoicing.

But the main mood is attack, whether the sun's:

> His lone might 'gainst all darkness opposing

or Bertran's own:

> When our elbows and swords drip the crimson
> And our charges 'gainst 'The Leopard's' rush clash.

Pound was proud of it in 1913: 'Technically it is one of my best, though a poem on such a theme could never be very important.'[51] It appealed to that pugnacity in him which Wyndham Lewis said made him so unsuitable for London society.[52] After the meeting with the young sculptor Henri Gaudier-Brzeska, whom Pound described as vanishing like a glimpsed Greek god on that occasion, he arranged to see him again and carefully chose poems to read to him which would be energetic enough to impress a man nearly ten years younger than himself; he chose *Sestina: Altaforte,* and it worked. He wrote to William Carlos Williams in 1913: 'Have just bought two statuettes from *the* coming sculptor, Gaudier-Brzeska. I like him very much. He is the only person with whom I can really be "Altaforte".'[53]

Pound made 'Altaforte' into a cipher for the kind of aggressiveness that comes across in the poem. The Romance roots of the name, meaning 'high-strong', could describe the bastions of Bertran's castle, Hautefort (in Provencal, *Altafort*);[54] but they could also describe the way Pound delivered the poem. When Pound's and Hulme's artist friends dined at the Tour Eiffel, Pound declaimed it so violently that the management put a screen round their table.[55] Gaudier-Brzeska seems to have been impressed on this occasion because Pound had dared to use the word 'piss' in a poem — presumably Gaudier's mis-hearing of 'all this our South stinks peace'(!),[56] which is another comment on the aggressive sounds in *Sestina: Altaforte*. The *Annotated Index to the Cantos* understandably takes 'Altaforte' in Canto LXXX to be a kind of metaphorical adverb meaning 'riotously, belligerently':

> As the 'Surrender of Breda' (Velásquez)
>   was preceded in fresco at Avignon
>   y cavals armatz with the perpendicular lances
>   and the red-bearded fellow was mending his
>   young daughter's shoe

'Me Hercule! c'est nôtre comune'
('Borr', not precisely Altaforte)[57]

What Pound actually meant was that the gentle red-bearded peasant who gave him hospitality was at Born, which is not precisely Bertran's castle Hautefort, despite the name. Velásquez's horsemen
with their phallic lances reminded Pound of the *cavals armatz,*
armed horses, that Bertran declared he loved to see ranged across
the battlefields of spring.[58] Pound's 'Altaforte' mood when he was
with Gaudier-Brzeska must have been 'phallic' also, for Wyndham
Lewis described Gaudier's statue of Pound with that word.[59] This
phallic state of mind in Pound has much importance for his Provence, and we should try to group the things with which it had affinities for him, and those to which it was opposed.

Pound later came to see the directing intelligence as a phallus. In
Blast No. 1, of 1914, he speaks of 'All MOMENTUM, which is the
past bearing upon us, RACE, RACE-MEMORY, instinct charging
the PLACID, / NON-ENERGIZED FUTURE.'[60] Commenting on
Gourmont's *Physique de l'Amour* in 1921, Pound said that the
human brain could be seen analogically as a large clot of genital
fluid; there were traces of this idea 'in the symbolism of phallic religions, man really the phallus or spermatozoid charging, head-on,
the female chaos; integration of the male in the female organ. Even
oneself has felt it, driving any new idea into the great passive vulva
of London, a sensation analogous to the male feeling in copulation.'
Intuition was the creative part of the process: 'And as Gourmont
says, there is only reasoning where there is initial error, i.e., weakness of the spurt, wandering search.'[61] But the 'direction of the will'
was necessary to prepare oneself properly for this intuitive leap; so
Pound conceded to the Buddhists in the later Cantos:

> But their First Classic: that the heart shd / be straight,
> The phallos perceive its aim.[62]

Therefore anyone who could get some shape into the universe was
taking a male role. Mussolini, a 'factive personality' like Malatesta,
was 'a male of the species'.[63] Pound did not see in all the troubadours the violent energy of Bertran de Born, and Bertran himself
soon faded out of the foreground of Pound's Provence, but his trou-

badours fit the metaphors that I am describing. Pound has the troubadour developing his knowledge of the 'universe of fluid force' by
attacking the great barrier between himself and that elemental
other, the female, and hence generating a tension that increases his
psychic sensitivity. From this come all the electrical metaphors for
creativity—sparks across polar gaps—in the early 'Psychology and
Troubadours'. Provence, Pound felt, had favoured this sexual tension because 'the living conditions . . . gave the necessary restraint';[64]
by 1928 he thought that the cause was not such a sociology but 'the
dogma that there is some proportion between the fine thing held in
the mind, and the inferior thing ready for instant consumption', but
that this was still in opposition to the Hellenic 'Plastic plus immediate satisfaction'.[65] Ritual reflected this resistance and this break-
through, so that the troubadour was in some sense a priest; his poem
was like a rite; and Pound in fact believed that a sexual rite was
behind the troubadours.[66] These are the patterns behind his whole
later thinking about Provence, as we shall see.

The phallic aggressiveness on the one hand, and the fear-struc-
tures that both Pound and Bertran detested on the other, fit the
Freudian distinction between genital and anal. Pound's whole aesthetic of the 'clean line' in visual art is an attack on the wobbly,
muzzed-over line, the line whose author will not admit to himself
where he intends it to go; the line should charge direct to its goal,
like the knights in *Sestina: Altaforte*. 'Que vos vers expriment vos
intentions / et que la musique conforme,' ['Let your verses express
your intentions, and let the music fit,'] as the Cantos say.[67] The associations of the wobbly line—dirtiness and messiness—arouse an
anger in Pound, as when he attacks 'bad and niggled sculpture
(Angoulême or Bengal)':

Against these European Hindoos we find the 'medieval clean line', as distinct from medieval niggle. Byzantium gives us perhaps the best architecture, or at least the best inner structure, that we know, I mean for propor-
tions, for ornament flat on the walls, and not bulging and bumping and
indulging in bulbous excrescence. . . .
Perhaps out of a sand-swept country, the need of interior harmony. That
is conjecture. Against this clean architecture, we find the niggly Angoulême, the architectural ornament of bigotry, superstition, and mess.[68]

Not only art, but also moral qualities and sciences—especially
economics—were either 'clean' or 'filthy' for Pound. British journal-

ism was an 'excrement' poisoning the human colon.[69] All this was related to sexuality: usury obstructed the natural desires of youth and
defiled the altar of the sex-rite, creating 'a species of monetary
Black Mass'; in a decent age usury was placed 'on a par with buggery'.[70] Pound, consciously or not, made the Freudian connection
between money-hoarding and anality. In *Sestina: Altaforte,* the
fearful crouch near the earth and try to protect what they have:

> The man who fears war and squats opposing
> My words for stour, hath no blood of crimson
> But is fit only to rot in womanish peace

just as in Pound's model for this, Bertran de Born, rich men stay in
their cellars to guard their gold.[71] Pound associated usury with
hoarding, and both with fear stemming from lack of faith in oneself
and in the abundance of nature; there was a hoarding of money
which caused art treasures to gather dust 'in the dealer's cellar',[72]
and a hoarding of knowledge which caused professors to sit 'on piles
of stone books',

> obscuring the texts with philology,
>   hiding them under their persons, [. . .]
> monopolists, obstructors of knowledge,
>   obstructors of distribution.[73]

and both come out as anal.

Two currents of metaphor seem to be joined in all this: (a) consti-
pation / messing around with one's own filth / refusal to void and
clean up; (b) buggery as diversion of the 'natural' current / coitus
reservatus or refusal to rish the phallic commitment. Thus in the
later Cantos we find these lines about the people's outcry against
Gondomar, Spanish Ambassador in London in the early seventeenth
century and therefore representative of wealth, obscurantism, repression, and intrigue:

> Gondomar 'devil in dung-cart'!

> Flaccus' translator wore the crown
> The jew and the buggar dragged it down
> 'Devil in dung-cart' Gondomar[74]

I think we shall see that these conjunctions of emotional areas are extremely important for Pound's Provence: they are the points *against which* he defined his troubadours' relations with their ladies / goddesses. Let us sort them out:

Anal	*Genital*
homosexuality	heterosexuality
instant satisfaction	resistance
confusing	distinguishing
plaster-moulding	stonecutting
Rubens creampuffs	Pisanello 'clean line'
usury	constructive credit
'hogging the harvest'	distribution
mumbo-jumbo	science
philology and scholarship	elucidation
parasitic priesthoods	interpretive cults
Buddhist 'facile abnegation', leading to fanaticism or to smugness	Catholic sense of one's relation to a vital universe of graded good and evil
darkness	illumination
clogging	flow
static harmonics 'like steam ascending from a morass'	'the sharp song with sun under its radiance'[75]

It will be seen that these sets of antitheses are part of every area of Pound's thinking. They are particularly important for us here because Provence was the *exemplum* of almost everything on the approved side, except perhaps the most energetically constructive cast of mind, which he found in Italy in Malatesta.[76] At moments, both sides of the basic opposition are stated by Pound in an hysterical way; there is a violence about the usury/buggery talk, and a certain unreality about the insistently clean encounters of the semi-divine in the Cantos.[77] Perhaps these aspects of life are by him separated out too much. His insistence that the business of life must be possible cleanly, without complication, weakness, or obsession with one's own problems, may have led to the later breakdown. The clean cutter, the aggressive fighter, demanded definite resistance, just as the troubadour needed tension and restraint; the *Rock-Drill* title 'was intended to imply the necessary resistance in getting a certain main thesis across—hammering' (Pound),[78] just as *Sestina: Altaforte*, forty-six years before, had spoken of this resistance almost

more than the overcoming of it, with its rhyme-repeat on 'opposing'
This is probably why Pound's view of history came to be not the various sluggishness and cupidity of all men fighting against their
momentary clarities, but a succession of identifiable Montforts and
Hamiltons betraying a parallel series of culture-heroes and secret
cultists. The real struggle for a man like himself was therefore to
keep up his will, not to be deflected, to propagandise endlessly until
the truth was heard. This feeling that the battle for truth was external may have led Pound into his impatience with others, especially
in the key area of economics, which was also the focus for the emotional complexes I have described. The young man's healthy intoler-
ance, probably cultivated even in those days, became mere irritabil-
ity, as when he rendered this Chinese:

> Tinkle, tinkle, two tongues? No.
> But down on the word with exactness,
>   against gnashing of teeth (upper incisors)
>   chih! chih!
>   wo chih[3] chih[3]
>   wo[4] wo ch'o ch'o, paltry yatter[79]

This probably helps to explain the peculiar business of Pound's
identification with Mussolini. Mussolini was, as Pound later
admitted, a 'bubble'; he was above all a voice, and Pound of all
people (as Zukofsky told him) should have known voices.[80] But what
Pound identified with was the decisiveness, and this is not so far a
step from the way he had created the pugnacious persona Bertran
de Born, and worn it to impress Gaudier-Brzeska with his vigour.

THE LATER POUND AND BERTRAN'S ART

By the time he came to write the Cantos, Pound's attitude towards
Bertran de Born was changing from the simple admiration of masculine vigour that comes across in Sestina: Altaforte. In the earlier
years he had thought of Bertran's verse as an expression of real involvement in real war, and an expression that had an effect on the
war. Hence its particular value: 'Villon's verse is real, because he
lived it; as Bertran de Born, as Arnaut Marvoil, as that mad poseur

Vidal, he lived it. For these men life is in the press. No brew of
books, no distillation of sources will match the tang of them.'[81] In
1910 Pound thought that Bertran's kind of war was important:
'Much of such song is, of course, filled with politics and personal
allusions which today require explanation. The passages on the joy
of war, however, enter the realm of the universal, and can stand
without annotation.'[82] But the essay 'Troubadours: Their Sorts and
Conditions' (1913) was a watershed. It begins as exactly the kind of
pretty tapestry about the troubadours that it claims not to be; but
then Pound seems to become appalled by the way his favourite
material must appear to his less whimsical friends (imagine Lewis
reading this article); and he tries to bring in a note of reality with a
piece about Peire Cardenal, a violent critic of thirteenth-century
corruption. At this point appear doubts about Bertran de Born,
though for the moment Pound shelves them by saying 'His time was
past':

And after this there is a passage of pity and of irony fine-drawn as much of
[Peire's] work is, for he keeps the very formula that De Born had used in his
praise of battle, 'Belh mes quan vey' ['It delights me when I see']; and, perhaps, in Sir Bertrans' time even the Provencal wars may have seemed like a
game, and may have appeared to have some element of sport and chance
in them. But the 12th century had gone, and the spirit of the people was
weary, and [Peire's] passage may well serve as a final epitaph on all that
remained of silk thread and *cisclatons,* of viol and *gai saber.*[83]

That was in 1913. Then came the First World War, the magni-
tude of whose disasters and the horror of which, when they finally
became known, had a big effect on Pound. He began to change his
ideas on the nature of war, and to look for the rot in the common-
weal that could have produced such a monster. In 1920 he wrote his
first damnation of the treachery, starting with lines which are remi-
niscent of Bertran's 'who will have come, some for wealth, some on
command, some for honour':

> Some quick to arm,
> some for adventure,
> some from fear of weakness,
> some from fear of censure,
> some for love of slaughter, in imagination,

learning later. . . .
some in fear, learning love of slaughter;

Died some, pro patria,
                non 'dulce' non 'et decor'. . . .
walked eye-deep in hell
believing in old men's lies, then unbelieving
came home, home to a lie,
home to many deceits,
home to old lies and new infamy;
usury age-old and age-thick
and liars in public places.[84]

The truth about what happened in the war took a long time to filter through, as so often happens, and in 1916 Pound could still write unreservedly of patriotism versus 'the Boche', and quote his dead friend Gaudier: 'Perhaps you ignore what is Rosalie? It's our bayonet, we call it so because we draw it red from fat Saxon bellies.'[85] In 1918 he still spoke of the war as 'civilization against barbarism.'[86] But when he came to rework this last piece in 1929, he felt obliged to add a footnote: 'I should probably be incapable of writing this paragraph now.' In that year he added a footnote to his early praise for Bertran's songs: 'This kind of thing was much more impressive before 1914 than it has been since 1920. The pagentry can still be found in the paintings of Simone Martini and of Paolo Uccello.'[87]

Was Bertran's poetry now valueless, and if so, how had it once seemed so important? Was its apparent value entirely in its realism, and when that was disproved, was there nothing left? Pound had implied in 1913 that war in the twelfth century might have been altogether a pleasanter occupation. But to that extent it must have been war within the limits of some temporary code and thereby, like all games, of limited interest as a subject for poetry. That is the judgement Pound seems to make on Bertran's wars in 1938, using the Chinese poets as a touchstone: 'The weariness and fact of war already there in the Songs of Tsao, *Odes* I.15. . . .

At any rate 3000 years ago the Chinese poets were aware of the unutterable dullness of warfare. The fine edge of chivalry is something utterly different from the weariness of plugging along in the mud, season after season.'[88]

But it will be noticed that Pound says nothing derogatory about 'the fine edge of chivalry'; nor is the comparison with Uccello any insult to Bertran. Pound probably felt that, seen thus, Bertran's world was of lesser significance to later ages than he had thought, since few ages and classes have benefited from the safeguards and privileges necessary to the kind of war implied by 'chivalry'. But Bertran had produced a very vivid and precise account of a particular kind of world, however narrow; an account that would not rot 'in the unhermetic jars of bad writing', to quote Pound on James.[89]

This seems to be Pound's conclusion in 1921, when he published Canto VII:

> Eleanor (she spoiled in a British climate)
> ''Ελανδρος and 'Ελέπτολις, and
>   poor old Homer blind,
>   blind as a bat,
> Ear, ear for the sea-surge;
>   rattle of old men's voices.
> And then the phantom of Rome,
>   marble narrow for seats
> 'Si pulvis nullus' said Ovid
> 'Erit, nullum tamen excute.'
> To file and candles, e li mestiers ecoutes;
> Scene for the battle only, but still scene,
> Pennons and standards y cavals armatz
> Not mere succession of strokes, sightless narration,
> To Dante's 'ciocco', brand struck in the game.[90]

This is a list of poetic skills. Pound said that Homer probably had his powers of imagination accentuated by being blind; here it is his auditory imagination that he speaks of, as when he wrote: 'I have never read half a page of the *Odyssey* without learning something about melodic invention.'[91] Ovid, with his lines about brushing away non-existent dust from the favoured girl's lap, had a precise eye for the manners of his Rome. These are faculties that can be developed. So can the ability to get them onto paper; so Pound tells the writer 'Get to your bench,' to the *amorosa lima*, the loving file, and the midnight oil:

> To file and candles, e li mestiers ecoutes

E li mestiers ecoutes is a mis-concocted piece of Old French, probably intended to mean 'and listen to the craft'.[92] Then in the next
four lines Pound captures the nature of Bertran de Born's limited
but living pagentry. 'Y cavals armatz', 'and caparisoned horses', we
have seen quoted in the later Cantos with a reference to the 'perpen-
dicular lances' of the military pomp in Velásquez's *Surrender of
Breda*. It is from the song in which Bertran celebrates the visual
pleasures of Eastertime warfare. 'Ciocco' is from an image in Dante:

> Then, as in striking burned brands
> Innumerable sparks leap up....[93]

Pound had already picked up this image in Canto V:

> Sparks like a partridge covey,
> Like the 'ciocco', brand struck in the game.[94]

It seems to sum up Bertran's main gift, creating images that contain
movement which have exactly the advantage over a

> mere succession of strokes

that the ideogram, Pound implied, has over the static images produced by his fellow-Imagists.[95] We shall see some of these moving
images when we come to the troubadours' writing about nature.

In later years Pound harnessed Bertran in the cause of distribu-
tive economics. The following passage from the *Guide to Kulchur* of
1938 puts together revenue-sharing and feudal gift-giving, the common factor being that each could prevent wealth from accumulat-
ing in a few hands, whence it could manipulate the public:

We have one Mohammedan fact that will take a headline in future histories. One of the early khalifs did pay a national dividend. He ran with an
empty treasury no national debt and a share-out....

Whig historians have not emphasized feudal distributism....

The praise of *largesse* in the troubadours is a fact in history. The attempt
of Frederic II of Sicily to enlighten Europe both culturally and economically was a MAJOR event.

Feudal dues have been stressed and the feudal duties (noblesse oblige)
have been overshadowed....

S. Malatesta gave away a lot of castles on, or shortly after, his accession. Such acts have a meaning and a social significance. Madox Ford used to talk very vehemently, but not very coherently, of the damage done in England by commutation of duty of overlords to their people into mere money payments.[96]

Pound believed that, whether the unit of government was the modern state or the mediaeval lord, a zero balance in the central bank was a good thing. A big reserve meant that money was not being used productively but was being held in large quantities either for defence or for attack in the exploitative game of international exchange rates. A national debt meant that a select group of bond-holders was making a free living out of government paper at no risk whatsoever, since the guarantee was the State; which guarantee, or reputation, could much better have been used by the State to issue money not backed by borrowing from private individuals. Worse, the bondholders acquired a dangerous economic-political power that was constantly increasing with the accumulation of interest paid to them by the State. These things can be applied with some reason to the mediaeval economy as well as to the modern; for the modern period, Pound's remedy was revenue-sharing, and in the mediaeval period he pointed to the constant propaganda for hand-outs that came from the troubadours. So in a late Canto Pound brought in Bertran de Born to a passage about a share-out by Alexander the Great:

> Báros metetz en gatge!
> > Alexander paid the debts of his troops.
> Not serendipity
> > but to spread
>
> 德
>
> tê   thru the people.[97]

Bertran's words are from the *tornada* where he tells the barons to pawn their castles before fighting, thus (according to Pound) fleecing the usurers and bringing their hoards into circulation. The *tê* that Alexander spread through his troops when he shared out his treasury is glossed in Pound's *Confucius* as ' "know thyself" carried into action' — presumably the kind of self-awareness that exists in a sensibility not corrupted by the habit of greed.[98]

So, despite all his reservations, Pound made quite a large claim both for Bertran's ability as a poet and for the ethos he represented. Bertran's poetics will be examined at various points in the following chapters. His ethos, and whether Pound should have cited it in a modern economic argument, is also a problem that a book like this should tackle, by seeing how it worked in his own time.

2. BERTRAN'S PROPAGANDA

Pound in his earlier years used Bertran as an *exemplum,* a demonstration of a possible way of living, just as Confucius used the Duke of Chou;[1] Pound's Bertran was a model for a certain dynamic confidence in pouncing on the pleasures of life. Let us consider how this image was constructed out of Bertran's poetry, and what relation that poetry had to Bertran's own times.

Bertran's propaganda is against fear, and the defences it builds, whether personal or political. He leaps into the horrors of war with gusto:

> The Count has demanded of me, via Sir Aramon
> to fix him up a song in which
> a thousand shields will be split,
> headpieces, hauberks, tunics chopped up
> and doublets ruined and torn.[2]

Were Richard not betraying him, he says, he would already have

> caught thrusts on my shield
> and turned my white banner red.[3]

War is for him in the same range of aesthetic delights as love, and where a hundred troubadours had made spring's coming the preamble to amorous expectation, Bertran proclaims that spring makes him think of war:

> The gay time of Easter pleases me,
> bringing leaves and flowers,
> and I am pleased when I hear the sounds
> of birds making their song ring
>   through the woodland,
> and I love to see the fields pitched
> with tents and pavilions
>   and I'm happy

to see in ranks in the countryside
armed knights and horses. . . .

When the fight starts we shall see
war-clubs, swords, coloured helmets,
shields, sliced, ruined,
and many a liegeman strike in the mêlée,
    so that dead men's horses
and those of the dying will wander aimlessly.
When he's in the thick of it
    let no man of birth
think of anything but splitting heads and arms,
for a dead man is worth more than a live prisoner.[4]

Bertran brings out all the freshness of the warrior life with his word-sounds; in

Trombas e corn e graile clar[5]

trumpets and horns and clear bugles

the thinness of *clar* and *graile* sets the bugles off from the fat trumps. Another poem was written when Bertran was on campaign and addressed to a princess in the comfort of her court,[6] and he contrasts his hardships with an imaginary inn stocked with good things:

Ges de disnar no fora oi mais matis,
Qui agues pres bon ostau,
E fos dedintz la charns e·l pas e·l vis,
E·l fuocs fos clars com de fau.[7]

It would not be quite time to dine
for a man who had taken good lodging,
where were meat, and bread, and wine,
and the fire clear as of beechwood.

Nothing could equal the gusto of those plosives and fricatives in accented syllables, setting down the pleasures of good food and warmth. In a few words Bertran's cadences can bring alive whole scenes of mediaeval warfare in a way that seems more real than anything before Breughel:

> Puois Ventadorns e Comborns e Segur
> E Torena e Monfortz ab Gordo
> An fach acort ab Peiregorc e jur,
> E li borges si clauen de viro[8]

In that, one can almost hear the 'clack' of the shutters, when the castles

> have sworn to a pact with Périgord,
> and the citizens are locking up all round. . . .

The townsfolk of one of Breughel's tableaus seem to scatter as Bertran rubs his hands, in these two lines:

> E platz mi, quan li corredor
> Fan las gens e l'aver fugir[9]

> and I like it, when the scouts
> make people and their goods flee. . . .

For those who have not the confident vigour to throw themselves into these pleasures, Bertran has only scorn; they do not know what they want, they are spineless, they are less than human. As they deserve to be, they are mere pike-fodder for Richard Lionheart, who

> sharpens them and hones them
> and plays them like a knife;
> but they are too thick on the ground, to the fore,
> and numerous, towards the edge,
> and more faithful than a prior;
> by courtesy of the sharpener
> they will all come to the life eternal.[10]

Philip of France's victims are like 'sparrows, and little birds' that he is hunting with falcons.[11] Bertran's own allies are like iron, and he the blacksmith; or they are like big, useless horses:

> Talairan doesn't trot or jump
> or shift from his stall[12]

Bertran's belief in the contagiousness of courage is such that he never flatters anyone's cowardice; he tries to shame his allies into a little firmness of purpose.

Bertran sees money-lust quite simply as a defence hiding a fear, leading to more fear: his contemporaries hoarded gold because they feared living by their courage:

> Don't think that a weak man
> will ever rise two steps in worth,
> — down in the cellar
> he can squat, quiet, and curled up,
> and let him stay there!
> for a thousand sterling marks
> he couldn't climb two steps,
> he's so afraid his loot should go missing.[13]

When he discovers that his allies have made a separate peace, he predicts how stingy they will get in peacetime:

> now the rich will act like doorkeepers,
> keeping their gates shut tight[14]

For war is what keeps money and life in general flowing. It makes the great spend freely:

> Don't take me for a brawler
> if I want one baron to hate another;
> that's the way that vassals and castle-holders
> will get more out of them;
> a great man is freer, more generous and *intime,*
> I give you my word,
> in war, than in peace.[15]

War makes the rich abandon their old men's pleasures and cultivate a little social life once more:

> I am very pleased that there is left neither truce
> nor peace among the barons,
> who just now were planting shrubberies.
> They like gardens and parks
> and indolence, with little company, so much
> that you'd think they were expecting assassins —

> you'd never get in where one of them was
> without a scuffle.[16]

And the usurers, arch-hoarders, can be plundered at will when there's a war on:

> Soon we'll see trumpets, tabors, banners, pennants,
> coats-of-arms and white and black horses,
> for the time will be good :
> we shall take the usurers' wealth from them.
> No pack-horse will travel
> safe by day, or citizen, without fear,
> or merchant coming from France:
> he who steals gladly will be rich.[17]

So Bertran believes in what Pound called 'confusion/Basis of renewals':[18]

> I like it, when I see the lords change round,
> and the old men leave their houses to the young[19]

Bertran's personal impulses certainly favoured this devil-take-the-hindmost freebooting, based on perpetual war; or he could not have got it so perfectly into verse. But he was also one of a group whose interests as a whole seemed to push them in that direction. They were the knights whose expectations of life, inherited from their culture, were becoming impossible to sustain in the economic conditions of the twelfth-century South. The 'norm' for a knight was that his life-style should be supported by the possession of land and the income deriving from it, though there were exceptions, like the 'household vassals', unplaceable younger sons maintained in some lord's castle.[20] But houses could simply dwindle: there was no effective principle of primogeniture in these regions — all properties were divided among all children — fiefs might be chopped up into twelfths, thirty-sixths, and even seventy-seconds.[21] Thus with Raimbaut d'Orange, a contemporary of Bertran's, a troubadour, and like Bertran the projector of a courtly, aristocratic ideal: his list of fiefs was impressively long, but the fiefs themselves were scattered and tiny, and the rights to them were endlessly subdivided.[22] Raimbaut had to mortgage his lands, and so did dozens of his contemporaries in these regions. Bertran de Born himself was probably caught by the same process, since he had to share his castle, Hautefort, with a brother he hated.[23]

There was another economic vice that was squeezing the poorer knights intolerably. The value of land was almost static, and the rent-income was fixed by ineluctable custom. Now, in the twelfth century, especially in areas like Languedoc, a commercial revolution was taking place: towns were growing, trade was booming, and prices were rocketing. This brought disaster to many a nobleman.[24] Men in Bertran's position were thus caught between the economics of the Middle Ages and those of the Renaissance.[25]

The propaganda for war was a common answer. In *Girart de Roussillon,* the Franco-Provençal *chanson de geste,* when peace has been concluded the knights put forward a plan to maintain a permanent army, with the obvious aim of earning their living by it.[26] 'Household vassals', and poor knights doing occasional garrison duty for some lord, were always ready to be led off to war, to have their pittances supplemented with plunder.[27] Peace was a situation where the 'new men' of the rising communes — the merchants — were in control; Raimbaut d'Orange and Bertran de Born could not understand the commercial revolution, and detested trade-based money.[28] Raimbaut, as Walter Pattison says, retreated simply into archaism, into trying to 'maintain a court of a rather archaic type, in which the new power of money could still be ignored, although at the ultimate cost of bankruptcy.'[29] Bertran retreated more specifically into the world of the heroic/epic *chanson de geste,* which offered to solve the problems of status and of economics at the same time. He inherited a social position that 'by rights' ought to have a power concomitant with its prestige; at every turn he was humiliated by lack of cash. In the *chanson de geste,* cash, and honour with it, came out of the blue — at least to those, like Bertran, who possessed the necessary virtues of courage, honesty, and loyalty. It came from above, from the lord one followed to war. In the Germanic tribes of Roman times, Tacitus had found this simple economic structure, the *comitas,* whereby the lord forever distributed to his vassals the plunder acquired by their valour in perpetual war. The poet of the Old English *Seafarer* lamented that it was dying:

> there are not now kings or emperors
> or gold-givers such as there once were[30]

But a glittering model for this generosity still existed in Bertran's time, in the *Song of Roland* and the other gestes, and Bertran took these for one of the chief items in his 'mental furnishings'.[31] He placed the economic reasoning and the cultural model side-by-side:

> I can't stop myself from sending out a song
> now Sir Yes-and-No's started fires, and drawn blood:
> a great war makes a greedy lord munificent,
> so I'm glad to see the kings' pomp,
> now they'll need pegs, cords, and tent-caps,
> and tents will be pitched in the field,
> and we'll meet in hundreds, thousands,
> and after us they will sing *gestes* of it.[32]

The last lines of this strophe[33] sound as stirringly as Henry V's 'And gentlemen in England, now a-bed, / Shall think themselves accursed they were not here', and a clear tradition links the two. Bertran lets the epic-Germanic formula for worthy kingship slip out with complete simplicity when he reproaches Richard Lionheart for his idleness:

> He toys with jugs and cups
> and silver
> pots, and casseroles,
> and hawks and hunts;
> and here he used to seize and give;
> let him not dodge
> troubles —
> mêlée and noise
> and turbulent war
> do him good.[34]

E sai tolia e donava, 'And here he used to seize and give.'

Whole aspects of Bertran's vision came from the *Chanson de Roland* and its descendants. When Geoffrey, brother to Richard Lionheart, and Bertran's quondam ally, died, Bertran filled Paradise with *geste* heroes in his lament, to keep the valiant prince com-

pany.[35] The vision of the *geste* authors themselves is described thus
by Paul Meyer:

> ...they had no idea at all of the power of the blows struck, or of the effects
> of the wounds they delighted in describing. At every moment there are
> people split down to the belt, arms and legs cut off with a sword-blow....
> *Chanson de geste* authors show us knights, unhorsed, getting back into the
> saddle after losing an arm, or still speaking and fighting while the grey
> matter is coming out of their opened skulls.[36]

Bertran likewise:

> soon we shall see fields littered with quarters
> of helmets, and shields, and swords, and saddles,
> and men split through the trunk right to the belt.[37]

His vision is straight from the *Chanson de Roland,* where Roland
kills Chernuble in this wise:

> He breaks his helmet where the garnets shine,
> cuts through his hair and his scalp,
> splits between his eyes and down his face,
> and the hauberk with its fine mail,
> and the whole body, down to the fork.[38]

Writers and artists of all ages, though deeply involved in war,
have transmuted it at some level of their consciousness from what it
is to what it ought to be. Wilfred Owen, now taught in school as
blunt reality, also has admixtures both of high Romantic bisexual
masochism and of melodramatic Darwinism.[39] In Bertran's time the
Chanson de Roland was far more influential, in determining how
artists showed battles, than the actual wars going on all around. In
visual portrayals of the Roland legend, as Lejeune and Stiennon
show, text governs iconography.[40] In one fifteenth-century minia-
ture 'With his invincible Durandal, Roland splits in two King Mar-
sile, who faces him here. The detail of the body, cut in two, reminds
one of an anatomy drawing.'[41] Charlemagne is faithfully shown
slicing off half of Palligan's head, helmet and all.[42] Bertran took in
wider *geste* attitudes also: like them, he never particularly cared

whose side a man was on, as long as he was 'handsome and strong
and swift and light', as the *Roland* describes the pagan Margariz.[43]
The *geste* was, for his age, what Henry Newbolt and his predecessors
were for the British Imperial officer: a set of attitudes breathed in
with the air.[44] When a Norman minstrel sang for William the Conqueror's men at the battle of Hastings, it was 'of Karlemaigne and of
Rollant' that he sang.[45]

Such a propaganda must have made life hard and sometimes hell-
ish for society at large. Paul Meyer describes warfare as it may be
seen through *Girart de Roussillon:*

After the victory, the prisoners are massacred, only keeping back the rich
barons who are worth a ransom.... That is the constant practice of the
whole of the Middle Ages. After the taking or the capitulation of a town,
the paid soldiers of the garrison are mutilated, to put them out of service.
... One kills the peasantry of one's adversary by the same reasoning as one
destroys his harvest or cuts down his vines or fruit-trees: thereby, one ruins
him....[46]

Laying waste land, crops and habitations, and killing, mutilating or
abducting everything that moved, was universal, partly because
wars so often settled down to an endless siege, and this was one way
of punishing or demoralising the besieged.[47] Bertran railed:

> they ruin and burn my land
> and raze my trees
> and mix the grain with the straw[48]

But he himself was not too closely involved with this sordid business;
it affected his income rather than his person. A knight could generally restrict himself to pitched battles, where his highly superior
equipment made him safe from attack by any but his social equals.
His meiny, slow, ill-equipped, untrained and difficult to move
across country, did the dirty work, and were butchered miserably by
the mercenaries whose use was pioneered by Henry II and Richard.[49]
They hardly entered the field of vision of Bertran and his literate
contemporaries.

The propaganda for war did not even solve the cash problem for
men like Bertran de Born. The cultural model demanded not only

that one receive in abundance from the lord one had supported
loyally; but also that one pass it on freely. For Bertran, a good court
had

> gracious welcoming and giving without fickleness
> and sweet repose and we're-so-glad-to-have-you
> and a large and well-maintained establishment,
> gifts, and equippings, and courteousness[50]

He was proud of his race's generosity:

> We Limousins and people who enjoy ourselves,
> who want men to give and laugh,
> shall vanquish sense with craziness[51]

like Tartarin de Tarascon, who inherited something of Bertran's
tradition. For Henry Fielding this attitude—again in part inherited
from the *geste* tradition, via many mediators—was one of the worst
vices a young nobleman could have. It did twelfth-century meri-
dional noblemen no good, as Paul Meyer observes:

Since their revenues, which were in any case very badly administered,
could not keep up with these growing expenses, it was necessary—in a
period when it was not easy to get into debt, for lack of lenders—to multiply extraordinary resources. The greed of the Latins, with their unbearable loquacity, was what first struck the Byzantines when they came into
contact with the Crusaders.[52]

Unfortunately, by Bertran's time the economy of the rising towns
was sophisticated enough to have moneylenders. Raimbaut
d'Orange, whose case is so close to Bertran's, suffered from them.
He was in trouble from the day he inherited his father's land. His
father had been unable to live within his income, and had left most
of his tiny fiefs in trust for thirteen years after his death, to pay off
his debts. Raimbaut pawned what he could as soon as he could and
raised the loans to the absolute limit; then when the thirteen years
were up, he started pawning again. When he died, he probably had
no more than a nominal claim to what he had inherited.[53]
In his poems, Raimbaut reviled the new rich of the towns, the

most common source of liquidity.[54] Bertran de Born recommended
that they be robbed wholesale on the highways. He also, apparently,
proposed to exploit the moneylenders:

> Barons, put in pawn
> Castles and farms and towns
> Before you make war on each other.[55]

As Pound explained it: 'thus if they won they could redeem them, if
they lost the loss fell on the holder of the mortgage.'[56] But moneylenders were not stupid. It was common enough to lend to kings and
princes — Henry II hired mercenaries on borrowed money at the age
of fourteen, to make a raid on his as-yet-unsecured patrimony, and
his son the Young King was to be constantly in debt.[57] But the lenders knew the risks, and charged far higher rates to kings and princes
than to municipalities. The Emperor Frederick II had to pay 30-40
per cent in 1319; the Angevin King of Naples agreed to 30 per
cent.[58] The aristocratic classes only hated the lenders more for this.
The illustrious William the Marshal one day met a clerk who had
eloped with his girlfriend. The conversation was cordial, until the
clerk mentioned that he intended to live from the interest on his
capital. Then the great warrior, close friend of the Young King and
as parasitical upon the community as he,[59] thought it a virtue to
seize the money:

> Said the Marshal: 'Usury!
> By God's sword! I don't like it . . . .
> Take the money from him, Eustace!'[60]

And with all these hypocrisies, and sufferings inflicted, the propaganda for chivalric war had yet one more drawback: it greatly
slowed the economic development that was to make the Renaissance
possible. City-states could not grow without specialisation; specialisation was impossible without transport, and incessant petty wars
helped to make transport prohibitively expensive as well as dangerous.[61]

None the less there are things to be said in favour of Bertran's
ethic and aesthetic.[62] We can see him as identifying with the values
of an age that was partly mythical and partly historical, and whose
breakdown before and during his time in certain ways represented a

definite decline. The *comitas* system, based on the distribution of plunder, had already by Charlemagne's time begun to give way to the classic feudal system: officials were rewarded with land to administer, and this land came to be regarded as a patrimony, provided that the heir always did homage for it to his overlord.[63] The *comitas* structure had given the bond of simple personal contact between warrior and lord; the feudal system placed the man often at a great geographical distance from his lord, and the idea that he owed the lord anything for what he had 'inherited' from his own father often became very weak.[64] None the less there could remain very strong personal and ritual bonds. There was a ceremony of homage which was no mere decoration, but legally essential. The kiss of homage suggests some feeling of mutuality, and the vassal was sometimes called the *dru,* 'lover', or *ami,* 'friend'. In the law books this bond was often taken to be more binding than the bond of kinship, and there was a universal assumption that what a man received from his lord he owed to his inferior.[65] There was more in the relationship than mere exploitation; and as we have seen, Pound, whose sympathies were often closer to feudal societies than to others, made something of this.[66]

By Bertran's time the personal tie was quickly losing its force, and being converted into a grudgingly-acknowledged claim of authority which was more and more expressed and satisfied in terms of money. Overlords became more interested in dues than in the loyalties of vassals.[67] Fiefs could be sold; services were commutable for cash; and where, as became common, a man owed loyalty to several lords, there arose the highly un-personal idea that his highest duty was to the lord of whom he held the richest fief.[68] By the period of Bertran de Born and the Plantagenet kings, as Bloch says, 'Fealty had become an object of trade.'[69] In earlier periods, when circulation of money was weak, it was not worthwhile to hoard coin; and since it was almost impossible to pay wages, payment in kind and by services created further ties between man and lord, and between man and land. In Bertran's time, society was coming more and more to be based on monetary values, on the acquisition of status and security by wealth; the economy came to be dominated not by the producer, but by the trader, as Bloch says,[70] and the usurer made money out of money.

Bertran grasped his values clearly, and rightly placed them in the

myth of the period of Charlemagne that is embodied in the *Roland,*
and in the realities of the age that was dying in his time. No doubt
he fused the two in his mind, seeing more of the *Roland* qualities in
the immediate past than were really there; but the important point
is the clarity with which he saw his values. He loved vigorous, open-
air action, the pleasures that went with it, and the human relationships that came from it. He took his delight in sound, colour, movement, sensitive discourse (as the love-poems show), free social interchange, and what a man does and feels in hunting and fighting. He
dissociated all these from substitutes in the culture around him,
sought after because they were tangible (and thus had instant pres-
tige-value) and static (and thus did not depend on the vitality of
one's perceptions). He despised the desire to amass wealth, the desire
to sit in solitary comfort and security, and the desire for man-to-man
relationships insulated by money. In other words, he knew what
pleasure was, as distinct from what the *bourgeois* and the alienated
regard as pleasure. This awareness is of the highest value, inasmuch
as without it no society can have an aim beyond the solving of immediate physical problems. Pound observed that the real aristocracy
believed ' "people shd. do what they like". This is good society. Personal codes used for themselves.' He placed its value very close to
that of the creative artist, and set it off clearly from 'the great mass
of the rich, organized in circles of snobbisms'.[71]

It is true that Bertran's cultural model was archaic and, taken as
a whole, useless even for his own period. The events that are the subject of the *Chanson de Roland* took place in 778, and the life-style
that Bertran admired certainly had some reality at that time; but
the *Chanson* was actually written a little before 1100, when ties to
territory were already coming to seem as important as personal
bonds. Bertran wrote his songs in the years just before and after
1200, when the rise of Renaissance-type urban economies was
already making his ethic a dangerous obstacle. The landless knights
in a lord's retinue, Bloch remarks, kept alive the features of the
ancient *comitas* system throughout the Middle Ages, and Bertran
was effectively one of these living archaisms.[72]

None the less the Italian Renaissance probably inherited something important from Bertran's ideal. Dante and his contemporaries
had a certain arrogance in aesthetic matters; knowing that the finest
perceptions cannot instantly be communicated in the language of

the democratic media, they still proceeded to cultivate these perceptions, for themselves and for 'those who knew'. They believed in a natural aristocracy, and even though some of them thought this was an aristocracy of talent, not of birth, they still used the vocabulary of a myth of blood aristocracy: a worthwhile woman was *gentile,* something between 'nobly-born' and just 'refined'. The myth of noble blood was tied to a myth of the court — 'aulic' is a key word in Dante's discussions of language;[73] and it is significant that the vocabularies of 'courtliness', of innate nobility, and of a certain conception of love are inextricably entwined in both the Provençal and the Italian lyrics, despite the fact that this idea of love has nothing inherently to do with court environments,[74] and that many of its celebrators in Northern Italy had no connection with a court.[75] This myth of inherent nobility, having its natural focus in a court, has its origins in the Provencal lyric, with the *geste* elements that that had subsumed, and in its younger sister the French romance. It was in all probability the myth of Bertran and his peers, the myth of the man of birth who cultivates genuine pleasures (including love) and the inherently noble gesture (especially of courage), which gave the Italian Renaissance the arrogance to rise above money- and prestige-grubbing. For us, Bertran can clarify a certain area of perception, that of the pleasures that he loved, and thus increase our sense of the possibilities.

3. HISTORY AND BERTRAN'S POETRY

Pound, when he began to say that the 'pagentry' and the 'fine edge of chivalry' were not so significant after all, had realised that the 'reality' Bertran 'lived' was partly moulded by a myth that was limited in value. But he never questioned whether Bertran really did and said, roughly speaking, what Bertran tells us he did and said. Nor did Dante, who also used Bertran's life, as it comes over in his poems,[1] as a moral example. Recent scholarship has alleged, on historical grounds, that Bertran was nowhere near the reality he claimed to be living. This of course calls into question the right of poets like Pound and Dante, who only know what Stock called the 'literary surface',[2] to use historical figures as moral examples. The reasons why good poetry is a reliable guide, in a certain way, to lived experience, are independent of any one case; but sceptics might be convinced by a careful look at this case as an historical problem. Do the documents suggest that Bertran was really involved in the kind of politics he writes about?

Bertran de Born is to be found with his head tucked underneath his arm 'in the manner of a lamp' in the eighth circle of Dante's Hell, because he 'gave the evil support to the Young King'; he 'turned the father and the sons against each other', and so 'separated persons thus united'.[3] Dante holds him chiefly responsible for the enmity between Henry II Plantagenet and his sons Henry 'the Young King', Geoffrey, Richard, and John. Splitting father from sons is breaking up part of the universal hierarchy; and so Bertran's head is removed from his trunk with this quasi-liturgical formula:

> And they were two in one, and one in two.

Dante shows his high seriousness by adapting *Lamentations* to describe Bertran's punishment:

See if any is as great as this.

But Dante does not confuse Bertran's ethics with his value as a
writer: when he selects the three great subjects for poetry, Safety,
Love, and Virtue, and says that 'valour in arms' is necessary for the
first of these, he cites Bertran as its greatest poet.[4] He then quotes
from *Non puosc mudar, un chantar non esparja*,[5] which is an excellent example of Bertran as provoker of strife between lord and
vassal.

Bertran seems to have been provoking strife throughout his
known lifetime. His first *sirventes* or verse-diatribe is about one of
the two main feudal struggles that went on throughout the later
twelfth century in the *Midi:* the struggle between the house of Barcelona (later united with Aragon) and the house of Toulouse, for
the County of Provence.[6] When, in 1181, Alfonso of Aragon broke
into the lands of Raymond of Toulouse, Raymond called for Bertran's poetic help.[7]

Alfonso's enemy lay between him and his prize, and this long
struggle would hardly have been possible had it not been that vassals
in the *Midi* were frequently disloyal. If by accident of inheritance or
acquisition a man held land 'of' several lords, as became common,
he could pretty much choose whom to support. This was useful; Pattison observes that 'Their decision was based on a definite principle:
when the vassal dared, he joined the enemies of his own overlord (or
if two suzerains were involved, the more remote and consequently
less exacting).'[8] This principle also made possible the other inter-
minable struggle that Bertran was involved in: the rebellions in his
native Limousin and Périgord. When Henry II Plantagenet had
united the vast territories of England, Normandy, Anjou, Brittany,
and Aquitaine, he seems to have envisaged a kind of federation after
his death in which his eldest son, Henry, would preside as King,
while Geoffrey and Richard held sway as subordinates in Brittany
and Aquitaine, respectively.[9] Geoffrey and Richard were put in
charge of their territories and the young Henry was crowned in London in 1170; he became known as 'the King, the King's son', and the
Midi knew him thenceforth as the *joven re engles*, 'the Young
English King'.[10] But his father would not trust him with territory,
and the Young King grew jealous of his brothers, who were actually
in possession of their lands. Their mother Eleanor fanned this dis-

content into a rebellion by them all in 1173, which their father put down with his usual vigour; Eleanor was placed under house arrest, and the brothers had to be content with things very much as before.[11] This could not last, and the Young King soon found an excuse to intervene on behalf of the Aquitainian barons against Richard's rule.[12] Here Bertran de Born spoke up, and taunted the Young King with the fact that Richard had taken his road tolls and was building a great castle on his lands:[13]

> Ah, Puy-Guilhem and Clérans and Grignol
> and Saint-Astier, you have indeed great honour,
> and so have I, if anyone will recognize it,
> and Angoulême has much more
> than Sir Carter who quit his cart;[14]
> he has no money, and takes none without fear. . . .

> Between Poitiers and l'Isle-Bouchart
> and Mirebeau and Loudun and Chinon,
> at Clairvaux, they've fearlessly built
> a fine castle, and put it in the middle of the plain;
> but I wouldn't want the Young King to know about it
> or see it — he wouldn't like it —
> though it gleams so white that I'm afraid
> he'd see it all the way from Mateflon.[15]

Bertran wants the Young King to go to war against Richard: there is little chance that he will ever be as powerful, and as much of a nuisance, as Richard is in Aquitaine. For exactly the same reason, the same poem tries to stir up the weak and far-off Philip of France into supporting the rebels by challenging his valour:

> We shall know for sure whether King Philip is like his
>   father [the unwarlike Louis]
> or whether he will follow the Charlemagne-like ways
> of Sir Taillefer, who does homage to him
> for Angoulême. . . .[16]

The largest group of Bertran's songs is concerned with this 1182-1183 rebellion against Richard in Aquitaine.[17] Henry II and Richard together had no difficulty in putting it down, but at one point

Bertran thought the Young King was making a separate peace, and reacted typically. Furiously he taunted the Young King,

> who has withdrawn his suit
> against his brother Richard, because his father tells him to;
> *force majeure!*
> since he holds and rules over no land,
> let him be King of the Cowards.

> He acts like a coward, living completely
> off allowances by number and by measure;
> a crowned king who lives on rations from another man
> hardly resembles Arnaut, Marquis of Bellanda. . . .

Bertran accused the Young King of treachery to his allies, of a torpor that would never conquer anything, and of jousting while his valorous enemy and brother

> lays seige to them and saps them,
> takes their castles and demolishes them and burns down
> on every side. . . .

> I would prefer that Count Geoffrey, to whom Broceliande belongs,
> had been the firstborn,

> for he is courtly—and that kingdoms and dukedoms
> had been at *his* disposal.[18]

The appeal is simply to pride, and thus far Dante seems to have interpreted Bertran's aims aright. The results were sometimes ignoble: at one point Henry II, unaware that the fighting was on again, was actually shot at by his son's men.[19] But these episodes came to an abrupt halt when fever and dysentery suddenly terminated the Young King's brief life. Immediately Bertran's tone towards him changed, and he launched the stately and magnificent *Si tuit li dol e·lh plor e·lh marrimen:*[20]

> If all the pain and tears and mournfulness
> and sorrowing and spleen and misery
> that ever men heard in this weeping world
> were put together, they would seem a nothing

against the death of the Young English King,
for which cause worth and youth stay sorrowing
and this world, murky, dark and shadowed over,
shorn of all joy, full of sorrow and grieving.

Weeping and sad and full of mournfulness
are stricken down the courtly knights-at-arms
and troubadours and jongleurs of good parts. . . .

Each stanza plants its feet in the first line with a kind .of violence
and, though the later lines vary the pattern, it is against the subliminal background of this heavy onward march, which is returned to
with the rock-like final syllable of each line. The inexorable cycle of
each stanza returns to 'the Young English King' in the final phrase
of every fifth line, marking a kind of climax and pause, after which
the last lines decline to the deliberately weak *ira* with a sense of res-
ignation. It is a brilliant piece of musical construction, and Pound
had only to follow the stress-patterns fairly closely (with the extended vocabulary that his Victorian poetickese permitted) to make
a poem (*Planh for the Young English King*) which was in its way an
addition to the resources of English verse. Into this lament, just as
he had into the lament for Geoffrey, Bertran introduced his vision
of the prince as chief among Rolandian 'companions', under the
protection of God:

May He forgive him, as is true forgiving,
and make him be with *companhos* of honour,
there where was never grief or will be grieving.

The barons of Aquitaine, who had strength to negotiate from,
quickly made their peace with Richard, and Bertran was left
defenceless. He complained bitterly to Geoffrey of this treachery,
with no effect, and Richard besieged the 'quite impregnable' castle
Hautefort. In seven days it was taken and handed back to Bertran's
loathed brother, whom he had kicked out.[21] That should have been
the end of Bertran's career, for Richard was savage to defeated
rebels.

But it appears that Bertran was on close terms with Richard—he
had addressed a poem the year before to Richard's sister, mention-

ing that he owed the introduction to Richard himself.[22] Now he wrote a poem to his lord, asking humbly for his castle back on the grounds that Richard had given him the kiss of peace, denying any intention to flatter, and throwing in a few vilifications of his allies:

> Have perjured themselves towards me
> three palatine Counts,
> and the four Viscounties
> of Limousin
> and the two greaseballs
> of Périgord
> and the three stupid Counts
> of Angoulême.... [23]

And it seems that Richard returned Hautefort to him.[24]

Bertran henceforth was Richard's loyal ally. He supported him in his struggle with Raymond of Toulouse, which almost led to a war between Henry II and Philippe-Auguste; when it didn't, he tried to taunt both his overlord and his enemy into rejoining the struggle, with slanders on their manhood.[25] In a later dispute between these two, Richard went over to Philippe-Auguste's side,[26] and it was after a humiliating peace in their favour that Henry II, harried and sick, was finally brought to his deathbed. There he learned that John Lackland, his youngest and the only one of his sons who had stayed loyal, was now a rebel; and he died, muttering 'Shame on a beaten king.' As Appel says, 'Bertran, who lamented the deaths of the Young King and of Geoffrey, sang no songs on the tragic death of their father.'[27]

Richard, now Richard I of England, and Philippe-Auguste of France were both under an obligation to crusade, and Bertran seemed briefly to raise his sights above local squabbles when he cursed them both for self-interested manoeuvring while Christendom lacked champions.[28] He himself refrained from crusading. When the long and disastrous Third Crusade was over, and Richard had been ransomed from his famous captivity, Bertran was there to welcome him back with news of more rebellions in Aquitaine; and here he exited from history, pausing in a last song to renounce the world and the sins that he had so enjoyed.[29]

This picture of Bertran's place in history, based chiefly on his

poems, seems coherent and detailed enough, and would clearly justify Dante's placing him among the *seminator' di scandalo e di
scisma*.[30] But was Dante taken in by Bertran's self-projection—and
Pound likewise?

Whatever influence Bertran wielded was not based on military
strength; he could raise no armies from his tiny fiefs,[31] and though
Hautefort was a strong castle, this no longer had much significance
in the new 'lightning war' that Henry II and Richard practised.[32] In
any case Hautefort was probably weakened from inside by the dispute with Bertran's brother Constantine.[33]

The Provençal biographers always took it that Bertran's influence
was personal, and based on his friendship with the Young King,
with Richard, and with Geoffrey. Of course it is possible that they
had no other evidence for this than Bertran's songs. All the later
prose writers in their turn took this assumption from the Provencal
biographers.[34] In his songs, Bertran always addressed the three
princes familiarly, sometimes abusively, or insultingly, and never
without plenty of peremptory advice on how to conduct their affairs.
He used nicknames like *Oc-e-No*, 'Yes-and-No', and *Rassa* (meaning unknown), more frequently than their correct names. He
boasted about his power with political figures:

> Every day I re-sole and trim down
> the barons (whom I intended to lay waste),
> and I melt and temper them. . . .[35]

and he taunted the princes with comparisons, as we have seen. In
1925 the American scholar Olin H. Moore suggested that all this
was so much empty posturing. He pointed out that we no longer
take the Provencal prose 'lives' and commentaries—the *vidas* and
razos—at face value: ever since the classic article of Gaston Paris in
1893, it has been shown again and again that *vidas* and *razos* were
often no more than imaginative developments from things found in
the poems—and what is worse, frequently misread.[36] If we are sceptical about the prose commentaries, Moore asked, why believe 'the
poetic statements of a highly imaginative troubadour'?[37] He looked
at the historical evidence, compared it with Bertran's statements,
and concluded: 'several passages in [Bertran's] *sirventes* . . . indicate

positively that the poet could not have been acquainted with the Plantagenet family.'[38] In view of the fact that this conclusion is on the way to becoming an accepted 'fact' of history,[39] we had better examine its bases one by one.

Moore remarks, first, that there is no reason simply to take Bertran at his word when he claims to have influence with the great; and this of course is true.[40] Moore then goes on to claim that all Bertran's remarks about the three princes conflict with what we know about them. In fact, however, we know very little about them. Moore's method here is to confront the *general* conclusions of modern historians about the characters of the princes with the *particular* remarks of Bertran. This is simply unreasonable: the sweeping nineteenth-century style of character-summary that he uses is hopelessly over-confident in view of our ignorance of the detail of these men's lives, and this very detail of course, had it survived, is what would supply the explanations for Bertran's attitudes to the princes. Moore claims, for instance, that some of the nicknames are inappropriate;[41] it would be more to the point to say simply that in the case of one nickname (*Rassa*) we have no idea at all what it means, and in another (*Marinier*) we have no idea at all why it was used.

Moore also observes that the laments for the dead princes are purely conventional: they do not contain 'one scrap of real historical information', and in one of them 'The name of the Young King could be substituted throughout . . . for that of Geoffrey.' But we do not find personal description or historical detail in any of the troubadour laments; such individualism was simply not of their time. A troubadour was far more concerned to assimilate his dead hero to the world of *geste* than to immortalise the colour of his eyes.[42]

More seriously, it is claimed that Bertran makes specific errors of fact in his songs. One such 'error' is a reference to Richard as the King, at a time when Henry II was still living; this turns out to be a misreading on the part of Moore, for Bertran there refers to Henry II, not to Richard.[43] The only other specific error alleged is when Bertran says the Young King has no lands or money—in fact, Moore says, he had been 'liberally provided' with both.[44] But if we consider the Young King's expectations—those, after all, of a young fool trying to act the part of a king—Bertran is clearly right: the Young King's allowance *parum erat ad explendam latitudinem cordis ejus,* as Robert de Torigni said, and he died heavily in debt.[45] These 'errors' are not Bertran's but those of the modern historian.[46] Even if we exercise the utmost care with evidence, we are at a tremendous disadvantage by comparison with Bertran, simply because of the 800 years that have intervened; and not one genuine error of fact has yet been discovered in all the thirty-nine highly allusive songs with which Bertran is credited.[47]

There are reasons for thinking that Bertran did exert an influence, in person and in his verse. When Bertran says that Raymond of Toulouse has asked him for a *sirventes* against Alfonso of Aragon,[48] it might be wise to believe him: in the twelfth-century *Midi*, not only did people listen to poetry, but they paid for it (many troubadours had no other support), and it was sometimes so damaging that laws were passed against *sirventes*.[49] When we consider the mental temper of an age that went into battle to the sound of the *Chanson de Roland*, we can understand why the song that resulted from Raymond's request to Bertran might have worked; the pomp of its sounds is magnificent in the original. Here is a version:

> And with us there will have come
> the great lords and barons
> and the most honoured companions
> in the world, and the most famous; . . .
>
> And as soon as we have arrived,
> the jousting will start on the plain,
> and the Catalans and the Aragonese
> will fall fast and thick
> —their saddles won't hold 'em up
> we'll hit them so hard.

The frank and arrogant independence of the ideal projected by Bertran would have been his chief attraction to an age so impregnated with the *chanson de geste*.[50] Moore doubts whether a petty lordling in Bertran's position would have dared to call the notoriously proud Young King 'King of the Cowards', but it is likely that the princes respected Bertran precisely because of his courage.[51] We see him slightly anxious about all this, but after all unrepentant, in this song, where he has just taunted both Richard and Philippe-Auguste with being in terror of each other:

I am not at this moment afraid of Yes-and-No,
for it worries him if I tell him off for anything;
but the French King is brooding too much,
and I'm afraid he will come down on top of me. . . .
but never at the siege of Troy
were there as many dukes, princes or emirs
as I have thumbed my nose at by singing.[52]

And the very returning of Hautefort to Bertran by Richard is a sign that there was more between these two than the distant relations of king and subject. It is known from a reliable contemporary chronicler that Richard, with his ally Alfonso, personally laid siege to Hautefort and took it from Bertran;[53] Bertran's songs say that he got it back soon after, and since the chronicle tallies with his account of events before, we can accept his word for the rest. It was very unusual for Richard to hand back a rebel castle; most non-royal castles were built either in defiance of or with intent to defy royal authority, and Richard and Henry II normally razed them.[54] Further, in 1183 the ever-savage Richard punished the rebels by having them 'captured, drowned, butchered, or blinded, knights being made to suffer hugger-mugger with foot soldiers'.[55] Bertran was doubly a rebel, since Richard appears to have supported the claims of his brother Constantine against him.[56] There can hardly be any explanation, other than Bertran's personal influence with Richard, for the peculiar fact that in spite of all this Richard proceeded to hand back Hautefort to Bertran.

So Pound, and Dante also, were probably right about Bertran's 'place in history'. This of course proves nothing about either poet's know'edge of the history of twelfth-century Aquitaine. But Pound at least believed that emotion cannot be faked; that the state of mind concomitant with real involvement differs from that concomitant with hopeful bluster, and that these states are communicated infallibly through art.[57] 'History', as far as Bertran's war-poetry is concerned, seems not to prove him wrong.

There is also the love-poetry, whose relation to lived events has likewise been questioned. Carl Appel says that it was Bertran's love-poetry that first established his personal contact with the Plantagenets,[58] and we first see him addressing a song to Henry II's daughter Matilda, introduced to him (so he says) by Richard. With his talk

of the 'Roman crown' and an 'Imperial cushion', Bertran flatters the
aspirations of Matilda's husband to be Emperor:

> . . .the Roman crown will be honoured
> if your head is circled by it.

> With the gentle look and the gay glance that she gave me,
> Love made me her slave.
> And my lord sat me near her
> on an Imperial cushion. . . . [59]

Matilda is to be found in another of Bertran's poems as 'the Saxo-
ness':

> There will never be a distinguished court
> where people don't amuse themselves, and laugh;
> a court without giving
> is no more than a baron-pen;
> and the ennui and the ill-breeding
> of Argentan
> would have killed me infallibly,
> but the pretty, loving person
> and the sweet gentle face
> and the excellent company
> and conversation
> of the Saxoness saved me from that. [60]

And in the same poem Bertran refers back to earlier loves in his
native country: to the three daughters of Raimon II of Turenne, two
of whom may be the 'Beautiful-Lord' and 'Beautiful-Cembeli' of
whom he takes his leave at the same time. [61] We do not know the
dates of these songs, or the date of the arrival of one Guicharde de
Beaujeu (whom he calls 'Better-than-good') in Bertran's country. [62]
The *razos* say that the famous song of the borrowed lady was composed to soothe the feelings of 'Beautiful-Lord' after Bertran had
welcomed Guicharde a little too enthusiastically. [63] If these poems
are at all serious, Bertran was a very successful lover.

But Stronski, in the famous preface to his edition of Folquet de
Marseille, suggested that the whole scenario of these Provencal love-
poems was imaginary. The amorous situations presented by the
troubadours, he said, were generally impossible for socio-historical

reasons — Folquet, for instance, was a bourgeois merchant, but his verses are chivalric and courtly. These poets' ladies were 'in general, pure imaginary phantoms'.[64] Appel likewise thought Bertran's verses should be taken obliquely. In one of the poems addressed to Matilda, Bertran says:

> Her happy,
> young, noble, loving person
> nowise deceives in beauty,
> nor does it make any illusion,
> but grows prettier for the man who uncovers it;
> and wherever a man took off more
> trappings
> he would want it more,
> because her throat makes night seem day
> and if one saw
> further down
> the whole world would grow more beautiful.[65]

'Would Bertran then have depicted a princess like Matilda, the daughter of a king, surrounded by her court, in such a manner as we find in these verses?', Appel asks. 'An unbridgeable gap separated the troubadour, lord of an insignificant castle, from the lady of royal rank (who, moreover, precisely in these months gave her husband a son, Otto). The troubadour was fifteen or perhaps even twenty years older than the beautiful young princess. Could his stormy words have been anything other than the expression of a purely poetic homage?'[66]

However, the *moeurs* of twelfth-century European nobility were not what these comments seem to suggest. The debauches of the grandfather of Henry II's wife (Matilda's mother) gave rise to speculation of incest in her parentage. Eleanor herself was accused, no doubt wrongly, of something close to incest; but also, probably correctly, of adultery, and this could have endangered the royal line — a matter of great concern to feudal society.[67] There was also plenty of crossing 'unbridgeable' social gaps. Henry II had numerous mistresses, all commoners, who no doubt contributed to the estrangement from Eleanor that caused such disaster in his later years. His bastard son Geoffrey, Bishop of Lincoln, was the offspring of a commoner; his affair with a hostage was the excuse for a rebellion; and his alleged liaison with Richard's betrothed caused her repudiation.[68] It was alleged that Richard interfered with the womenfolk of his vassals and this led to another rebellion.[69] The Plantagenet family was not especially peculiar: Bloch remarks that 'The noble's marriage, as we know, was often an ordinary business transaction, and the houses of the nobility swarmed with bastards.'[70]

Appel appears to suggest that there were actually physical obstacles, in that Matilda was pregnant and Bertran was in any case too old for the girl. Bertran himself certainly did not feel too old—he was over fifty when he wrote another poem, whose evident sexual passion Appel notes.[71] Pregnancy is no reason why Bertran should not have hoped or intended to make love to the young princess—whose husband, in fact, was absent on a pilgrimage at the time.[72]

We need not claim that Bertran slept with every lady to whom he addressed a passionate poem; or that he slept with Matilda because he appreciated her beauties; or that if he had, the fact would add the slightest interest to his works. But works of art have their precise natures because of the differing 'pulls' in them, the possible futures implied, irrespective of graphic detail. An allusion to a woman's form in *Comus* would carry a different charge from that of any such allusion in *Les liaisons dangereuses,* and yet the latter work contains very little post-Lawrentian anatomising. One has to consider the effect of the whole work.

Bertran wrote his share of 'pure' courtly love aspiration, like this poem where he says that Guicharde has

> authorised me her love,
> when she wishes to have a knight,
> for she will admit as a confidant
> the man whose worth is greatest.... [73]

The aim of this poetry is certainly 'the admiration of a finely educated, even spoilt, courtly circle of listeners', in Appel's words,[74] though the emotion is a little factitious. But Bertran was not an average troubadour, if such an animal ever existed. One has only to imagine his words in the mouth of the most 'courtly' of the great troubadours, Bernart de Ventadorn; these, for example:

> the boredom and the ill-breeding
> of Argentan
> would have killed me infallibly....

The thought is too particular, the assertion of the poet's own tastes too forthright. Even when Bertran sees himself as his lady's chosen 'confidant', there may be ambiguities: he uses the terms *prejador* and *chastiador* with very similar senses in other poems, but they seem to require an unusual knowledge of the lady:

> Rassa, I have a lady who is fresh and fine,
> pretty and gay and young,
> with yellow-brown hair, a ruby complexion,
> her body white as the whitethorn flower,
> her elbow soft, and her breast hard,
> and her spine seems like a rabbit's.... [75]

The naive sensuality of this, in the original, is very close to Villon's 'Belle Heaulmière'.[76]

One part of the Provençal legacy—working through the *Vita Nuova,* Petrarch, and the rest—left at the beginning of our century a feeling that love was either the 'true' variety that occurred with ladies as blank as Shakespeare's heroines, or it was simple rutting. Appel said of the 'borrowed lady' poem that 'No genuine passion would, in a quarrel with the beloved, imagine for itself a replacement made out of the sorted fragments of the other beautiful women'; so, rather than consign Bertran's love to the category of rutting, he called it just 'a surpassing piece of gallantry'.[77] But there are various kinds of love, and more than one of them have been acceptable to different women at different times. Bertran's string of compliments to fine women, all subordinated to his praise for the chosen one, could well have worked as a means to an end. In the last lines of the poem Bertran makes a compliment even out of his self-restraint, with his vocabulary of pure greed; his purpose was pleasure, but the pleasures of the intelligence and those of the senses are not mutually exclusive.

Bertran's character has not fared well at the hands of scholars, and the purpose of the foregoing has been to redress the balance somewhat, and to show that Pound's interest in him was not a juvenile vacuity. It is now very easy to place the early Pound in his period: to see him as a flowery post-Pre-Raphaelite looking, in an area that was traditional Pre-Raphaelite fodder, for things to turn into Pre-Raphaelite art. We have seen him doing this with Bertran de Born. As he grew older, and his sense of the 'recurrent' in history became more solid, he converted Bertran less into a figment of such a fragile period. But at all times of his life his urge was to increase the sense of available life-impulse, even if his youthful idea of it was comparatively shallow. With his steady antipathy to scholarship, he never succumbed to the academic desire to show that 'there's nothing in it' — nothing in Bertran, nothing in the troubadours, except a series of self-serving games. It is worthwhile spending a little academic effort to show that there was something in Bertran de Born, as Pound claimed.

PART TWO

4. FROM WILLIAM IX TO DANTE

❦❦❦❦❦❦❦❦❦❦

Pound wrote a history of the Provençal civilisation in Canto VI. Canto VI is very short — only two-and-a-half pages — but it is very selective. The way its parts are put together amounts to a view of the way in which the Provençal culture worked. The Canto begins with the first known troubadour, William IX of Aquitaine (1086-1127); moves to the marriage of his granddaughter Eleanor with Louis VII of France, to her second marriage with Henry II Plantagenet, and her relations with Bernart de Ventadorn; and shifts finally to Sordello, one of the last great troubadours, an Italian, whose lady Cunizza was known to Guido Cavalcanti. What the Canto says is that there was a continuity of culture and awareness of human possibilities from the circle of William IX of Aquitaine right through to the circle of Dante, and that this continuity depended on personal influence and contact.

Pound believed that there was a special quality of communication effectible only in person. Hence his 'Vortices', the circles of high-powered artistic interaction that he was always founding. He believed that a man's art-product was continuous with his general development, since art could not deceive; and since people communicate through their whole behaviour, personal communication could be very rapid. So he tried to meet all the great artists living in his time.[1]

Pound considered that people underestimated the effect that a few well-informed persons can have on the process of history, and that governing classes in fact generally govern for good or evil by their superior knowledge of what is going on.[2] Hence the struggle throughout his life to keep up an effective personal system of news-gathering, one that would select the key events and facts, and not clog up his time with what was essentially repetition. The family ought to be one of the best channels for keeping up this kind of awareness, once established; Pound said that he could write the history of the United States by writing the history of five families.[3]

These ideas, spread out a little, lead to a belief in aristocracy, and to culture as coterminous with race.[4] As Pound became more and more keyed up about his failure to alter the immediate course of history, he exaggerated the sense of direct conflict, and finally seemed to have traced all movements in history back to key groups of people working for good on the one hand and for evil on the other. In the chain of awareness, starting in Greece, that was eventually to 'cause' the troubadours' cult, an event as localised as the visit of Scotus Erigena to Provence could be one link.[5] In the chain of devils operating throughout history, we have 'the enormous organized cowardice' of police, Jewish financiers, and bankers.[6] By this time, in the late thirties and forties, Pound was so combative that he was claiming much too much both for any one individual's knowledge at any moment of the total state of affairs, and for any one individual's effect on it. In the sixties he admitted as much.[7] But his ideas about personal contact speak for themselves, and we should see how they shaped his idea of Provence.   The *Cantos* as a whole begin with the great metaphor of Odysseus's journeyings in search of understanding. In Canto I he is going to Hell to find the way home; or he is returning to the ancients to draw on their wisdom for current use. Elsewhere he is voyaging out onward in search of cultural contacts, like Pound going to Venice and London, or like Hanno in Canto XL escaping from a metaphorical Victorian England:

> (AGALMA, haberdashery, clocks, ormulu, brocatelli,
> tapestries, unreadable volumes bound in tree-calf,
> half-morocco, morocco tooled edges, green ribbons,
> flaps, farthingales, fichus, cuties, shorties, pinkies
> et cetera
>   Out of which things seeking an exit
>
> PLEASING TO CARTHEGENIANS: HANNO
>
> that he ply beyond pillars of Herakles[8]

The 'first troubadour', William IX of Aquitaine, does both these things at the beginning of Canto VI:

> What you have done, Odysseus,
>   We know what you have done. . . .
> And that Guillaume sold out his ground rents
> (Seventh of Poitiers, Ninth of Aquitain).[9]

William 'sold out his ground rents' in order to go crusading.[10] He started out on the First Crusade in 1101, and got as far as Jerusalem, but on the way he lost most of his army. On this journey — during which it is possible that he was imprisoned by the Saracens — and on his campaign against the Moors in Spain in 1120, he might have made the contacts with Arab culture that Pound says are visible in Provençal poetry.[11] Canto VIII says:

> And Poictiers, you know, Guillaume Poictiers,
>   had brought the song up out of Spain
> with the singers and viels.[12]

Pound's economics are sexual: distributing the available wealth fertilises, and hoarding it is, for him, like sodomy, 'life-denying'. In Canto VI, William IX of Aquitaine fertilises economically, culturally, sexually, and ritually:

> And that Guillaume sold out his ground rents
> (Seventh of Poitiers, Ninth of Aquitain).
>   'Tant las fotei com auzirets
>   'Cen e quatre vingt et veit vetz....'
> The stone is alive in my hand, the crops
>   will be thick in my death-year....

In that William is said to have sold rights, or tried to pawn all his territories, to raise money for crusading,[13] he showed that he preferred increasing his knowledge of the world to sitting on acquired wealth. His sexual activities are in the song that Pound quotes in Provençal:

> I fucked them as much as you will hear,
> A hundred and eighty-eight times....[14]

Because, in his more complete state of existence, William embodied his people's contact with the gods and nature, he becomes one of Frazer's sacrificial kings, renewing the natural cycle: 'the crops / will be thick in my death-year....'

The man of courage and developed sensibility — as ruler, lover, and poet — fertilises. The effects persist: in this case he has founded a dynasty of culture. This is how Canto VI gives the dynasty:

> Till Louis is wed with Eleanor
> And had (He, Guillaume) a son that had to wife
> The Duchess of Normandia whose daughter
> Was wife to King Henry e maire del rei jove. . . .

First it mentions the marriage of William's granddaughter, Eleanor of Aquitaine, to Louis VII of France.[15] Then it follows the Provençal 'life' of William IX, with its errors. It goes back to William's son and to the son's daughter, Eleanor again, who married Henry Plantagenet after her divorce from Louis. By Henry she was *maire del rei jove,* mother of the Young King who was friend to Bertran de Born.[16]

Next Canto VI says what happened to Louis and Eleanor on the Second Crusade:

> Went over sea till day's end (he, Louis, with Eleanor)
> Coming at last to Acre.
> 'Ongla, oncle' turned Arnaut,
>   Her uncle commanded in Acre,
> That had known her in girlhood
>   (Theseus, son of Aegeus)
> And he, Louis, was not at ease in that town,
> And was not at ease by Jordan
> As she rode out to the palm-grove
> Her scarf in Saladin's cimier.

Taking the phrase he has used for Odysseus, in Canto I,[17] Pound tells of Eleanor's Odyssey, out to the Holy Land, where she had an affair with her uncle that seems to have set her spirit free from the chains of her marriage to Louis.[18] There is also an apocryphal story of an affair between Eleanor and Saladin,[19] and Pound even seems to suggest, via the reference to Arnaut Daniel's 'nails and uncles' song, that Arnaut seduced Eleanor under her uncle's nose.[20]

Theseus suddenly appears in the middle of this passage because he was the hero who carried off Eleanor's other incarnation, Helen of Troy; he thus forms an earlier incarnation of Raymond of Antioch, Eleanor's uncle. The line 'That had known her in girlhood' suggests that Pound was following his seventeenth-century gossip-column source in taking Eleanor and Raymond to have been in love earlier on. (Eleanor was only five or six when Raymond left Poitou.)[21] For the Canto, it is as if an early liaison was put off for twenty years, just as the liaison between Theseus and Helen was broken off till the girl should have been brought up to fit age by Theseus's mother.

Then Eleanor's marriage collapsed, and her patrimony (the great dukedom of Aquitaine) went to her next husband; as Canto VI relates it:

> Divorced her in that year, he Louis,
> > divorcing thus Aquitaine.
> And that year Plantagenet married her
> > (that had dodged past 17 suitors)
> Et quand lo reis Lois lo entendit
> > mout er fasché.

Pound gives Louis's reaction in a concocted Old French: 'And when King Louis heard it / he was very angry.'[22] Being, by comparison with the Plantagenets, an ineffectual commander and ruler, Louis could do little.

Canto VI then quotes from a 'document' (apparently put together by Pound)[23] representing an agreement between Louis and Henry II.

> Nauphal, Vexis, Harry joven
> In pledge for all his life and life of all his heirs
> Shall have Gisors, and Vexis, Neufchastel
> But if no issue Gisors shall revert....

The territory of the Vexin was a disputed and strategic area on the border of Normandy. By this agreement, Henry the Young King ('Harry joven') was to marry Louis's first daughter by his second wife, and the land was to go as the dowry. Louis regarded it as an arrangement for the future, since his daughter was three years old at the time, but Henry Plantagenet pushed the marriage through and took the dowry. The same piece of territory, still in dispute, comes up in an actual document of much later, when another political betrothal-settlement between these two families was finally cleared up, and Canto VI proceeds to quote from this document:

> 'Need not wed Alix...in the name
> Trinity holy indivisible.... Richard our brother

Need not wed Alix once his father's ward and. . . .
But whomso he choose . . . for Alix, etc. . . .'[24]

This concerns another son of Henry's, Richard Lionheart, who in
about 1169 had been betrothed to Louis's daughter Aélis. Twenty-
two years later they were still unmarried, and the successor of Louis
VII, Philippe-Auguste, was obliged to take back the girl and cede
the Vexin to the Plantagenets yet again.[25] As in the Malatesta Cantos, Pound is trying to show that the people who re-energize culture
are not recluses, dead from the neck down, but activists, involved in
life's messy struggles.

Canto VI, with the space of a line for pause, switches immediately
from the Plantagenet family's politicking to its cultural affairs. The
troubadour Bernart de Ventadorn has been banished by Eblis, lord
of the castle in which he grew up, for showing too much interest in
Eblis's wife. The lady herself is being guarded close. In the Provencal 'life' of Bernart, from which most of this is taken, Bernart simply
goes to Eleanor (the 'Duchess of Normandy') as to another patron-
ess.[26] Pound has Bernart seeking the help of Eleanor, by asking her
to certify to Eblis that he, Bernart, is safely distant, so that the lady
may be let out:

> Eleanor, domna jauzionda, mother of Richard,
> Turning on thirty years (wd have been years before this)
> By river-marsh, by galleried church-porch,
> Malemorte, Correze, to whom:
>> 'My Lady of Ventadour
> 'Is shut by Eblis in
> 'And will not hawk nor hunt
>> nor get her free in the air
> 'Nor watch fish rise to bait
> 'Nor the glare-wing'd flies alight in the creek's edge
> 'Save in my absence, Madame.
>> "Que la lauzeta mover"
> 'Send word I ask you to Eblis
>> you have seen that maker
> 'And finder of songs so far afield as this
> 'That he may free her,
>> who sheds such light in the air.'

By placing all this at Malemort, Pound seems to have identified
Eleanor with the 'Audiart of Malemort' who appears in his *Dompna*

puois translation.[27] This makes Eleanor, according to the Provençal prose, a friend of the Maria de Ventadorn whom Pound seems to identify with Eblis's wife. If Pound was thinking of all these points, he must have realised that the situation gets complicated when Bernart proceeds to fall in love with Eleanor herself— *& ella de lui,* 'and she with him', as the Provencal *vida* has it. The phrase *domna jauzionda,* 'joyous lady', is used by Bernart of a lady whose identity we do not know; Pound makes it apply to Eleanor.[28] The adulteries are as complicated as those in the stories of Guilhem de Cabestanh, Peire Vidal, Savaric de Mauléon, and Peire de Maensac in Cantos IV and V; but the atmosphere of clarity, summer, and illuminate nature is the same in all of them, because the protagonists respect 'the sacrament (which is the coition and *not* the going to a fatbuttocked priest or registry office).'[29] This atmosphere is in the poem by Bernart de Ventadorn that Canto VI quotes at this point, *Quan vei la lauzeta mover:*

> When I see the lark move
> its wings for joy against the light,
> so that it forgets itself and lets itself fall. . . .[30]

But in Canto VI these complications are not developed into the theme of Eleanor/Helen the destroyer that is present in other Cantos. Canto VI returns all the time to creativity, the personnel being poets and patrons of poets.

Now the great cultural Vortex that William IX of Aquitaine began at the beginning of the twelfth century is carried past the time of his granddaughter and into *Duecento* Italy. Pound believed that the Italian *dolce stil novo* poetry of the late thirteenth century —the period of Dante, his friend Guido Cavalcanti, Guido Guinizelli, Cino da Pistoia, and Lapo Gianni— was the direct descendant of the Provencal verse. Here he 'demonstrates' this by atmosphere. The clarity of the Bernart section, which is a faithful remaking of the tone-colour of some of the best Provençal verse—for example, the lines of Bernart quoted—is completed by a line borrowed from Guido Cavalcanti:

> who sheds such light in the air.[31]

The line is a century out of place, but it fits.

The atmospheres of these sections are continuous with one another, and that is the effect of the cultural 'dynasty' that Pound is proposing; but at this point there is a gap in the dynasty itself. Canto VI goes straight from Eleanor to a thirteenth-century Italian troubadour, Sordello, who wrote in Provençal but who has no particular demonstrable connections with the house of Aquitaine. Pound takes the communications between Poitou, Languedoc, and Provence proper at the beginning of the thirteenth century, and Italy a few decades later, for granted, which seems reasonable. Canto VI says *E lo Sordels si fo di Mantovana*, 'And Sordello was from Mantua' — Mantua is in northern Italy, but the *vida* is in Provençal, just as Sordello's writings and (as I shall try to show) a whole culture in northern Italy at this time were in Provençal.[32] This is Canto VI's version of Sordello's 'life':

> E lo Sordels si fo di Mantovana,
> Son of a poor knight, Sier Escort,
> And he delighted himself in chançons
> And mixed with the men of the court
> And went to the court of Richard Saint Boniface
> And was there taken with love for his wife
> > Cunizza, da Romano[33]

After following the Provençal vida as far as Sordello's seduction of Cunizza, Canto VI switches to a document which describes what Cunizza did in old age 'in the House of the Cavalcanti':[34]

> That freed her slaves on a Wednesday
> Masnatas et servos, witness
> Picus de Farinatis
> and Don Elinus and Don Lipus
> > sons of Farinato de' Farinati
> 'free of person, free of will
> 'free to buy, witness, sell, testate.'

Pound points out, here and elsewhere, that Cunizza showed a great charity in freeing her slaves during her lifetime; and that this took place in the house where Cavalcanti, who must have known her, grew up, and was witnessed by 'Don Elinus and Don Lipus' — Cavalcanti's relatives. Now Cavalcanti, as Pound also points out, was Dante's 'first friend', and must have helped to form his mind. The line Sordello-Cunizza-Cavalcanti-Dante completes this cultural dynasty which stretches in Canto VI from around 1100 to around 1300, working through personal influence.

Cunizza, like Eleanor, was not one to deny herself pleasures, and Pound quotes from a chronicler's account of her abduction by Sordello:

> A marito subtraxit ipsam . . .
>> dictum Sordellum concubuisse:

'took her away from her husband. . . . Sordello said to have slept with:'.[35] This was one of many escapades in her emotional life, to which the *Cantos* come back later. The effect of her grace and spontaneity comes through in this song by Sordello which Canto VI next quotes from and which has a quiet and obsessive beauty:

> 'Winter and Summer I sing of her grace,
> As the rose is fair, so fair is her face,
> Both Summer and Winter I sing of her,
> The snow maykth me to remember her.'[36]

The 'dynasty' that Pound sets out in Canto VI renewed itself in each generation not by anxious conservation of disembodied images of the past, not by a kind of cultural classicism, but by cultural/monetary/sexual fertilisation by courage, which is why the Provençal poetry was not a static but an evolving art. To judge by the protagonists, the heritage of the past can only be refertilised by those capable of living in the present; culture is not a dead thing; 'Knowledge is NOT culture.'[37] After Cunizza, in Canto VI, there comes an example of the dead reworking the dead, which is what happened in Provence after the Albigensian Crusade:

> And Cairels was of Sarlat. . . .

The *vida* tells us that this obscure troubadour was

of Sarlat, from a town of Périgord, and he worked gold and silver and designed arms; and he made himself a jongleur and travelled through the world a long time. He sang badly and composed badly and played the viol badly and spoke worse, and wrote down words and music well. He was for a long time in Romania, and when he left there, he returned to Sarlat, and there he died.[38]

'Without character you will / be unable to play on that instrument', as Confucius says in Canto XIII;[39] Elias Cairel presumably lacked the inner impulse, and in that he 'wrote down words and music well' he was probably perpetuating the life of that mass of inferior material that threatens to engulf live culture at any time. The spirit is the same as that of the *bourgeois* of Toulouse, with their 'Consistory of the Gay Science' that Pound attacked for having encouraged sterile imitation through all the 700 years since Giraut Riquier, the last real troubadour, died.[40]

The last lines of Canto VI go back to the world of heroes and demi-gods and gods who are gods 'by speed in communication':[41]

<blockquote>

Theseus from Troezene,
Whom they wd. have given poison
But for the shape of his sword-hilt.

</blockquote>

At this point in the myth, Theseus is saving himself from his turbulent family: the wife of Aegeus his father has tried to have him poisoned. This is a parallel to the destructive side of the life of women like Cunizza and Eleanor of Aquitaine who made the Plantagenet family seem like the Atreides. It prepares for the beginning of the next Canto:

<blockquote>

Eleanor (she spoiled in a British climate)[42]

</blockquote>

So Canto VI makes assertions about Provencal culture and, by extension, about culture in general. It says that those who begin new movements and renew old ones are not 'recluses, dead from the neck down'. It can be taken as saying that they are not literary men. The requirement is: first, the passion; then, the need to get it across, which drives its possessor to dedicated craftsmanship, so that in the end he is 'literary' with complete seriousness. Beginning from a delight in manipulating the forms of expression, with a vacuum as to motive, is to be avoided. Elias Cairel is the literary exemplum of this latter: the scholar who merely remasticates the forms that other men's passion took in writing. Louis VII is the extension of this in other fields of behaviour, where a man marries, crusades, and plays power-politics, without feeling intensely enough about any of these things to bring them to fruition. The *mout er fasché,* 'he was very angry', when Henry took away his Eleanor and his Aquitaine, is one of several emblems of his general impotence. As in Hemingway, the man who is as it were 'potentially' potent is the man who has the passion first and finds the forms for it secondly, whether in shooting or in making love; the man who thinks about the forms first is Robert Cohn.[43] This strand is continuous in Pound from much earlier days, when the poems constantly assert that it is the soul's moment that matters, not this mere body or these mere words, which shall shrivel away and leave a core of passion; and when his criticism self-consciously asserts that Pound would much rather lie and contemplate on the floor of Catullus's villa than turn out explanatory prose.[44] In the later years Pound adopted much tougher personae for the same purpose of announcing that he was not literary: that what came first was having a job to do, and that the mastering of a dozen usable styles was just a means towards its execution. Thus when the *Cantos* say

> War, one war after another,
> Men start 'em who couldn't put up a good hen-roost[45]

it is clear that the implied persona knows perfectly well how to build a good hen-roost and spends a reasonable proportion of his time in doing things like that. The good writer is the master of necessary technologies, one of which happens to be the apparatus of writing, like Hemingway punching away in a standing position at his Corona typewriter (or *mitrailleuse*), the boxer/soldier and poet *à ses heures.*[46] The hero of Canto VI, William IX of Aquitaine, has an alter ego, Sigismondo Malatesta, and Pound took Hemingway's advice, on the ground, about Malatesta's military tactics. But here it is Hemingway as armour for Pater. The core is still passion-as-Beauty, which Pound very early in his career saw in the Middle Ages, in Bertran and the rest, and which he spent a lot of his working life trying to find an impregnable armour for, to protect it against the harshness of twentieth-century realities. The troubadour 'Beauty' was one with the object of his religion, and we see both the Beauty and his constant testing of it against the modern world in the later Cantos:

'mi-hine eyes hev'
                well yes they *have*
        seen a good deal of it
            there is a good deal to be seen
        fairly tough and unblastable[47]

So the whole Canto is anti-literary in this sense; and this does not contradict Pound's life-long literary professionalism.[48] The personae of Canto VI are, on the one hand, men and women of action (William IX, Eleanor, Henry II) or passion (Bernart, Sordello) or both, who are as it were literary by accident; and on the other hand, scribes, and the impotent. A thread uniting the scribes and the impotent is their link with the Church,[49] and this is shown much more strongly in the Malatesta Cantos where it is the Pope and his agents who express the general distortion of their faculties in their 'best bear's-greased latinity'[50] as they try to do Malatesta down. They are the professionals, the archivists, the manipulators of forms, the precursors of the *Quarterly Review* and *Times* reviewers whose bottled-up perversion Pound immortalised in the Hell/London Cantos.[51]

The Canto carries the passion and the protective toughness in its movement: we see Eleanor in conjunction with the warrior-politicker Henry, and the aesthetic revelation is in then seeing the same Eleanor in passionate and sensitive involvement with the troubadour Bernart. Passion and toughness are both also in the language. The political bargainings and marriages are delivered in Pound's throwaway syntactical subordination — '*Till* Louis is wed with Eleanor'; ellipsis — 'Divorced her'; switching of tenses and addressees — 'What you *have done*'; and clumsily repetitive officialese — '(He, Guillaume)'. All this gives the impression that one is having *the essential* thrown at one in whatever form the recounting voice has stumbled across it in authoritative documents — authoritative, because (such at least is the effect) not written with us in mind at all, but strictly for immediate functional purposes. This, it seems, is the thick of the action; it has complete, casual authenticity. Having established its toughness, its capacity to handle any level of reality a cynical (especially a modern) world may throw at it, the Canto moves into delicate incantation and archaism:

'And will not hawk nor hunt
nor get her free in the air

which is the protected core of passion in which the same personnel
move. Both the movement and the language-contrast are then repeated for Sordello: tough hagglings and vicissitude followed by
delicate lyric of passion. So the burden of this Canto is a presentation of this Paterian passion with its protective Hemingway toughness as, together, the real instigators of culture: it is the recurrence
of and contact between people who have them, as opposed to the
scribblings of the methodical, which can constitute durable cultural
dynasties.

But as well as being a statement of universalised cultural values
that we can find elsewhere among Pound's generation, this constitutes an historical assertion, and one that can be tested in historical
terms. Is it or is it not true that the continuity of the Provençal culture depended on the type of personal energy Pound shows forth;
and did the energies of these or similar figures multiply and feed
each other to the extent that they amounted to a different entity, a
'dynasty', having its own laws and acting as a separate factor in their
lives? The question is a huge one, because of the scope of time and
event involved, and because of the fortuitously selective way in
which material has survived. But in principle it is as resolvable as
the question: was institutional momentum a factor in State Depart-
ment policies during the Eisenhower era?—or as any similar historical question. As well as its major historical assertion, Canto VI also
carries a number of minor but related assertions, all of which are, in
the light of views generally held in these fields, controversial: that
William IX was a 'complete man' and an instigator of culture, not a
loud-mouthed buffoon who accidentally wrote a handful of sensitive
lyrics, and thus invented a tradition as a by-blow; that Eleanor of
Aquitaine was connected with a literary Vortex, and that her literary interests were not entirely narcissistic; that the background of
Dante and Cavalcanti was steeped in Provençal, and did not owe its
knowledge thereof to a few isolated surviving anthologies. The
merits of all these claims may be discussed in historical terms, and I
propose so to discuss them in the remainder of this section. I shall
pursue them as far as I am able in the attempt to see whether they

link up to form a coherent view of the culture as a whole, tending to support the picture of a 'dynasty of energy' that Canto VI projects.

The scholar who has been following the source-material for Canto VI, as I give it in the footnotes to this chapter, may well view these aims with some scepticism. The source-material that Pound can be shown to have had on his desk comprises:

(a) Pound's own copyings from the Paris manuscripts;[52]
(b) Five scholarly collections of texts in the original;[53]
(c) One scholarly translated collection of historical documents;[54]
(d) One collection of gossip about historical figures;[55]
(e) ?? One scholarly history;[56]
(f) ?? One school textbook.[57]

In all this, the only soundly based historical record is Zeller and Luchaire's excellent but tiny (duodecimo) selection of translated documents, with brief introductory paragraphs, covering the complex events of the years 1180-1226: *Philippe Auguste et Louis VIII: La royauté conquérante*. To the list of works that have left a verbal trace in Canto VI, as given above, we may add a small clutch of historical works used in preparation.[58] In the earlier published version of Canto VI, Zeller and Luchaire's tiny work provides the skeleton for the whole poem, since its sixth, eighth, eleventh, twelfth, thirteenth and fourteenth documents[59] appear in that order in the Canto (excepting only two anticipations of the fourteenth document), interpolated only with small passages of narrative from elsewhere, and followed only by the Bernart passage as it appears in the final version. Of these passages of narrative from elsewhere, a part may be from a schoolbook that Pound speaks of having used; but the largest part is from another duodecimo, fatter but a great deal less historical, called *Intrigues galantes de la Cour de France*. This book is one of a spate that appeared in the latter years of the seventeenth century, anonymously or pseudonymously, and with fictitious imprints disguising their Dutch manufacture, servicing a market for quasi-historical intrigues among the celebrated.[60] Its first volume scutters from the Dark Ages to the late sixteenth century in 317 pages, under businesslike headings like 'Amours de Faramond, Premier Roy de France' and 'Amour Incestueux de Clotaire'. Its picture of Eleanor as a female Don Juan is based on a mixture of fictions and free amplifications, some the work of others and some perhaps its own, and these form the substance of the passage in the first published version of Canto VI.

These two little volumes are no longer the skeleton in the final version of the Canto.[61] But the connection with material that an historian would normally handle has become even slighter, as Zeller and Luchaire's contribution has shrunk, with only slight compensations in the new Sordello matter: Rolandino's chronicle (two lines) and the act of manumission in Zamboni (six). There is a stronger element of Pound's own myth-making: William IX as fertility-king, Arnaut commenting on Eleanor's uncle, the hyperbole in Eleanor's having 'dodged past 17 suitors', the interpolation of 'once his father's ward and . . .', and the suggestion that the Sordello song is connected with Cunizza. This element, added to the rapid alternation between sources, makes the whole weave so tight that it is now Pound's own, and it is impossible to say now that it is more based on one source than another.

So the source-material that Pound was in contact with was a very particular mix, in which literary texts, poems and 'lives', had a big part. But his methods of using this mix complicate the issue even more. They are all directed towards a particular mode of communication. The Canto does not try to prove; in each case, in order to prove, it would be necessary to deal with contrary arguments and exceptions. It picks out key events, focuses of action, whether literary events, personal or political ones. It tries to suggest by the 'quality' of these events, the intensity of the life in them, that they are pivots. It does this by staying close to documents. It assumes that the sense of life that appeared to Pound in a particular nodus as he waded through the documents can be communicated to the reader, either by quotation, by finding a translation-equivalent, by creative forgery, or by retelling in a modern idiom. Pound quotes the key lines of William IX and of Bernart de Ventadorn direct. He translates and chops up the Sordello poem and various legal documents. He fakes the comment on Louis's anger, and, legitimately reading items from one agreement with the Plantagenets into another, proceeds to make up the text of the document that does not exist from the one that does. He has William IX selling out his 'ground rents', like a modern property speculator: an excellent situational equivalent. And finally, like the Provencal *razo* writers before him, he fabulates from the song that has struck his imagination, putting a particular historical interpretation on the 'nails and uncles' of Arnaut, the 'Audiart' of Bertran de Born, and perhaps even the lark-song of Bernart de Ventadorn.

This is a method both for arriving at perceptions about eras of history, and for communicating such perceptions. The truths here may be 'recurrent' or even 'permanent' (according to Pound's classification), and thus Pound's presentation of them may amount to myth; but in the first instance they may apply in the local and particular historical area. Thus Pound is right to call this a 'method of historiography'.[62]

First, in source-material, there is no clear line between the literary and the historical. The Act, or Treaty, of which one might believe (say) 95 percent of the details, is often in part a work of propaganda.[63] It grades into the reasonably sober chronicle, like Rolandino's, of which one might believe 80 percent of the detail; into the gossipy chronicler, like Benvenuto da Imola for instance, perhaps 50 percent believable; and into the Provencal *vida,* perhaps 30 percent of whose details, at a wild guess, might be believable. Yet even the Provençal *vidas* contain many particulars that, to our great surprise, have been corroborated quite convincingly, and many others that we can therefore infer to be in all probability sound. Finally we arrive at the Provencal lyric itself, for which the same claim can be made in an even more diminished degree. All this certainly does not prove that all sources are reliable to the same degree for the same purposes. It proves that if one is interested in accuracy of detail, these sources are reliable in differing degrees, a point which historians have long accepted in principle, though they have often failed to apply it in practice;[64] but that no source is unusable for historical purposes just because it is usually called literary.

But Pound was not interested in historical accuracy of detail except secondarily. Just as he loathed analyses of literature that argued *a priori* and refused to contemplate the effect of the whole work or passage (compare the anecdote of Agassiz and the fish[65]), so in historical matters he considered the effect of the whole, and scorned a rationalist apprehension of detail. Schliemann had no 'sound' evidence for the location of Troy, but he had evidence that he could use, in literature, the tones of which he could judge and put together with the scraps of other information that seemed to him significant. He, and not the methodical sceptics, found Troy. Pound's reading of Provencal culture is a reading of the tones of its literary artefacts, documentary remains, and quasi-historical anecdotes, helped by a strong element of personal observation and gathering of legend on the spot, in Languedoc, in the manner Pound so much admired in Frobenius. Canto VI is a fusion of these, intended to communicate the overall tone of a way of life, distinguishable by us from that of the Edwardian era or that of the Third Reich. This tone may have implications as radical in Provencal studies as did Schliemann's discovery in the Hellenic field. It is not as easily verifiable as the location of Troy, and yet Pound drew from it a corollary that has been verified just as concretely as that location. Pound's Troy in Languedoc was the heretic centre of Montségur, and he discovered that it was a sun-temple at the same time as he was preparing for Canto VI. He was led to this discovery by the same development of Frobenian observation and intense reading as led to Canto VI. Here and at all later points, his reading of the troubadour lyric and documents, and his use of the Montségur discovery, colour each other.[66]

There is no point in arguing that Pound's written sources are correct because they are contemporary, or nearly—though some of Pound's early remarks suggested that there was.[67] And no one of these materials gave him precisely the tone that he believed was right; this would come out of a selection and working of them. Pound's poem is not its sources.[68] Pound does not want the coy and breathless narrative tone of Vanel's *Intrigues galantes* as they show Eleanor hopping from lover to lover; what survives into the final Canto VI is the unease of Louis, and the scarf in Saladin's helmet, and that is what Pound wants. (It is glamour, but not Vanel's kind of glamour.) There are also, of course, the many occasions when Pound *does* want the tone (or something relating to the tone) of his original, whether this original be a contemporary or some cultural intermediary that Pound is interested in,[69] and when he uses its words or some cunning English equivalent to capture this. But the strength of this appearance of quotation is varied deliberately by the devices that Pound uses, in some cases (as with the *Intrigues galantes*) fading altogether, so that the unprepared reader may not be aware that it is a quotation at all. It is probable that there is always *some* Poundian modulation even in the most nearly verbatim of his quotations—it often takes the form of fake-careless quoting, or quoting that is genuinely careless but by overall policy.[70]

So all this digging away at Pound's sources might serve only to show that there is no necessary relation to the sources at all. With such a high degree of personal intervention, of manipulation, Pound perhaps might as well (as far as his reader is concerned) have made up all the quotations and source-references, in the manner of more recent literary illusionists and *blagueurs*.[71] The part-fiction of quotation, it might be said, exists only within the poem itself, and might as well be pure invention. But this quasi-quotation would have no meaning at all without our 'external' experience of the tones of pieces from similar periods; and our sense of it will always be affected by further reading *and* further living. And secondly, if we knew that the whole were a tissue of fiction, our apprehension of it would be altered. Canto VI and similar Cantos have a necessary relation to our sense of what history actually consisted of.

Pound's 'reliable', 'semi-reliable', and 'apocryphal' sources are used neither for the historical accuracy of their detail nor (necessarily) for the tone that they place on events; they are used for what Pound has read 'between the lines' of them, and for what he can fuse together from them to communicate this perception, which always depends partly on our sense of the relation that his 'quotations' from them have to the events that they witness. This fusion may or may not amount to an historical thesis; the only proof of the pudding is in the eating. It seems to me that it stands up to historical testing, and the following chapters will try to show that it does.

Pound has left a comment on the method of Canto VI, written when the Canto was still in its first published form. At this stage it was concerned in a good part of its bulk with the manoeuvring between Richard Lionheart and Philippe-Auguste over the Crusade, and how these squabbles produced a treaty that settled a thirty-year squabble over dowries and border territories.[72] Pound noted, first, what he had been reading: a nineteenth-century Catholic school history-book, the *Intrigues galàntes de la Cour de France*, and the collection of translated documents made by Zeller and Luchaire. He observed:

Their styles differ, the ex-cathedra statements are inharmonic, but I have found no contradictory statement of facts. The relations between Philippe,

Coeur-de-Lion, and the King of Sicily, and their entourages at the start of the crusade in 1191 are as bad as anything in a Henry James novel; the eliminations of the "meagre" historical record have left nothing any simpler than the relations between our friends X., N., and G. Eleanor deserves as much attention as Ninon. But side by side with human and intimate detail one has the constant burning of allegory.[73]

When the historical record is pared down to the greatest possible degree, as in Zeller and Luchaire's selection ('the "meagre" historical record'), the complexity of human relations that remains is equal, Pound is saying, to anything in our 'sophisticated' modern world; equal even to that recorded by James, who left in so much that other artists pared away.[74] The corollary of this is that the mutually contradictory 'ex-cathedra statements' of the authors of such works as he used are redundant. *A fortiori,* history-writing in the classic manner is also largely redundant, since it contains so largely of ex-cathedra opinions. The art of writing the 'lucid prose' of admired historical narrative is an art of homogenisation: it relates all events and personality to the one consciousness (the historian's), whether distancing them by adroitly nuanced irony, or identifying with them through restrained praise; and it attributes to this consciousness the authority to judge all action, while discreetly reserving the grounds (which must be a statement of the historian's own values and experience) for doing so. Therefore such supple monuments as Luchaire's *Innocent III* were not for Pound. Pound was instead a re-anthologiser of anthologies, crystallising his feelings about periods or people when he found the perfect selection of documents, as in the *Provenzalische Chrestomathie* of Appel that his Provençal work is so often based on, or Zeller and Luchaire's pithy choices, or De Lollis's collection in the appendix to his Sordello, the major source for Canto XXXVI as well as (probably) parts of Canto VI. Pound, one of the first poets thrown up by post-Germanic university 'philological' studies and the great national libraries, saw over-information as a threat to culture in our century.[75] The anthology, a 'selection of flowers', was his weapon against it—the published form of the loose-leaf file that Pound said should become the critic's tool—and the anthologiser was a heroic performer of 'drainage'.[76] A canto like Canto VI is a greatly refined anthology. It is a method of seizing the life of documentation direct, based on the assumption that mere 'facts' in overabundance are the enemy: 'Knowledge is NOT culture'. Neither the finding of good and truly 'representative' anthologies nor the further re-fusion of them should be despised, since both demand a maximum of understanding.

Pound's technique may in the end stem from an organising consciousness as powerful as that of the classic historian, but on the page it relies on a different kind of authority, that of our own sense of its authenticity, its particular location in culture-time. It does so in order to create the strongest possible casing of 'reality', or sense of being at grips with things-as-they-are, to protect that troubadour 'Beauty' of Bernart and Sordello which is the centre of Canto VI: to establish that these people are not mere sentimentalists, but have their feet as firmly on the ground as you or I. It loses in intelligibility: parts of Canto VI cannot be understood without the help both of the earlier published version and of historical explanations. But when elucidated it also presents an important historical vision, which remains to be by us tested.

5. WILLIAM IX OF AQUITAINE

Pound's history of Provence in Canto VI takes William IX of Aquitaine to have been one of the great originators in 'Provence' and hence in Western Europe. He is 'rhymed'[1] with Odysseus, the 'live man' of whom the gods would have said 'That man is one of us.'[2] He is also rhymed with Malatesta, being shown not as a 'flat-chested highbrow'[3] whose sensibilities had developed acutely on one plane at the expense of all others, but as a man whose faculties had come to fruition in harmony with each other and with the inner impulse.[4] Neither William IX nor Malatesta, according to Pound, was a Descartes cogitating in bed, a Pascal lamenting the need to leave his study, or the 'rational' appetiteless man lampooned by Franklin.[5] The surviving documentation about William IX's personal life is by no means as rich as that for Malatesta. Had it been, perhaps Pound would have rhymed William more elaborately with the Malatesta he shows in Canto VIII, poet and *condottiere*. But the two are quite clearly parallelled:

> He, Sigismundo, *templum aedificavit*
> In Romagna, teeming with cattle thieves,
> with the game lost in mid-channel,
> And never quite lost till '50,
> and never quite lost till the end, in Romagna,
> So that Galeaz sold Pèsaro 'to get pay for his cattle'.

> And Poictiers, you know, Guillaume Poictiers,
> had brought the song up out of Spain
> With the singers and viels[6]

The image of Sigismondo Malatesta had been besmeared, apparently for good, by his enemy Pope Pius II,[7] and in the same way William IX of Aquitaine had seemed permanently diminished because his record was set down by men of the Church, with which he had been at odds throughout most of his life. William IX was indifferent and uncooperative towards the Church, and his scandalous private life perfected its hostility.[8] The chroniclers, all churchmen, made of him what their mental apparatus permitted them to. They had the Pauline reaction to sex, and in the book of rules that was their passport to heaven, this matter, together with the dignity of the Church, occupied a large space. In their chronicles they drew disproportionate attention to these obsessions, and thus presented information in such a distorted, trivialised way that we feel the objects of their interest must themselves have been trivial. William IX emerges from their accounts as one of those funny, jerky little puppets we think of as typically 'mediaeval'. Just as he had with Malatesta, and by exactly the same methods, Pound set out to 'rewrite' William IX, by going behind both the scandalous anecdote of the chroniclers and the generalising prose of nineteenth-century historians. He found nuggets of verse, deed, and document, and let their juxtaposed energies interact to show the 'field of force' William IX of Aquitaine. To see what Pound did, we must assemble earlier pictures of William IX from the histories and chronicles.

The ancestors of William IX had fixed their dynasty in Poitou in 902, and it was to last until Eleanor's marriage to Henry II gave the patrimony to the Plantagenets in 1152.[9] When William's father died at war in 1086, he left his son territories that stretched (at least in theory) almost from the Loire right down to the Pyrenees, and from the Atlantic coast almost as far as Clermont-Ferrand.[10] They amounted to about one-third of modern France, which was considerably more than either the Dukes of Normandy or the Kings of France — the two chief neighbouring powers — disposed of; and these lands were very rich. But Aquitaine's feudal structure had always been loose, and William's family had kept its hold only by ceaseless struggle.[11] When William inherited he was fifteen years old. He later complained: '. . . when my father had journeyed from this world, as many know, I was left, to all intents and purposes a boy. Then my barons, who should have helped me, fell off from loyalty to me, and began to harm me greviously. . . .'[12] But he survived this crisis with small loss of territory, helped by powerful tutors,[13] and set aside his tutors when he reached the age of twenty.[14]

Three years later he married Philippa of Toulouse, probably with designs on her territories. In 1096 the idea of liberating Jerusalem was in the air, and emotion ran high when Pope Urban came to Poitiers to preach crusade. Chroniclers recorded portents. Raymond,

Philippa's uncle, was fired with zeal and departed for the Holy Land; but instead of following him, William IX proceeded to invade his lands.[15] Somehow William avoided being censured publicly by the Pope, but the tone of his relations with the Church was already set.

Soon there was news of quick successes in the Holy Land, and Jerusalem fell to the Crusaders under circumstances that were universally held to be miraculous.[16] William IX changed his mind about crusading. We have seen that Pound says 'Guillaume sold out his ground rents';[17] one story is that he sold his wife's rights in the County of Toulouse, and another is that he mortgaged all his lands to William Rufus, King of England, to raise money for crusading, only to be frustrated by the King's sudden death.[18] The chroniclers thought him a wastrel[19] and scorned all his crusading efforts. To one he was a mere buffoon; for another 'he brought nothing to the Christian name; he was a rabid lover of women; therefore he was inconstant in his works.'[20] William of Malmesbury said of this 'foolish and lubricious man' that 'before he came back from Jerusalem he wallowed in the sty of vices as if he believed all things to happen by fortune, and not to be ruled by Providence.'[21] For them all, his crusading was merely an excuse for foreign vices, and events retrospectively proved his godlessness. His army was ambushed in Asia Minor, with terrible loss of life. He reached Antioch and safety with, it is said, only six companions, and having lost everything he was forced to depend on others for his needs during the rest of his ill-starred crusading.[22] The whole expedition was a blow to his prestige, when rivals and vassals were returning home in triumph; but William, say the chroniclers, made his sufferings into witty songs on merry tunes to delight his noble compeers.[23]

For the next twenty years, William was chiefly occupied with controlling his northern vassals, who exploited the friction between the great houses of Aquitaine and Anjou.[24] But his father had been heavily involved in Spanish affairs, and because he shared the loyalty of many vassals with Christian kings in Spain, William himself was obliged to take a hand there.[25] In 1120 he scored a great victory against the Muslims, having gone with 600 knights to help Alfonso of Aragon; and for men of his own time, at least those who did not loathe William on moral grounds, this victory probably outweighed the disasters of the Crusade.[26]

But meanwhile William had been busy with the more private

activities that were permanently to antagonise the Church. In 1114 he was excommunicated, apparently for keeping a mistress — William of Malmesbury says that he threatened the officiating bishop with his sword and then clapped him in irons, where the poor man died.[27] He had begun a liaison with the Viscountess of Châteller-ault, surnamed 'Maubergeon' or 'Dangerosa', whom he installed in a tower of his palace. This led to a war between William and his son, which only ceased, it is said, when William's wife died in her convent.[28] William of Malmesbury recounts that the Duke adored his Maubergeon so much 'that he had a picture of her placed on his shield, saying thereupon that he wanted to bear her in battle, as she bore him in bed.'[29] Again he was excommunicated, and this time (we are told) he said to the bishop: 'You will comb waves into the hair that has fled your pate before I will give up the Viscountess.'[30]

The chroniclers accumulated anecdotes. In one, William IX searched for an abbess for a priory of prostitutes that he had founded; in another, he set out *incognito* to ascertain which was the most pleasurable of all the professions, and finally settled for that of merchant, going to all the fairs and sampling the delights in the inns.[31] Certainly he cannot have been in the most sacred of odours when he died in 1127. But the Provencal *vida* sums up his life less heavy-handedly than the chroniclers:

> The Count of Poitiers was one of the most courtly men in the world and one of the greatest deceivers of women, and a good warrior and capable in womanising; and he was capable in composing and singing. He travelled a long time throughout the world to lead women astray. He had a son who had for his wife the Duchess of Normandy, who bore him a daughter [Elea-nor of Aquitaine] who was wife to King Henry of England, and mother of the Young King and Sir Richard and Count Geoffrey of Brittany.[32]

THE SONGS

Eleven songs attributed by the manuscripts to William IX have survived,[33] and one of these is among the best from Provence. This is its literal content:

> Since a wish to sing has taken me
> I shall make a song, that gives me sorrow;

I shall serve no more
in Poitou or Limousin.

For now I shall go into exile,
in great fear, in great danger,
I shall leave my son at war,
and his neighbours will harm him.

So sad it is to me leaving
the rule over Poitiers;
I leave to the care of Fulk of Anjou
the whole land and his cousin.

If Fulk of Anjou does not help him
and the King I hold my honour from
all and general will harm him,
felon Gascons and Angevins.

If he is not wise and valiant
when I have left you,
they will soon have thrown him down
seeing him young and weak.

I ask the grace of my fellow
that if I ever wronged him he pardon it me;
and I ask the same of Jesus from His throne
in the language of *Oc* and in Latin.

I had prowess and delight,
but now we two part,
and I shall go to Him
with Whom all sinners find peace.

I have been very elegant, I have had a good time,
but Our Lord does not want it any more;
now I can no longer carry the burden,
I have come so close to the end.

I have left everything I have always loved,
chivalry and pride,
and because it pleases God I accept it all
and pray Him to take me to Him.

> I ask all my friends that at my death
> they come each one and honour me greatly,
> for I have had joy and delight
> far and near and at my hearth.
>
> So I leave joy and delight
> and red squirrel, grey squirrel and zibeline.[34]

This song was written not on the eve of William's departure for the Crusade, or on the eve of his actual death, but in 1111-12, when he was seriously ill with a war wound.[35] The specific referents do not matter; it is a statement of accounts by a man who believes himself to be about to die, and no critic has ventured to say otherwise.[36] It is the more effective in that the poet almost accidentally registers the emotions that move him. He must cease to exercise his functions as vassal to King and God—'I shall serve no more'[37]—for his patrimony. His care is for his son and for the harmony of his friends. These concerns are silent witnesses to the fact that William is to be alone. In theory the 'peace' that he will find at the knees of his Lord will compensate for his loss, but the poem registers no specific joys in heaven. The delights of William's past life are recalled to the companions he shared them with; they must come together in his memory. Like the poet of the *Seafarer,* William accepts the call of his *drihten* as an inevitability that it would be ignoble to complain against, but it is a dark solitude that the Lord beckons him to. This noble Epicureanism is expressed with great control: the stanza is short, the lines are brief, and there is a strong alternate beat, so that the 'breath' is never allowed to wax emotional.[38] The last line of each stanza rhymes not with the first three, but with the last lines of all the other stanzas, so that there is a return to a dead final beat; here is how the poem ends:

> Tot ai guerpit cant amar sueill,
> Cavalaria et orgueill;
> E pos Dieu platz, tot o acueill,
> E prec li que·m reteng' am si.
>
> Toz mos amics prec a la mort
> Que vengan tut e m'onren fort,
> Qu'eu ai avut joi e deport
> Loing e pres et e mon aizi.

Aissi guerpisc joi e deport
E vair e gris e sembeli.

It is probable that Pound was thinking of these last lines in the *Pisan Cantos,* when he recalled the memory of all the companions whom he, like Odysseus, had lost on the terrible voyage home—the brave men he had known in the London of his youth. He took words for the 'Lordly men' from the *Seafarer,* drew on Bertran de Born's lament for the Young King, and echoed themes of transience from Villon and Froissart.[39] Thinking of Nancy Cunard he echoed William's song:

Nancy where art thou?
Whither go all the vair and the cisclatons[40]

In his memory he reworked his own past into a fused pre-feudal, Rolandian 'companionage' and feudal chivalric splendour.

But this song of exile was not William IX's most significant product in relation to later history. The troubadours have given us two donations: the remaking of Western poetic technique and 'Courtly Love';[41] William IX is the only person who could claim to have originated both.

Courtly love is that attitude of man towards woman in which he believes that her existence is on a higher plane than his own; in which he believes that she can give him something like a key to his existence; and in which he believes that receiving this key would go along with being allowed into the intimate circle of her life.[42] It is a worship of woman, in a strict sense: it assimilates her position to that of a deity.

Courtly love is a 'colour'; in any useful definition it is not the mass of the troubadour culture, including anything the troubadours might have said or done and everything descended from them; it is a psychological position which is to be found here and there, now dominant and now subordinated, weaving in and out of the cultural product. In this poem by William IX it is completely dominant:

I am gladdened through by the love of
a joy that I want to delight in more,
and since I want to return to joy
I must, if I can, go to the best of them,

for she honours me more, without question,
than one could see or hear of.

I (you know this) must not boast
and cannot furnish myself with praise,
but if any joy ever came to flower
this one will bear fruit more than any of them,
and amaze beyond all,
as a dark day grows bright.

One could never imagine
how she is, in one's wishing or desiring
or thinking or wondering;
such a joy can find no equal,
and a man who wanted to praise it justly
would not do it in a year.

Every joy must bow down before her
and every pride obey
my Lord, for her beauty in welcoming
and her fine delighting look;
and a man who could seize her love's joy
must live another hundred years.

A sick man can be healed through her joy
and a sound man die of her displeasure,
and a sane man go mad
and a handsome man lose his handsomeness
and the most courtly man fall low;
and any serf grow courtly.

Since no-one can find a finer lady,
nor eyes see, nor mouth speak of,
I want to keep her for my uses,
to refresh my heart within
and renew my flesh,
so that I may not grow old.

If my Lord will give me her love
I am ready to take her in gratefulness
and keep her secret, serve her,
do and say what pleases her,

hold her value dear
and further her praises.

I dare not send her anything by another,
I have such fear lest she should grow angry,
nor dare I urge my love in person,
so much do I fear doing the wrong thing;
but she must choose the best for me,
since she knows it is with her I shall be healed.[43]

The whole situation comes from the lady's divine powers in relation to the poet. She is the source of joy—an ineffable joy, since she
is on a higher ontological plane. Hyperbole on this subject fills five
stanzas. Her spiritual powers come through on the physical plane, so
she has control over total states: she can give eternal youth, cure illness, and raise a man to an inherently noble (that is, courtly) condition. For these gifts, since they are transcendent, the poet is willing
to do anything, and since her level of wisdom is infinitely higher
than his, he fears that everything he does, including adoring her,
may be ridiculous and a bore. It goes without saying that this state
of the emotions in William IX and his successors was presumably as
transient as most human emotional states, and yet it took a certain
hold, and grew to be one of the recurrent strains in their culture.

William calls his lady *midons,* which I have translated as 'my
Lord'. This *midons* is, as Pound said, 'inexplicable':[44] it is used
almost exclusively by the troubadours, of their ladies, and in the
later troubadours we find it everywhere—Bernart de Ventadorn
uses it twenty-three times.[45] Its etymology is (?*mi-*) *dominus,* 'my
master, lord', but since it is used only of women—its pronoun is 'she'
—glossarists have difficulty in giving it a gender.[46] Though Mary
Hackett has shown that it was not felt to mean on the *primary* level
'my quasi-feudal lord' by the troubadours who used it, these men
knew their Latin and must have been aware of its origins and peculiarity;[47] in fact it was clearly their collective emotions and expectations that drew what amounts to a metaphor from the area of lordship, just as it is the collective metaphor-making process that establishes 'baby' as a term for a girlfriend and that creates and transforms language constantly. In the same way, knowing that *Dominus*
was the standard term for God, and that *don,* 'lord', was also used
for God,[48] they must also have felt some connection with religious

adoration. William IX echoes the Scriptures when he says

> Every joy must bow down before her
> and every pride obey
> *Midons*. . . .

and

> no-one can find a finer lady,
> nor eyes see, nor mouth speak of. . . .[49]

The incantatory fifth stanza of this song enumerates powers that were invoked every day in the Virgin and the saints.[50]

William IX is, metaphorically, his lady's feudal vassal as well as her worshipper.[51] So that there are three structures in parallel: the feudal, the courtly-love, and the religious; the psychological structure of each followed that of the others, so that it was difficult to think of any of them without transferring the feelings that belonged to the others. The lady was to lover as God to man, and as feudal lord to vassal; feudal lord to vassal was as God to man.[52] Our socio-economically minded age would say that the forms of feudal society must have shaped relationships in the other two spheres, but it is as likely that aesthetics and ethics mould economics as vice versa. Of course, courtly love was not 'religious' in the sense of being part of any Christian ethic; it was a religion in its psychology. The courtly lover did not think of his lady as the Church thought of her, but as the Church thought of God.[53]

Where did William of Aquitaine acquire this emotionality? One scholar has said that it was invented as a mechanism for social climbing; the noble lady's favour would give status to her lover.[54] In fact there is no reason for thinking that the lady's social status was typically any higher than that of her poet.[55] Another has said that William invented it to attract the women who were getting bored with his bawdy, of which we shall see examples.[56] One of the longest-lived ideas is that he took it from the Arabs.[57] There are reasons for thinking that the troubadours could have learned literary techniques from Arabic verse, as Pound suggested.[58] We have seen the ample opportunities that William in particular had to see the Moorish culture of Spain, and it is argued that there was a great deal of cultural interchange between the Moslem and Latin worlds.[59] But the evidence of specific borrowings by William IX of literary techniques from the Arabs is very slight — the piece of 'hispano-Arabic' that he is supposed to have put in the mouth of his erotic pilgrim playing dumb, whom we shall see later, is most probably the work of a fourteenth-century scribe.[60] So one cannot argue that, having cribbed from the Arabs their manner, he must also have borrowed their matter; even if one were certain that something like 'courtly love' were stronger in the Arabic world and literature than elsewhere at the time.

For Peter Dronke has shown, by citing extensively from vernacular poetries, that 'the feelings and conceptions of *amour courtois* are universally possible in any time or place and on any level of society.' There was no need, he says, for 'the character of European secular songs' to have been determined 'from outside, by another culture, at one particular point in time'.[61] One can argue that the emotions of courtly love may exist in any one life, and hence in the concerns of any culture, fleetingly, or may become psychologically durable beyond the scope of the situation that produced them.

There is a moment in approaches of a sexual nature (however sublimated) to another person, when everything that is connected with this other person seems to have a fuller existence than the normal; when the rhythm of one's own faculties and hence the sense of one's own existence seem to be accelerated and sharpened by awareness of the magic generated by said person, and to be capable of infinitely greater acceleration and sharpening exactly to the extent that one is allowed nearer to her (taking a 'her' to be the object) and accepted by her as part of her concerns. There may be purely cultural factors in this. Our inherited courtly-love expectations tell us that we should feel these emotions about the beloved; or our capacities seem to be augmented merely because we are pleased at fitting a socially approved role. But the emotions I have described do not seem to be limited to individuals particularly conditioned by cultural eras in which a courtly-love inheritance is dominant: see, for instance, the poems from scattered cultures cited by Dronke.[62] They can arise in personal situations that attract no particular cultural approval, as when persons past middle age fall in love. Any biological textbook will provide examples of a similar general quickening of behaviour, during sexual approach, in other species.

The sense of renewal, the augmentation or imminent augmentation of possibilities is a constant in the courtly-love emotion. The obvious analogy is what one feels when spring comes, the emotion occurring when one becomes aware of birds singing outside the library at an unexpected hour, the light lasting longer than one had come to expect, the dense scents on the air. Both sets of emotion are the result of stimuli acting on our sex-related faculties. In so far as the Provencal poets were not merely 'looking for something to write', their concern was chiefly with these emotions. The relation could be reversed, with a lady sighing for proximity with the magic aura of a certain man — this situation is found in the Provençal lyric, for example in the works of the Countess of Die. It could no doubt have been homosexual, involving either gender; the lines from Sappho that Pound compares to Arnaut Daniel seem to be relevant here.[63] But the courtly-love lyric begins from, and loses any meaning when it entirely loses contact with, a relation which is in some form one of sexual attraction.[64]

These emotions may be a brief and marginal concern in most lives, and in a preponderance of the infinite variety of cultures that inhabits the earth's surface; but at certain times they have become central, and cultural momentum has perpetuated their centrality (even though in any rational view they are as arbitrary a choice for the pivot of a culture as the Egyptian interest in the after-life, or the man-lord relationship of *Beowulf*, seem to us, or as our post-Lawrentian 'complex relationship between equal individuals' must seem to the inhabitants of Maoist China). But our own culture is affected by assumptions inherited from the troubadour lyric via the French romance; Dante and his Beatrice; Petrarch and his Laura; Wyatt, Shakespeare, Donne, Rochester, and their paramours; Walter Scott and even the generations of Joyce and Henry Miller, who resurrected anti-idealist earth-goddesses but still seemed to make the solving of life's problems coincide with finding the Right Woman. If courtly love as I have described it seems 'obvious', and therefore no explanation of anything, it is because we are still in that wood and have little with which to compare its trees.

The courtly-love 'awakening' being like that of spring, and this connection being not only aesthetic but physiological also, it is natural that the troubadours should have opened a very large proportion of their love-lyrics with lines about nature in spring-like moments. The Germans have a word for this feature of the Proven-

çal lyric: the *Natureingang,* the 'nature-entry' or spring-opening.
Now as one spring-opening is not necessarily the same in emotional
content as another—Giraut de Calanso's

> as the sun turns snow into
> sweet water, so soft is its shining[65]

having its particular weight, not like others' we shall see—so the
common or generalised images chosen by a whole culture have their
own particular weight, and are not like another's. The Provençal
lyricists had seized upon a particular emotional moment as 'their'
moment: the moment of prospective contact with the creature with
whom one has fallen in love; not the moment of being cuckolded, as
in the country blues, or the moment of penetration, as in Indian
temple sculptures. The moment of spring is therefore an appropriate image, because it is gentle, non-immediate, softened. The
courtly-love moment is a moment of suspense, or at least an intermediate moment, and once the poet has begun to understand its
psychological fecundative possibilities, he may be tempted to try
to prolong it; whence certain problems in later Provençal love-
poetry.

One might conclude that these connections also explain why
courtly love first became important (for our tradition) in the Provençal-speaking areas. In Languedoc and Provence, spring and
early summer are more available, more attractive, more able to
open up one's faculties than in harsher or more sweaty climates—as
in Pound's description of the way in which, in the 'Tuscan aesthetic'
(and by implication the troubadours'): 'The senses at first seem to
project for a few yards beyond the body. Effect of a decent climate
where a man leaves his nerve-set open, or allows it to tune in to its
ambience . . . .[66] This might seem to be a reason for Pound why
courtly love arose in 'Provence', rather than for example in
Morocco, where he describes the sexual relation as 'eugenic':[67] in a
hot land, the sexual moment cannot be, as in Provence, so prolonged that it is sometimes not even recognised as sexual. But Pound
in fact based his myth of the Provencal culture on a cult of spring
and a cult of woman *already* combined: 'a certain Madonna Primavera, who, as Dante does not remark, had set the dance in Langue
d'Oc and in Lemosi';[68] and which, transmitted deviously from

archaic Greek times, took a particular hold in Provence and then in Italy, and might have been helped in that by the Mediterranean climate. The fact that 'the birth of Provençal song hovers about the Pagan rites of May Day'[69] was for him merely the most striking evidence of this fusion of woman-cult and spring-cult at the moment that it reached Provence; the origins of the fusion itself must still be cultural, not climatological.[70]

Without claiming that William of Aquitaine invented courtly love, or borrowed it from one source, one can say that he was most probably the moving power that got Provençal poetry — with its particular forms, techniques, and ethic — off the ground, by the example of his status and his brilliance;[71] and this is what Pound believed.[72] The elements of this cultural product may exist in scraps everywhere, but it was Provence that developed it to a high degree, and this demands some explanation. Pound's myth in Canto VI makes William of Aquitaine's personal drive the beginning of a chain that was continued by personal drive; the fact that Provençal society was a fertile bed, prepared for this action, was for him the result of efforts by individuals like William IX who had spread 'the awareness' through the various levels of society for the previous thousand years.[73]

Even apart from questions of origin, such an account of the central courtly-love emotions leaves problems. The first is that, as has so often been noticed, the ladies have no features. They are phantoms, as Stronski said many years ago; the troubadours were merely playing elegant verbal games.[74] A more recent claim is that the troubadour songs are articulated in such a way as to evoke an emotion which is not that of a man in love with a particular person, equipped with a will and an identity of her own, but that of a man projecting a set of his own (but socially acquired and orientated) expectations onto a woman of whose personal identity he has no real awareness beyond this projection. Frederick Goldin, in a cogent series of articles over the last ten years, has developed the thesis that the poetry is thus the very subtle articulation of a whole class's ideal self-image, handling very cleverly its own built-in capacity to become meaningless: the knight/troubadour projects onto the lady his own expectations of what knights should be, in the form of the virtues he has her requiring of him.[75] It seems to me that this description almost, but with important caveats, fits certain troubadours like Bernart de

Ventadorn and Sordello; but only becomes entirely true when the poetry of the troubadours becomes entirely empty—that is to say, when they are writers 'looking for something to write'. But I shall go into this in more detail when I discuss Bernart de Ventadorn.

The central event of courtly love as I have described it had occurred with William IX of Aquitaine, and it was a human and personal phenomenon, as this next poem shows:

> With the sweetness of the new time
> the woods leaf, and the birds
> sing each one in his dialect
> according to the strophe of the new song;
> so it is right that one should take pleasure in
> what one wants most.
>
> From the place that delights me most
> I see no messenger or seal
> so that my heart neither sleeps nor laughs,
> nor dare I move an inch,
> until I know about the truce
> —whether she is how I wish.
>
> Our love goes like
> the hawthorn branch
> that shudders on the tree
> at night, in the rain and frost,
> till the morning, when the sun spreads
> through the green leaves and twigs.
>
> I still think of a morning
> when we made peace to the war,
> and she gave me so great a gift:
> her loving and her ring.
> God let me live so long yet
> that I have my hands in her cloak.
>
> I have no fear that strangers' talk
> may cut me off from my good neighbour,
> since I know about words—how they go
> with a short remark that spreads;
> let others go prattling about love;
> we have its bread and knife.[76]

This time there is no dying of the lady's wrath, or living a hundred years on her smiles. The metaphors are on a more human scale: the lady transforms the poet's world as spring transforms the land. A large part of the meaning comes from the third stanza, where the poet introduces the image of the hawthorn with 'Our love goes like', and then leaves it to function on its own; Dante did the same when he picked it up in his *Inferno:*

> As the little flowers, bent and closed
>> by the night frost, after the sun brightens them
>> erect themselves all open on their stems:
> so I made myself, from my spent forces. . . . [77]

The event, like this opening of the flower, may happen again; it is 'our love', not so overpowering to conceive of that it must be put into a system of abstractions and pushed into an indefinite future, and the lady has become 'human', as Pound said of Gottschalk's Christ in 'Psychology and Troubadours'.[78] Pound picked this poem out of all his Provençal reading as being one of those that, after a decade of translating, seemed to him worth preserving; and he included it in his *Homage à la Langue d'Oc* under the title 'Avril'.[79]

William IX wrote other courtly-love poems that have survived, but the tones in them are inconsistent, to the extent of cancelling each other out and leaving the poems either empty or impenetrable. The rhythms are so simple and light, and some of the remarks so facile, that important emotions are not engaged; but these things are not taken quite far enough to produce parody. If one could confidently render *Farai chansoneta nueva*[80] as follows — using a slight freedom, certainly — one would be certain that William were parodying courtly love before it was well out of the cradle, and merely amusing himself with a lot of the metaphors that were to become standard:

> I shall make a pretty poem
> Now, before it comes on snowing;
> My love says 'I want to know him,
> If true loving's in his heart';
>> She's to know that I'm not going,
> However many storms she start.

Witness these presents, I deliver
Up myself, herself knows whither,
Sound of mind and cool of liver,
Though I love my pretty sweet;
I can't live unless it's with her,
I die unless she lets me eat.

Your white is white as ivory,
No other's like this bribery;
If you won't show connivery
(Tell me that your love is mine),
I'll die, by pious Gregory;
Please kiss me under sheets or vine.

What good, sweet pearl of my world's oyster,
If you take your love, and foist a
'Pure' love on me, from your cloister?
Know this, that I want you so
I shall drown, if I get moister,
If you won't wipe out all this woe.

What good if I should take the habit,
Cast off by my pretty rabbit?
Joy is ours, if we can grab it,
If your love for me is true.
Sing this song of mine, don't blab it,
Daurostre, when it reaches you.

My heart now is never mended,
Your love always makes it bleed.
No-one like you is descended
From Adam's ancient, noble breed.

This version is in fact almost literal, and follows the metrical form
very closely—giving AAABAB CCCDCD instead of AAABAB CCC-
BCB. Such a set of rhythms would clearly tend to take a song out of
the realm of serious statement, unless it were part of a heavy verbal
irony—as in Cummings's 'I sing of Olaf glad and big'—or unless
there were indications that the unfortunate poet had intended something weightier. But the original is slightly less jerky in its cadences,

slightly more smoothly *cantabile;* and some of my images are more 'curious' than William's; so that the original is facile in a slightly less clear-cut way. My version can stand only as an attempt to point towards the problem of the tones in William's courtly-love songs.[81]

William of Aquitaine also wrote a group of songs that until recently would not have been mentionable in decent company—Jeanroy left a number of delicate gaps in his translations. In one of them, William compares his two mistresses, in castles dependent on him, to a pair of horses that cannot abide each other.[82] Another tells how a lady has been confined by her menfolk, but has availed herself of the man nearest to hand—wouldn't you drink water if you could get no wine? A third seems to say that William himself has tried to keep 'cunt' captive, but it has only made itself more available—the levelled forest grows up thicker.[83] The heavy metaphorisation contains no wit, none of the sudden uncogitated touches that come from the mind in a creative state.[84] But there are two songs in which William hits the mark, and the better of them is this:

> I shall make a song, since I'm sleeping
> and walking and staying in the sun.
> There are women with bad ideas,
> and I can tell you which:
> the ones that despise
> knights' love.
>
> A woman commits a great mortal sin,
> if she doesn't love an upright knight;
> but if she loves a monk or a clerk
> she goes wrong;
> by rights she should be burned
> with a brand.
>
> In Auvergne, past Limousin,
> I was on my way quietly, alone;
> I came across Sir Guari's wife
> and Sir Bernart's;
> they greeted me simply
> in St. Leonard's name.
>
> One of them said to me in her native speech
> 'God save you, sir pilgrim;

you certainly appear to me of good neighbourhood,[85]
from what I see;
but we see going through the world too many
lunatics.'

Now you will hear what I replied:
I never said to her 'bat' or 'but'
or spoke of iron or wood
but just this:
'Babariol, babariol,
babarian.'[86]

Lady Agnes said to Lady Ermessen:
'We have found what we were looking for.
Sister, for the love of God, let's shelter him,
for he really is mute,
and what we do, from him, will never
be known.'

One of them took me under her cloak,
led me to her room, to the stove.
Know that this was good and fine to me,
and the fire was good,
and I warmed myself willingly
at the big coals.

They gave me capons to eat,
and know that there were more than two of them;
and there was no cook or cook's boy
but just us three,
and the bread was white and the wine was good
and the pepper thick.

'Sister, this man is cunning,
and he won't speak because of us:
let's bring our red cat
right now,
for he'll make him talk fast
if he's fooling us at all.'

Lady Agnes went for the nasty creature,
and it was big and with long whiskers;

and I, when I saw it with us,
was scared of it,
so that I almost lost my valour
and my boldness.

When we had drunk and eaten,
I undressed as they wished.
They brought the cat behind me,
evil and wicked;
one of them dragged it down my side
right to my heel.

By the tail she immediately
drags the cat and it scratches;
they gave me more than a hundred wounds
at that time;
but I still wouldn't move
if someone had been killing me.

'Sister', said lady Agnes to lady Ermessen,
'He's dumb, for it's obvious;
sister, let's get ready for a bath
and to retire.'
Eight days and still longer I stayed
in that cauldron.

I fucked them as much as you will hear:
a hundred and eighty-eight times,
so that I almost broke my gear
and my harness;
and I can't tell you the trouble,
it took me so bad.

I could never tell you the trouble,
it took me so bad.[87]

The narrative is paced to raise the interest and not to over-prolong
it. Situation is presented with economy of images, delivered in
sound-shapes that reinforce them:

> Et eu calfei me volontiers
> Als gros carbos.

> And I warmed myself willingly
>   at the big coals. [88]

The rhythm is light, and the short last lines ironical:

> I almost lost my courage then
>   and hardiment.

> Q'a pauc non perdei la valor
>   E l'ardiment.

William IX has brought together all the concerns of his psyche that crop up and are overplayed in his other poems: sexual play as combat, where the combatants are like horses, dominating or being used:

> I almost broke my gear
>   and my harness.

and 'cunt' as a blind force that no man can compete with. [89] This content is neither thrown away nor inflated, and William has rendered his personal 'matter' with the force of an archetype. Pound took it as such for the drama of his Cantos, played between a series of super-males and the great female chaoses they try to inseminate some order into, when he set William the fertility-king at the beginning of troubadour history:

> 'I fucked them as much as you will hear
> 'a hundred and eighty-eight times.... ' [90]

But critics have generally found this range of emotion in William hard to swallow. How could the tender, humble suppliant be the same man as he who talked of women as horses that he knew how to rule without effort? He could not; and so while one school of critics has thought of him as schizophrenic, a 'two-faced troubadour', [91] another has actually claimed that there were two authors. [92] Both schools have shared one vocabulary, in which 'tender', 'sincere', and 'delicate' are constantly contrasted with 'boaster' and 'cynical'. [93] With 'cynical', critics evidently refer to William's recurrent feeling that women are controlled only by their sexuality and become

uncontrollable; also to his intention to act on this feeling, to enjoy
himself by whatever devious means are necessary. William, they
seem to consider, is a 'boaster' when he announces that he has the
ability to act on these feelings, to take advantage of this female psychology. They call him 'sincere' when he wishes not to exploit, but
to make a 'disinterested gift' of himself;[94] and they call him 'tender'
when he entertains nice thoughts of women. They clearly feel that
William's desire to 'lay' his women is necessarily exploitative, and
that women never entertain similar desires. They obviously also feel
that, by contrast, courtly love has no connection with sex or any
other body-based emotion, but is a motiveless donation of the self.
In so far as the critics have seen William as one writer, he is a kind of
Augustine, yawing between these extremes.[95] Gourmont no doubt
would have commented that 'a sensibility without egotism is a meaningless concept, since by its definition the sensibility is the faculty of
feeling, and one can only feel with the body that one personally pos-
sesses.'[96] But to examine these associations of ideas further would be
more a work of post-Victorian sociology than an elucidation of William IX of Aquitaine.

POUND AND WILLIAM IX

In his early works, Pound made very little of William; *The Spirit of
Romance* says 'his fame rests rather upon deeds than upon the eight
poems that have survived him', though 'Troubadours: Their Sorts
and Conditions' gives him the credit for having had the energy to
make verse-writing 'the best of court fashions'.[97] In the early Cantos,
William is the instigator of a cultural line and the importer of new
techniques from Spain.[98] For Pound's opinion of the qualities of
William's verse itself, we have only a translation in the *Homage à la
Langue d'Oc* of 1918, with later comments, and a long parenthesis
added to *The Spirit of Romance* in 1929.[99]

The translation is from the song that I have translated as 'With
the sweetness of the new time'.[100] Perhaps its lack of any living precision shows that Pound was not interested.[101] His old teacher Felix
Schelling reviewed this collection of translations, and when Pound
replied he made it clear, first, that he saw William as 'satyric (the
"leer" can be his, quite correctly)', and secondly that the archaisms
in his versions were intended to reflect what he saw in the originals.

The Latin behind the *Homage to Sextus Propertius,* with which they were printed,[102] was 'modern', coming from an era like our own; but the era of the Provencal was a great distance away from us.[103]

When Pound added a note to *The Spirit of Romance* in 1929, he kept this very important distinction, but reversed William IX's position in it. The 1910 version had said:

The culture of Provence finds perhaps its finest expression in the works of Arnaut Daniel. Whatever the folk element in Provençal may have been, it has left scant traces.

But now Pound qualified this:

(What now strikes me [1929] is that Guillaume de Poitiers is the most 'modern' of the troubadours. For any of the later Provencals, i.e. the highbrows, we have to 'put ourselves into the Twelfth Century' etc. Guillaume, writing a century earlier, is just as much of our age as of his own. I think it quite likely that all sorts of free forms and doggerel existed and that nobody thought it worth while to write them down. Guillaume being a great prince, snobism took note even of his spontaneity.)[104]

I think one can define Pound's 'modernism' as 'awareness of root causes' — especially causes in biology and economics; that awareness whose precise antithesis for the modern era is sentimentality, the generating of untied emotion. But what has this got to do with courtly love? Remy de Gourmont wrote, and Pound translated, the *Physique de l'Amour* to show how

Love is physical, all love has a physical basis, because only the physical exists and the soul is a Sorbonne invention; but love develops in so many manners, bodily, spiritual and mixed, tempestuous or tempered, that it requires separate chapters. . . .

as it says in Gourmont's *Lettres à l'Amazone.*[105] The *Physique de l'Amour* places all the variations of male-female relationship that we feel to be peculiarly human in a huge context of variations among animals and insects. The human development, according to Gourmont, is not the highest but merely one of many; and all our 'idealistic' love-play is biological in origin.[106]

Pound developed this basis in a commentary on the *Physique de l'Amour,* and characteristically he was most interested in the 'spiritual' offshoots of sex. He took as his title-piece Gourmont's remark that 'Perhaps there is a certain correlation between complete and profound coition and cerebral development.' Trying to explain the connection between coition and the development of the higher faculties, he cited a line from Propertius that he always used to show how the troubadour's lady acted as a 'magnet', bringing his faculties into order:

Perhaps the clue is in Propertius after all:

> *Ingenium nobis ipsa puella fecit.*
> [My genius is no more than a girl.]

There is the whole of the twelfth century love cult, and Dante's metaphysics a little to one side, and Gourmont's Latin Mystique.... [107]

Pound's essay on Gourmont will show how Gourmont had helped him to make these connections:

Physique de l'Amour (1903) should be used as a text-book of biology. Between this biological basis in instinct, and the 'Sequaire of Goddeschalk' in *Le Latin Mystique* (1892) stretch Gourmont's studies of amour and aesthetics. In Diomède we find an Epicurean receptivity, a certain aloofness, an observation of contacts and auditions, in contrast to the Propertian attitude:
> 'Ingenium nobis ipsa puella fecit',

this is perhaps balanced by '[Without you, I believe that I would not love much any more and that I would no longer have much confidence either in life or in myself.]' (In *Lettres à l'Amazone.*)[108]

This is a series of distinctions: (a) sex as a biological force, (b) sex as giving rise to a number of pleasures to be savoured by a fine palate, and (c) sex as the orderer of the higher faculties, as the troubadour's lady shaped his spirit, and as Propertius's lady shaped his. In William IX of Aquitaine, these would be (a) the songs of horses and 'cunt', (b) the farewell to the world, remembering its pleasures, and (c) the songs of courtly love. Pound continues on Remy de Gourmont:

... in, let us say, an indication of him, one wants merely to show that one has himself made certain dissociations; as here, between the aesthetic receptivity of tactile and magnetic values, of the perception of beauty in these relationships and the conception of love, passion, emotion as an intellectual instigation; such as Propertius claims it; such as we find it declared in the King of Navarre's

'De fine amor vient science et beauté';

and constantly in the troubadours.

(I cannot repeat too often that there was a profound psychological knowledge in medieval Provence, however Gothic its expression; that men, concentrated on certain validities, attaining an exact and diversified terminology, have there displayed considerable penetration....)[109]

The 'profound psychological knowledge' and the 'validities' are the courtly-love relationship and the awareness that springs from it. For Pound this is a quasi-religious relationship, and includes awareness of the gods and goddesses: there is no clear break between the ordering of the higher faculties and perception of the overall 'coherence' which is divinity operating within the universe.[110]

Awareness of these biological connections is a 'modernism'. Propertius knew of them. Gourmont knew of them and thus 'prepared our era', in contrast with James and Hardy, Swinburne and Yeats, to whom no 'modern' could have spoken his mind.[111] This modernism is to be distinguished from two kinds of archaism: that present in the nineteenth-century culture Pound had inherited and which he came to detest, and that present in the works of certain later troubadours and in other mediaeval work which he found not incompatible with beauty.

In the Romantic era one put into one's work 'the tone of time'[112] or the mist of half-grasped emotion because one felt that the highest things should not be explainable; that that which could be explained belonged to the lower atomic/Darwinian/industrial/middle-class universe, from which the Romantic and post-Romantic struggled to lift himself by force of 'soul'. Hugh Kenner has described how Pound attacked the mist of 'time' in his *Homage to Sextus Propertius:* by making his *Propertius* an inextricable mix of periods, of Frigidaires and wine jars, so that it was permanently contemporary, the aura of The Past being constantly burst in upon.[113] *Moeurs Contemporaines* was published with the *Propertius* and with the *Homage à la Langue d'Oc,* and in it Pound attacked the mist of half-grasped emotion with the classic weapon of irony:

> Its home mail is still opened by its maternal parent [. . .]
> It is an officer,
>   and a gentleman,
>   and an architect.[114]

The 'archaism' of the later troubadours is more difficult to define. Pound did not condemn it along with the nineteenth-century 'fugg'. When he described William IX of Aquitaine as 'the most "modern" of the troubadours', he did not mean that William's poetry was more important to him than the later work. He never did as much with William as with the later troubadours; the highest place in Pound's most religious poetry, the later Cantos, is reserved for Bernart de Ventadorn, and perhaps (through his lady) for Sordello — both 'highbrows'. One could say that these writers were 'concentrated on certain validities', the courtly-love relationship, which we know to develop out of sex as a biological force; they had lost sight of these lower connections, but their development was none the less legitimate and not a distortion of natural processes. The 'archaism' in them was an over-elaboration into something of a closed system.[115]

William of Aquitaine in fact wrote some of the 'later' kind of poetry — for example in the piece that I have used to illustrate the basis of courtly love. But he also wrote poetry that shows a clear grasp of what moves men in instinct, poetry that includes the 'vair and fair' of Epicurean pleasure and sense of transience, and poetry that shows the basis in instinct as part of a series of emotions moving the whole man in harmony with nature: as the sun unfreezes the hawthorn, he may

> live so long yet
> that I have my hands in her cloak.

Pound connected 'all sorts of free forms and doggerel' with William IX's 'modernism'. The song of the two women and the cat, like several of William's songs, is in a kind of stanzaic scheme which was probably picked up from a universal European substratum of folksong.[116] The 'matter' is the matter of folk-balladry, like the 'encounters' of Cavalcanti's songs and the English 'as I went out one morning' genre.[117] Folk poetry has always tended to have a more direct and open contact with 'root causes' than the culture of higher

society; which is why bringing slang and low talk into modern poetry
was one of the things that marked it out as modern, though the subject might be a Renaissance Pope:

> Damn pity he didn't
>   (i.e. get the knife into him)
> Little fat squab 'Formosus'[118]

So Pound always renewed his contacts with folk-language even at
the highest spiritual moments—like the death-agony of Herakles in
Women of Trachis.[119] These things can coexist in a developed sensibility. We can destroy once and for all the idea that there was some
terrible and unlikely split in William of Aquitaine, by pointing out
that they did coexist in another 'libertine', the Earl of Rochester.
His parody of Etherege, 'I F-ck no more then others doe', has an
archetypal solidity of perception, and uses folk language mixed with
courtly style to construct it.[120] It is certain that 'Absent from thee',
and other products of the pure courtly-love tradition, were written
by the same Earl of Rochester.[121]

6. ELEANOR OF AQUITAINE

The cultural 'dynasty' thus magnificently founded by William IX of Aquitaine might not seem to have kept its momentum in the years that followed. William's son, William X (who reigned from 1127 to 1137) was not a troubadour himself, and was the patron of two troubadours only, Cercamon and Marcabrun.[1] But the troubadour art was not yet widespread, and these two are a large proportion of the total in that generation: 'of the 450 troubadours whose names are known to us, none appears to be earlier than 1100, and only six go back to the first half of the 12th century.'[2]

At this period, Eble II of Ventadorn still lived; but unless he was the author of William IX's decent verses, which is unlikely, nothing of his survives. His fame is scattered in various testimonies, like this from Bernart de Ventadorn:

> I shall give up being a singer
> and belonging to Sir Eble's school,
> for my singing is no good to me....[3]

When Cercamon wrote the funeral lament on William X in which there are echoes of the exile lament of William's father, he addressed it to Eble II.[4] The chronicler Geoffrey of Vigeois gives Eble the magnificent title of *Ebolus Cantator* (in English merely 'Eble the Singer'), saying that 'through his ability in composing songs he had won the great esteem of William.'[5] He illustrates this friendship between William IX and Eble of Ventadorn with a laborious anecdote about their competitions in extravagance.[6]

So far as is known, Bernart de Ventadorn took his name from the court of Eble II, where he is said to have grown up and to have fallen in love with one of the wives of Eble's son.[7] Thus Eble II had founded another cultural dynasty, which lasted in fact as long as poetry in Provence kept its standards. The second wife of Eble V, Maria de Torena, who died in about 1220, was one of the 'three of

Turenne' praised by Bertran de Born; she held a literary court of some importance in these last days of Provence's greatness.[8] Therefore when Pound wanted to contrast a product of the 'factive paideuma'[9] with the vegetable cyclism of *tovarisch* — his emblem of the revolutionary proletariat — he chose the castle of Ventadour. Solid stone building is an emblem of the constructive drive throughout the Cantos — whether in Malatesta's Tempio, in the Usury Cantos, or at Montségur — but at Ventadour the bees have superseded the builders:

> Nothing I build
> And I reap
> Nothing; with the thirtieth autumn
> I sleep, I sleep not, I rot
> And I build no wall.
> Where was the wall of Eblis
> At Ventadour, there now are the bees,
> And in that court, wild grass for their pleasure
> That they carry back to the crevice
> Where loose stone hangs upon stone.
> I sailed never with Cadmus,
> lifted never stone above stone.[10]

ELEANOR

While Bernart de Ventadorn was growing up in the menials' apartments at Ventadour, when *Ebolus Cantator* was still alive and receiving the poetic homage of Cercamon — perhaps even when Eble's old friend William IX, 'the troubadour', was still living at Poitiers[11] — an important person was born at the court of Poitiers. Eleanor of Aquitaine was the daughter of William X and of Aénor of Châtellerault.[12]

Eleanor's father died in 1137, leaving the fifteen-year-old girl in possession of his huge territories. To ensure a succession she had to marry; if she married, her possessions would pass to her husband's heirs. Her whole life was an effort not to be the nullity this position suggested. But in the first instance, she had no choice: before he died, her father had committed her to the care of Louis the Fat of France, who quickly had her married to his young son, and then

died. When she reached Paris, Eleanor found herself Queen of
France, while the young Louis VII—at sixteen years old—was master of a kingdom twice as large as the one his father had possessed.[13]

No doubt Eleanor was not at home in Paris. She and her entourage were culturally strangers there—they continued to speak in
their southern dialect.[14] While Louis made various ineffectual and
humiliating attempts at kingship, she was yet unable to play any
independent role. The young king loved her 'vehementer . . . et fere
puerili modo', but for a long time they had no children: she complained to Bernard of Clairvaux that 'God had closed her womb so
that she might not bear; she had now lived nine [in fact seven] years
with the King, and had indeed conceived in the first years, but had
aborted, and from then on had remained sterile, and now despaired
of fertility.'[15] Bernard promised to pray for her, and in 1145 her first
child was born.

But it was very soon after this that Bernard made his appeal for
the Second Crusade, and Louis VII, for reasons much more pious
than those that had moved Eleanor's grandfather, decided to go.
Louis was unable to leave Eleanor behind, and she was not a dutiful
housewife.[16] Because she had to go, the ladies of many barons had
to follow her example; they could not go without their maids, and
'hence the scandalous spectacle offered by our army', for 'warlike
arms and young women's encampments do not go together.'[17] The
troubadour Marcabru railed against the looseness of camp-fol-
lowers, probably intending those on the Crusade, and chroniclers
lamented the 'many vilenesses abominable to God that thence
arose'.[18]

The overland journey of Eleanor and Louis was just as disastrous
as her grandfather's had been. There was an important interlude at
the court of Manuel Comnenus in Byzantium; this 'lover of wars,
tourneys, theatre, medicine, and theology, but also of drinking, ele-
gantly corrupt and not disdaining incest' probably opened the eyes
of Eleanor and her entourage and led to a renewed sense of the cos-
mopolitanism that had withered in the Paris of Louis VII.[19] But on
the gruelling trek to Antioch which probably averaged between ten
and twenty miles per day, Turkish raids and natural disasters
brought a sense of failure to Louis's army even before it reached its
goal.

In Antioch the presiding spirit was Raymond, Eleanor's uncle, and the cultural affinities of his companions were much closer to Eleanor's native Poitou than to the France of King Louis. Louis himself was shocked by their undedicated way of life, and began to feel that he had been lured to the Holy Land on false pretences. Raymond committed an error of tact by giving military advice to Louis—advice which, had it been followed, would have prevented further disasters. And now there grew up an excessive and even scandalous familiarity between Eleanor and her uncle.[20] Louis was paralysed by wrath and indecision. His attendant clerical eunuch told him that the name of France and his patrimony could only be saved if he took Eleanor away forcibly, and this he did. They embarked from Acre in 1149.

Eleanor now began to demand an annulment on grounds of consanguinity. She was dissuaded for a while by the Pope, with whom they stayed on the journey back, and she conceived another child; but the child proved to be a girl, and the King at last gave way. It is difficult to imagine why, since in political terms he and his house had everything to lose. Eleanor must have made herself such an unbearable nuisance that they would sacrifice anything to get rid of her.[21] In the event they sacrificed half the patrimony: Aquitaine. They did not realise what else they had done, but it quickly became clear. Eleanor at once set off for her own lands,[22] where she would be free from the insipidity of Louis's clerical entourage and rule her own house. She was now a valuable property: any single man who could drag her before a priest was master of Aquitaine.[23] At Blois she encountered Count Theobald, second son of Stephen of England's brother; but she escaped, avoided an ambush prepared by the young Count Geoffrey of Anjou, and reached Poitiers. She then acted decisively, by intimating to Henry, the young Duke of Normandy, that she would consider a proposal of marriage. He hurried to Poitiers and the thing was done.

But Henry had more to his name than the dukedom of Normandy, as Eleanor knew. His father had established the house firmly in Anjou. For seventeen years, Stephen of Blois had been struggling to establish his legitimacy as King of England, but had been frustrated by the persistence of the daughter of King Henry I, Matilda. The Henry whom Eleanor had just married was the legitimate son of Matilda, and the crown of England was in prospect. Two years later Stephen died, and Henry came into his own: he was now Henry II Plantagenet of England, master of territories from the Scottish borders to the borders of Eleanor's lands in the Pyrenees.[24]

Henry was eighteen when they met in 1151; Eleanor was nearly thirty.[25] With her experience and her personal attractions she must have thought that she could rule her new husband, who would be 'prince consort of Aquitaine', as Labande puts it; instead she became another of his political instruments.[26] She began to establish a court at Poitiers; but Henry took her off to Normandy, and then, for the coronation, to farthest Britain.[27] She was essential to Henry for the production of heirs, but since she immediately began to produce male children and continued to do so, her importance declined. By 1166 she had had eight children by Henry, three of them girls, and seven of them still living, which in mediaeval conditions was remarkable.[28] Henry obliged her to accompany him — or be left behind by him — in an endless series of epic rides, displaying the decisive energy and ability to surprise that alone permitted him to hold the kingdom together. It was no life for a queen; Labande quotes this typical entry from a contemporary chronicle, for spring 1165:

On the King's orders, the Queen came to Normandy, bringing with her her daughter Matilda and her son Richard; but, the King returning to England to march against the Welsh at the head of a large expedition, the Queen stayed on the Continent.[29]

She laboured without much success to keep some scraps of the power that she felt her inheritance entitled her to.[30] The great opportunity came in 1170. Henry had at last decided that Poitou and Aquitaine would never allow themselves to be governed by foreigners — his deputies — backed up by his lightning punitive expeditions; the only way was to delegate power in his major counties to his sons. Richard, at the age of twelve, was made Duke of Aquitaine, and was sent off to rule from Poitiers with Eleanor as his regent. This was one of the high points of Eleanor's life, and she appears to have made the most of it, opening the doors of her palace at Poitiers to a great *concurrence* of artistic talent. She was detaching herself emotionally from Henry, and coming closer to her son Richard; and at such a distance from the dominating King, and surrounded by the appurtenances of her own personal power, she began to entertain even larger ideas of the possibilities of her position. News of Henry's inveterate, and insultingly public, infidelities no doubt pushed her onwards. At any rate she then organised her sons—Henry, Richard, and Geoffrey, aged eighteen, fifteen, and fourteen, respectively—into an alliance with Louis VII of France, in which each tried to assert autonomy from the head of the family. Henry II was not daunted, and it took him very little time to crush the revolt. He caught his wife, disguised as a man, on the road to Paris, and executed or mutilated her followers. Via his secretaries he addressed to her homilies on the relative status of man and wife, using the image that Dante was to use for Bertran de Born: he was the head, she the limbs. Eleanor suffered much for her attempt, spending the next sixteen years under house arrest.[31]

For most of this time she remained in the Babylon of miserable England, where the cooking and the singing were null.[32] There was a short respite in 1184, when Henry brought her out to use her as moral blackmail to try to get Richard to abandon a revolt in Aquitaine. Richard submitted, and she returned to captivity. In this period she was also afflicted by the death of her two sons, Henry the Young King and Geoffrey. At last, in July 1189, the King died, and Eleanor can have had little cause for grief. Richard was now King; he immediately liberated Eleanor, and she triumphantly toured the kingdom, granting amnesties and exercising the power that now fell to her in virtue of the fact that her eldest son was preparing to go off on crusade.[33]

Richard I Lionheart was as shortsighted a king as he was brutal, and Eleanor had much ado to put right the omissions and wrongs that he committed, both preparing for his crusade, during his two-year absence, and after his return. She successfully fought the danger that came from her son John's alliance with England's chief enemy, Philippe-Auguste of France. In 1191, now aged seventy, she crossed Europe, including the Alps, in midwinter, and reached Messina to arrange the marriage of Richard, which was essential to the safety of the dynasty. When Richard allowed himself to be captured in Germany on the way back from the Holy Land, she had her secretary address a series of blistering letters to the Pope: 'Eleanor, by the wrath of God Queen of England. . . .' When finally the Pope intervened, she had to take the money to Germany to free her hot-headed son. But this period of arduous and effective action in support of Richard was not to last for long. Richard was struck by a crossbow-bolt, and Eleanor had to watch helplessly as he died.[34]

Though Eleanor had carefully arranged for Richard to have an heir, she now declared for Richard's brother John. In this she may have been moved by her hatred for Constance of Brittany—recorded in Shakespeare's *King John*—for Constance would have been the young Arthur's regent. Eleanor, well into her seventies, accomplished a series of exhausting tours to prop up John's regime. She was now at the apogee of her powers, though she retired whenever possible to the convent of Fontevrault, which she had long ago chosen for her resting-place. From Fontevrault she heard of the lunatic action of her son John, who in August 1200 abducted Isabella of Angoulême, which gave Philippe-Auguste his chance to declare forfeit all the Plantagenet lands south of the Channel and ultimately gave rise to the Hundred Years' War. Arthur her grandson, allied with Philippe, attacked Eleanor in 1202, and she narrowly escaped by sending for John's help. Then in April 1203 she received a cryptic message from John intimating that he personally had murdered the young Arthur, and it was amid the resulting collapse of John's power in Normandy that Eleanor finally died, aged 82, at Fontevrault.[35]

The conjunction of Henry and Eleanor was disastrous, though it is useless to speculate that either would have been happier with another partner. Henry II was a great soldier and ruler: at the same time as displaying the extraordinary energy that alone could hold together his restless and far-flung dominions, he was laying the foundations of aspects of the English legal and administrative systems that were to last for centuries. Thomas Becket was one of his few major mistakes.[36] Eleanor clearly had tremendous ability in government, but Henry would allow no interference from her. He did all he could to separate her from Aquitaine, the heart of her independence.[37] He used her as a symbol at the innumerable plenary courts, from Bordeaux to Lincoln, but gave her no power. The last straw was probably when it became clear that her regency in Aquitaine, beginning in 1170, was to be under his strict supervision.[38] One may surmise that the results for his relationship with her and with his sons had more damaging effects on his dynasty than even the affair of Thomas Becket.

But in the brief flowerings that Henry allowed her, Eleanor's influence was enormous. Henry himself was outstanding among kings of his time for learning in languages and literature,[39] but it is probable that his endless movements prevented any filtering through of this culture to those he moved among: all writers remark how little the 'Plantagenet renaissance' of his reign affected the barbaric English.[40] Works of historical-mythical narrative of the greatest importance were dedicated to him, but it is quite likely that Eleanor's was the influence that suscitated them.[41] Eleanor's cultural world had been far from that of her first husband, who was dominated by clerics: the key influences over Louis VII were Abbot Suger, Bernard of Clairvaux, and possibly the eunuch Thierry Galeran. Eleanor of course had grown up at the court where her grandfather, William IX of Aquitaine, had given the Provencal lyric its momentum, and where her father had still been at its centre; these lyrics were regarded as filth by all contemporary churchmen who spoke of them.[42] It is to clerical writers that we owe Eleanor's early reputation of a Messalina which inspired many apocryphal stories. She was alleged to have had an affair with Saladin in the Holy Land, though he was ten at the time; she was said to have tried to seduce the saintly Gilbert de la Porrée, but Gilbert excused himself on the grounds that his hands would be too soiled to eat with.[43] The distance between the two worlds is apparent. Eleanor's heart lay in Aquitaine.[44] There men were more interested, it is true, in food than in moralising, but they were also capable of cultivating refinement of emotion; and it is rightly said that what happened in the contact between South and North that Eleanor caused was that Aquitaine taught France and England to converse.[45]

Eleanor's first chance came after her marriage to Henry II in 1152. With her sense of what was possible no doubt still heightened by the cultural shocks experienced in Byzantium and at Antioch, and with a man at least temporarily suited to her tastes and of different expectations from those of Louis, she was able spiritually to expand. Troubadours and *jongleurs,* as well as the French *trouvères,* came to England after the coronation. One of them was Bernart de Ventadorn, who addressed at least one song to her, and it is likely that in England Bernart met Chrétien de Troyes, whose work contains reminiscences of Bernart's lark-song.[46] In the situation of this cultural contact, the Provençal lyric fathered the French lyric, which in turn gave rise to the narrative genre. The *Roman d'Enéas,* for example, adds a long love-episode to the *Aeneid* material, and this new matter owes everything to Ovid, who thus makes his entrance into Northern letters; but Ovid, 'King of the Middle Ages', had been present in troubadour writing for some time, in the songs of Marcabru, of Rigaut de Barbézieux, of Jaufre Rudel, and — extensively — of Bernart de Ventadorn himself.[47] It is true that Eleanor has only one definite contact with the troubadours, but the practice of the *senhal* or anonymous poetic name may conceal more. When Eleanor went into captivity, a long allegorical address lamented the silencing of music in her lands; it is evident that she surrounded herself with poets and musicians,[48] and the rise of such a woman, with Aquitainian tastes and expectations, must have drawn the prestige of Aquitainian culture with it. It is pleasant to think of Eleanor as being herself the model for the 'April-like queen'· who fools her annoying husband in one of the first Provencal pieces that Pound read.[49] Carl Appel, describing the intense literary activity connected with the court of Henry II and Eleanor, observed that very few pieces of troubadour poetry survived from before its period. In particular, Bertran de Born's poetry only survived from after his contact with the Plantagenets. He concluded that this 'glittering' court had the critical effect of pulling Provencal poetry together from the relatively spontaneous manifestation it had been into a self-conscious literary art.[50]

It is possible that the historical-mythical narrative owes much more to Eleanor than to Henry; that in commissioning the *Geste des Bretons* (or *Brut*) of Wace, which gave greatly extended publicity to the Arthur material, Eleanor was responsible for the entry of that great 'matter' into mediaeval letters.[51] In offering her patronage to Thomas and his *Tristan* poem (if it was she, rather than Henry) she introduced a second great 'matter' into Europe;[52] and in acting as midwife to Benoît's *Roman de Troie,* she helped to transfer the third great 'matter' from the realm of scholarly curiosity to the aristocratic life of letters, where it could act on the European intelligence.[53] It is also possible that Eleanor had an influential connection with Marie de France, creator of another new genre, the *lai*.[54]

The influence of Eleanor's children was no less pervasive. Her daughter Matilda of Saxony, in entertaining the hopes of Bertran de Born, allowed the German poets in her entourage to hear something new and important for them.[55] Richard Lionheart was a friend of Bertran and of Peire Vidal, and a patron to Gaucelm Faidit if not to many others; in patronising important French poets also, he bridged cultural gaps as his mother had.[56] He entertained Arnaut Daniel at his court in England,[57] and himself wrote one extremely beautiful poem that has survived, from his captivity in Germany.[58] Henry 'the Young King' showed an interest in Bertran de Born's work in Provençal as well as in that of Marie de France in French.[59] At the court of Geoffrey of Brittany, Provençal poets met French, and Geoffrey exchanged *tensons* with poets of both tongues.[60] Marie de Champagne, Eleanor's eldest daughter, may not have been in contact with Eleanor after the divorce from Louis, when she was aged seven, but the example of her powerful and wayward mother must have been present almost as a myth in the court of Champagne. Gace Brulé, one of the first great *trouvères* (the French followers of the troubadours), was commissioned to write by Marie. Marie is responsible almost single-handedly for the courtly romance: she commissioned Gautier d'Arras to write his *Eracle* and gave to Chrétien de Troyes the matter and the commission to write his *Lancelot*, or *Le Chevalier de la Charrette*, creating the Lancelot who, as Lejeune says, 'codified in French the whole doctrine of the troubadours on the vassalage of love.'[61] The court of Eleanor's second daughter, Aélis of Blois, was another meeting-place of troubadours and *trouvères*, and her fourth daughter, Eleanor, made the court of Castille a centre of troubadour patronage.[62] The only one of Eleanor's offspring who was a complete nullity in letters was John Lackland, who was brought up away from his mother.[63]

Eleanor of Aquitaine had an enormous influence on contemporary letters, but it is a mistake to ascribe to her everything that was achieved between 1150 and 1173, as her best advocate, Rita Lejeune, has done.[64] Yet even this exaggeration is preferable to the attitude of Jeanroy, who represented the peak of Provençal scholarship when Pound's work on Eleanor was being published: Jeanroy dismissed Eleanor as a gatherer of flattery from fawning hacks.[65] None the less there is one body of work for which Eleanor can have no responsibility. This is the 'Judgements' of the 'Courts of Love' which Eleanor and Marie de Champagne are alleged to have presided over, as recorded by Andreas Capellanus (and by no other). These tediously fanciful constructions belong to a quite different tradition from the art that is most plausibly associated with Eleanor. The songs of Bernart de Ventadorn deal, at their best, with fine emotional distinctions; these 'judgements' deal with codified moralising, and have much more in common with the more gothic of the late *razos* (the Provencal prose commentaries on songs). There is no evidence that such palavers as Andreas describes ever took place, still less that Eleanor was connected with them.[66]

POUND'S ELEANOR

In the *Cantos,* Eleanor is one of a small group of high-powered women who spread order and destruction with equal effectiveness. The order is usually spiritual-cultural, and the chaos is political and physical. In Canto VII, Eleanor is first equated with Helen of Troy; then she is the woman whose shadow makes a clear translucent shape for Arnaut (who seems to have become her lover?) watching her at Buovilla. Here and elsewhere, Pound makes this particular vision into an emblem of a god-like super-perception.[67] After that she seems to become Helen again, with the reference to Poe's Nicean barks, but this time she brings clarity:

> Ελέναυς, ἔλανδρος, ἐλέπτολις
> The sea runs in the beach-groove, shaking the floated pebbles,
> Eleanor!
>   The scarlet curtain throws a less scarlet shadow;
> Lamplight at Buovilla, e quel remir,
>   And all that day
> Nicea moved before me
> And the cold grey air troubled her not
> For all her naked beauty, bit not the tropic skin,
> And the long slender feet lit on the curb's marge
> And her moving height went before me,
>   We alone having being.[68]

Eleanor's destructive aspect comes repeatedly with Aeschylus's pun about Helen of Troy: *helandros, helenaus,* and *heleptolis—* 'man-destroyer', 'ship-destroyer', and 'city-destroyer'. In Canto II:

> Seal sports in the spray-whited circles of cliff-wash,
> Sleek head, daughter of Lir,
>   eyes of Picasso

Under black fur-hood, lithe daughter of Ocean;
And the wave runs in the beach-groove:
'Eleanor, ἑλέναυς and ἑλέπτολις!'
        And poor old Homer blind, blind, as a bat,
Ear, ear for the sea-surge, murmur of old men's voices:
'Let her go back to the ships,
Back among Grecian faces, lest evil come on our own,
Evil and further evil, and a curse cursed on our children,
Moves, yes she moves like a goddess
And has the face of a god
        and the voice of Schoeney's daughters,
And doom goes with her in walking,
Let her go back to the ships,
        back among Grecian voices.'[69]

Many threads from this passage bind Eleanor and Helen together. The 'let her go back' comes in with the chaos that follows Arnaut Daniel's calm and order in Canto XX, and with it come Circe, Helen of Troy, and Parisina d'Este.[70] Parisina was beheaded with the natural son of her husband for their adultery; in Canto VIII she is linked with the doom of the house of Atreus, cursed because of Helen of Troy.[71] Parisina is seen paying for the upkeep of 'this tribe' of poets, in the courtly-love line that began with William IX of Aquitaine.[72] Her parallel, the concubine Pernella, appears in Canto XXIX with Cunizza, Sordello's lady (as Venus), and with woman as 'a chaos / An octopus / A biological process'.[73] In Canto XXIV Parisina's husband, Niccolò d'Este, 'in his young youth' visits Cyprus (the island of Venus) 'where Helen was abducted by Paris', and proceeds to the places in Palestine which Eleanor visits in Canto VI.[74] All this is woven in with several falls of Troy, including two in Provence: the 'Troy in Auvergnat' of the Peire de Maensac story, and the heretic centre of Montségur —

        And that was when Troy was down, all right,
            superbo Ilion. . . .[75]

As is very clear from the way he used Bertran de Born, Pound believed in differentiating the sexual roles. In the Cantos, the most typical heroes and demi-gods are very 'male' males, and the most typical heroines and demi-goddesses are very 'female' females. The image of these females is neither Victorian nor geisha-like. But since they are instinctive rather than constructive, and since they have this pull on men—

> Sleek head, daughter of Lir,
> eyes of Picasso
> Under black fur-hood

—their effects are gigantic one way or the other. Eleanor's 'place in history' has already told us about the disorder she helped to cause. The order she spread can be seen from her place in culture.

A VORTEX AT THE ANGEVIN COURTS

Each of the troubadours Bernart de Ventadorn, Bertran de Born, and Arnaut Daniel was at the Angevin courts at one time or another, and it is highly probable that each knew the others. Noting this, and working from his assumptions about the way in which artists gather cultural influences (assumptions visible in the way Pound himself worked with fellow-artists), and observing further certain qualities about the writing of Bernart, Bertran, and Arnaut —Pound concluded, I think, that these three troubadours were connected particularly closely and that they were in close personal relations with Eleanor.

There is historical evidence for this, which can be considered elsewhere.[76] From what we have seen so far about Eleanor's position, the assumption is a likely one. Effective patronage does not consist of laying out artistic specifications and paying for praise by the line; it consists of helping towards an artist's upkeep and of being a fit audience, and it may not leave much evidence.[77] The ways in which poets benefit from each other are not necessarily obvious. But poets are neither the isolate souls of the Romantics nor the sociological functions of the Marxists. They learn from each other, as Pound argued for so long:

No man ever knows enough about any art. I have seen young men with most brilliant endowment who have failed to consider the length of the journey. *Anseres,* geese, as Dante has branded them, immune from learning. . . .

What we know about the arts we know from practitioners, usually from their work, occasionally from their comments.[78]

The kind of cooperation we would *not* expect to find is described by Pound:

Dear Vogel: Yr. painfully evangelical epistle recd. *If* you are looking for people who agree with you!!!! How the hell many points of agreement do you suppose there were between Joyce, W. Lewis, and yrs. truly in 1917; or between Gaudier and Lewis in 1913; or between me and Yeats, etc.?[79]

So if we find that Pound thought of these three troubadours (Arnaut, Bertran, and Bernart) as a group, existing in fruitful inter-relation, we should not look for the evidence in a shared life-style or propaganda, but in the detail of their craft, and in the 'atmosphere' or aesthetic that emanates from between their words. This aesthetic seems to have most to do with an attitude towards the natural setting that becomes part of the 'nature-openings' that Pound described as a 'metaphor by sympathy' for the rest of the poem, and that were in fact near the centre of Pound's own interest in the Provencal lyric. Beginning with the apparently very un-Pound-like case of Bernart de Ventadorn, we shall see how these 'nature-openings' acquire their importance.

7. BERNART DE VENTADORN

Everything that is known about Bernart, and some more, is in the Provençal *vida:*

Bernart de Ventadorn was from Limousin, from a castle of Ventadour, of low breeding, the son of a serf and of a woman who baked bread, as Peire d'Auvergne says of him in his song, when he slanders all the troubadours:

> The third, Bernart de Ventadorn,
> who is lesser than [Giraut de] Borneil by a thorn,
> in his father he had a good serf
> who always carried a bow of laburnum;
> and his mother heated the oven
> and his father gathered the brushwood.

But whoever he was son of, God gave him a handsome person and an agreeable one, and a noble heart, from which nobility came in the beginning, and gave him sense and wisdom and courtliness and noble speaking; and he had finesse and the skill of finding good words and gay tunes.

(And the Viscount of Ventadour, his lord, liked him and his composing and his singing very much, and honoured him greatly. And the Viscount of Ventadour had a beautiful, gay, young and noble wife; and she liked Sir Bernart and his songs very much, and fell in love with him and he with her, so that he made his verses and his songs about her, the love he had for her, and the worth of the lady.)

And God gave him such success, because of his fine manner and his gay poetizing, that she wished him well beyond measure, so that she kept no sense, nobility, honour or merit or shame in it, but fled her sense and followed her will, as Arnaut de Mareuil says:

> I think of the joy and forget the foolishness,
> and flee my sense, and follow my will.

and as Gui d'Ussel says:

> for thus it happens to true lovers,
> that sense has no power against desire.

And he was honoured and esteemed by all good people, and his songs honoured and appreciated. And he was seen and heard and received very willingly, and great honour and great gifts were given him by the great lords and the great men, so that he moved in great trappings and great honour.

Their love lasted a long time before the Viscount, her husband, perceived it. And when he had perceived it, he was very sorry and sad; and he made the Viscountess, his wife, very sad and unhappy; and he had Bernart de Ventadorn given leave that he might leave the country.

And he left and went off to Normandy, to the Duchess who was then lady of the Normans [i.e. Eleanor of Aquitaine], and she was young and gay and of great worth and merit and great power, and she was very interested in honour and merit. And she received him with great pleasure and great honour, and was very happy about his arrival, and made him lord and master of her whole court.

(And Sir Bernart's verses and songs pleased her very much, so that she received and honoured and welcomed him and did many things to please him.)

And as he fell in love with the wife of his lord, so he fell in love with the Duchess, and she with him. For a long time he had great joy of her, and great happiness, until she took King Henry of England as her husband and he took her away beyond the English Channel, so that he never saw her again, or any message from her.

(And he left Normandy and went to the good Count Raymond of Toulouse, and was with him at his court until the Count died. And when the Count was dead, Sir Bernart abandoned the world and composing and singing and the delights of the world and entered the Order of Dalon; and there he finished.

And the Count, Sir Ebles of Ventadour, who was the son of the Viscountess that Sir Bernart loved, told me, Sir Uc de St Circ, what I have written about Sir Bernart.)[1]

It was not Bernart's life that interested Pound, apart from the one incident in this story that he took into Canto VI. Nor did he find a great deal to say about Bernart's verse, though all that he did say was of the highest praise: 'What is to be said for the quality of *Ventadour* in the best moments, or of *Sordello*, where there is nothing but the perfection of the movement, nothing salient in the thought or the rhyme scheme? You have to have known Provençal a long time perhaps before you perceive the difference between this work and another.'[2] He contented himself always with asserting that Bernart was a master in the use of sound.[3]

I feel sure that most of the very few men of intelligence whom
Pound has ever persuaded to read the troubadours must have come
away from Bernart with a headache.[4] The literal meaning of his
poems is easy to grasp, having neither complexity nor much variation. *Trobar leu* (easy style) songs, as Pound had admitted, 'are apt
to weary you after you know them; they are especially tiresome if
one tries to read them *after* one has read fifty others of more or less
the same sort.'[5] The modern 'intelligent layman', if he should ever
read Ventadorn, would come upon him in a volume containing
forty-five of his poems. Lacking distractions (such as would have
punctuated the performance in a mediaeval castle), and in the
absence of music to bring out some differentiation in the movement,
he would read it straight through. Presumably he would not have
the awareness of troubadour sound-values that Pound said he had
acquired only after 'long domesticity' with music.[6] He would probably digest the work of Bernart's lifetime at a sitting, and call for
something more solid.

His impression of Bernart's 'mental furnishings' might not be
favourable. The emotional situation is static not only over the work
as a whole (Bernart cannot be blamed for the way his work is presented after 800 years), but even in the individual poems. The first
factor guaranteeing permanent stasis is the *enveyos,* or jealous one,
who occurs (in the plural) in many poems without ever being specified.[7] The enviers intend not to calumniate Bernart to his lady, but
to betray them both to her husband — we assume:

> Oh God, how good would be the love
> of two lovers, if it could be
> that not one of these enviers
> should ever know of their friendship.[8]

The persistent snooping has even parted Bernart from his lady, in
one song:

> But deceiving heartless flatterers
> have sent me away from her country,
> because the man whom I would have
> expected to hide us, if he knew
> we were both of one heart,
> makes himself a spy.[9]

So Bernart recommends deceit to his lady:

> we ought to talk with hidden meanings,
> and, since boldness is no use to us, let astuteness
> serve our turn![10]

And he then finds himself praising the virtues of this situation into which he has been 'forced':

> For it would not seem that a man
> who takes his ease in love, loves,
> since one becomes dependable through secrecy
> and thereby reaches nearer to joy. [11]

So it seems that Bernart wants (when, that is, he can gain his lady's approval) to remain under permanent suspicion. Such conditions make liaisons difficult. But closeness is not desired:

> Let her not love me
> as a lover (*per drudaria*), since it would not be right[12]

Some other mysterious token is all that Bernart asks for:

> but if it pleased her
> to accord me some favour,
> I would swear to her
> by her and by my faith
> that the favour she accorded to me
> would not be known from me. [13]

He is obviously more interested in secrecy than in love of whatever kind, just as the unfortunate client to whom Belle-de-Jour is introduced in Buñuel's film only wants to be punished for *offering* to make love.

Bernart also likes a certain self-abasement:

> for at court I shall be courtly towards you
> among ladies and knights,
> and open and gentle and humble. [14]

There is something more actively humble in the Provençal present

participle *umilians* than in the English 'humble'. Bernart thinks it is
a bearing that of itself ought to evoke a favourable response in a
lady, and, as so often with the troubadours, he starts to moralise
when he finds it does not work:

> A man who goes around womanizing
> with pride and deception gets more love
> than one who pleads every day
> or is too humble;
> for Love scarcely wants the man who
> is open and loyal, as I am.[15]

In lines like these, Bernart's ecstasies seem like those of a lapdog:

> For with the favourable regard alone that she turns to me,
> when she can or when circumstances permit it her,
> I have so much joy that I am not even aware of my existence,
> because I turn and spin and whirl so.[16]

The *enveyos* are a built-in mechanism for thwarting Bernart's
designs, and for punishing him when they succeed. But his own attitude towards the lady has the same effect. He thinks he is likely to be
punished if he ever has the presumption to reveal his love for her:

> I love my lady, hold her dear,
> fear and serve her so much
> that I have never dared speak of myself to her,
> I ask nothing of her, and send her nothing.[17]

In that poem, one could say that Bernart is still protecting his lady's
reputation from the *enveyos*. In this one, it is quite clear that he is
simply afraid of presuming too much:

> for now she has given me the heart and the desire
> to seek, if I could,
> such a thing that, if the King sought it,
> he would have been extremely bold. . . .
> From me she shall never know what afflicts me
> and no-one else shall say anything.[18]

As if that were not enough bogeys, Bernart also has a fear lest his
lady realise her own value — and hence his own worthlessness:

since she is so gentle and perfect and pure,
I have a great fear in case she should take cognisance of her value . . . . [19]

And

> I should really kill
> the man who ever made a mirror!
> When I really think about it,
> I have no worse enemy.
> The day she looks at herself
> and thinks of her value,
> I shall never receive
> her or her love. [20]

What is special about the position of Bernart (and his countless cultural descendants) is the tightness of his prison, the number of foolproof devices guaranteeing permanent failure. He sees virtue in his position, as we have seen; in fact enough to be able to reproach the lady when she fails to respond. He recognises that he is victim to the obligatory madness:

> Still, I know that it is normal in love
> that a man who loves well has hardly any sense. [21]

but he still imagines that his strange condition places moral obligations on the unfortunate lady. And just in case anyone should think of telling him to improve his situation, Bernart insists that he enjoys it:

> In the world there is only one thing
> through which I could gain joy;
> and I shall never have it from her,
> and I can never want it from another.
> Nevertheless through her I have value and wisdom,
> and I am gayer and my heart is more gracious through her,
> for if she did not exist, I would never enter the struggle! [22]

What puts a man in this extraordinary position, and makes him write endless songs about it? Bernart gives us a good number of reasons why he should *not* sing: the need for secrecy, fear of the *enveyos,* desire not to impose himself on the lady—so that the lady's identity is never revealed directly. Yet he composes songs for public consumption. The reason implied in the fictional situation of his songs is that he requires our sympathy, and needs the release of declaring his sorrows. Bernart must sing, he tells us, to comfort the other lovers in a barren season;[23] or again, he is so sad that he can't sing (or so he sings to Lemozi and us, the sympathetic audience).[24] When he tells us that his former lady was false, and that his new lady is complaisant (speaking of them both in the third person), and then turns to address this new lady herself—yet still clearly speaking for our hearing[25]—he is using us, the audience, as a kind of sympathetic sounding-board. If the message does not reach the lady at all, we are like Pyramus's wall, and in any case we reinforce the message with our implied sympathy, like the mute witnesses to an estrangement addressed in songs that tell us to see that the lady is wearing her coat so warm, etc.

We might turn from the situation implied by Bernart's songs to look at his historical working situation. Bernart, in common with many other troubadours, had neither lands, a notary's job, nor a position in the clergy with which to support himself. It seems reasonable to suppose that his songs were his living.[26] It was usual, in troubadour poetry, to address songs to ladies who sounded as though they ought to be of terribly noble birth, but our expectation in this is just a side-effect of the ethic/aesthetic qualities seen in them by the troubadours; in any case, the ladies are rarely identifiable from within the songs.[27] We may assume that there was no more a particular lady behind any one of Bernart's songs than there need be behind any modern love-lyric. If we imagine Bernart as a professional, we realise that his first requirement was to keep up an output on the subject of love every night of his working life. The props I have described would certainly have helped to keep up a level of imaginative belief in the love-situations he sang of, which were thus bound to be static and repetitive. He had to preserve the lady's anonymity in case, at the operative time, there was no lady. He could not develop elaborate romances in his successive songs, for rumour would soon say whether they were true. To cover these real reasons for vagueness, we have all the fictional devices of the troubadour lyric. Most particularly, some kind of tension was necessary to hold the audience's interest; it could not be a narrative tension; and so we have all the static devices of conflict, like the *enveyos,* and the fear of being found inadequate. The basic tension is the fact that Bernart is parted, eternally, from his lady, and he knows how to give this all the immediacy it needs for the audience in the hall:

> But I am here, far away,
> and I don't know how she is![28]

But all this implies that the mediaeval audience were much more naive than the modern critic; that they needed to believe (literally) that the troubadour standing there in the straw and spilt wine was enacting, for their sakes, the heartaches of a situation he was (literally) going through in those very days, or had been when he composed the song. There is no reason for thinking this. All literatures can be explained away by reference to the survival requirements of their practitioners; the explanation is false as long as the literature has any power, for it does not begin to explain this power over contemporary audiences or over us. It is better to try to understand the emotions involved in whatever reality it is that we participate in, at the level at which (observing empirically) we *do* imaginatively participate in it, rather than at levels at which we ought to; and to see if this imaginative participation breaks down anywhere, and why.

Taking Bernart's song-fiction as a whole, we find that it contains strong elements of narcissism and also of masochism. He presents us with feelings of sudden elation caused by a very passive relation with an all-powerful woman; alternatively, and very frequently, when things go wrong, with feelings of abjectness, distraction, and frustration. Bernart's sensuality, rather like that of the 'caressable Greeks' as Pound called them, is mixed with self-abasement:

> With my hands clasped I come for her pleasure,
> and wish never to move from her feet again,
> until for pity she brings me to where she undresses[29]

Again,

> She will be doing wrong, if she doesn't send for me
> to come to where she undresses,
> so that I may be by her command
> near to the bed, next to its edge,
> and may take off her well-fitting shoes,

> on my knees and humble,
> if it pleases her to stretch out her feet to me.[30]

The lady seems to be partly a means whereby he can watch himself being watched by her:

> I never had power over myself
> or was my own, from that time onwards
> when she let me see into her eyes
> in a mirror which pleased me greatly.
> Mirror, since I saw myself in you,
> sighs from deep down have killed me,
> because I lost myself as did
> handsome Narcissus in the spring.[31]

Provided we restrict ourselves to troubadours like Bernart, there seems to be something in Leslie Fiedler's opinion that the troubadour's lady is a resurrection of the Great Mother: 'The themes of self-punishment and self-destruction are inseparable (in the West at least) from the worship of the Female, who represents the dissolution of consciousness as well as that of ecstasy.'[32]

The lady from whom Bernart gets his ecstasy or his humbling is not only not named, and not given any physical differentiation, but also has no features of psychology, of emotion or behaviour, in regard to Bernart or anyone else, that would give us a strong sense that Bernart saw her as an individual existing outside his own feelings about her. She is proud and silent towards him, but tricks him into believing that she still loves him;[33] or she has a flighty heart, which he in wrath will imitate by loving anyone who wants him, while the new lady by contrast has done him 'so much honour' and from the beginning has been 'noble and of good company'.[34] But if the lady in question is being vile, she goes through a certain number of motions, and if she is being good, she goes through an equally limited set of motions, each equally absolute and all-embracing in its approvability and capacity to confer enlightenment and honour on Bernart.

One feels in fact that it is this capacity to confer desirable emotions on Bernart, whether of elation or of humiliation, that is all that matters to Bernart about her. It is a very subtle but important shift of emphasis from what I have described[35] as the core of the

courtly-love emotion. There, the poet's thoughts have focused on a
lady because she is wonderful in herself and has an inexplicable and
awe-inspiring capacity to make things meaningful, including (as a
side-effect) the life of the poet; the power emanates from the lady,
she is felt as entirely other than and above the poet, all depends on
her will:

> ...I dare not move an inch
> until I know clearly about the truce,
> whether she is how I wish.

But in the past she has exercised her will favourably to him, and
since this is put in simple, personal terms, there is nothing to make
us suspect that her independence is only respected as long as it fits
socially preordained norms:

> I still think of a morning
> when we made peace to the war,
> and she gave me so great a gift:
> her loving and her ring.
> God let me live so long yet
> that I have my hands in her cloak.[36]

With Bernart, however, one sometimes feels that his attention
focused on the lady specifically and solely because she seemed capable of remaking him in an image that he had fixed before he met
her. Worse, this pre-fixed self-image was not even a very interesting
one; it was the lowest common denominator of a number of socially
fashionable expectations. It was not that he, Bernart, his own man,
spontaneously felt his existence to be heightened by her, but that he
came to her requiring to be 'remade' by her; but he does not in fact
allow her to remake him in any image other than the one he has
brought along, which is not one that he has generated himself, but a
series of unimpeachable blandnesses like 'honour', clearly social in
origin. This reinforces our feeling that he has no strong sense of his
own individuality, which is exactly what begins the whole circular
self-defeating process. It combines passivity with a sort of social
narcissism, that is to say an interest chiefly in how one appears, this
appearance being judged entirely in borrowed terms. I have defined
courtly love as a kind of worship, in which a man believes that a par-

ticular woman's existence 'is on a higher plane than his own; in
which he believes that she can give him something resembling a key
to his own existence. . . .'[37] A man who has no strong sense of his
own existence in the first place may well make this idea of relative
value into something rather monstrous, a distorted grovelling with
regrettable compensations—like the sudden petulant antifeminism
that Bernart indulges in.[38] It is a mutual validation by two entities
neither of which begins with anything intrinsic. This is what courtly
love tends to become, and we shall see this strain again in Sordello.

From here it is a short step to accepting the argument of Frederick
Goldin, that the image projected by the troubadour onto his lady is
in fact a social ideal, and the whole troubadour lyric a social process; that the lady is only allowed to be a mirror, a validating reflection of the troubadour's self-image as a perfected member of a class,
and hence an ideal self-image of that class as a whole, towards
which the class strives as a focus of its common life.[39] The qualities
that the lady's approval allows the troubadour to see in himself, and
the qualities in her that enable her to be an object to strive towards,
and to confer this approval, are on the same plane, and are such
socially approvable things as generosity, graciousness, and the like.
Goldin argues that the troubadours had taken the ancient but currently dominant Augustinian *topos* of the mirror, in which a man
might see himself truly, but through which (for Augustine) he ought
to peer in order to perceive God; and had turned it into an end in
itself, giving it a life beyond its own blankness by fusing it with the
lady, to whom they could attribute an interest-sustaining capacity
for conferring approval as from outside. But the paradox was obvious: if the lady could only be motivated by her socially approvable
qualities to confer approval for his socially approvable qualities—
qualities determined by the poet as member of a class in the act of
writing—then she did not have a will of her own, and in fact could
not have any personal interest in the troubadour. Or if he became
aware of her womanliness and individuality, then he would realise
that she could not have the perfection (in identification with the
social image) that alone would authorise her to confer approval; she
would be a mere (fickle, etc.) woman. The troubadours sustained
this paradox, Goldin suggests, by an ingenious juggling, often within
the single poem. They would successively address themselves to fic-
tive audiences consisting of the lady and the sincere troubadour's

friends (before whom no doubts could be admitted, since the troubadour's validation depended on his adoring without qualification
or reserve); of the vulgar mockers (who could not imagine that any
such ridiculous self-prostration could be sincere); of the false lovers
(who cynically borrowed the troubadour's words in order to get
equal approval from the lady); and so on. Goldin believes that it is
this tension between complete doubt and heroically persistent faith
in the embodiment of the ideal in the lady that provides much of the
subtlety and psychological interest of the troubadour poems.

But as I have suggested, the mediaeval audience might have been
just as subtle at working out the varying levels of fictional reality as
we are. There remains, for us as for them, a level at which we imaginatively participate in the poem's situation; perhaps a dominant
level, with harmonic levels above and below. If we can think of it all
as a subtly self-serving group self-projection onto a mere reflecting
surface, so could they; obviously they did not, primarily; nor, except
when we are writing critical monographs, do we. For the mediaeval
audience and for us, the lady exists, out there, separately. That is
the enduring underlying fact of the poem's situation.[40] Once that is
admitted, one can say that the troubadour does not take much
notice of her individuality; but that can be said of many relationships in the lives we know, and does not deny that they are personal
relationships, however strong the admixtures of social poses. The
elements that I have picked out from Bernart's poems show that
they imply psychological situations, situations of a (however sublimated) sexual relationship, that are quite in accord with a personal
psychology in the poet which would want to minimise the lady's separate existence.

The situation implied by Bernart's poems is bounced off his lady
towards his narcissistic self first, and towards himself as a member of
a group only secondarily. Bernart, in wishing to find approval for
himself, can only use borrowed, currently fashionable validators;
and this brings in groups outside himself. But there is no evidence
that Bernart's self-approval image was that of a 'class', or of any
group beyond that of the lady (hopefully), the immediate audience
(or elements of it), and perhaps us, the eternal audience, like Dr.
Eckleburg's eyes. Goldin clearly implies an historical audience when
he says that 'the chief professional concern of the courtly poets' was
'to preserve the unity of a social class', and specifies that this class

was in fact 'a ruling class'.[41] By strange contrast, Koehler believes that the whole courtly-love lyric was the invention of a class specifically excluded from the ruling class: the poor knights (like Bertran de Born and Raimbaut d'Orange), who sought by its means to by-pass their financial and social humiliations. He even argues that the great Duke William IX of Aquitaine supported this movement because he needed the political support of this class![42] It is impossible in fact to think of all the producers of troubadour poetry as belonging to, or aspiring to, the same class. Even if they did, the troubadour lyric would be quite ineffective as a projection of a socially unifying ideal: imagine what Bertran de Born would have thought of the self-image projected by Bernart de Ventadorn and reflected by Bernart's lady. Leaving aside his opinion of Bernart's craftsmanship, he could only have thought of Bernart as the least knight-like man he had ever heard sing.

If one explains the troubadour lyric as a group ideal-self-image projection, one must also explain why this mechanism should have been hitched onto the sexual relation; why the adorer and the adored are of opposite sexes, which they are (in Provence) even when the adorer is a lady.[43] Why do the troubadours call it *amors?*[44] The social self-reflection argument can only take account of the sexual relation when it is that 'vulgar carnality' in favour of which the true, the social idealisation of courtly love is switched off, whenever the troubadour becomes aware of the element in himself and his audience which laughs at the baselessness of his purity.[45] But a sexuality (not usually seen in these simple terms of taking to bed or not taking to bed) is infused in the whole of the courtly-love relationship. To talk of the courtly love lyric without taking note of this basic emotional level is like talking about the level of self-idealisation in 'See that my grave is kept clean' without noting that it assumes the possibility of death, and that death is associated with solitude and fear. Without taking into account the chief emotional 'subject', there can be no account of the way in which the sophistications of the song grew out of it.[46]

The troubadour's lady only really becomes a social mirror when the whole poem is such a 'going through the motions' that the entire act of writing is felt as the adopting of a borrowed, not experienced, posture.[47] But in all periods there have been second-rate writers who have used the form of a personal utterance for what begins and ends as a social act; they do not thereby create a new form which is valid as a social act.[48]

The question to be asked is how much bending from the developed norm, how much infusion of symptoms of the poet's own personal obsessions, in the form of images that would not have occurred to another, or odd pacings of the breath, is necessary before we feel that an individual is speaking, that the things he speaks of, however superficially similar to another's subject-matter, are his own? When it seemed that the poetry-reading public were about to take George Oppen as 'another William Carlos Williams', Pound noted that 'the cry for originality is often set up by men who have never stopped to consider how much. I mean how great a variant from a known modality is needed by the new writer if his expression is to be coterminous with his content.'[49] *His* content is the compound of his concerns, and, since he is an unrepeatable individual, it differentiates him from anyone else. This line of thought in Pound goes back to the *virtù* of the individual which he tried to define in 1912 as that which the writer must somehow discover in himself and get down on paper.[50] It was such a combination of trace-elements, slight in themselves, that led Pound to feel that the troubadour lyric was more than a programme. Bernart's concern with feet and with unclothing seems to be one trace of his *virtù*, but not the most important. Without modifying the obvious characteristics of the form, the poet can bend it subtly through image and cadence. The troubadours often modify both elements most effectively in the 'spring-opening', the *Natureingang* that begins so many poems. So that if we are looking for the individual thumbprint—that in which the emotions and implied situation are different from those of a class—we had better look very carefully at the 'spring opening'.

Consider the effect of these opening lines by Bernart:

> Can l'erba fresch' e·lh folha par
> e la flors boton' el verjan,
> e·l rossinhols autet e clar
> leva sa votz e mou so chan,
> joi ai de lui, e joi ai de la flor
> e joi de me e de midons major;
> daus totas partz sui de joi claus e sens,
> mas sel es jois que totz autres jois vens.

> When the fresh grass and the leaves appear
> and the flower buds on the branch,
> and the high clear nightingale
> lifts its voice and intones its song,
> I delight in him, and I delight in the flower
> and in myself and more in my lady;
> from all sides I am enclosed and wrapped in delight,
> but that is true joy which vanquishes all others.[51]

In the first four lines, a few simple and unqualified nouns are isolated with such art that each becomes a complete image, grouped in such a way as to allow the others to exist like intact things — to borrow Zukofsky's terms.[52] Plosives (c, b, p, t), chiefly unvoiced and mixed with many liquids (l, r) and unvoiced fricatives (s, f, tz), make the aural picture delicate. This is the sound-aesthetic that the troubadours called *trobar prim*, of which Linda Paterson has collected fascinating examples.[53] Meanwhile a pattern of *f*s interwoven with *b*s and other consonants interweaves with another pattern, the shift of vowel-direction from *er, e, o, ar* in the first line to *or, o, e, a*. (Speak the lines aloud and listen for these movements). These first four lines establish the poet within a Nature that is gentle, clear-cut, and delightful; and at the same time establish the ground-tone of his emotions. The poet now comes to his statement about the lady, and the metric begins to open out. From the ecstatic holding-back in the first four lines, each of four stresses with a masculine ending, it relaxes into the five-stress

> joi ai de lui, e joi ai de la flor
> e joi de me e de midons major

The counterbalance of verbal elements has now become more obvious, and likewise the bending of the expectation of simple repetition, set up by

> joi ai de lui, e joi ai de la flor

and subtly not fulfilled by the sounds of

> e joi de me e de midons major

The poet then repeats, for emphasis, that the 'joy' is flooding in from all sides, and ties off the whole stanza with a redirecting and culminating of the sense that would be the envy of any sonneteer trying to fit his fourteen lines:

> but that is true joy which vanquishes all others.

So one can distinguish two grades of sound-craftsmanship here. The first is that in which, by an alchemy that only the mouth, the ear, and the visual memory can unravel, something like a mimetic aural picture is built up which precisely reinforces the emotional direction of the imagery.[54] The second is that in which there is musical invention only; invention being that capacity to hold our interest by introducing new patterns, delaying or varying their fulfilment, and so on, in which for example Bach rarely fails even when he has 'nothing to say'. In this song by Bernart, this latter type of craftsmanship takes over from the first as soon as he shifts from the natural scene to direct description of his relationship with the lady. The song is now smoothly *cantabile,* while keeping the progression of emotional shape that goes in each stanza with the opening out from the four-stress line to the five-stress; yet always brilliantly inventive in the sound-values:[55]

> Ai las! com mor de cossirar!
> Que manhtas vetz en cossir tan:
> lairo m'en poirian portar,
> que re no sabria que·s fan.

This complicated intervolution is saying no more than:

> Alas! how I am dying of troubled thoughts!
> For frequently I ponder so much that
> thieves could carry me off,
> for I would have no idea what they were doing.

Bernart's successful songs are a combination of what Pound called 'poetic lyricism', the true and rare reinforcement of image/thought by sound, and 'melopoeic lyricism', the independent brilliance of sound-invention.[56] The first is almost always restricted to the de-

scriptions of nature; the second occurs in the direct reference to the
lady. It goes without saying that many of his songs have neither.

When I say that Bernart's finest art is reserved for his nature-
descriptions, I do not want to suggest that he is not interested in the
lady. What I suggest is that the nature-opening is in fact the best
expression, a better expression than most of the verse, of his relationship with the lady. The spring-opening is everywhere in the troubadour lyric, and very frequently finely individual, and it almost
always serves as an introduction to expounding the state of the troubadour's feelings about the lady. It is, as Pound said, 'an interpretation of the mood; an equation, in other terms, or a "metaphor by
sympathy" for the mood of the poem.'[57] The spring opening is at
one and the same time the best evidence of the troubadour's craftsmanship; the best proof of the individuality of his 'breath' and his
emotions, and of the interpersonal nature of his emotions, for its
tone always connects with his position vis-à-vis the lady; and, since
we are obliged to generalise, the best evidence of the sexual nature
of the whole business.

We may see all this in the most famous of Bernart's songs, the
song of the lark:

> Can vei la lauzeta mover
> de joi sas alas contral rai,
> que s'oblid' e·s laissa chazer
> per la doussor c'al cor li vai,
> ai! tan grans enveya m'en ve
> de cui qu'eu veya jauzion,
> meravilhas ai, car desse
> lo cor de dezirer no·m fon.[58]

> When I see the lark move
> for joy its wings against the light,
> so that it forgets itself and lets itself fall
> for the sweetness that comes to its heart,
> oh! such a great envy comes to me
> of anyone I see happy,
> I am surprised that on the spot
> my heart does not melt with desire.

The light floods, for the lark; but not for Bernart, who (as Goldin
says)[59] has discovered that all the things he saw in the lady were read

into her by himself, that he was in fact only seeing himself in her:

> I have never had power over myself
> and have not been my own man, from the moment
> that she let me see into her eyes,
> in a mirror that pleased me greatly. . . .

He reproaches her for being no more than a mirror for his self-image; but at the same time he blames her (in the most banal family-comedy terms) for being a mere woman and not setting her aspirations (which reflect on her aspirations for him, the sights she sets him to aim for) high enough:

> In this my lady shows herself a woman,
> and I blame her for this,
> that she does not want what one ought to want,
> and what one forbids her, she does.

So Bernart, like the pop-song lyricist locking himself away from the day, rejects the world in sobbing phrases:

> So I leave her and give her up;
> she has killed me, and I answer her as a dead man,
> and go away, since she does not retain me as her liege,
> a wretch — into exile — I don't know where.

But though Bernart is unhappily not like the lark, the lark is his image of what he would like to be. When things are going well, that is his manner of loving, or of being loved. The magic moment is the focusing of the lady's attention on him, when 'the sweet passivity of his will' (to borrow Goldin's phrase)[60] releases in him an ecstasy, with its floods of light, its melting, as the lark 'forgets itself and lets itself fall'. It is as individual and personal an image for Bernart's kind of sexuality as the frost-on-hawthorn in William IX of Aquitaine's song, or the rose-in-snow in Sordello's.[61]

Since Pound felt as he did about the individual breath in poetry, it is natural that he should have been interested in the spring-openings of the troubadour lyrics almost more than in any other aspect of them. It is also interesting to find that three of the troubadours with whom he most concerned himself — Bernart de Ventadorn, Arnaut Daniel, and Bertran de Born — should have surprising continuities

with each other's successes in the spring-opening, and that they
should have been the ones Pound connected mythically with Eleanor of Aquitaine, on whom he based so much of his feelings about
Provençal culture.

The ethoses or implied modes of living in the verses of Arnaut,
Bertran, and Bernart are different. But they shared elements of an
aesthetic, which Pound describes in the case of Arnaut:

that fineness of Arnaut's senses which made him chary of his rhymes, impatient of tunes that would have distorted his language, fastidious of redun-
dance, made him likewise accurate in his observation of Nature.

For long after him the poets of the North babbled of gardens where
'three birds sang on every bough' and where other things and creatures
behaved as in nature they do not behave.[62]

Pound was not unaware of the element of convention in the
'spring-opening': he noted simply that in 50 percent of the Provençal verse it 'determined the tone' of the rest of the poem.[63] If a comprehensive list of the elements of nature in Arnaut's verse were to be
compiled, it would not be very long; nor would there be found any
precise descriptions of the behaviour of hoopoes and ravens, such as
one might expect when Arnaut is called 'accurate in his observation
of nature'.[64]

But a great deal depends on the way the conventional elements
are presented. The human form is a convention in sculpture; after
thousands of years its possibilities for the precise definition of emotion are not yet exhausted. No one would deny that the precision of
the definition, in the case of sculpture, is a matter of cubic milli-
metres of stone; likewise in poetry it depends on the relations of
minute components of music, syntax, associations, and the rest. The
fact that Arnaut puts birds in the first strophe of his poem X out of
Y times is at least as insignificant as the fact that Giacometti has
sculpted Z human figures with one foot; the fact is meaningless
without the feeling.

Pound was therefore talking of something else. In the *Guide to
Kulchur* he spoke of a 'real knowledge' that allowed him to tell one
painter from another, and that differed in kind from memorisable
facts. This knowledge was not merely passive, but affected 'every

perception of form-colour subsequent to its acquisition.' Further, there were types of writing that communicated a knowledge which was closer to this kind of knowledge than to what one gained from memorisable facts; which was why Confucius demanded that his students read the Odes themselves, rather than any list of facts or maxims that might seem to be equivalent to them.[65] The communicable content of poetry therefore is of a different order from that of any objects it may happen to mention.

In Arnaut, it was 'observation of nature' not merely listed, but built into cadence, that Pound was interested in. He said of Petrarch: 'As far as any question of actual fineness of emotion or cadence or perception he is miles behind Ventadorn or Arnaut Daniel.'[66] Such fineness can be found in Bernart de Ventadorn, in lines like this:

> ni l'erba nais delonc la fon[67]

> nor [when] the grass appears by the spring

The liquid consonants and back vowels of *delonc la fon* seem to bring across the resonant acoustics of water. The effect is similar but less pastoral in these lines by Villon:

> Echo parlant quant bruyt on maine
> Dessus riviere ou sus estan[68]

> Echo speaking when one makes noise
> above a river or a pond

The cadence of Bernart's

> part la fera mar prionda[69]

> beyond the wild deep sea

is more obviously united with its subject: it accelerates and becomes jerky with *fera mar* and seems to plunge with *prionda*. Note how the word *prion*, 'deep', has a very different sound and a different effect when used in this line in the masculine, giving a flatness and a hopelessness:

m'an mort li sospir de preon[70]

the sighs from deep down have killed me

or here, from the poem with the grass by the spring, where it gives the feeling that Bernart is drowning:

tro aras, qu'en sui tan prion

until now, when I am so deep in it

One might not expect such subtlety in Bertran de Born's war-poems, but it is there:

Be·m platz lo gais temps de pascor,
Que fai fuolhas e flors venir;
E platz mi, quan auch la baudor
Dels auzels, que fan retentir
    Lor chan per lo boschatge[71]

The delightful time of Easter pleases me,
bringing leaves and flowers,
and I am pleased when I hear the sounds
of the birds making their song ring
through the woodland

There is an extraordinary subtlety in the echo and reverberation of *retentir,* and the way the back vowels back up the hollowness of the woodlands in the last line. Bernart has a similar effect:

Can par la flors josta·l vert folh
e vei lo tems clar e sere
e·l doutz chans dels auzels pel brolh
m'adousa lo cor e·m reve[72]

When the flower appears among the green leafage
and I see the weather clear and serene,
and the sweet song of the birds through the woods
softens my heart and comes back to me

The sound is *through* the woods — the birds are seeking something — and this is felt in the hollow sounds as the line slows down, *dels auzels pel brolh.* Arnaut Daniel also has something similar, but his frogs, *ranas el riu,* are more Disney-like with their quick croaking:

> Lanquan vei fueill'e flor e frug
> parer dels albres el ramel
> e aug lo chan que faun e·l brug
> ranas el riu, el bosc auzel[73]

> When I see leaf and flower and fruit
> appear, on the branches of the trees,
> and I hear their song that they make, and the noise,
> frogs in the stream, birds in the wood

And one ought to point out the masterly mimetic cadence in Bernart's song of the lark which seems to pause and hang for a moment as the lark hangs suspended before its fall:

> que s'oblid' //   e·s laissa chazer

> so that it forgets itself //   and lets itself fall

What Pound learned from his 'long domesticity' with Provençal sound-values must be diffused in many parts of his verse, but there are places where one can suggest a direct link. There are these lines by Bernart:

> que pois l'arma n'es issida,
> balaya lonc tems lo gras.[74]

> for after the grain has dropped out of it,
> the cornstalk sways for a long time.

Arma also means 'soul': the heart has dropped out of Bernart and he still lives on. The sense and the sounds of emptiness are the same in Canto VII, where culture has died and there is no one to activate it — no Eleanor:

> Thin husks I had known as men,
> Dry casques of departed locusts
>   speaking a shell of speech.... [75]

In these brief visions of circumambient nature, the capacities of the words are so precisely arranged that they reinforce each other as it were exponentially, as Pound put it: 'thus three or four words in exact juxtaposition are capable of radiating this energy at a very high potentiality.'[76] Here the energy is a sense of order and clarity in nature. It is present in the second line of this strophe by Bertran de Born:

> S'abrils e fuolhas e flors
> E·lh bel mati e·lh clar ser
> D'un ric joi cui ieu esper
> No m'aiudan et Amors
> E·lh rossinholet qu'auch braire. . . .[77]

> If April and leaves and flowers
> and the fine mornings and clear evenings
> and the nightingales I hear making a noise
> and Love don't help me
> towards a great happiness I hope for. . . .

Bertran may have learned it from Arnaut:

> L'aur'amara
> fa·ls bruoills brancutz
> clarzir
> qe·l dous'espeis'ab fuoills[78]

> The bitter breeze
> makes the branched thickets
> lighten
> that the soft breeze thickens with leaves

Pound saw how Dante had learned it from Arnaut:

> The simile shows how well he had followed Arnaut Daniel:
> 　　As the spray which boweth its tip at the transit of
> the wind, and then of its own power doth raise it again;
> so I while Beatrice was speaking.
> 　　It is no borrowing, but it is Arnaut's kind of
> beauty.[79]

Pound himself learned it, and put it for example into his great Canto on Arnaut:

Wind over the olive trees, ranunculae ordered,
By the clear edge of the rocks
The water runs, and the wind scented with pine
And with hay-fields under sun-swath.[80]

Pound paid a great deal of attention to the details of sound that
these three troubadours were masters in. He needed to learn their
craft, and he believed that these elements of texture were as important as considerations of structural form; which probably, one fears,
receive more attention because they are easier to talk about.[81] Pound
considered in fact that often the whole of a work of literature existed
solely as a build-up for one of these moments when the matter is
stated in a perfect cadence of a line or two, or in a juxtaposition of
images of equivalent power, or in both combined.[82] Hence one of
his methods for building the Cantos: to arrange these one-line keys
to the power of the writings he considered important.

When a singer wanted an ad hoc translation of Bernart de Ventadorn, to sing to his music, Pound refused to swamp the jewel of the
poem in literary mud:

Kattegorrikaly DAMN the woman. I refuse to spoil one of the best bits of
Provençal by making a rush crib in twenty minutes to order. Meaning is all
tied up with sound.
First strophe is about new leaves and flowers bring back fragrance to the
heart.
Second — insomnia — due to natural cause usual at the season.
Then — where man's treasure is there will his heart be also.
Then — and if I see her not, no sight is worth the beauty of my thought —
which is the trouvaille — can't spoil it by botched lead up.
There *is no literal* translation of a thing where the beauty is melted into
the original phrase. Tell the brute to take a literal photo of the Venus de
Milo.[83]

The one part that he was willing to translate in this letter was the
'find':

> s'eu no vos vei, domna, don plus me cal,
> negus vezers mo bel pensar no val[84]

and that was because he had actually found an adequate equivalent
for it in English; so adequate that it went into the Cantos in these
words:

>And if I see her not
>No sight is worth the beauty of my thought.[85]

Pound would not have wanted to swallow Bernart de Ventadorn
whole, self-abasement and all. But he was interested in the way that
this centre of psycho-sexual attraction, Bernart's lady, seems to concentrate his faculties, even by becoming an internalised object of
contemplation:

>And if I see her not
>No sight is worth the beauty of my thought

and hence to clarify his perception of the surrounding natural order,
of which the 'nature-opening' suffused with divine light becomes an
emblem. We shall see how the fourth line of Bernart's lark-song is
modified to

>ab lo dolchor qu'al cor mi vai

>with the sweetness that goes to my heart

in Canto XCI, to concentrate these themes around the goddess as
Elizabeth I of England.[86] In the first of the Pisan Cantos there is the
passage:

>With the four giants at the four corners
>and four gates mid-wall Hooo Fasa
>and a terrace the colour of stars
>pale as the dawn cloud, la luna
>   thin as Demeter's hair
>Hooo Fasa, and in a dance the renewal
>   with two larks in contrappunto
>   at sunset
>   ch'intenerisce
>a sinistra la Torre
>   seen through a pair of breeches.
>*Che sublia es laissa cader*
>between NEKUIA where are Alcmene and Tyro
>   and the Charybdis of action
>   to the solitude of Mt Taishan
>femina, femina, that wd/ not be dragged into paradise by the hair,

under the grey cliff in periplum
the sun dragging her stars[87]

In the concentration camp at Pisa, Pound thinks of the legend of the resurrection of Wagadu, and also of the resurrection of Italy, until it be a celestial city like Ecbatan with its 'terrace the colour of stars'.[88] He watches the sun go down and thinks of Dante's lines about sunset 'that softens' ('ch'intenerisce') travellers' hearts and turns them towards their homeland.[89] He is thinking of his solitude by the Pisan mountain that he always compares to Taishan in China, and hearing the two larks in counterpoint reminds him of Bernart's lark 'that forgets itself and lets itself fall' (*Che sublia es laissa cader*), which takes his mind in contemplation to eternal woman, thought of here with despair.[90] It is this registering of nature's clarities that Pound takes to be the true emblem of Bernart's emotions about the lady; and it is a continuity in these emblems that picks out Bernart, Bertran de Born, and Arnaut Daniel for him as the three craftsmen of the Eleanor 'Vortex'.

8. ARNAUT DANIEL

✣✣✣✣✣✣✣✣✣

Arnaut Daniel's work contains the main reasons for Pound's later interest in the troubadours. These can be called *'trobar clus* as rite' and 'woman as focus of the poet's intelligence'. To explain these two concepts is to explain Pound's whole view of the troubadour poetic, and perhaps most of Pound's own poetic effort. *Trobar clus,* which means 'enclosed', perhaps hermetic composition, is the name given to the art of those troubadours who put hidden meanings in their songs; at times Pound took it that these meanings were not strictly esoteric, but simply deep. He saw this *trobar* as an act of worship. He believed that Provence's discovery was the way in which the love of a woman and the effort to 'get across to her' raised the artist's perception to the divine. The artist became a priest. The connection between these two ideas is religious but not particularly Christian, and comes from the benevolent, divine, and ordered nature of the universe, which it is the whole purpose of the Cantos to show.

In his person Arnaut Daniel seems an unworthy vessel for such high purposes, but as so often the information is anecdotal, scrappy, and unreliable. He seems to have been an impoverished gentleman of the lowest rank, unable either to enjoy the privileges due to his 'quality' or to gain any social compensations from his art. He 'flourished' poetically between about 1180 and 1200,[1] that is, in a period roughly spanning the last ten years of Henry II Plantagenet's reign and the whole of Richard Lionheart's. His Provençal biography says that he was a *gentils hom* 'and learned letters well and became a *jongleur*' — that is, an itinerant singer of songs composed by others.[2] A literate gentleman would normally either live on his rents or enter the Church. Other manuscripts of the *vida* perhaps explain this strangeness in Arnaut's career when they say 'And he learned letters well and delighted himself with *trobar* (composing) and abandoned letters and became a *jongleur*'.[3] We may see him at work in this lowly profession (if it is the same Arnaut) when Bertran de Born says:

Take my 'old-and-young' *sirventes*
to Richard, *jongleur* Arnaut, so that it may guide him.[4]

There is a possibility that Arnaut was on close terms with Richard
Lionheart, as these lines might suggest, and as is claimed flatly by
the *razo* to one of Arnaut's songs. It talks of a competition in *caras
rimas* (tough rhymes) with another *jongleur,* under the chairmanship of Richard. Though I think that this anecdote was concocted
by misreading one line in the song, the *vidas* and *razos* have not
often been proved wrong in the persons they associate together.[5]
Benvenuto da Imola, a commentator on Dante, was a great con-
cocter of stories,[6] and he is the source for another charming anecdote about Arnaut:

. . . while he was growing old in poverty, he made a very beautiful song that
he sent via a messenger to the King(s) of France and England and to the
other western princes. In it he asked that just as he, with his efforts, had
aided them in the matter of pleasure, so they with their wealth should help
him in the matter of utility. When, after this, the messenger brought back
a lot of money, Arnaut said: 'Now I see that God is not about to abandon
me.' And immediately he donned the monastic habit and was thencefor-
ward of most virtuous life.[7]

*Jongleur*ship had not brought Arnaut to wealth or to power, as had
happened for instance with Raimbaut de Vaqueiras and Sordello.[8]
We gather as much also from a brief controversy of wit in which
Arnaut was involved. One of the *vidas* tells us that 'Raimon de Durfort and Sir Turc Malec were two knights of the Cahors area, who
made *sirventes,* verse-polemics, about the lady who was called Lady
Aia—the one who said to the knight of Cornil that she would not
love him, if he did not trumpet in her bottom.'[9] The 'knight of Cornil' refused the demand,[10] and was reproved for unchivalrous behaviour by Raimon and Turc. Arnaut Daniel then came to his defence, protesting (in as vulgar a manner as he well could) that the
idea was repulsive;[11] and Raimon replied to Bernart, with this
oblique stab at Arnaut:

You are even more of a wretch
than Arnaut the scholar,
whom dice and gaming-boards undo;

> he goes around like a penitent,
> poor in clothing and in cash.... [12]

We deduce very little further detail of Arnaut's life from his other songs, which are of love in the more usual troubadour sense. The *vida* can only add the name of his lady—which might well be, as so often, apocryphal: [13]

And he loved a noble lady of Gascony, the wife of Sir Guillem de Bouvila, but it was not thought that the lady ever did him pleasure in the matter of love; for which reason he sings:

> I am Arnaut, who gather the wind
> and use the ox to hunt the hare
> and swim against the rising tide. [14]

ARNAUT'S CRAFT

The above lines of Arnaut's verse raise the question of *trobar clus,* the 'hermetic composition'. *Trobar clus* could be a misnomer for what Arnaut does, and though Pound used the term, his concept of what it meant in Arnaut probably changed according to whether his idea of history was more conspiratorial or less. In his less embattled periods I think he saw that there is nothing hermetic in what Arnaut says. [15] There is a perfectly intelligible literal meaning for every line of his verse, except in a few cases where the manuscripts are probably corrupt or the idiom lost.

There are troubadour songs, like for instance William IX of Aquitaine's *Farai un vers de dreyt nien,* which have no such intelligibility, and in which critics have seen ciphers of great complexity. [16] There are times in Arnaut's verse when one is tempted to see private references, intended specifically for the beloved and adding a mystery to the song; such as in the ox/hare metaphor we have seen, which occurs again:

> Love and joy and place and time
> make me bring my wits back into order
> from that stupidity I was in the other year
> when I was chasing the hare with the ox....

and again:

> ...I am so learned [in the arts of love] that I can
> stop the current of the rising tide
> and my ox is much faster than a hare.[17]

In the song of 'nails and uncles', which appears to be the first and original sestina, the infolding and obsessive rhyme-scheme builds up an intensity in the rhyme-words ('nail', 'uncle', 'enters', 'soul', 'chamber', 'rod') which makes one wonder what strange love-situation they could have come from.[18] Otherwise, Arnaut's art is straightforward *trobar ric*, 'rich/dense composition'. He practised an hermetic art only in the sense that the kind of truth he tried to express could be received by those 'educated' in love, like himself,[19] and by no others.

Perhaps 'straightforward *trobar ric*' is an impossibility. Arnaut's poetry is very difficult to read. He is not a poet whom one can pick up and read unseen, given a reasonable acquaintance with Provencal; as one can, for instance, Arnaut de Mareuil. Arnaut Daniel uses one new rhyme per ten lines,[20] as compared for instance with Raimbaut d'Orange, also renowned for the density of his style, who uses one per fourteen-and-a-half; with Giraut de Borneil (one per fifty-six-and-a-half); and with Peire Cardenal (one per twenty-five). This shows how far Arnaut avoids the usual *amor/dolor* vocabulary, the equivalent of our 'true/you/blue'; the number of these easy rhymes was limited in Provencal, though perhaps less so than in English. Many a Provencal poet felt able to turn out poems with seven easy rhyme-sounds per strophe, repeated in the same order in all following strophes; which was even easier than in English, even without sticking to morphological tags, as Folquet did in one of his songs: *-ar, -er, -ar, -er, -ens, -ens, -an, -an.*[21]

Branching out into untried rhyme-schemes can bring with it a new order of consciousness in poetry. If you are going to rhyme on a word meaning 'sausage', as Pound commends Villon for doing,[22] you must discover (in most Provencal rhyme-schemes) six or so other words, just for the first stanza, that rhyme with this impossible word and whose exact senses you can employ meaningfully. You then have to bring in many ideas unknown to the average love-poem to make use of your 'dossage', 'fossage', and so forth; hence a greater concreteness and, if the requirement of decent sense is properly fulfilled, a greater precision of emotional definition.

Alfred Jeanroy accused Arnaut of being governed by this demand
without fulfilling it, and of dragging in words willy-nilly to satisfy
the rhyme-scheme, regardless of meaning; and he noted twenty
words in Arnaut's poems that are not to be found anywhere else in
Provençal, suggesting either that Arnaut had to cook them up *ex-
tempore* or that he had to hunt among dialects and rarities.[23] A
tough rhyme-scheme does not automatically have this effect; it
merely requires a much greater training and concentration, brought
into focus by the poet's need to communicate his subject, so that the
form shall be wrested to his uses; and the choice of the form must be
dictated by whether its rhythm-value emotionally fits the subject. In
Arnaut's case, Jeanroy's remarks are discredited when he piles together a number of Arnaut's images, clearly implying that they
come from only two poems, and then calls them 'bizarre'; which,
heaped thus, they are. There is in fact no 'piece built round the
rhymes -*ocs, -ancs, -im*' where the author brings in *cocs, flancs, noi-
rim* ('cook', 'flank', 'nourishment'), and nowhere do we see 'Me-
leager, Flanders, the Ebro, Lucerne and the Puy-de-Dôme appear-
ing pell-mell'.[24] Jeanroy has grabbed bits from seven different
poems, bits which all have a reasonable meaning in context. As for
Arnaut's unique words, most probably they were only rarities in
their time, and poetry has never been restricted to the 5,000 most
common words in the language.

The moments of contact with fresh perception in Arnaut are as
frequent as in Villon, though the range and the bulk are smaller.
With a poet who demands that the modern reader reach for the dictionary at every third word, and who is full of unfamiliar forms, one
does not expect to grasp the emotional structure — the way parts recall and expect other parts — quickly. With a poet whose word-forms
remind the English reader at first sight of a series of hawkings and
spittings, and who in any case specialises in 'hirsute sounds' more
than almost any English poet, one does not expect to hear the word-
music soon.[25] But Provençal has its own sound-laws, which as Pound
said do not conform to Dante's rules for Italian;[26] and when one is
sufficiently familiar with Arnaut, his 'rightness' becomes apparent.

His particular strength is in the rhyme-music that occurs when a
song like IX (in the traditional numbering),[27] one of Arnaut's best,
lays down seventeen different rhyme-sounds and then proceeds to
pick them up in the same order in the five following strophes. Pound

has described this effect in Arnaut: as the seventeen end-sounds are repeated in each verse, the pattern of these sounds gradually establishes itself and is intensified in the 'auditory memory', so that one becomes conscious of its subtler elements only by the fourth or fifth verse and then hears it set out in full clarity at the end, as it were like a horizontal chord. Pound describes it as 'a *sort of* counterpoint' against a pattern of sounds already established and held in the auditory memory. This effect, he says, was developed to a high art both in Arabian music and in Provençal verse, and it was because Dante was still aware of it that his opinions of Arnaut as compared to other troubadours have differed so much from those of unmusical modern scholars.[28]

This effect has no equivalent that I know of in English literature.[29] Pound's translations of Arnaut, though Murray Schafer calls them 'matchless for their sound',[30] are weakened by the same thing that destroys Arnaut's less effective songs, namely a lack of intensity, a feeling of triviality, in the subject matter. Often the subject matter of Arnaut's original is softened by Pound's vocabulary. Arnaut sometimes has this softness, when he falls into the legalising and moralising with which troubadours so often overwhelmed their ladies. But Pound often kills even Arnaut's successes, as in this passage which we have already seen, where the cadence gives sharpness to the forest scene:

> Lanquan vei fueill' e flor e frug
> parer dels albres el ramel
> e aug lo chan que faun e·l brug
> ranas el riu, el bosc auzel. . . .[31]

and where Pound softens the vocabulary:

> When I see leaf, and flower and fruit
>   Come forth upon light lynd and bough,
> And hear the frogs in rillet bruit,
>   And birds quhitter in forest now. . . .[32]

Pound explained this stage of his development in his essay 'Guido's Relations': 'I was obfuscated by the Victorian language';[33] he had found it impossible to get round the imprecise image-making built into that dialect. Meanwhile Arnaut's delayed echo is still unavailable in English. Pound was right to call the troubadour work 'an art between literature and music';[34] my example from his Arnaut versions shows that when the image- and association-content of the words is inferior, the music is castrated.

When the 'mental tone' set up by Arnaut's music fits with that of the imagery and the verbal qualities, the result is an addition to one's experience. Despite his reputation for being laborious, he has a remarkable lightness of touch, often achieved with that very 'hirsute' or 'shaggy' vocabulary (Dante's term) that I have spoken of. One might compare these lines from Basil Bunting:

> Brief words are hard to find,
> shapes to carve and discard:
> Bloodaxe, king of York,
> king of Dublin, king of Orkney.
> Take no notice of tears;
> letter the stone to stand
> over love laid aside lest
> insufferable happiness impede
> flight to Stainmore,
> to trace
> lark, mallet,
> becks, flocks
> and axe knocks.[35]

In this the consonants that bring the rhythm to abrupt halts in 'lark, mallet, / becks, flocks / and axe knocks' are used to produce their own bounding music; not 'sprung' à la Hopkins, the only English poet considered by the wider public to have rhythms at all, where the shaggy consonants reinforce the jagged effect of stress deliberately distorted by pattern; but a music produced by the organic stress-patterns of English syllables in their natural order.

It happens that there are very similar sounds in Arnaut:

> e·ls letz
> becs
> dels auzels ramencs
> ten balps e mutz. . . .[36]

and again:

Doutz brais e critz,
lais e cantars e voutas
aug dels auzels q'en lur latin fant precs
qecs ab sa par.... [37]

Arnaut's verse, like Bunting's, has strong alliterations ('over love laid aside lest', and so forth), and Pound thought that Arnaut might have borrowed this effect — as Bunting did — from Anglo-Saxon.[38] If one could imagine the lines from Bunting repeated, in order of rhyme-sound, in line-length, and even (often) in cadence, through five-and-a-half following stanzas, then Bunting's free verse would have become Arnaut's *trobar ric* by exactly the same process as, Pound says, caused the stanza originally to be invented: 'when a man was singing a long poem to a short melody which he had to use over and over.'[39]

The music communicates what may be called 'body-information', and so, when it is properly fused with the rest of the poetry, the knowledge communicated is more complex than that presented by verse that is only ideology. As it involves the whole art of the poet to put this perception into words, so it is beyond the critic's power to do more than I have here, that is, to suggest what the reader may look for; and again, so it involves no small part of the reader's intelligence and perceptivity to 'receive' the poet's work adequately.[40]

In this sense, art is private. There are those who feel the active force in a painting, and there are those who are coming to feel this force; but those who feel force in no painting can have no real use for paintings, and no amount of the systematisations and allegorisations that fill the Warburg Institute will remedy the defect. Similarly, there is no way for a man who feels the energy in a poem to make his friend feel that energy. This is the sense in which, it seems to me, Pound's ideas about Arnaut and the *trobar clus* have lasting value. When we come to the heretics of Provence we shall see that at times Pound thought Arnaut and the others were esoterical in the strict sense; those ideas did not win out in his view of the troubadour culture.

In *The Spirit of Romance,* in the chapter dating from 1912, Pound divided Provençal verse roughly into *trobar leu,* 'easy composition', and *trobar clus.* Of the *trobar clus* canzoni he said that 'they are not always intelligible at first hearing. They are good art as the high mass is good art.' They must be 'approached as ritual', because their purpose and effect 'make their revelations to those who are already expert'.[41] It was the *trobar clus* as ritual that most interested him.

'TROBAR CLUS' AS AN INCANTATION

The harmony of the universe, as Pound saw it, was reflected in a strong sexual dialectic. To explain this, one could start with one of Pound's mature theological formulations:

(1) The intimate essence of the universe is *not* of the same nature as our own consciousness.

(2) Our own consciousness is incapable of having produced the universe.

(3) God, therefore, exists. That is to say, there is no reason for not applying the term God, *Theos,* to the intimate essence.[42]

The important thing about the 'intimate essence' is its otherness — the sense we have, faced with certain experiences, that their quality is something quite unfamiliar, untainted with our acquaintance, of an order beyond our own conception or fabrication. Perhaps this feeling is inseparable from a sense of order or 'rightness' that we sometimes have, faced with particular natural or even artistic phenomena. Perhaps, in particular, these feelings are associated with sexual feelings, and occur most during what Gourmont calls 'la copulation complète et profonde'.[43] The troubadour's lady made him feel this otherness and this rightness. The song was an enactment of them, a sort of parallel or analogy or ritual formulation that the poet could repeat like his rosary prayers, so that the lady and the song became almost interchangeable as emblems of what Pound would have called the divine. Pound used the term *mantram* (which normally means a Vedic text used as a prayer or incantation) when he glossed a passage from Richard of St. Victor:

. . . by naming over all the most beautiful things we know we may draw back upon the mind some vestige of the heavenly splendour.

I suggest that the Troubadour, either more indolent or more logical, progresses from correlating all these details for purpose of comparison, and lumps the matter. The Lady contains his catalogue, is more complete. She serves as a sort of *mantram*.[44]

The term, and the idea of a ritual formula encapsulating the sense of *Theos,* were still there when Pound was working on the philosophy/religion of Confucius, many years later. The West, he said, needed Confucius because both faith and the capacity for clear statement had been lost. The first chapter of the Confucian *Ta Hio* should be used as a *mantram,* developed and concentrated in order to guide meditation into contemplation, in the terminology Pound took from Richard of St. Victor.[45]

In 1920 Pound published a poem (*The Alchemist*) in the style of Gourmont's *Litanies,*[46] where he used names that had been given a ritual depth by troubadours in their poems. The Provençal names, for example in the following passage, had a depth about them both because of the structures that the troubadours had built around them, and because sometimes they were invented names, designed to keep an affair secret, or to seem to do so:

Sail of Claustra, Aelis, Azalais,
As you move among the bright trees;
As your voices, under the larches of Paradise
Make a clear sound,
Saîl of Claustra, Aelis, Azalais,
Raimona, Tibors, Berangèrë,
'Neath the dark gleam of the sky;
Under night, the peacock-throated,
Bring the saffron-coloured shell,
Bring the red gold of the maple,
Bring the light of the birch tree in autumn
Mirals, Cembelins, Audiarda,
                              Remember this fire.
[. . .]
Midonz, gift of the God, gift of the light, gift of the amber of the sun,
                Give light to the metal.[47]

This poem is an incantation by its rhythm, its parallelism, its

colours and its appeal to the mystique of the names and of alchemy;
but Pound probably also hoped that it was an incantation in that it
used the names like chemical formulae, which he saw the troubadours' songs had made them into, standing for perceptions of the
total order: 'The equations of alchemy were apt to be written as
women's names and the women so named endowed with the magical
powers of the compounds'.[48] *The Alchemist* also shows how the
many women, individually of divine status in their relationships
with their poets, become the one Goddess. The ladies in it are not
differentiated by any reference to their persons. They are repeatedly
all taken in under the one title *midonz,* the Provençal name that the
troubadours often used for their ladies, whose associations are with
words meaning 'my lord'.[49] Likewise Pound does not individuate
any beloved woman in his Cantos, though sometimes a beloved is
obviously present; he makes his many goddesses into aspects of the
one Goddess.[50] The one woman to whom the troubadour, or Pound,
actually (but, for the reader, 'accidentally') addresses his poem, contains the essence — representative of the divine order — perceived in
all women through her.[51]

A crux in Arnaut Daniel shows how, for Pound, the troubadour's
lady was literally his Goddess, and the poem his incantation. Editors
have struggled with it almost more than with any other part of
Arnaut. One could translate it thus:

> wealth
> does not take me away from you,
> nor does it make me leave,
> because I have never loved
> anything so much, with less vainglory,
> but I desire you
> more than God those of Dome [*cill de Doma*].[52]

It is not clear where and what Dome is, and the last clause could
mean 'more than God loves her / those of Dome' or 'more than she /
those of Dome love(s) God'.[53] One can see what Pound thought in
this translation:

> Averse
> Me not, nor slake
> Desire, God draws not nigh

> To Dome,* with pleas
> Wherein's so little veering.

He added this footnote:

*Our Lady of Puy-de-Dôme? No definite solution of the reference yet found.[54]

His idea had come from Canello, Arnaut's first editor, who compared this passage in Arnaut to another where

it was said that Arnaut's lady is the most beautiful there has been in the world since Mary; and here it seems to be said that Arnaut loves his lady more than God loves the Virgin Mary, 'her of Dome'. We thought, in fact, that here there might be a reference to a sanctuary of the Virgin on the Puy de Dôme, or in some other place bearing the name of Dome, Provençal Doma; and that the troubadour might be etymologising as it were on Doma, seeing in it a variation of domna [i.e. 'lady'; the word used for the Virgin also].[55]

If this is right, Arnaut's lady has superseded the Virgin to a blasphemous, perhaps a heretical degree; Arnaut is saying 'I love you more than God loves the Virgin', and otherwise equating the two with the domna/Domna/Doma pun. The idea was most striking to Pound. In 1909 he told the Poets' Club: 'The boldness of the comparison . . . is such that no translation can diminish it. Its arrogance may well have delighted [Dante], who summoned the rulers of the third heaven to listen. . . .'[56] The third heaven is that of Venus, and Pound said in 1912: 'The rise of Mariolatry, its Pagan lineage, the romance of it, find modes of expression which verge over very easily into the speech and casuistry of Our Lady of Cyprus [i.e. Venus], as we may see in Arnaut, as we see so splendidly in Guido's "Una figura della donna mia." '[57] Pound meant that the troubadour's lady and Venus were goddesses for the same reasons that the Virgin was a goddess. To help explicate Arnaut's crux, he called on 'those who fear to take a bold line in their interpretation of the Cill de Doma' to re-read the poem by Cavalcanti he mentions in the quotation above: Una figura della Donna mia.[58] In this poem, Cavalcanti explains to his friend that the image worshipped at the Church of Orsanmichele, the image that is the great refuge of sinners, that comforts

those who languish, that cures the sick and casts out demons, that
makes blind eyes see clearly (*ed occhi orbati fa vedere scorto*), and
much more, is an image of his beloved:

> but the Brothers Minor say it is idolatry,
> for envy, because the image is not near them. [59]

Pound was obviously right to say of this poem that 'its blasphemous
intention is open to the simplest capacity', [60] and to link it to the 'He
(who watches you) seems to me to be equal to a god' of Catullus and
its model in Sappho. [61]

THE LADY WISDOM

Pound had his reasons for dwelling on this obscure point in Arnaut.
To understand them, it is necessary to look at the way the whole
courtly-love lyric developed. Modifying the argument of Peter
Dronke in his *Medieval Latin and the Rise of European Love-Lyric*,
we may distinguish three stages.

The first has occurred in many cultures, but it was the psychological core of the Provencal lyric and everything that has developed out
of it: the feeling of the lover that to approach near his beloved
would be to rise to a higher level of existence. We have seen this
'primitive' stage in William IX of Aquitaine. [62]

The second stage is in Arnaut Daniel, for example in the *cils de
Doma* crux as Pound interprets it. [63] The element of worship in
courtly love made it potentially a rival religion to Christianity; now
it has come to include Christianity in itself, or to regard Christianity
as just an extension of itself. The parallels between the man-woman
relationship and the man-God (or man-Virgin) relationship are
obvious, and the poet has begun to ring all sorts of changes among
them. His lady's standing is equal to the Virgin's; God created his
lady to body forth all the virtues that mankind can possess; the poet
is faithful to her, as a cleric to God; may God give him a vision of
her (naked); God's grace permitted him to perceive her virtues. [64]
For the Provencal poets of the late twelfth century, God comes out
as a sort of patron for the lady, or a spiritual goal of about equal
standing with her; in fact usually she is taken more seriously than He

is, and He is only there as a kind of hyperbolic reference. But this religious reference is a very important extension of the range of metaphor and relationship handled by the courtly-love lyric.

By the third stage, in the time of Guinizelli, Cavalcanti, and the other *dolce stil novo* poets, the metaphors are much more complex. The basis is that the lady is the source of wisdom for her lover. So, as God informs the Virgin, who informs mankind; as the sun shines on the moon, which shines on the earth; as God illuminates His Church, which illuminates man; so the lady irradiates the understanding of her lover. Further, there were theories of psychology, developed for example out of Aristotle's *De Anima* and reaching through Avicenna and Albertus Magnus to Cavalcanti and his generation, which postulated two parts of the intellect. There was the 'intellect possible', shared by all men, which would enable them to pierce through the surface of things and see them as they really were; but it was activated to differing degrees in different men by the 'active intellect', which descended through divine grace. This active intellect was constantly figured by the poets as their lady.[65]

What had happened was that the basic metaphor or relationship-dynamic had developed into a world-system, with so many intricate parallels and ramifications that it had to be treated by its users with the seriousness and precision of a science, since it contained the key to all causes and effects, ethics based on them, and so on. The life of this system was in the vigour and precision of its images and metaphors, which depended on the degree to which the things they derived from mattered to the poet. So at its apogee this complex development was still tied to the perception of natural phenomena, such as the light of the sun and moon, and above all the visionary quality of the poet's lady, now seen as Lady Wisdom.[66]

It is easy to see that Arnaut has reached the second stage of this process. Everywhere he uses feelings about the Virgin to convey his sense of his lady's position:

> Since the dry rod [*verga,* i.e. the Virgin] flowered,
> or nephew or uncle descended from Adam,
> I do not believe that such a fine love as the one that is
> entering my heart was ever in body, or even in soul. . . .[67]

His lady is the successor of the Virgin:

> never, since St Paul wrote an Epistle
> or since the Fast in the Wilderness
> has even Jesus been able
> to make such a creature, for she possesses together all
> the virtues that most exalt the One men call Virtuous. [68]

Mary was said to have been a 'new Eve', in that she demonstrated for the first time the virtue that is in woman; but Arnaut says of his own lady

> I can never travel far enough through fields, valleys,
> plains and hills, to find in one person
> such qualities, all good:
> God wished to select and establish them in her. [69]

It certainly smells of blasphemy when Love commands Arnaut: 'after God, honour and exalt her'—that is, 'your lady';[70] Arnaut's age was extremely conscious of the worship owed to Mary.[71]

Obviously Arnaut used the Christian vocabulary to strengthen the feeling that to approach his lady was to reach a higher level of being. But Pound suggested that he also prefigured the Italians:

Cossir, solatz, plazers ['thinking, solace, pleasure'], have in them the beginning of the Italian philosophic precisions, and *amors qu'inz el cor mi plou* is not a vague decoration. By the time of Petrarca the analysis had come to an end, only the vague decorations were left. And if Arnaut is long before Cavalcanti: —

> 'Pensar de lieis m'es repaus
> E traigom ams los huoills crancs,
> S'a lieis vezer nols estuich.'

leads toward 'E gli occhi orbati fa vedere scorto,' though the music in Arnaut is not, in this place, quickly apprehended.[72]

Arnaut was using the metaphor of sunlight as love, perhaps as wisdom:

> and even though the cold wind blows,
> the love that rains in my heart
> [*l'amors q'inz el cor mi plou*]
> keeps me warm when it is most wintery.[73]

Perhaps his lady was the source of wisdom: 'It rests me to think of her, and I've both my eyes cankered when they're not looking at her (*Pensar de lieis m'es repaus...*).'[74] Pound said that this image led towards *E gli occhi orbati fa vedere scorto,* which is Cavalcanti's line 'And she makes sick eyes see clearly' from the poem about the Madonna of Orsanmichele.[75] It is clear from other parts of Arnaut that, for him, wisdom equalled the light of the vision of the lady:

> I thank God and my eyes for this,
> that through their knowing
> joy came to me....[76]

and again:

> So clear was
> my first light
> in choosing
> her whose eyes my heart fears....[77]

So that Arnaut was not so far from the Italians, and from the Dante whose lady appeared to him as a vision granted to him by divine grace to lead him up to Paradise: *Ecce deus fortior me, qui veniens dominabitur michi,* 'Behold a god stronger than me, who, approaching, will reign over me.'[78]

ARNAUT IN THE CANTOS

In the Cantos, Arnaut shows the highest development of the cult of the Goddess. The cult moves him to a scientific precision, and permits him to see the true vision of the Goddess, as well as the pattern of the divine radiation of wisdom, which is related to the universal patterns lying underneath the surface structure and showing through in metamorphoses.

In 'I Gather the Limbs of Osiris', Pound had called Arnaut 'accurate in his observation of nature'; we have seen this accuracy in his cadences and those of Bernart de Ventadorn and Bertran de Born.[79] Pound said in 'Osiris' that the true artist 'discovers, or better, "he discriminates". We advance by discriminations....' All science for

Pound was 'the sorting of things into organic categories', or the 'discerning that things hitherto deemed identical or similar are dissimilar; that things hitherto deemed dissimilar, mutually foreign, antagonistic, are similar and harmonic'.[80] For this discernment the writer and the scientist needed both energy and accuracy, that is, power and the ability to direct—which Pound saw as sexual qualities. The bad painter in a corrupt era would hedge or wobble, not admitting where he intended the line to go to. The good writer would 'cut' with his content and his rhythms: 'the full man's words have an edge of definition',[81] and 'Thing is to cut a shape in time', since poetry is 'between literature and music'.[82] The mediaeval period was particularly disposed towards this kind of precision:

> Let us say that mediaeval thought (or *paideuma*) was at its best in an endeavour to find the *precise word* for each of its ideas, and that this love of exactitude created some very fine architecture, and that when it got into song (or, if you like, when it came out of song) it produced a very exact fitting of the melody to the shape of the words.[83]

Arnaut was one of its best exponents: 'You can connect that fine demarcation with demarcations in architecture and re usury, or you can trace it alone, from Arnaut and his crew down to Janequin, where a different susceptibility has replaced it . . . .'[84]

For Pound, the art of making significant poetry and music was not self-generating and self-justifying. It depended on perception of the given universe. But there was no barrier between exact perception and rendering of the universe on the one hand, and the higher regions of art and religion on the other. What allowed one into these regions was not an extra ingredient provided by freak qualities of soul, but just the full development of sincerity, or honesty with self, by work with the given nature-embedded materials. Coke the lawyer, 'the clearest mind ever in England',[85] did not need a separate dispensation or terminology to let him walk in Paradise with more normal saints; the universe having its own divinity, to be an adequate interpreter was enough.

Canto XX shows Arnaut the scientist walking in a Confucian kind of Paradise. Pound has gone to visit Emil Levy, the maker of the great standard Provençal dictionary, the *Supplement-Wörterbuch* to Raynouard's *Lexique Roman*.[86] His 'excuses' are that he wants to

show the old man a find from the Ambrosian library in Milan, and
to ask him about the *di noigandres* problem in Arnaut Daniel—
though we can see that he also wants to make contact with 'the
elders' as part of his search for the best in the tribal past. The setting
is Germany, but it runs over into an imaginary landscape in a very
ordered Nature:

> The boughs are not more fresh
> where the almond shoots
> take their March green.
> And that year I went up to Freiburg,
> And Rennert had said: 'Nobody, no, nobody
> Knows anything about Provençal, or if there is anybody,
> It's old Lévy.'
> And so I went up to Freiburg,
> And the vacation was just beginning,
> The students getting off for the summer,
> Freiburg im Breisgau,
> And everything clean, seeming clean, after Italy.
>
> And I went to old Lévy, and it was by then 6.30
> in the evening, and he trailed half way across Freiburg
> before dinner, to see the two strips of copy,
> Arnaut's, settant'uno R. superiore (Ambrosiana)
> Not that I could sing him the music.
> And he said: 'Now is there anything I can tell you?'
> And I said: 'I dunno, sir,' or
> 'Yes, Doctor, what do they mean by *noigandres*?'
> And he said: 'Noigandres! NOIgandres!
> 'You know for seex mon's of my life
> 'Effery night when I go to bett, I say to myself:
> 'Noigandres, eh, *noi*gandres,
> 'Now what the DEFFIL can that mean!'
> Wind over the olive trees, ranunculae ordered,
> By the clear edge of the rocks
> The water runs, and the wind scented with pine
> And with hay-fields under sun-swath.
> Agostino, Jacopo and Boccata.
> You would be happy for the smell of that place
> And never tired of being there, either alone
> Or accompanied.
> Sound: as of the nightingale too far off to be heard.

Sandro, and Boccata, and Jacopo Sellaio;
The ranunculae, and almond,
Boughs set in espalier,
Duccio, Agostino; *e l'olors* —
The smell of that place — *d'enoi ganres.*
Air moving under the boughs,
The cedars there in the sun,
Hay new cut on hill slope,
And the water there in the cut
Between the two lower meadows; sound,
The sound, as I have said, a nightingale
Too far off to be heard.
And the light falls, *remir,*
from her breast to thighs.[87]

Levy has the civility of the 'old men with beautiful manners' of the pre-Victorian generation that Pound saw in London;[88] and Pound is with him as a deferent disciple, like Confucius's disciples in Canto XIII, where they move in a similarly green and ordered world. Levy also has the wisdom of the Poundian writer/scientist, or the Confucian *literatus,* in that he has not jumped to easy conclusions; Pound was fond of the *Analects* passage that says: '1. Even I reach back to a time when historians left blanks (for what they didn't know), and when a man would lend a horse for another to ride; a forgotten era, lost.'[89]

So far we have seen the scholar/scientist applying his sincerity to a detail of his subject, Arnaut Daniel. Now the Canto moves from Germany into an ideal landscape, in which the meaning of this detail is defined by atmosphere; just as, Pound said, the 'Nature-opening' in most Provencal songs is 'an equation, in other terms, or a "metaphor by sympathy" for the mood of the poem'.[90] Levy was in fact the man who had suggested the best solution for the *di noigandres* problem. The relevant stanza in Arnaut is this:

Now I see scarlet, green, blue, white and yellow
the orchards, plains, hedges, hillocks and dales,
and the song of the birds sounds and resounds
with sweet harmony in the morning and late.
This puts it in my heart to colour my song
with a flower, such that its fruit be love,
its seed joy, and its scent protection from distress.[91]

'Protection from distress' is Levy's suggestion for *d'enoi gandres*. It adds another dimension to Arnaut's allegorical flower, whose seed is joy, its fruit love, and its scent the protection of oneself from distress. It is clear that the highest of these is the fruit, love. 'Protecting oneself from annoyance' is some kind of process that goes along with the development of this fruit from its seed in joy. It is defined in the atmosphere of the landscape in Canto XX:

> You would be happy for the smell of that place
> And never tired of being there, either alone
> Or accompanied.

This set of ethical distinctions can probably be understood from the translation of Confucius that Pound published three years after Canto XX.[92] The seed is joy, which is 'the tendency...to love an agreeable and seductive object'; the byproduct is the scent, protecting oneself from annoyance—'the tendency to escape from a disagreeable odour'. These tendencies must be respected, since together they permit one to 'clarify and render sincere one's intentions'. It is a matter of uncluttering one's processes by seeking out stimuli that do not act as a recurring irritant on one's inner nature— one is less likely to achieve the calmness necessary to understanding what one is really up to in life, for instance, in a work-situation that continually arouses anger. Canto XX's setting 'demonstrates' or provides a 'metaphor by sympathy' for the scent of the flower, *enoi gandres,* protecting oneself from irritants, in the serenity of the place.

The difficult first step may be to admit to oneself which stimuli are in tune with one's inner nature. But his faculties once uncluttered by this *enoi gandres,* one is enabled to perceive more precisely, and one learns from these newly clear perceptions how to seek out yet more uncluttering stimuli, which help to clarify one's emotions further; so that perhaps by some such process of feedback the poet reaches a vision far surpassing what could have been expected from the original step of clarification, difficult as that (Pound implies) may be. The clarity reaches the divine, the vision of the lady becomes the vision of the Goddess, and the vision of immediate nature becomes a vision of the total ordered coherence which is Pound's idea of Godhead. So the fruit in love must be understood in the highest sense, the 'DUM SPIRO AMO', 'while I breathe I love' of

John Adams in Canto LXX, or Pound's remark that 'the greatest is
charity' in Canto LXXIV.[93]

The Canto then shows Arnaut's vision of the Goddess and the
multiple metamorphoses related to it. In its ideal landscape there
float the names of various painters — painters of Venus, Hugh Kenner has said — and hence the images of the Goddess as they have rendered her.[94] At the end of the passage come the lines:

> And the light falls, *remir,*
> from her breast to thighs.

In the poem from which this word *remir* is taken, Arnaut wishes to
lie with his lady in a chamber where they may agree

> that kissing and laughing I should uncover her pretty body
> and that I should gaze at it against the light of the lamp.[95]

The stanza begins with an address to God, 'by whom were absolved/
the sins that the blind Longinus committed'; and it asks God to permit him this vision of his lady. It was Longinus who pierced Christ's
side on the cross; God forgave him and granted him sight. As Kenner says, 'Arnaut boldly proposes a sin that shall culminate, like
Longinus', in vision: and the light, and the paradisal *tan gran joi,*
help lend her lovely body, *seu bel cors,* the force of "Hoc est corpus,"
a revealed miracle, to adore.'[96] The lady is the vision of Wisdom.

But the nature of this vision takes it also into the realm of Pound's
metamorphoses. The air in Canto XX is full of things that are and
are not:

> sound,
> The sound, as I have said, a nightingale,
> Too far off to be heard.

The *Ligur' aiode* with which the Canto begins is glossed by Pound as
a sound and a light.[97] The visions have a super-real sharpness:

> By the clear edge of the rocks
> The water runs

and the phrase *e que·l remir,* 'and that I should gaze on it', is intended to fit with these things. Pound seems to have understood it as

something like 'and that glows'. He made it equivalent to the image
in Golding's Ovid:

> As when a scarlet curtaine streynd ageinst a playstred wall
> Dooth cast like shadowe, making it seeme ruddye therewith all.

The following lines from Canto VII bring together Eleanor of Aquitaine, Ovid, and Arnaut — lover of the wife of Guillem de Bouvila:

> Eleanor!
> The scarlet curtain throws a less scarlet shadow;
> Lamplight at Buovilla, e quel remir[98]

So the phrase comes into this world of preternatural clarity as the
halo around a back-lit silhouette; like the 'diafan' formed 'from
light on shade' in Pound's translation of Cavalcanti's philosophical
canzone, which is his image for the way love is formed by the
imprinting of the lady's image on his memory. He glosses 'diafan'
with the image from the *Paradiso* of Dante: 'thus we see the moon
sometimes girdled, when the air is impregnated, so that it retains
the line that the halo makes.'[99] This fits with the multiple sets of
vision and non-vision, and illusory clarity, with which Pound defines
the mediaeval aesthetic in his work on Cavalcanti:

We appear to have lost the radiant world where one thought cuts through
another with clean edge, moving energies '*mezzo oscuro rade*', '*risplende in
se perpetuale effecto*', magnetisms that take form, that are seen, or that
border the visible, the matter of Dante's *paradiso,* the glass under water,
the form that seems a form seen in a mirror, these realities perceptible to
the sense, interacting, '*a lui si tiri*' . . . . [100]

Mezzo oscuro [luce] rade, 'in the midst of darkness shines infrequently', *risplende in sè perpetuale effecto*, 'shines in itself, an eternal Effect', and *a lui si tiri*, 'draws to itself', are all from Cavalcanti's
Philosophic Canzone, translated in Canto XXXVI. The first of
them belongs with a group of images for light of a quasi-divine
clarity.[101] The 'form that seems a form seen in a mirror' is a reference to Beatrice's explanation in the *Paradiso* of why the beings in
Paradise seem, but are not, as dense as those on earth.[102]

This concentrated ideogram in 'Cavalcanti' sets out to describe

the mediaeval precision, but makes this seem indistinguishable from
the aesthetic of metamorphoses. The 'glass under water' suggests the
great pattern of crystal, wave, and jewel imagery in the Cantos;
fluid becomes glass and crystal, and crystal is like the sign of the
gods, because it is a frozen metamorphosis, a held moment of appa-
rition. Metamorphosis in Pound is the making visible of that otherness which is the divine in the universe:

> 'as the sculptor sees the form in the air . . .
> 'as glass seen under water,
> 'King Otreus, my father . . .'
> and saw the waves taking form as crystal,
> notes as facets of air,
> and the mind there, before them, moving,
> so that notes needed not move.[103]

It is the making visible of deep patterns, 'magnetisms that take
form', which make one thing 'essentially' like another and different
from a third. Thus after the first fall of Montségur in the Cantos the
'form' of Provence becomes visible:

> and I saw then, as of waves taking form,
> As the sea, hard, a glitter of crystal,
> And the waves rising but formed, holding their form,
> No light reaching through them.[104]

So the 'wave in the stone' that recurs in visions of Provence in the
later Cantos[105] is an emblem of the Provençal manifestation of the
gods.

Into this complex of wave and crystal imagery comes another detail from Arnaut Daniel, not used in Canto XX, that ties it all to the
Platonic world-scheme of the divine illumination of wisdom through
the lady. Pound took Arnaut's words *e lo soleils plovil,* translated
them 'and the sun rains', and used them in the middle of the succession of Provençal visions and metamorphoses, Peire Vidal and Guilhem de Cabestanh, irradiated with sunlight in Canto IV:

> Thus the light rains, thus pours, *e lo soleils plovil*
> The liquid and rushing crystal
>   beneath the knees of the gods.[106]

So the ideogram of mediaeval precision overlaps with that of meta-morphosis, which overlaps with the ideogram of Platonic illumina-tion, including in it the anthropomorphic mythology of sun and earth as male and female, Erigena's concept of the universe as a manifestation of God, and so on. In the later Cantos:

> Ra-Set in her barge now
> > over deep sapphire
> but the child played under wave...
> > e piove d'amor [it is raining love]
> > in nui [in us]
> > a great river, the ghosts dipping in crystal
> > & to Pinella.... [107]

This Ra-Set is Pound's composite goddess of the solar and lunar cycles; [108] this love is raining in the hearts of Cavalcanti's maidens; [109] and Cavalcanti 'sends' to Pinella 'a river in full flood / Stocked with Lamia-nymphs....' [110] Love is a river of divine illumination pour-ing from the sun, so that indeed, as Pound says, Arnaut's 'love rain-ing in my heart' is 'not a vague decoration'. [111] The following passage from Canto XCIX, based on the Chinese *Sacred Edict,* develops Arnaut's vision:

> To see the light pour,
> > that is, toward sinceritas
> of the word, comprehensive
> > KOINE ENNOIA
> all astute men can see it encircling. [112]

All these things overlap with yet one more important concept that Pound developed with Arnaut's help: that the troubadour vision of illuminating wisdom was made possible by the troubadour chastity. We have seen the considerable ideogram that Pound built up in his prose around Cavalcanti's poem of the Madonna of Orsanmichele and Arnaut's *cill de Doma,* the Virgin of Dome. [113] He picked up Cavalcanti's line *E gli occhi orbati fa vedere scorto,* 'and (she) makes blind eyes see clearly', and compared it to the lines from Arnaut that he translated thus: 'It rests me to think of her, and I've both my eyes cankered when they're not looking at her....' [114] This line 'It rests me to think of her', *Pensar de lieis m'es repaus,* comes into a passage in the Cantos which is full of light and crystal and the female eyes that draw, beginning with the fourth line of Bernart de Ventadorn's lark-song:

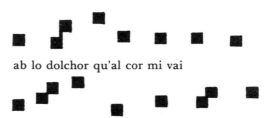

ab lo dolchor qu'al cor mi vai

AB LO DOLCHOR QU'AL COR MI VAI
that the body of light come forth
from the body of fire
And that your eyes come to the surface
from the deep wherein they were sunken,
Reina — for 300 years

This 'Reina', Queen, coincides with Elizabeth I of England, who appears with Arnaut's line:

The GREAT CRYSTAL
doubling the pine, and to cloud.
pensar de lieis m'es ripaus
Miss Tudor moved them with galleons[115]

The crystal is described with words from Dante (*convien che si mova / la mente, amando*) where it is natural that 'the mind, loving, should move towards the [divine] essence, wherein is such super-abundance that every good outside it is only a light of its radiating.' This core of light, Pound's as well as Dante's central image for divinity, is shown at the beginning of the Canto with the 'nature-opening' of Bernart's song of the lark, its flooding of light recalled but not stated in the *ab lo dolchor qu'al cor mi vai*, 'with the sweetness that comes to my heart'. The 'It rests me to think of her' indicates the virgin Elizabeth/Artemis's power of ordering perception not only in herself, but through the poet's secondary *mantram*, his internalised vision of her. Love strikes in *dove sta memoria*, 'where memory liveth', as Pound repeats from Cavalcanti's canzone.[116] Because the troubadour derives his vision from this inner icon, he has a chastity, not a chastity that keeps him from taking part in the central rite of coition,[117] but that regulates sex and keeps it 'holy', with its power of illumination unweakened.[118] Pound set the troubadour ethic against the Greek, which was 'Plastic plus immediate satisfaction'.[119] This ethic of sex and chastity made him combine Venus and Diana at the centre of his troubadour-derived religion.[120] He took from the troubadours' works a series of lines that contained this ethic. Bernart de Ventadorn's

> And if I see her not
> No sight is worth the beauty of my thought[121]

are quoted in the original at the beginning of the Canto about Levy, Arnaut Daniel, and the goddess,[122] and they come back in an important passage about the Provencal heretics.[123] Sordello's lines meaning 'Alas, and what are my eyes doing to me / For they do not see what I wish' and 'When I really ponder in my proud thoughts [What she is like. . . .]' come into Cantos passages about his relationship with Cunizza, who becomes an equivalent of Venus in Pound's heavens.[124] What these lines say is: 'When I have not you, I have the thought of you, and I want nothing else till I may have you again.' This is the discipline of Pound's rite; this element of chastity was one of the chief things that drew him to the troubadours. As we have seen, he thought Propertius's 'My genius is no more than a girl' contained 'the whole of the twelfth century love cult', and he used that line as a title for Arnaut's verse which ends

> Arnaut has waited and will wait a long time,
> for by waiting a true man makes a great conquest.[125]

9. SORDELLO

Pound's respect for both Browning and Dante gave him good reasons to be interested in Sordello. But in the early years of studying the troubadours he brushed over him; he tended to think of writing as either noble-and-difficult or easy-and-slick, and Sordello was easy.[1]

But when Pound came back to the troubadours he followed Dante's lead even more carefully, and his opinion of Sordello improved. In 1937 he wrote, 'With Sordello the fusion of word, sound, movement is so simple one only understands his superiority to other troubadours after having studied Provençal and half-forgotten it, and come back to twenty years later.'[2] He explained further:

> Only after long domesticity with music did I, at any rate, see why Dante has mentioned Sordello, or has he even done so in *De Eloquio?*
>
> Above other troubadours, as I feel it *now,* Sordello's hand (or word) 'deceives the eye' honestly. The complete fluidity, the ease that comes only with mastery in strophes so simple in meaning that they leave nothing for the translator.[3]

One might think that Arnaut Daniel is an acquired taste; but now Pound spoke of his 'merits that can be picked out, demonstrated, explained'; Sordello was for those who had 'direct perception of quality'.[4] Writing about his great praise in the early days for Arnaut, he now said 'A more mature judgment, or greater familiarity with Provençal idiom might lead one to prefer the limpid simplicity of some of Sordello's verses.'[5]

So the history of Pound on Sordello is like the history of Pound on Bernart de Ventadorn: late appreciation of a mastery in music that can only be hinted at, not shown. The two troubadours also have a lot in common in their 'content'.

The first impression that Sordello's poetry gives is bland, not only in sound but in thought; there is rarely an idea or a phrase that has not been smoothed by use in another troubadour's work. Sordello himself says he belongs to the school of *trobar leu,* the easy style:

I like to make, with easy words,
a pleasing song and one with a light melody,
because the finest lady one can choose,
to whom I hand myself over and surrender and give myself,
does not like and is not pleased by master-class poetry;
and because it doesn't please her, from now on I'll make my singing
easy to sing and agreeable to listen to,
clear to understand and delicate, whoever has the delicacy to pick it out.[6]

Sordello does not include the striking nature-imagery that even Bernart de Ventadorn opened with; he sticks more or less closely to the casuistry of love. Sometimes he admits that he is interested in love-making, perhaps, obliquely, but everything is so surrounded with fear of doing the wrong thing it is difficult to know what Sordello is at:

And if love makes me want anything
you should not do,
for pity's sake I wish to ask you
that you should not do it;
for I prefer to live in torments
than that your worth [*pretz*] should be devalued,
lady, for anything you might do for me;
because I have enough from you, whom I desire,
if only you sincerely permit me
to love and serve you.[7]

Sordello has aetherialised his lady into nothing but a source of moral worth, and when he meets someone who thinks of women as flesh and blood, they cannot even speak the same language. Montanhagol asks him which is best: that he should know his lady's heart, or that she should know his. Sordello answers:

'Montanhagol, it would please me
a hundred times more
that she for whom I die living
should know . . .
my heart, that she holds in torment,
than that I should know hers;
because if the truth should show to her
how I am tormented for her,
she would take pity on it,

or all her heart would be
hard as stone, cold as ice . . . '

'Sordello, it is truly much better
that you should know the heart and the feelings
of her whom you love truly
— whether she loves you or is fooling you;
because often under a fine appearance
great falsity hides,
and, if you find yourself being fooled,
you will seem too mad
if, after that, you love unloved . . . '

'Montanhagol, I don't take it
as any trickery from her
whom I love and serve loyally,
even if it pleases her to kill me . . . '[8]

They are the adepts of two different faiths: Montanhagol of all
the mediaeval beliefs that woman was a sink of iniquity, and Sordello of the religion of Courtly Love. It is difficult to say which is
narrower.

The kind of casuistry that Sordello shared with Bernart de Ventadorn also brought a 'morality' into love. For them, moral value in
the troubadour depends on the quality of lady he chooses and on his
devotion; but moral value in the lady depends on the quality of man
she deigns to accept and on her pity on his devotion. This is a little
circular; did nobody start off with intrinsic value, inspiring devotion
or acceptance from their partner? Hence the terms become somewhat vague, and both in their etymology and in their use there is a
suggestion that words like *pretz* mean 'high reputation' or 'the fact
that I, or people generally, esteem you'. The *reductio ad absurdum*
would be something like this: 'I love you, and you have *valor*, so that
it is unthinkable that you should refuse me, because a lady who has
valor never refuses a knight who has *valor*, what though my only
valor be this, that I have set my sights on a lady of such great *valor*
as yourself.' Thus:

. . . because I love what is uniquely estimable [*de bon pretz*],
I prefer to love her uselessly
rather than another who might deign to take me to her;

but I don't serve her unrewarded,
because a real lover never serves unrewarded
when he serves with his heart in an honoured and valued [*prezan*] place;
wherefore the honour is a reward to me for the fact
that I don't seek the overplus, though I'd certainly accept it.[9]

Sordello is in Bernart de Ventadorn's prison, and he uses the same apparatus to lament it:

I hate mirrors, for they are too harmful to me
in relation to her who makes me languish in her prison,
and when she looks at her body and her shapes,
thinking what sort of person she is, she thinks little of my torment. . . .[10]

A large part of his verses is taken up with considering how little, when he thinks of the great worth of the lady who is the cause of his torments, he cares about his torments[11] — he only regrets that when she has killed him there will be no one to sing her praises properly.[12] We can see the beginning of the Petrarchan war games, with their glances as darts of love, their wounds, their sallies and retreats of spirits, at moments in Sordello.[13] Sordello tells us how part of his fineness consists in not wanting the wrong thing, because he could not love her half so much, loved he not honour more; because of this fineness he should and sometimes does feel secure against all rivals, since she is bound to love the finest of her lovers.[14] This concern with his own state is what really marks him out as a later troubadour, sharing the Gothicness of expression that Pound speaks of[15] with Bernart and with Arnaut. We find in William IX of Aquitaine that he expresses a desire for a presence that he feels would transform his world, and he expresses his pain at its lack. It is we, the readers, who can see the effects of this want on him. But with the later troubadours we find them in 90 per cent of their verse expressing, not their desire or its unfulfilment, but their observations as to the effect of its unfulfilment, held as a permanent state, on themselves. It makes me, they observe endlessly, into an *amans fis*, a 'fine lover' — Sordello talks of his 'fine joy', of himself as one of the 'fine courtly men', of his 'fine heart' that she has stolen, and of handing himself over to her 'fine and true'.[16]

Though there is much scope for fun at the expense of these contortions, they led Sordello to a very high development of his art. The prison of love was his 'subject'; it fitted his nature, as we can see; he refined the weapons of poetry to a point where he could use them on it with psychological exactitude. He invented an intricate causative logic which dominates the poem and expresses his entrapment. *Quar,* 'because', *per que,* 'wherefore', and their equivalents begin almost every clause. In a typical Sordello stanza the reasoning that constitutes his prison builds up continuously in a complicated series of subordinations, weaving through the gentle rhythms and imposing its continuity on them with many enjambments, until it reaches a perfect stasis in the last line, often containing both a verbal and logical paradox and a highly developed cross-play of sounds. He is held in a languishing happiness:

> Now towards the time of May
> when I see leaf and flower appear
> to reach my duty
> I shall sing in the best manner in the world,
> worthy lady, since I cannot cease,
> since I turn back to see you, from singing,
> but because I don't see you my life seems death to me,
> and singing pain, and pleasure unhappiness
> [*e chanz dolors e plazers desconortz*].[17]

Sordello only hits the gentle plaintive rhythm that is his 'voice' when he uses a line that is longer than that of most troubadour songs; most of his groups of lines that do not have or lead to this metric length are of little strength. He needs leisure to develop his peculiar soft ennui. When he hits this rhythm he begins to interweave his sounds and verbal contrasts to an extraordinary degree.[18] The following stanza, for example, has an intense cross-play of verbal contrasts, which I have italicised:

> As the *ill* person who cannot *keep well*
> when he is *cured,* so that the *illness takes* him again
> and *makes* him *worse* in this *second sickening*
> than it *made* him before, so it has *taken* me and *takes* me
> with the *illness* of love with which I have *sickened again:*
> because I did not *keep* myself from it when I had got away,
> now I have such an *illness* as I will never be *cured* of
> if the beautiful one through whom I have it doesn't *cure* me.[19]

The way in which the verbal play fits into the ambulation of sounds can only be heard in the original:

> Si co·l malaus qe no se sap gardar
> qan es garitz, per qe·l mals lo repren
> e·l fai trop peig en son recalivar
> qe non a faich, aisi m'es pres e·m pren
> del mal d'amor dun sui recalivatz:
> qar no·m gardei qan eu n'era escapatz,
> ar ai tal mal dun jamais non garai
> si no·m garis la bella per cui l'ai.

The whole of Sordello's real content, that is the content in which he differentiates himself from other poets and makes us 'smell' his individuality, is this logic through which he points out to his beautiful captor one by one the interconnected reasons why it is through her that he is trapped. On rare occasions it focuses so sharply on the nature of the captor that it produces a most beautiful 'sympathetic parallel' to her in the nature-imagery that traditionally starts the Provencal poem:

> Atretan dei ben chantar finamen
> d'invern com faz d'estiu, segon rason,
> per c'ab lo freitz voill far gaia canson
> que s'en pascor de chantar cor mi pren,
> quar la rosa sembla lei de cui chan,
> aultresi es la neus del sieu senblan:
> per qu'en andos dei per s'amor chantar,
> tant fort mi fan la rosa e·l neus menbrar.[20]

We have seen Pound's attempt at this in Canto VI;[21] he caught the obsessive repetitions, but it was beyond even his art to catch the sound of Sordello's invention, the winding syntax:

> I must sing as finely
> in winter as I do in summer, according to reason,
> for with the cold I want to make a gay song,
> since if the desire to sing takes me at Easter,
> because the rose resembles the lady I sing of,
> equally the snow is like her;
> so that in each season I must sing for her love;
> so much do the rose and the snow remind me.

SORDELLO AND CUNIZZA, HISTORICALLY

Pound did not dwell on the beauty of Sordello's work; it was the story of Cunizza, Sordello's sometime lady, that impressed him and made her one of the lights at the centre of his Paradise.[22] One of the Provencal *vidas* sums up the story:

> Sordello was from Sirier in Mantuan country, the son of a poor knight who was called Sir El Cort. And he delighted himself in learning songs and in composing; and he stayed with the good courtiers, and learned all that he could; and made *coblas* and *sirventes*.
>
> And he came away to the court of the Count of San Bonifacio; and the Count honoured him greatly. And he fell in love with the wife of the Count, in the manner of pleasure, and she with him. And it happened that the Count did not get on with her brothers, and estranged himself from her. And Sir Ezzelino and Sir Alberico, her brothers, had Sordello abduct her from the Court; and he came away to stay with them; and he was with them a long time in great happiness.
>
> And then he went off to Provence, where he received great honour from all good men, and from the Count and the Countess, who gave him a good castle and a noble wife.[23]

Though this story is suspiciously like the *vida* of Bernart de Ventadorn,[24] we know a great deal more about Sordello. Like William IX of Aquitaine, he was a political figure, which both attracted public attention to his deeds and provided a different kind of documentation.

Sordello had made a poor start in his career—we know of it chiefly from his competitors, the troubadours who infested the courts of northern Italy around 1220.[25] They accused him of being a gambler, and of being a *jongleur,* willing to sing anyone's songs for handouts.[26] No doubt he had risen above these circles by the time he met Cunizza. Sordello had been at the court of Azzo VII d'Este,[27] and from there he went to the court of Azzo's friend, Rizzardo di San Bonifacio, in Verona. At the beginning of the year 1222, the Da Romano and the San Bonifacio had concluded a peace in their lengthy and bitter struggle, and as a sign of trust had married off Cunizza da Romano to Rizzardo di San Bonifacio, while Zilia di San Bonifacio went in marriage to Ezzelino II da Romano.[28] Cunizza is the lady to whom a love-judgement is referred in one of Sordello's songs, a *partimen* with another troubadour.[29] The two houses were back at war by 1226, and the troubadours were soon spreading the news that Sordello had carried Cunizza off.[30] The chronicler Rolandino, whom Pound uses extensively, relates that Ezzelino II

In the sixth place begot the lady Cunizza, the order of whose life was thus: — At first she was given as wife to Count Rizzardo di San Bonifacio; but in a while, on the orders of Ezzelino her father, Sordello, a man from his retinue, took the lady away from her husband secretly, and with her it was said that he lay while she was staying at her father's court. And when Sordello had been driven out by Ezzelino, a certain knight, Bonio of Treviso by name, loved the lady, and took her away from her father's court secretly, and she, excessively in love with him, went around very many parts of the world with him, having much pleasure and spending a great deal. At last they both returned to Alberico da Romano, the brother of the lady, who ruled and reigned in Treviso, against the will of Ezzelino her brother, as it was said and became apparent; and there this Bonius stayed with the said lady Cunizza, though the wife of Bonius was still living and staying in Treviso.

This was not the end of Cunizza's affairs:

Bonius was finally killed by the sword on a certain Sunday, when Ezzelino apparently wanted to snatch the city of Treviso from the rule of his brother. When, after all this, the lady Cunizza had fallen as far as to her brother Ezzelino, he married her to Sir Aimeric, or Rainier, of Braganza, a nobleman. But afterwards, when war broke out in the Marca [Trevigiana], Ezzelino had his kinsman killed with certain noblemen of Braganza and elsewhere in the Marca. Yet again Cunizza, after the death of her brother Ezzelino, got married, in Verona.[31]

Sordello also proceeded to other affairs. The other Provençal *vida,* which calls him 'very treacherous and false towards ladies and towards the barons with whom he stayed', says that after the liaison with Cunizza he secretly married one Otta di Strasso, and had to stay armed in Ezzelino da Romano's house to protect himself from her brother and from Cunizza's people.[32] He then travelled westwards to Provence; a song by Uc de Saint-Circ describes his expertise in seducing his way through the courts.[33] He stayed with the great patron Savaric de Mauléon, in Aquitaine, and visited St. James of Compostella. By 1241 he was with Raimon-Bérenger of Provence,

beginning a new career in politics.[34] His famous song of the 'three
disinherited men' curses the Count of Toulouse, the King of
Aragon, and the Count of Provence, each beaten in recent struggles.[35] Another famous *sirventes* starts out as a lament on the death
of Blacatz, a nobleman of Provence who was a patron of troubadours, and turns on the cowardly princes of Europe to tell them they
need to eat the dead man's heart, for his courage.[36] This poem
immediately raised Sordello's status; his name began to appear
among those of great vassals.[37] But Raimon-Bérenger died in 1245,
and Sordello transferred his loyalties to the new master of Provence,
Charles of Anjou,[38] and he began to appear in the acts of this prince
as *miles*, 'knight'.[39] When Charles of Anjou set off to conquer the
kingdom of Sicily in 1265, Sordello probably went with the land
army, but Charles seems to have ditched him, for we find his name
in this surprising letter to Charles from Pope Clement IV:

...many people presume that having subjected them to labours beyond
their capacities, you are defrauding your Provençal men of their pay....
Your knight Sordello is languishing at Novara; even had he not deserved
well of you, he ought to be bought out, and how much more should he be
ransomed for his merits; and many others who have served you in Italy
have returned naked and poor to their homes.[40]

Sordello was soon released and back in favour: Charles began to
shower him with gifts. First came a castle; then after the battle of
Tagliacozzo, that secured the Kingdom of Naples for Charles of
Anjou, more fiefs; then more castles, and even, it seems, a cloth-
works.[41] Sordello was worth 200 ounces of gold per annum, and was
a *familiaris* of one of the great princes of Europe.[42] At the height of
his prosperity he died, at some time around 1269.[43]

As for Cunizza, one would have presumed that she was dead by
the time that Sordello returned to Italy, were it not for an act which
survives from that very year. Boni describes how Sordello 'returned,
changed, to a changed Italy, where many of those he had known or
at whose side he had lived had disappeared'. Rizzardo di San Bonifacio was dead. Ezzelino da Romano had died of wounds received at
the battle of Cassano d'Adda; his brother Alberico had been betrayed to the Guelfs, who had butchered him, with his wife and children, at San Zeno. Only Cunizza still lived. When the Romano

house fell, after her third marriage, she had found refuge in Tuscany with her relatives on her mother's side. On 1 April 1265, being
a guest at the house of Cavalcante de' Cavalcanti, she signed an act
of manumission freeing her brothers' slaves, violently execrating
those who had handed over Alberico and his family to their deaths,
and finally (as Boni does not say) freeing them also.[44]

SORDELLO IN DANTE AND POUND: THE SCOURGE OF PRINCES

Most readers take their knowledge of Sordello from Dante, where in
the *Purgatorio* (as Pound notes in *The Spirit of Romance*) Virgil
says: ' "But see there a soul, that stationed / entirely alone looks
towards us. . . ." ' Dante describes Sordello:

> O Lombard soul,
> how you were proud and disdainful,
> and honest and slow in the moving of your eyes!
> It said nothing to us;
> but let us go on, only watching
> in the manner of a lion when it rests.
> But Virgil went on towards it, asking
> that it show us the best way up;
> and it did not answer his question;
> but questioned us
> about our countries and our lives.[45]

Sordello and Virgil, fellow-Mantuans, embrace, and on these implications of past glory Dante builds a great invective against modern
Italy.

Pound picks up the tone of this famous picture of Sordello Man-
tuan, the lion in repose, when he describes Henry James:

> And the great domed head, *con gli occhi onesti e tardi*

'with the honest and slow eyes'. Pound is thinking of Henry James
the rebel, the teller of uncomfortable truths, whose club (with that
of Browning) had beaten what little intelligence London possessed
into its skull, and whose death, as Eliot said, would cement the new

Anglo-American *entente,* in this comparison with Sordello.[46] For Sordello appears 'before hell mouth' in Canto XVI, and Pound's Hell is London:

> And in the west mountain, Il Fiorentino,
> Seeing hell in his mirror,
>   and lo Sordels
> Looking on it in his shield;
> And Augustine, gazing toward the invisible.[47]

Pound also takes Dante's Sordello to scourge the princes of Europe as described by Thomas Jefferson in 1822:

> a guisa de leon
> The cannibals of Europe are eating one another again
> quando si posa.[48]

The authority of Jefferson, observing from his retirement, is like that of Sordello: 'in the manner of a lion / . . . when it rests.'

But Pound notes that 'Sordello's right to this lonely and high station above "the valley of the kings" has at times been questioned. . . .'[49] Sordello's right to his position in Purgatory depends not on his political importance, which has not been questioned,[50] but on his moral stature; and it has been said that in his political songs the attacks are unjust and the themes hackneyed.[51] We find it difficult to care about the cowardice of princes, but this is the constant theme of Sordello and other troubadours. The theme is a fusion of two currents of feeling: the first is that a prince's highest duty is to defend his patrimony, and the second, in the case of a great proportion of songs by Sordello's contemporaries, is that the expansionism of 'the Church and the French' is a usurpation.[52] The princes in question would realise the hopes of their peoples simply by making good their claim to what belonged to them as of 'right', custom, or divine law.[53] This vindication of territorial rights had been elevated, for example by Bertran de Born, into an equivalent of 'honour'. To us it seems a strange localisation of honour, but at least it was an ethical concept, and could be seen as embodying systems of personal values; for all these troubadours it was the one obstacle to mere greed, and in particular, at this time, the greed of the Church and the French, making itself felt most particularly in the Albigensian Crusade.[54] Originality of theme and treatment was not something the troubadours saw in the same light as the twentieth century; what Sordello does in his Blacatz *sirventes* is to invest his polemic with the solemnity of mourning in these majestic hexameters with their heavy ending, tones no doubt picked up from Bertran de Born's lament for the Young King:

> Planher vuelh en Blacatz en aquest leugier so
> ab cor trist e marrit, et ai en be razo,
> qu'en luy ai mescabat senhor et amic bo,
> e quar tug l'ayp valent en sa mort perdut so....[55]

> I want to lament Sir Blacatz with this slight tune
> with a sad and low heart — and I have good reason,
> for in him I've lost a good lord and friend,
> and since in his death all ways worth anything are lost....

CUNIZZA IN PARADISE

Cunizza, of whom we know no more than the scraps I have related, is to be found in Dante's Paradise, where one might not particularly have expected her. She introduces herself:

> In that part of the evil Italian land
> that is between the Rialto [that is, Venice]
> and the sources of Brenta and Piava
> rises a hill, not very high,
> from which once descended a spark [Ezzelino da Romano]
> that caused great destruction to the land.
> From one root were born both I and it;
> I was called Cunizza, and I shine here
> because the light of this star [Venus] overcame me.
> But joyfully I pardon myself
> the cause of my fate, and I don't lament,
> which would probably seem strange to your people.[56]

It has indeed seemed strange to people here below that Cunizza should not lament the sins we know she committed. Thus Hauvette:

Dante seems to have known nothing about the gallantries that marked the youth of Sordello; this impression is the stronger in that the poet has put

Cunizza in Paradise, naturally in the heaven of Venus, but without any allusion either to Sordello or to the other lovers of this joyous lady. It seems therefore that Dante was passably ill-informed here.[57]

In this strange reasoning it is natural that Cunizza should be in the heaven of Venus, but apparent that Dante knew nothing of her amours or her first lover's. Critics are quite aware that the heaven of Venus is the sphere of sensual love, but cannot admit any connection, since God is the very opposite of sensual love; one, for example, can only guess that Dante put her there because she freed her slaves.[58]

But Dante's Cunizza after all has the authority of being in his Paradise, and she says specifically that she pardons herself 'the cause of my fate, and I don't lament.' She makes it quite clear that the 'cause' of Her 'fate' is that

> the light of this star [Venus] overcame me

and warns us that we will find this surprising. Pound gave the words of Dante's poem the attention they ask for. In *The Spirit of Romance* he connected this passage with the words of Folquet de Marseille:

> Here, in defiance of convention, we find Cunizza:

> Out of one root spring I with it; Cunizza was I called, and
>   here I glow because the light of this star overcame me.

> In Canto IX, lines 103-106, [Folquet's]

> Yet here we not repent, but smile; not at the sin, which
>   cometh not again to mind, but at the Worth that
>   ordered and provided,

> we have matter for a philosophical treatise as long as the
> *Paradiso*.[59]

The sin that Folquet speaks of is the ardour of his love, which he has described at length. We know quite a lot about the career of this man from troubadour to heretic-hunting bishop, and he seems to have been just as deep in the pleasures of love as Cunizza;[60] his words, dismissing his sins, are almost identical with Cunizza's.[61]

The early commentators on Dante could see that he had made

Cunizza into Venus: 'Rightly the poet figures himself finding this lady in the sphere of Venus; for if the noble Cypriots dedicated their Venus and the Romans their Flora, each a most beautiful and splendid whore (*formosissimam & ditissimam meretricem*), how much more worthily and nobly could the Christian poet save Cunizza.'[62] They had no doubt that she liked to have lovers: 'It is to be known that the said lady Cunizza is said to have been in love at all times of her life, and her love was of such generosity that she would have held it great ill-breeding to think of denying it to anyone who asked courteously.'[63] There is no doubt that they were right. Pound is no doubt also right in deducing from the evidences of her life a 'grace' of character:

Cunizza, white-haired in the House of the Cavalcanti, Dante, small guttersnipe, or small boy hearing the talk in his father's kitchen or, later, from Guido, of beauty incarnate, or, if the beauty can by any possibility be brought into doubt, at least and with utter certainty, charm and imperial bearing, grace that stopped not an instant in sweeping over the most violent authority of her time and, from the known fact, that vigour which is a grace in itself. There was nothing in Crestien de Troyes' narratives, nothing in Rimini or in the tales of the ancients to surpass the facts of Cunizza, with, in her old age, great kindness, thought for her slaves.[64]

Using his methods of argument by juxtaposition, Pound suggested that such grace was an influence which would propagate itself (as in Canto VI's line of descent), and that it was incompatible with any crudeness of cultural manifestation. This passage on Cunizza in the *Guide to Kulchur* is immediately followed by a whole string of examples of the mediaeval clarity and precision: Sordello's verse, the exactitude of mediaeval theology, the beauty of Romanesque architecture descended from Byzantium, and its relation to Moslem building and to certain buildings in Poitiers. All this amounts, Pound says, to an 'anti-usura paideuma'.[65] The connection between Cunizza and these things is that a sharper awareness of emotional distinctions will lead one to sharper distinctions elsewhere.[66] That is why Pound felt that the troubadours were 'raised' by their ladies; that is why Dante's Beatrice, who ultimately leads him to Paradise, was first worshipped for her material beauty.[67]

Though each of the demigoddesses in the Cantos has her adequate worshipper, for whom she creates emotional clarity, each at some point causes destruction. In the Pisan Cantos Pound remarks:

> and the greatest is charity
> to be found among those who have not observed
> regulations[68]

Both clarity and chaos come into Sordello's Cantos XXIX and XXXVI.

Canto XXIX is about woman-born disorder and clarity. It begins with the chaos wrought by Pernella, the concubine of Aldobrando Orsini,

> Bringing war once more on Pitigliano[69]

which rhymes with the chaos in the house of Este wrought by Parisina, a parallel to Eleanor of Aquitaine in Cantos VIII and XX.[70] It notes the complaints of Sextus Propertius against his girl's infidelities,[71] and then moves to the document whereby Cunizza freed her slaves:

> Liberans et vinculo ab omni liberatos
> ['freeing the freedmen from every chain']
> As who with four hands at the cross roads
> By king's hand or sacerdos'
>   are given their freedom
> —Save who were at Castra San Zeno. . . .
>
> Cunizza for God's love, for remitting the soul of her father
> —May hell take the traitors of Zeno.[72]

Pound interpolates two lines from Rolandino's chronicle:

> And fifth begat he Alberic
> And sixth the Lady Cunizza.[73]

Then he returns to the document of emancipation:

> In the house of the Cavalcanti
>   anno 1265:
> Free go they all as by full manumission
> All serfs of Eccelin my father da Romano
> Save those who were with Alberic at Castra San Zeno

And let them go also
The devils of hell in their body.

Finally he goes back to Rolandino's account, pausing only to put in
the line from Dante's words by Cunizza in Paradise — 'The light of
this star o'ercame me':[74]

And sixth the lady Cunizza
That was first given Richard St Boniface
And Sordello subtracted her from that husband
And lay with her in Tarviso
Till he was driven out of Tarviso
And she left with a soldier named Bonius
nimium amorata in eum ['excessively in love with him']
And went from one place to another
'The light of this star o'ercame me'
Greatly enjoying herself
And running up the most awful bills.
And this Bonius was killed on a sunday
and she had then a Lord from Braganza
and later a house in Verona.

'This star' (Venus) predominates in this short life of Cunizza, and
Pound makes it merge with the grace that freed her slaves. After the
Cunizza passage, Canto XXIX shows examples of American sub-
urban social life and the unsatisfying sexual *moeurs* of the Twenties
young. Then comes a diatribe against woman:

a chaos
An octopus
A biological process
                    and we seek to fulfill....
TAN AIODAN, our desire, drift....
                    Ailas e que'm fau miey huelh
                    Quar noi vezon so qu'ieu vuelh.

We 'seek to fulfill' 'our desire', like the cock parading his feathers
and his noise, with all kinds of attractions, including song; the biological pull results ultimately in the scrap of Sordello's song that
Pound quotes: 'Alas, and what are my eyes doing to me / for they do
not see what I wish.'[75]

Canto XXXVI begins with Pound's final translation of the 'Philosophic Canzone' of Cavalcanti. Cavalcanti's neo-Platonism in this
song puts a particular emphasis on Love's place in the memory:

> Where memory liveth,
>   it takes its state
>   Formed like a diafan from light on shade[76]

Sordello, Cunizza his *mantram,* and Sordello's temporal affairs — as
being part of Cunizza's sphere of influence — are placed with this
Cavalcanti. After the canzone the Canto introduces Scotus Erigena,
who gave Pound the idea of a material universe as lights radiated by
God.[77] It considers oppositions to him: the later Church which confused him with contemporary rationalist heretics; and Aquinas and
Aristotle, 'greek-splitting' metaphysicians.[78] Then there is the rite of
coition, which is behind what Pound thought of as a continuous cultural stream that produced the balanced part of the Western 'paideuma', including both Erigena and the troubadours; and Sordello
appears:

> Sacrum, sacrum, inluminatio coitu.
> Lo Sordels si fo di Mantovana
>   of a castle named Goito.[79]

'The rite, the rite, illumination in coition' is a Latin dictum of
Pound's;[80] 'Sordello was from Mantua country' is from the *vida.*[81]
Then Pound cites Sordello's dealings with Charles of Anjou: receiving castles, complaining about the things he has already received
(including a cloth-works), and being helped out of prison by a letter
to Charles from the Pope:[82]

> 'Five castles!
> 'Five castles!'
>   (king giv' him five castles)
> 'And what the hell do I know about dye-works?!'
> His Holiness has written a letter:
>   'CHARLES the Mangy of Anjou....
> ..way you treat your men is a scandal....'[83]

Pound quotes from the document giving various castles to Sordello,

and notes that he sold them all soon afterwards (in fact they may
have been sold after his death):

> Dilectis miles familiaris . . . castra Montis Odorisii
> Montis Sancti Silvestri pallete et pile . . . .
> ['Beloved knight of our retinue . . . the castles of
> Monte Odorisio, / Monte San Silvestro, Paglieta
> and Pila . . . .']
> In partibus Thetis ['In the district of Thetis'] . . . . vineland
> > land tilled
> > the land incult
> > pratis nemoribus pascuis
> > ['meadows groves pastures']
> > with legal jurisdiction
> his heirs of both sexes
> . . . sold the damn lot six weeks later,
> Sordellus de Godio.
> > Quan ben m'albir e mon ric pensamen.[84]

The last line is the key: it is the interiorised icon, the troubadours'
version of Love's place in the memory, the goddess that they preferred to any passing pleasure, from this stanza by Sordello:

> When I consider well in my proud thoughts
> [Quan ben m'albir en mon ric pensamen]
> of her to whom I give myself up and surrender myself, what kind
> > she is,
> I love her so much, because her worth is beyond that of the delightful
> > women that exist,
> that in the matter of love I esteem each one as nothing,
> and since I know no other in the world so worthy
> of whom I might take pleasure lying kissing;
> for I do not want to taste any fruit
> through which the sweet should turn sour for me[85]

SORDELLO, CUNIZZA, AND THE PROVENÇAL CULTURE IN ITALY

We have seen how Canto VI shows a culture that begins with William IX of Aquitaine, reaches its next focal point in his grand-

daughter Eleanor, and passes via Sordello and Cunizza to Guido
Cavalcanti and the young Dante. It is a kind of cultural dynasty
which passes on a certain awareness by personal contact, and which
refertilises this awareness by personal energy and courage. At the
stage of Sordello and Cunizza, the key phrase is 'in the house of the
Cavalcanti'—it occurs both in Canto XXIX and in the *Guide to
Kulchur*.[86] It is implicit in Canto VI:

> Cunizza, da Romano,
> That freed her slaves on a Wednesday
> Masnatos et servos, witness
> Picus de Farinatis
> and Don Elinus and Don Lipus
> sons of Farinato de' Farinati[87]

These witnesses are the sons of Farinata degli Uberti ('Farinata
de' Farinati' in the document), most aristocratic of the Florentine
ghibellines, whose lofty spirit is recorded in Dante's *Inferno:*

> ...he raised his chest and brow
> as if he held Hell in great scorn.
> ...When I reached the foot of his tomb,
> he looked at me a little, and then as if disdainfully
> asked me: 'Who were your ancestors?'[88]

Though Farinata certainly has to ask about Dante's antecedents
because he is sometime dead, his interest in family fits both with his
own politics and with Pound's feelings about 'dynasty'—in the later
Cantos Pound hints that his own friend degli Uberti still carries the
Farinata distinction.[89] The point of introducing Farinata's sons into
Canto VI at this point is that in 1267, two years after this act freeing
Cunizza's slaves, Farinata's daughter Bice married Guido Cavalcanti.[90] These things show how close were the two houses, and reinforce the connection between Cunizza and the Cavalcanti.

Guido Cavalcanti was about twenty years old at the time of his
unfortunate marriage.[91] He was by that amount older than Dante,
who was born in 1265; and Pound says that 'His mind was in a way
the matrix against which the mind of the young Dante formed
itself.'[92] Sordello was the last great representative of the troubadour
culture, and Cunizza had formed his genius. She survived into old

age and was living at the house of Cavalcante de' Cavalcanti during the formative years of his son Guido. These connections are implicit in Cantos VI and XXIX.

One could take these connections as a suggestion, as an emblem or hypothetical representative example of the kind of thing that happened when the Provencal culture died and the Italian culture was born. I believe them to be significant when taken this way. They are an excellent illustration of the enormous part the troubadours played in the creation of the Italian *Duecento* aesthetic. This image of a culture that 'begins when one HAS "forgotten-what-book"',[93] transmitted by the energetic activity and the personal influence of persons who believed in its value, is far more plausible than the usual idea of an Italian literature which started up from nothing and happened across a few Provencal curiosities. The other way of taking Pound's thesis is the literal way—so that without Cunizza, there would have been no Divine Comedy. In his more conspiratorial moments Pound may have believed these emblems as literally as this, but I do not think we should allow this to hide the great value that they have as emblems.

But a preponderant view of researchers into Provencal and Italian culture has assumed that when Dante 'flourished' no information on the Provencal verse was available beyond that in a few enormously expensive collector's anthologies, such as a man like Dante could never have hoped to buy. This view must be examined in detail.

The surviving songs, fragments of songs, and pieces of prose describing them and their authors, that are what we now have of the troubadour culture, are contained in ninety-five song-books. More than half of these are Italian; none of them goes back earlier than the thirteenth century.[94] It is usually assumed that Provencal verse was oral, and then at some (late) stage was written down in *chansonniers,* like the ones that survive, for the benefit of wealthy collectors; that these *chansonniers* were few in number, and were all that was available by way of troubadour poetry and information to poets of Dante's generation; and that they gave rise to more copies in due course, and the ones we now possess are perhaps second or third or later generations descended from them.

This is unlikely for various reasons. The first is that when the assumptions are applied, and we try to write the history of these *chansonniers* as if they existed alone and gave rise to more anthologies without the help of any outside sources, the detailed evidence produced is a mere chaos. The second is that what we know of the general conditions of the Italian and troubadour cultures suggests that they possessed much more than a few anthologies; that types of communication much less formal existed and constituted a general ambience of knowledge which is usually ignored by researchers. Once we allow, for example, that the troubadours used the ordinary scrap or sheet of paper, the science of manuscript genealogy becomes a mere diversion and the supposed gap between Provence and Italy is bridged.

A prime example of the views I have described is Salvatore Santangelo's *Dante e i trovatori provenzali*.[95] It is not Santangelo's purpose to claim that Dante knew almost nothing about the troubadours; his assumptions about the nature of mediaeval communication make him presuppose this. His aim is simply to find out the sources of what he thinks Dante did know about the troubadours. He uses the normal method of manuscript genealogy, namely the method of comparative readings. This consists of looking for features of spelling, information, and treatment that are shared by the manuscripts in question and (preferably) by no others. A sufficient number of these shared peculiarities should prove that one of the manuscripts was derived from the others, or that they all came from the same source; or, in this case, that the bits of information Dante gives us about the troubadours were taken from the source Santangelo proposes.

In the first part of his book, Santangelo uses certain supposed contradictions of information to 'prove' that Dante did not know one of the most obvious possible sources for his information on the troubadours: the *vidas* and *razos*.[96] In the second part, with the same method, he tries to prove what (hypothetical) source Dante did know. Let us examine the detail of the method in this second part. First, by shared readings, Santangelo establishes a new and 'more accurate' grouping of manuscripts with common ancestors.[97] Then he examines the readings in Dante's bits on the troubadours, and finds that they concur more or less with those in one of the groups he has constituted.[98] There are difficulties, and so he proposes that Dante's source was not the source of his group, GQU_cV^2PS, but the source of that source.[99] Thus:

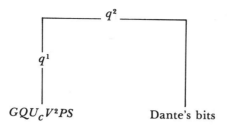

$$q^2$$

$$q^1$$

GQU_cV^2PS Dante's bits

We can show the actual pattern of corroboration in Table 1.

Table 1

Reading	Manuscript held to be related to Dante's source						
	G	Q	U	c	V²	P	S
1	X	X	X				
2		X		X			
3	X	X	X	X	X	X	X
4	X	X	X	X	X	X	X
5	X		X				X
6			X		X		
7			X				
8		X	X	X		X	
9		X	X				
10			X	X			
11	X						
12	X		X	X		X	
13			X				
14	X		X	X		X	X
15			X				
16							
17	X	X	X	X	X	X	X
18							X
19							
20	X	X	X	X	X	X	X

As may be seen, there is no pattern. At least, there is no significant pattern that Santangelo has cared to point out. The reason is that once he has established a point as a corroborated reading, he has no interest at all in the nature of the point. For example, item 20 is Dante's remarks on the metric of Arnaut Daniel; they are supported (according to Santangelo) by the songs of Arnaut cited in all seven manuscripts. Item 18 is the song by Sordello which is the reason, Santangelo says, for his place in the *Purgatorio*; it is given only in manuscript *S*.[100] Why is it that the copiers of all seven manuscripts kept the songs by Arnaut that were in their supposed source, when six of them seem to have thrown out the Sordello? We have no idea. Hence what justifies us in saying that the unanimous corroboration on the one item is more significant than the almost total non-corroboration on the other?

In the nature of things we can have no idea why some points are corroborated and not others, as will be seen if we look at these points in detail. Santangelo uses corroborations of three kinds: spellings, availabilities, and orders of citation.

For example, item 15 in the table is a corroboration of spelling. Dante's *De Vulgari Eloquentia* names a troubadour as 'Namericus de *Belnui*'. This agrees, more or less, with manuscript *c*, which has *Bellinui*. So Santangelo argues that Dante's source was probably the source of manuscript *c*. Item 3 is a point of availability. Dante does not cite Peire d'Alvernhe's poems, and we find that these poems are not in manuscripts GQU_cV^2PS, so it is argued again that the source of these manuscripts is likely to be Dante's source. Item 6 is an example of corroboration by order of citation. Dante only cites one of Bertran de Born's poems, and this poem is the first in order of Bertran's poems in manuscripts UV^2. So it is argued that the source of these manuscripts is probably one and the same with Dante's.[101] These kinds of corroboration are the bedrock of the whole science of manuscript genealogy, and in particular of the whole of Santangelo's picture of the relations between Italy and Provence.[102] Let us examine them.

The significance of single-word variations of spelling in the Middle Ages was negligible. As is well known, a concern for exact consistency of spelling is something quite recent. This is not to say that mediaeval spelling was completely idiosyncratic; scribes' sense of the phonetic value of the Roman letters seems to have been constant enough for modern scholars to gain a very good idea of the pronunciation of local dialects from the way they were written. But that is a general consistency over whole passages, not one that would make a scribe worry about single words. It does not tie a scribe to the spelling used in the sheet of parchment he is copying. We tend to assume, as Chaytor says, that

the medieval scribe adopted exactly the same mental attitude that one of ourselves would assume if he were occupied in copying a manuscript for his own purposes. This was certainly not the case, for the reason that we gain the majority of our information and ideas from printed matter, whereas the medieval obtained them orally . . . he brought not a visual but an auditory memory to his task. [103]

The scribe very often also had his own personal way of doing things. He might have some learning in the subject matter, and a taste for editing, like the fourteenth-century Narbonnais who went through the songs he put into manuscript *C*, polishing up diction and putting in bits of his own doubtful information. [104] He might be a man with his head full of Provencal verse, a genuine amateur of the subject and not just of its philological trimmings, like the scribe who seems to have transferred the rhyme-endings from one of Bertran's famous songs into the *razo*-passage describing it. [105] Jean Misrahi, struggling with the manuscripts of *Erec et Enide,* said:

The evidence points either to considerable and almost systematic individualism on the part of each scribe or else to equally considerable and crisscross 'contamination' of all the MSS. Until we have more direct knowledge of the habits and procedures of medieval scribes occupied in copying vernacular texts, we cannot definitely know. It seems probable, however, that both sources of MS. variation were ever present in varying degree. The 'mechanical' sources of scribal errors, as exposed by Vinaver, are responsible for only an infinitesimal fraction of the total number of variants in any text of which we have several MSS. As yet we know with certainty only that the MSS. very frequently disagree.

Hence:

Until we know why in each individual case, or, in other words, until we can see the reason for each textual variation, any method that we may use to tabulate them with a view to establishing distinct 'families' of MSS. is foredoomed to failure. [106]

The great *chansonniers* we possess are the product of men who cared, on whatever humble level, about the culture they were transmitting; not the product of a clutch of robots scribbling to order, copying the quirks of their predecessors to the letter. These men also had many more sources, from which to make their individualistic choices, than we now know of.

There are the corroborations of availability: the arguments that, for example, since *Per solatz . . .* by Giraut de Bornelh, which Dante cites, is in QUcP, Dante's source is likely to have been a relative of these manuscripts.[107] These points depend completely on the idea that Dante had no sources of information other than the ancestors of the *chansonniers* we now possess.

We know that books, in mediaeval times, were expensive. The ordinary troubadour would have a great deal less chance of buying one book in his lifetime than the modern factory worker has of buying a car. Many of the troubadours — Arnaut Daniel is an example — were reputed to be poor. But Stronski, than whom few have been more deeply read in the troubadour works, said that a troubadour like Folquet de Marseille 'knew about the activity of every one of his colleagues' — and, as he shows, imitated endlessly.[108] The *chansonniers* that have survived to us are nearly all illuminated Rolls-Royces of books, made for wealthy men. Is it possible to conceive that such books were the source wherein an Arnaut read the works of a Bertran de Born?

Boutière and others suggest 'oral transmission' — it was the *jongleurs* who communicated the songs.[109] There is no reason to rule this out. Oral memory is thought to have been more efficient in the Middle Ages than it is now.[110] In a *razo* of Arnaut Daniel, a *jongleur* spends the whole night reciting his song to learn it (from a parchment?) for oral delivery, and Arnaut learns it by listening.[111] But there is no reason why the culture of the troubadours should have depended on oral memory. Even this *jongleur* must have been learning his song from something. Many of the troubadours were educated in monasteries; the *vidas* say specifically that some of them were good scribes; and Ovid, who had not yet been translated into the Romance languages, is scattered all over their works.[112] Their literacy was quite adequate. It seems probable that songs like Arnaut Daniel's more difficult pieces could not have survived for long orally.[113] The men of the Middle Ages probably approached documents with auditory mental habits, but they must also have been at ease with pen and paper, and ad hoc documents, scraps of paper, and pieces of parchment were no doubt in use constantly. A well-known manuscript of Provencal poetry has an illumination showing an ecstatic poet composing at a desk with pen and parchment. Another manuscript illumination shows Jean Bodel reading his *Congé* to friends, from a parchment. There is a strophe in Jaufré Rudel where he announces, as if it were something unusual, that

> Without a parchment letter
> I send the poem, which we sing
> in simple vernacular,
> to Sir Uc Brunenc, via Filhol. . . . [114]

It is obvious that the air was full of bits of paper covered with songs, in the circles that cared for them; Dante, like the compilers of the anthologies, must have had at his disposal a lifetime's accumulation of the pieces that interested him. Dante, his friends, the minor poets, and their predecessors in Italy and Provence were interested in the Provencal work, for itself, as song; they sought things out, they selected and propagated; they were not a series of passive receptacles who happened to stumble across things and copy them out to kill time. So that, finally, the 'evidence' of the corroborated orders of citation is an absurdity. If we say that a particular poem by Bertran de Born is first in order of his songs in UV^2, and, since Dante only cites one of Bertran's poems, we can conclude that Dante is likely to have used a relative of UV^2, we are saying that Dante was like any reviewer of poetry who has read only one poem in the book: the first. The existence of Dante as a poet, and the whole history of Provencal and Italian poetry, show otherwise.

The transition from Provence to Italy shows the drive of interested persons throughout. Northern Italy in about 1220 was flooded with the troubadours who had been forced out by the Albigensian Crusade. They were protected by the heads of many illustrious Italian houses, who themselves wrote good verse—not in Italian, but in Provencal.[115] In about the same period the 'Sicilian school' of Italian verse began to grow up, being influenced by the troubadours and Italian patrons of troubadours who congregated around Frederick II in 1220.[116] Later, in the forties, the supply of troubadours was drying up and the Provencalising Italians were fading away, but the Italian 'sweet new style' of Cavalcanti, Cino da Pistoia, and the

rest was about to be born. Now men became very concerned to get
the Provençal down in more durable forms of writing. It was an
Italian who urged Uc Faidit to compose his 'Provençal Grammar';[117]
and an Italian, Ferrarino di Ferrara, who

was a *jongleur* and understood composition in Provençal better than any
man who was ever in Lombardy and understood better the Provençal
tongue. He knew letters very well, and was a better scribe than any man in
the world and made many and beautiful books. . . . He was always in the
Este household. When it happened that the Marquis had a celebration at
court, and the jongleurs who understood the Provençal tongue came to the
Marquis, they all went around with Ferrarino and called him their master.
. . . And he made an abstract of all the songs of the good troubadours in the
world. . . .[118]

It was an Italian, Sordello, who wrote some of the best verse in the
Provençal language, and he was at the house of the Este and also
with the da Romano, with Cunizza. Ezzelino da Romano protected
troubadours, among whom Guilhem Raimon:

> When I came from Hungary
> Sir Ezzelino laughed
> because I was crazy
> with greetings and with messages. . . .[119]

Alberico da Romano, Cunizza's other brother, was a patron of troubadours, wrote his own excellent verse, and caused to be made one
of the great *chansonniers* that survives.[120]

Yet it is assumed that Dante, in the generation following, was a
fumbling beginner in the subject of Provençal verse — that he merely
happened across one *chansonnier,* without which, one supposes,
there would have been no Arnaut or Sordello or Folquet de Marseille in the *Comedy.* It is said for instance that Dante could not
have known any document containing the *vidas,* since the *vidas* say
that Giraut de Bornelh was 'master of the troubadours' and Dante
says otherwise.[121] Obviously Santangelo thinks that Dante wrote his
fierce diatribe against those *stolti* who considered Giraut the best
troubadour because he thought that was what the public expected
to hear. It is argued again that Dante could not have known the
vidas because they say nothing that could have told him Provençal

was the first of the Romance poetic languages. But Dante's teacher was Brunetto Latini, who wrote an encyclopaedic work in French[122] and lived in France for many years.[123] Latini's life-span (ca. 1220-94) covers almost exactly the birth and apogee of the Italian love-lyric; in his youth the 'Sicilians' were making their first fumbling imitations of the Provençal, while men like Sordello, Lanfranc Cigala, and Bonifazio Calvo conceded so much to the prestige of the Provençal lyric that they wrote all their poetry in its foreign tongue. If tradition could not have told Dante that Provence had originated the Romance love-lyric, then normal human communication must have suffered a temporary lapse in Renaissance Italy.[124]

Pound knew that the Italian poetry did not come out of a desert of fortuitous encounters, but out of the interested drive of poets and patrons; and as always he looked for examples. He knew that Sordello went right across Provence proper and Languedoc, and he observed that Cavalcanti did so also. He speculated that in Languedoc or in Spain Cavalcanti might have met Giraut Riquier, 'last of the troubadours'.[125] In Canto VIII he refers to another link in the chain begun by William IX of Aquitaine:

> And Poictiers, you know, Guillaume Poictiers,
>   had brought the song up out of Spain
> With the singers and viels. But here they wanted a setting,
> By Marecchia, where the water comes down over the cobbles
> And Mastin had come to Verucchio,
>   and the sword, Paolo il Bello's
>   caught in the arras
> And, in Este's house, Parisina
> Paid
> For this tribe paid always, and the house
> Called also Atreides'[126]

'Paolo il Bello', the hero of the Paolo and Francesca story in Dante's *Inferno,* was drawn with Francesca into sin by reading about Sir Lancelot, which like the Tristan story was a 'matter' that probably first came to light at Eleanor of Aquitaine's court.[127] One-hundred and fifty years later, the tribe fathered by William IX of Aquitaine was still being kept by Parisina d'Este. Parisina was interested in the matter of Tristan, as Canto XXIV notes, and Ella Noyes has her reading *istorie francesi* with Ugo before their beheading by the irate

Niccolò d'Este.[128] The house of the Este, with certain other Italian courts, was instrumental in preserving the poetry of the troubadours. Sordello was at the Este court, like Ferrarino di Ferrara; in the high Renaissance the Este librarian was using the Provençal *vidas* for his own researches.[129] Jean de Nostredame did his version of the *vidas* for the Malaspina court; Aldus Manutius and Pietro Bembo were interested in the Provençal material; so likewise was Leone Strozzi and various members of the Medici family.[130] There is no doubt that it was such activities in the noble Italian houses right through the early and high Renaissance that saved Provençal poetry from incineration until the Romantic interest took over.[131]

PART THREE

10. THE HERETICS OF 'PROVENCE'

Everyone believes that Pound connected the troubadours with Manichaeism. Clearly he thought that there was a religious basis to the troubadour culture, and that it had to do with the Albigensian Crusade against 'Manichaean' heretics, which ended in the burnings at Montségur. In the later Cantos, Montségur is a temple dedicated to the sun; and Zarathustra and Manes, both sun-deities, occur in them. Obviously, the critics conclude, (a) these heretics were Manichaean and (b) these Manichaeans were behind the troubadours.[1]

But the religious cult that Pound saw in Provence was not the cult of the Zoroastrians or the Manichaeans or the 'Cathars' or any other dualist and ascetic religion. These dualisms all held that the material world came from the Principle of Evil, and must be renounced; Pound wrote endless attacks on asceticism, the mortification of the flesh, and the renunciation of this world.

These statements by Pound have been generally available at least since 1964:

It is equally discernable upon study that some non-Christian and inextinguishable source of beauty persisted throughout the Middle Ages maintaining song in Provence, maintaining the grace of Kalenda Maya.

And this force was the strongest counter force to the cult of Atys and asceticism. A great deal of obscurity has been made to encircle it. There are a few clear pages in Davidsohn's *Firenze ai Tempi di Dante*. The usual accusation against the Albigeois is that they were Manichaeans. This I believe after a long search to be pure bunkumb. The slanderers feared the truth. I mean they feared not only the force of a doctrine but they feared giving it even the publicity which a true bill against it would have required.

The best scholars do not believe there were any Manichaeans left in Europe at the time of the Albigensian Crusade. If there were any in Provence they have at any rate left no trace in troubadour art.

On the other hand the cult of Eleusis will explain not only general phenomena but particular beauties in Arnaut Daniel or in Guido Cavalcanti.[2]

Pound made it clear in 'Cavalcanti' that he did not believe the troubadours to have been ascetic. The essay moves almost unnoticeably between Provence and Tuscany, and between Arnaut Daniel and Cavalcanti; and it sets out to distinguish the usual idea of 'mediaevalism', that is 'idiotic asceticism', from the desire in Provence and Tuscany to bring the whole perceptible world into one's aesthetic and ethic.[3]

On the basis of this distinction, one can find plenty of hints about Provence. Pound never (to my knowledge) used the term 'Cathar', which is now the commonest term for the heretics of Provence; and he hardly ever used 'Albigensian' or 'Manichaean'. The subject of the Provençal heresy was near the centre of his arcana. In his religious poetry he borrowed Dante's warning:

> O you who are in little vessels,
> Wishing to hear. . . .
> Don't set out to sea, for perhaps,
> Losing me, you would be lost forever. . . .[4]

So these matters are approached mysteriously:

> and they dug [Scotus Erigena] up out of sepulture
> soi distantly looking for Manichaeans.
> Les Albigeois, a problem of history,
> and the fleet at Salamis made with money lent by the state to
>   the shipwrights
>   Tempus tacendi, tempus loquendi.[5]

'A time for being silent, a time for speaking.' But with more hints we can piece the meaning together:

The Duce and Kung fu Tseu equally perceive that their people need poetry; that prose is NOT education but the outer courts of the same. Beyond its doors are the mysteries. Eleusis. Things not to be spoken save in secret.

The mysterious self-defended, the mysteries that *can* not be revealed. Fools can only profane them. The dull can neither penetrate the secretum nor divulge it to others.

Pound explains that what I have called 'natural esotericism' does not apply merely to some separate, mystical area: it applies to every branch of knowledge, including what is called 'science'. No understanding in any area can be acquired by those who will not labour to eliminate the habitual stupidities in their whole approach to life. 'Eleusis' contains the summation or concentration of the wisdoms thus gained. Pound goes on: ' "*Il sait vivre,*" said Brancusi of Léger. This must also be said of the catachumens before they pass the third door. It is quite useless for me to refer men to Provence, or to speculate on Erigena in the market place.'[6]

Let us examine the things that Pound refers to. Eleusis: he believed that at this Greek religious centre the 'mysteries' consisted of a celebratory sexual rite, involved with the cycles of nature.[7] Erigena: Scotus Erigena, a ninth-century philosopher, said that the universe was a radiation from God; Pound thought that Erigena had been in Provence, where an Hellenic awareness of the gods survived.[8] Pound puts these things together with 'les Albigeois' (the Albigensian heretics) and Provence. But by 'Provence' does he mean the culture of the troubadours?

It is clear that he does: 'Says Valli, all these [Italian poets associated with Dante] were Ghibelline. . . . "Something" behind it? Certainly "something" behind it or beyond it. Which the police called "Manichean" knowing nothing either of Manes or of anything else.'[9] That refers to the Italians rather than to the troubadours; but in these matters Pound treated Dante's contemporaries and the troubadours almost as identical:

Erotic sentimentality we can find in Greek and Roman poets, and one may observe that the main trend of Provencal and Tuscan poets is not toward erotic sentimentality.

But they are not pagans, they are called pagans, and the troubadours are also accused of being Manichaeans, obviously because of a muddle somewhere. They are opposed to a form of stupidity not limited to Europe, that is, idiotic asceticism and a belief that the body is evil.[10]

That is quite clear: there was a religious cult behind the troubadours; but it was not Manichaean, it was the very opposite of ascetic, in fact it derived from the cult of Eleusis. Pound had set out all these ideas quite openly, years before he took up this esoteric approach, in the 'Psychology and Troubadours' lecture, published in 1912.[11]

He extended them in an article called 'Terra Italica', published in the *New Review* for 1931-32 and recently reissued. This article starts as a review of a series of brochures then being published in Italy by Eduardo Tinto which, Pound says, clarifies the subject of pagan ritual. Pound completely reverses the usual charges, making the mediaeval Church ascetic and dualist, and the heresy a cult of cele-bration. First he notes the tremendous elasticity and absorption-power of what-was-called-Christianity in its formative stages in Imperial Rome, and suggests that it may have acquired almost the whole of its later character from the cults it absorbed during this period; and Mithraism was one of the most powerful cults then being practised. Mithraism, he observes, 'is for the modern mind the least interesting, is in fact thoroughly boring. It gave, so far as one can make out, nothing to civilization' — he even denies that it gave bullfighting its pageantry; Mithraism only contributed the kill-ing. But he traces a great deal of the mediaeval Christian outlook to such ascetic/dualist cults:

Aquinas and Co. received a great deal from Mithra or from some religion or religions to which the Mithraic celestial map bore marked resemblance. Even the more unpleasant type of present day Christian can be found admiring the ritual and the frame of the Mithraic mind.

'The celebrant immolated victims' would seem to be the main theme. It produced nothing to match the grace of the well-curb at Terracina.

Pound explains the relation in mediaeval culture between the Eleu-sinian cult of beauty and the Mithraic cult of pain, implying quite clearly that the Eleusinian cult was *not* absorbed by the Church. It remained a source of heretical troubles for the Church (Pound seems to have the Albigensians in mind), but more important, a per-sistent source of beauty, 'maintaining song in Provence, maintain-ing the grace of Kalenda Maya.' The Mithraic aesthetic, on the other hand, *was* absorbed into Christianity, since the Church 'later emerges riddled with tendencies to fanaticism, with sadistic and masochistic tendencies that are in no way Eleusinian.'[12]

Pound then continues, in the paragraphs I have already quoted, to say that 'The usual accusation against the Albigeois is that they were Manichaeans. This I believe after a long search to be pure bun-kumb.' The argument is that it was the Church that absorbed dual-ist characteristics from Mithraism, and that the troubadour culture was quite free from them — it had neither the theology of Manichaeism (which was dead) nor its ethic (mostly identical to that of Mithraism, and to be found at that time in the bosom of the Church).[13]

It has been thought that Pound considered the Provençal culture to be associated with a dualist ascetic cult, which is impossible. The reason for this mistake was that every historian has seemed to agree on the point that the heresy connected with the Albigensian Crusade was 'neo-Manichaean' or at least dualist. But Pound was rewriting this part of religious and social history, and we must look at the evidence in detail, and judge his revision.

THE VISIBLE HISTORY OF THE HERETICS

The story of the heresy which centred on Languedoc and Aquitaine begins with an assortment of local perversities that the Church attempted to suppress each in its turn. By the later years of the twelfth century there was a consistent feeling that this whole area was setting itself outside the Church, in favour of some evil heretical doctrine. A long and bloody Crusade, the first to be authorised against a Christian country, reduced it to obedience, and the Inquisition indefatigably pursued the heretics who remained. The Crusade began in 1209 and was pursued almost continuously for twenty years; the Inquisition continued relentlessly in the South throughout this unhappy century. When the Crusade began, Languedoc was rich and powerful. A society of petty lords pursued their disorderly ideals, in the same way as did Bertran de Born's rivals in Limousin; a central power at Toulouse, marrying into intimate relations with Capetians and Plantagenets, played those houses off against each other for its own complete independence; wealthy cities like Montpellier, Narbonne, and Toulouse traded with the giants of the world on equal terms. When the Crusade was over, a hundred castles had been beseiged and the defenders slaughtered, cities had been decimated by dysentery and street fighting, fires and looting had destroyed the moveable wealth, and agriculture had been wrecked by the endlessly moving armies for reasons of strategy and vengeance. Innumerable barbarities had numbed the spirit of the people; there was no longer any surplus to support the culture that had been; the surviving troubadours had to move on.

Heretic activities as early as 1022 have been connected with 'Catharism' in Western Europe;[14] but it was in the first half of the twelfth century that prophets of assorted kinds began to appear in France, the Low Countries, Germany and England, and churchmen began to warn of a revival of the ancient errors of Manes and of Arius. Towards the end of the twelfth century, the fears of the Church focused on the area of Languedoc. The popes delegated full powers to a series of legates in that region, to try to persuade the Counts of Toulouse and their vassals to back up the local clergy. Innocent III took an intense personal interest in the question, even instigating local debates with heretics; but his zeal accomplished nothing, and finally Raymond VI of Toulouse was excommunicated for his obstinacy. In 1208 the papal legate was assassinated,[15] and Innocent then preached a crusade. In July 1209 the Abbot of Cîteaux led an army, with barons and bishops of the North at its head, across the Rhône.

The citizenry of Béziers in their pride sallied out to meet it; the rabble of the Northern army overwhelmed the city, and the Crusade was provided with its first 'miracle'. It was in this rout, when men hesitated for fear of killing Catholics along with heretics, that the Abbot of Cîteaux uttered his famous command, *Coedite eos, novit enim Dominus qui sunt ejus,* 'Kill them, God will know which are His.'[16] The lord of Beziers and Carcassonne had gone ahead to Carcassonne to prepare that city, but an equally swift disaster overtook him there. After brief, but bitter, fighting, he was defeated by conditions:

> If the number of the people massed inside had not been so great,
> Who had fled there from all over the country,
> They would not have been taken or conquered in a year,
> For the towers were high and the walls battlemented;
> But the crusaders had taken away their water and the wells had dried
> With the great heat in the height of summer.
> With the smell of men who had fallen sick,
> And the great number of beasts ready flayed in there,
> Brought from all over the country and shut in there,
> With the loud cries that from all sides
> Women and children, filling the houses, uttered, —
> Flies tormented them all with the heat, —
> They had never suffered so much since they were born.
> Eight days had not passed since the King of Aragon had left

When a powerful crusader called for a parley.
The Viscount went out there, with a safe-conduct,
  With a few of his men.[17]

In obscure circumstances the Viscount became a hostage and died
in the hands of the crusaders. The population fled and the crusaders
marched in to take over the abandoned wealth, and the fief of Raymond VI's principal vassal was vacant.[18]

By right of this new kind of warfaring, the Crusaders claimed the
fief and offered it to their leading barons; when these refused, it
went to the unknown adventurer Simon de Montfort. Simon was
equipped to an exceptional degree with ambition and piety,[19] which
he had need of; as the Northern barons melted away he found himself in charge of the Crusade. First he had to reduce the cities that it
was politically expedient to attack; and that accomplished, he had
to pulverise the local networks of intransigent Southern society and
the dozens of castles that were its strongholds.[20] One by one, these
must be reduced to submission — their defenders slaughtered,
maimed, or disinherited — and filled with the adventurers lured to
the South by the lands that Innocent III had offered 'to the greed of
the first occupier'.[21] Through 'miracles', disasters, and endless set-
backs, Simon pursued this sordid and terrifying war for the next
eight years. He circumvented the traditional warfare of the South,
based on the 'impregnable' castle, by virtue of the fact that he and
his mercenaries had nothing to lose. Unknown men who came for
indulgences and gain, they had no worries about the wasting of their
own lands; all was gain for them. Raymond of Toulouse, who
should have led the South's resistance, was always caught by an
impossible dilemma. If he chose to fight with all his forces, he risked
destroying everything he was fighting for; he might save the South
by humbling himself to the Pope, by negotiating, by appealing to
feudal law. But all these might fail, and he might have missed his
chance to destroy the viper in the midst of his people. This latter is
what happened, as he vacillated. For the Abbot of Cîteaux and his
colleagues, on the other hand, though not necessarily for the Pope,[22]
things were simpler: Evil was evidently more real to them than
Good, and they were more interested in eliminating heretics than in
preserving anything at all — as is quite clear from the language of
their 'official chronicler'.[23]

None the less the war might have dragged on for ever had it not

been for the foolish bravado of Raymond's principal ally, King
Peter of Aragon. Arriving in great style before Muret, he passed up
the opportunity to take the entrapped Simon without difficulty, and
tried to fight a battle out of the *chansons de geste*.[24] He was killed,
his forces panicked, and thousands were massacred. After Muret the
nobles of the South fought on, but they had no strength from which
to bluff or negotiate.[25]

Hope for the South seemed to dawn with a new generation of
leaders. Innocent III died in 1216, and the young Raymond VII,
son of Raymond VI of Toulouse, reconquered Languedoc amid
wild enthusiasm. Simon de Montfort's head was removed by a mis-
sile in 1217; and a few years later his son gave up the struggle and
headed for Paris, with the father's corpse sewn up in a cowhide.
These were false signs. The country was essentially exhausted, and
when Louis VIII led a new Crusade in 1226, it could not resist for
long. By the Treaty of Paris, 1229, Raymond agreed that his daughter and only heir was to marry the King's brother, so that Languedoc would pass to France; and from that point it was only a question
of 'mopping up.'

Heretic-hunting was an important part of this 'pacification', and
it is from this process that we have acquired much of our picture of
the heresy. The traditional procedure for pursuing heretics had
been that the local bishops followed up their suspicions, conducted
their own examinations, and sentenced. This the clergy in Languedoc would not do, partly because of corruption, partly because of
close involvement with the local society.[26] The only real answer was
to shift the power of inquisition from the local clergy to the Pope's
direct representatives. Finally this power was given, in 1233, to an
ideally suited organisation, the Dominicans, a newly founded order
of wandering friars, noted for their zeal and responsible only to the
Pope. This was the birth of what is commonly known as 'the Inquisition'.[27]

This historical sketch will help in understanding how the 'classic'
picture of the 'Cathar' heresy is affected by its origins. These origins
are, in general, (1) reports of the local conflicts between Church and
heretics before the Crusade, (2) the Registers of the Inquisition, (3)
tracts by the Catholic polemicists of the thirteenth and fourteenth
centuries, and (4) the 'Cathar texts'. From these sources a picture of
the heresy has emerged that is accepted by most writers, though not

by Pound; and I shall summarise it as it is stated by Jean Guiraud.

Guiraud takes it that, like their 'ancestors' the Manichaeans, the 'Cathars' were much concerned with the Problem of Evil. If God is good, why does He permit evils that do not contribute to any overall, much less to an individual, justice? The answer is that He did not create the world. Some 'Cathars' took the creator of the world to have been an evil god, equal in status to the good god; some held that he was a lesser god, and called him Satan. Satan was thought to have envied God his glory, and to have waged war against Him, with a number of angels. Many 'Cathars' believed that human souls were the spirits of these fallen angels, imprisoned by Satan in bodies. These souls transmigrated, so that they would be imprisoned in flesh until such time as they had completed their purgatory on earth. Having children, of course, just lengthened this purgatory for another soul. As for the Catholic Church's doctrines, the 'Cathars' believed that the God of the Old Testament — a mendacious work — was a devil, that Christ did not truly participate in the Divinity, that the Virgin Mary was one of the emanations of God, and that Christ was adopted, not begotten, by God.[28]

The heretics' ethics were based on this sense that the flesh was evil. The purpose of human life was to reunify souls imprisoned in human bodies with the spirit-world; that is, to end life in this world. If it were possible, the 'Cathars' would have liked the race to commit suicide. Human weakness being what it was, they contented themselves with individual efforts in that direction: with the *endura,* or fast to the death. For theological reasons they abstained from meat and other animal foods. They aspired to complete and perpetual chastity, as tending to shorten the life of the race. None the less generally they were extremely debauched, because they considered sexual promiscuity much less heinous than marriage — it created less offspring, made the sinful bond less permanent, and did not sanctify human ties with a family. The heretics condemned punishment, wars, and oaths.[29]

The *consolamentum* or initiation was the chief 'Cathar' rite. It took place after a spiritual preparation lasting a year; or, if the believer were near to death, as a kind of absolution. The believer, or *credens,* was received through this initiation into the class of priests, who were known as *perfecti.* These *perfecti* became wandering preachers, usually travelling in twos, and they enjoyed a high reputation for purity of life. The liturgy, ceremonial and hierarchy of the 'Cathar' church were very simple, and no fixed setting was thought necessary for its activities.[30]

Such are the doctrines with which the heretics of Languedoc have been credited; nothing could be further from Pound's conception. Thus reconstructed, it has been possible to find origins for this 'Catharism', in a line of descent stretching from the *echt* Manichaeism of the third century AD to the Bogomil and Patarin doctrines that existed continuously in Bulgaria and Bosnia-Herzegovina from the tenth to the fifteenth century. It is thought that the Bogomils had contact with northern Italy, whence their dualism spread to Languedoc.[31]

I believe that in fact such a picture bears almost no relation to a general aesthetic or ethic among the population of Languedoc in the eleventh and twelfth centuries, being a compound of fragmentary evidence grossly distorted by interested observers.

THE EVIDENCE FOR 'CATHARISM'

It seems fairly probable that 'Catharism' as accepted was concocted by the Church of the twelfth and thirteenth centuries. The Church observed various heretical symptoms, often ascetic in tone, scattered all over Europe over a long period of time. For reasons of its own psychology, which we shall look at, it regarded these as one huge interrelated web, manifestations of a common conspiracy and doctrine. When Languedoc and the surrounding territories became alienated from the Church, their underlying doctrines were automatically assimilated into this Great Web by the Church's theologians; the more easily because some features of the Languedocian heresy's ethos were easily mistaken, by men of a certain turn of mind, for asceticism. First, let us look at the kind of evidence that penetrated into the Church's consciousness, in so far as it has survived. Then we can see why and how it was converted into the monolith 'Catharism'.

The Italian historian Raffaello Morghen was probably the first to question the assumption that any heresy showing its head in Europe between the tenth century and the Crusade must be part of this monolith. He began with Adémar of Chabannes, who discovered

'Manichaeans' in the heretics of Aquitaine in 1018-28. Like the rest of Adémar's 'Manichaeans', these unfortunates seem to have professed a bundle of doctrines so individual that not one single thread runs continuously through them all. The heretics of Goslar, as Morghen observes at the end of his survey, were called 'Manichaean' because they refused to kill a chicken.[32] J. B. Russell took up the work of examining sources, and found that in most cases the doctrines of the heretics were totally individual or incompatible with 'Catharism', right up to the middle of the twelfth century. Sometimes they had been supposed 'Cathars' simply because scholars thought that this was the prevailing heresy: 'but', as Russell says, 'this is precisely what is questionable.'[23]

However, we then come to the 'heretic council' at Saint-Félix-de-Caraman, supposedly held in 1167; almost all scholars regard this as the turning-point after which the existence of 'Catharism' in the South cannot be doubted.[34]

The document recording this council was published in 1660 by one Guillaume Besse, who said that he took it from a manuscript of 1232, which is now lost. It gives the 'CHARTER OF NIQUINTA, Antipope of the Albigensian heretics, containing the Ordinations of the Bishops of his sect, made by him in Languedoc, communicated to me by the late M. Caseneuve, Prebend of the Chapter of the Church of St.-Etienne de Toulouse, in the year 1652'.[35] In a Latin which the most recent editor, Father Dondaine, calls 'half barbaric',[36] the Charter relates how 'Papa Niquinta' came to Saint-Félix where a 'magna multitudo hominum et mulierum Eccl. Tolosanae' had congregated to receive from him the consolamentum. Various men were elected bishops by their districts, and then 'Dominus Papa Niquinta' gave these men the consolamentum and ordained them. In his sermon he spoke of the seven Churches of Asia, mentioning the 'Eccl. Romanae, et Drogometiae et Melenguiae, et Bulgariae, et Dalmatiae', saying that they were established thus to eliminate administrative discord; and he laid down the demarcations of the Languedoc churches for the same purpose. The postscript of the Charter says that one 'Dominus Petrus Isarn' and one 'Petrus Pollanus' transcribed it in 1232.

Yves Dossat has shown that almost none of this holds water. The consolamentum is supposed to have elevated the believer to the rank of perfectus; at Saint-Félix the 'Pope' is shown giving it to bishops.

Father Dondaine has suggested that this shows the religion was undergoing a change at this point; but there is nothing in the text to support him. The travels of 'Pope' Niquinta and his conversion of Marc to absolutist dualism are confirmed by two texts, though one is likely to be derivative; but their dates disagree with those given by the Saint-Félix document, and they are unaware of any council at Saint-Félix. The heretics from the Val d'Aran are named incorrectly, and no other source shows that there were heretics in that area. Other sources show the heretics disagreeing over demarcations that were supposedly settled at Saint-Félix. The document is supposed to have been copied in 1232 by Peter Isarn, who is known to have been a high dignitary among the heretics—hence rather an unlikely scribe, and who in any case was burned in 1226. Dossat notes the barbarism of the language, which is supposed to fit the ignorance of the heretics; he points out that there were many notaries among the heretics, and calls the barbarism 'affected'. Finally, the *Ecclesia Melenguiae* arouses suspicion both because the Milinguians were unknown in mediaeval Europe and because they are known not to have been dualist. Dossat suggests that the author of the fake was Guillaume Besse, who had all the necessary facts within his reach and who in his time published at least two other forgeries.[37]

No other text of any kind mentions this 'council'; we may therefore assume that it did not take place.[38] But since some of the movements in it are corroborated from other sources, we might conclude with Dossat that the general picture of 'Cathar' development is not much altered. I conclude that, lacking this particular 'proof', the picture is altered, since all the other information comes through the late Catholic polemicists, who were reconstructing the past according to their own logic and needs.[39]

Armed with this famous Council at Saint-Félix-de-Caraman, even those scholars who are sceptical about the previous heresies take everything after mid-century to be 'Cathar'. Russell accepts that the heretics whom Evervinus fought against at Cologne in the 1140s were 'Cathars'. The reasons: that they claimed an ancient descent in 'Greece and other lands'; that they were vegetarians; that they baptised by the laying on of hands; and that they were divided into two grades, like the *perfecti* and *credentes* of the 'Cathars'.[40] All these supposed connections with the 'Cathars' are of the kind that the same scholar dismisses when he deals with earlier heretics. No one has yet traced an important dualist sect in Greece; all sects like to provide themselves with an ancient history, and all persecutors like to connect their victims with ancient evil. Vegetarianism (as Russell shows) goes along with the contemporary reformism both inside the Church and outside it.[41] The imposition of hands was part of the common fund of ritual on which all nascent sects drew; even at this period it was in use by the Church for reconciling heretics, having been regarded by St. Augustine 'and the mediaeval tradition' as in initiation.[42] And of course almost every religion divides itself into priesthood and believers.

With the 'anti-Cathar' sermons of Eckbert of Schönau there are inconsistencies; these are explained by saying that the sect developed, and had an 'inner circle' and an 'outer circle'.[43] This device is used with great freedom by the two great Catharologists, Jean Guiraud and Father Dondaine;[44] it allows the writer to fit obviously harmless beliefs in with the hydra he is pursuing. Russell adds a twist: that the 'inner circle' were watering down the doctrines that the weaker brethren would have been unable to stomach in their pure state. Similarly Father Dondaine: 'The Cathar doctors were very careful not to unveil completely those of their doctrinal errors which were most opposed to Catholic faith; the success of their preaching in Christian circles was at this price. This dissimulation is one of the saddest stains on mediaeval neo-manichaeism.'[45] This dissimulation, or the supposition of it, has also been of the greatest help to Father Dondaine in his ingenious reconstruction of the Cathar monolith from the confusion of the sources. But, as Morghen points out, it does not fit with the way in which heretics entered into public debate quite readily.[46] In fact Eckbert of Schönau's 'Cathars' used the Book of Moses, which the 'real' 'Cathars' are supposed to have detested; they rejected baptism on quite un-'Cathar' grounds; and they had a rite called 'making the body of Christ'—who was not, we are told, an important deity for the 'Cathars'. And Eckbert's descriptions of his heretics are probably falsified by a factor which runs through all of this: he knew and drew on St. Augustine's works about the original Manichaeans. The 'Catharism' of the four other pre-1167 cases is equally unlikely, but Russell generally supports it because they were so near in time to Saint-Félix.[47]

Christine Thouzellier has examined the heretical manifestations between the 'council of Saint-Félix' and the Albigensian Crusade. The assertions of Raymond V of Toulouse and the Catholic heresiologists are taken as read, though the heretics themselves do not say anything dualist in the public debating—with the exception of one final recantation at Le Puy in 1181. In thirty years of Catharism's 'fullest development', this evidence is not striking.[48] When Pope Alexander III sent Peter of Saint-Chrysogonus to find heretics in Languedoc in 1178, the legate, acting with the full support of the Pope and the nominal support of Raymond V and numerous barons, found only one heretic, but failed to get him to confess to dualism.[49]

The history of the Albigensian Crusade gives no hint of ascetic dualist doctrines of any kind, unless it be by the phrase 'those of Bulgaria' for the heretics; but 'Bulgar' had through the previous century become a standard expression for 'heretic'.[50] The Registers of the Inquisition, which begin from after the Crusade, give us over a period of many decades a few clear points of dualist doctrine: 'God is very good and in this world nothing is good, therefore He made nothing of what is in this world', according to the most coherent witness; and *Deus non fecit visibilia*, 'God did not make what is visible', is repeated hundreds of times.[51] But to back up these moments of clarity there are only innumerable inexplicable vaguenesses, assorted idiosyncrasies, and downright contradictions; in fact the number of clear anti-dualist remarks seems to be about equal to that of the clear dualist statements.[52] One can hardly wonder that this source of evidence, which might have been one of the most precious, is falsified, when the Inquisitors believed 'they had a knowledge of the heresy much deeper than that of those arraigned before them'.[53] They simply did not want to learn anything from their victim except where to find more victims. The flights, ambushes, and betrayals related in the testimonies should tell us about the 'Cathar' ethic in action; they tell us about the *consolamentum* and other rites, but there is no evidence at all of an ascetic way of life, unless we interpret thus the alleged frequent attacks on marriage.[54]

In the fragmentary evidence from all over Europe from before the period of the Albigensian Crusade, we can sometimes detect a common ascetic psychology, but we can detect no common theology, Manichaean or otherwise, and we can detect no sign whatever that the various heretics were connected in any way. We are dealing with local phenomena. In the quasi-independent evidence from Languedoc from the period of the Crusade and after, stemming from chroniclers and Inquisition witnesses, we can detect no generally shared theology, and no trace whatsoever of an ascetic psychology. By now the phenomenon appears to be general in Languedoc, but it does not in the least fit the classic picture of 'Catharism'. There remains the evidence from the Inquisitors and the other Church polemicists, who are the real source of this classic picture of the heresy in Languedoc.

THE INQUISITORS AND POLEMICISTS: WHY AND HOW THEY CREATED 'CATHARISM'

The Church was in a state of shock and reaction. Its very struggle for its own liberties over the centuries, as Gordon Leff has suggested, made it eventually appear 'as one more privileged body — a collector of taxes as well as the keeper of men's souls'.[55] Success within the Church became more a matter of administrative skill than of piety. Canon Law had developed and enshrined dogma and petty authority, and Innocent III, its greatest exponent, had finished centralising the great corporation on the foundations of this autonomous legal system.[56] When in the course of the Albigensian Crusade we see the great barons of Languedoc pleading for the return of their rights — *territorial* rights — before the Pope and his council, the Pope having unilaterally declared them open to any Christian conqueror, then we see the fruition of the struggles of a succession of militant popes for temporal arbitrage.[57] In the course of the Crusade, indulgences, pardons and anathemas were handled as purely political weapons.[58] The supreme temporal weapon, death (usually by burning) as a punishment for heresy, came to be permitted by the Church because Innocent III, disturbed by heresies in the territories where he intended to lay the foundations of the Church's temporal states, found a legal way of assimilating heresy to lese-majesty, which is surely the supreme incarnation of arbitrary authority.[59] As Manselli concludes, the Church had thus reached 'the anguishing conviction that heresy could not be vanquished in a free debate and by the power of truth, but that it must in the end be crushed by force.'[60]

By the end of the twelfth century one could say that the Church was in a state of 'dynamic conservatism': its desire to remain the same exceeded inertia, and it began to overreact, losing any sense of its own long-term best interests, which clearly lay in reform.[61] Monastic orders had been set up in former times as a valve for radicalism; new ones were not permitted now, and the Franciscan and Dominican orders quickly became embedded in administration.[62] The Inquisition was an instrument of overreaction. Its secrecy was a deliberate way of encouraging men to denounce their neighbours before they themselves could be denounced.[63] Terror of unbelievably harsh imprisonment, or of the stake, hung over all. The object of the Inquisitors—who were judge, prosecutor, and jury—was not to prove external acts, but to find internal heresy, which included failure to believe in any aspect of the Church's teaching or rituals.[64] The currents of devil-fear, arbitrariness, and sadism in this had always been present in mediaeval 'justice', particularly in its dealings with freaks and local heretics; but now they became an institutionalised and prominent part of the Church's life.

The hunting of heretics did not attract balanced men. St. Bernard was one of the earlier ones, and in his ethic pain seems to be more real than anything else: the pains of hell with which to terrify weaker brethren, and physical pains with which to castigate his own unruly flesh.[65] In the lives of Bishop Fulk of Toulouse, of St. Dominic, and of Innocent III, we see an intense self-discipline going along with the dedication to the rooting out of heresy; we see no trace of any delight in existence. The world is damned by human corruption, and these men are so appalled by the visible hand of the Devil in it that they can make no distinction between kinds of human behaviour except to group anything that appears in the least disobedient to Mother Church in the camp of the Evil One. For the 'official historian' of the Albigensian Crusade, as Dossat says,

Almost the whole of the South belongs to the side of Evil. In the first rank come the heretics, 'members of the Antichrist and firstborn of Satan', 'anchored in their malice', such as Theodoric, 'son of perdition and straw for the eternal fire' and Bernard de Simorre 'the famous heresiarch', with all of whom the Abbé des Vaux-de-Cernay disputed several times. One can add to them Bertran de Saissac, tutor of Viscount Trencavel, Pierre-Roger, lord of Cabaret, and Raimond, lord of Termes.[66]

This man rejoices when heretics are burned, and along with the other churchmen of the Crusade seems to show no interest in converting them.[67]

The 'Cathar church' is constructed to a considerable extent out of the fantasies of such men. Guibert de Nogent is used by modern historians as evidence for the *moeurs* of the Cathar heretics. Here is part of his testimony:

> They condemn marriage and propagation by intercourse.
> Clearly, wherever they are scattered over the Latin world, you may see men living with women without the name of husband and wife in such fashion that one man does not stay with one woman, each to each, but men are known to lie with men and women with women, for with them it is impious for men to go to women.
> They abstain from all food which is produced by sexual generation.
> They have their meetings in underground vaults or secret cobwebby places, without distinction of sex. After they have lighted candles, some loose woman lies down for all to watch, and, so it is said, uncovers her buttocks, and they present their candles to her from behind; and as soon as the candles are put out, they shout 'Chaos' from all sides, and everyone fornicates with whatever woman comes first to hand....
> If you review the heresies described by Augustine you will find this like none of them so much as that of the Manichaeans.[68]

Alain de Lille is another contemporary source of 'information'; he tells us that the 'Cathars' are so called 'because, it is said, they kiss the rears of a cat, in the semblance of which, they say, Lucifer appears to them.'[69]

The heretic-hunters were fanatical ascetics and often terrified of their own desires;[70] it is natural that one of the most fertile sources for their writings about heretics should have been gossip and fantasy about dark, perverted, underground sex. Guibert de Nogent's stories about the 'Cathars' have the same psychological quality as his stories about Jews and Moslems—unnatural lusts, sperm libations, and so on—in fact the churchmen's denunciations of the Templars, two centuries later, contain exactly the same kind of fantasies.[71]

The other most fertile source in the writers' imaginations was the idea of the International and Eternal Conspiracy. Morghen describes it as ' "heresy", considered as the immutable and eternal trap set up by the devil for the Church of God, coexisting with the Church herself and articulated in its most diverse manifestations right from its origin: a new Hydra. . . .'[72] All disobedience to the Church belongs to the same plot. The Inquisitor Moneta of Cremona published what Father Dondaine calls 'the most complete theological critique [of 'Catharism'] to have come out of the Catholic ranks'.[73] This is how he described Catharism:

The congregation of Cathars is not the Church of God, nor did it take its origin from the same source, but rather from the Pagans, or the Jews, or the Christian apostates. For there was a certain pagan, Pythagoras by name, who said that the souls of men entered into other bodies, that is to say of men or cattle, to which error many pagans agreed, and were called Pythagoreans, whom the Cathars . . . imitate; in this error were also certain other traitors, namely Zarden and Arphaxat, from whom all the Cathars, right through until this error, are derived, who said that the giver of the Law of Moses was the Prince of Darkness. There were also among the Jews the Sadducees, who denied the resurrection of their bodies; all the Cathars take their origin from them. There was a certain other person, Manes by name, who posited two principles and two creations and two natures, from whom certain people are called Manichaeans and certain of the Cathars took their principles from these. . . . There was also a certain person, Tatianus by name, after whom certain Tatians are called . . . whom the Cathars imitate. Likewise the Valentinians, after Valentinus, who said that Christ received nothing from the Virgin.[74]

The churchmen of the period before the Albigensian Crusade were faced with scattered perversities in various parts of Europe; these were mostly reactions against the splendour and mystification of the Church, and hence were often fundamentalist, reformist, and with ascetic tendencies.[75] The churchmen called them 'Manichaean' because they assimilated them to the Manichaeans attacked by St. Augustine; they constantly referred to Augustine for 'information' on their own contemporaries.[76] They called them 'Arian' because of the legendary heretics of the fourth century.[77] They called them 'Catharist' because of a celebrated canon of the Council of Nicea (AD 325) condemning Arianism.[78]

When the Inquisitors and polemicists of the period of the Crusade and after arrived on the scene, the 'identity' of the International Heresy was already established. Churchmen working in Languedoc in the early thirteenth century had only to read the works of their predecessors in Flanders or Germany a century before, and they knew exactly what they were dealing with: neo-Manichaeans. Inquisitors working in the North of Italy came across assorted reformist sects and put together their doctrines according to a mixture of gossip, fantasy, and what they had read about heretics, and everybody assumed that this was a True Description of the heresy as found at the other heart of the web, Languedoc. From there onwards the process was self-perpetuating. The Catholic polemicists 'read each others' books' to an extraordinary degree. Raynier Sacchoni (who published a condensed version of a heretic text that appears to tally with the doctrines in the 'Book of the Two Principles') and Moneta of Cremona are the two most 'authoritative' sources on 'Cathar' doctrines. If we look for corroboration of their information, we find that they are supported on many points by a crowd of Catholic polemicists writing all through the thirteenth century and the next. But nobody bothers to reproduce the texts of these polemicists for information on the 'Cathars', since they do nothing but repeat the information of Sacchoni and Moneta.[79] Inquisitors copied and recopied Sacchoni into their source-books.[80] We read that such-and-such an Inquisitor was 'learned in heresy'—having read the works of his fellow-churchmen.[81] Like the Inquisitors at Carcassonne, they knew all about the heretics before ever meeting one. From the centre of all this mutual misinformation comes the 'Book of the Two Principles'. It may be a genuine text, though the period was very productive of pious forgeries; but even if it is, there is clear evidence that it was not known to heretics beyond a restricted circle.[82] It seems probable that on such sparse and doubtful bases the whole impressive edifice of Inquisitorial heresiology was built.

HOW IT MAY HAVE BEEN IN LANGUEDOC

First, let us establish a distinction with the aid of Father Dondaine:

The error of the Cathars was to conceive of Evil as a reality opposed to Good, and not as a defect in Good; it therefore has a cause, and is anterior to man and the world. Sin was before us and corrupted everything, and man and nature are subject to its law. The soul, a divine spark, originally good, can only escape the empire of Sin by the total rejection of the sensible world.[83]

That is the psychological basis of all dualist asceticism, translated into theology. It is rigorously to be distinguished from an ideal of poverty as a means of keeping the faculties uncluttered. This ideal is the poverty of the Zen priests or of St. Francis, and it comes from a belief that the beauty or 'innerness' of the given universe is God's. Father Dondaine describes such a Christian view: 'Creation is not fundamentally bad, it is at the service of man to help him return to God; to condemn it would be to insult its Creator.' To have an intuition of this view, he says, we should consider St. Francis of Assisi, who was contemporary with the Albigensian Crusade: his way of life was 'ascetic', but we can feel the 'vibration of his soul before the manifest beauty of Creation'.[84]

St. Francis was not a dualist. He practised poverty, but it was not a symptom of a psychology that made Evil more real than Good, and demanded that the body and the world be flagellated and nullified as a manifestation of the Devil. To borrow Pound's distinction about another man, 'He believes that "*la povertà*" is holy, but does NOT believe that "*la miseria*" need be perpetuated. That is a lesson to the loose users of words.'[85]

It is fairly well established that the leaders of the sect that dominated in Languedoc practised poverty.[86] It is also perfectly clear that they inculcated in the people who followed and protected them no sense that wealth was evil, that the body was evil, that misery was a road to salvation.[87] Hence there is every reason to suppose that they practised poverty simply as a way of keeping the senses clear.

It is perfectly clear on the other hand, from all their writings and their actions, that the men who dominated in the Church's struggle against them believed wholly in the wickedness of this world. They fit Father Dondaine's description of 'radical pessimists' to the letter, whatever may have been their theological lip-service to the idea that the Creation is not evil. And this is what renders them quite incapable of making the distinction between 'holy poverty' as a hygiene of the faculties, and misery as a virtue. They cannot conceive of the beauty of the given world; how can they conceive that certain disciplines may help one to perceive it? To them, authority, fear, and punishment are the Real; what rebels against these is automatically Evil, and as black as the vilest devils of hell.[88]

The obstinacy of the people of Languedoc came largely from hatred of the foreigner. 'The Church and the French' was the usual Southern phrase for the crusaders. These latter had no local responsibility; for those who could not understand their hatred of the evil heresy, they were merely robbers; they spoke a foreign language, tried to impose French law because they could not understand the written law of the South, and, like the Manchus in nineteenth-century China, they forbade intermarriage with the native women. The hatred of the whole South for them was so intense that Simon could not be sure of any place where he was not actually present at the time, and found it extremely difficult to get capable men to withstand the Southerners' hatred and garrison his castles, so that he had to forbid his fellow-adventurers from returning to France without his permission.[89] Simon returned this hatred: when it seemed that he would lose Toulouse once more, he tried to burn it to the ground rather than let the inhabitants triumph.[90]

There is no sign in Languedoc of the social psychology that usually accompanied messianic movements for holy misery in the Middle Ages; social cohesion seems to have been high.[91] Nor is there any sign of revulsion for worldly splendour among the nobles or *bourgeois,* many of whom associated openly with heretics.[92] 'Paratge', the war-cry of the South, is almost identical with Bertran de Born's ethos of 'high-lineage-expressed-in-noble-action', than which nothing could be less ascetic; in the middle of that war, when they have a free moment, it is of 'arms and love and gifts' that the Southern barons talk.[93] Between these pleasure-lovers and the heretics there seems to have been complete respect. Between the often corrupt and pleasure-loving clergy and the heretics there seems to have been complete toleration.[94] Again, a large and detailed body of evidence about the behaviour of the heretics and their protectors comes from the two authors of the *Chanson de la Croisade Albigeoise* — both professing Catholics, one for, one against the Crusade, but both unimpeachable witnesses;[95] yet not once in their thousands of lines do they speak of such theological monstrosities as the Inquisition polemicists would have us believe in. Thus we can say that neither in the documented behaviour of the people, nor in the reactions of nobles, clergy, or balanced chroniclers, is there any sign of heresies that to the Middle Ages were immensely peculiar and fascinating: two gods, desire for extinction of the race, murky rituals, and the like. It seems more probable that the dominant ethic of the South was the one that is visible in its cultural products, troubadour lyrics, and Romanesque churches, where physical beauty is a manifestation of spiritual strength.

MONTSÉGUR AND POUND'S VIEW OF THE CULT IN 'PROVENCE'

Pound believed that a celebratory cult was 'behind' the troubadours, and Montségur is the first important element in the myth in which he embodied this belief. Montségur is a huge and anonymous-looking stone building at the top of a steep and isolated peak in the lower Pyrenees. According to the Registers of the Inquisition, it was rebuilt specifically for use as a heretic centre,[96] and in the desperate period after the treaty of Meaux it harboured heretics who helped Raymond of Toulouse's seneschal to massacre a group of Inquisitors.[97] When Raymond's revolt against France had failed, a royal army laid seige to Montségur. The seige lasted many months, until the 1st or 2nd of March 1244; when the 'castle' fell some 210 heretics refused to repent and were burned at the nearby town of Bram.[98]

The Registers of the Inquisition tell us only that Montségur was a centre of communication for the heretics; the comings and goings, even during the siege, seem to have been very frequent. We might conclude that it had no particular spiritual importance. After all, the heretics had other places of refuge. Throughout this period, the castles of Aguilar, Fenouillet, Peyrepertuse, and Quéribus, at least, were held by nobles who were openly heretical. These places, dominating great sweeps of the dry Corbières, look almost as impregnable now as they must have in the thirteenth century; to reduce the last three of them took the forces of France fifteen years after Montségur had capitulated.[99]

But Fernand Niel has demonstrated that Montségur was not an ordinary castle at all. As a tourist and an alpinist he became interested in the problems of the siege of Montségur, and from there he proceeded to the archaeology of the place.[100] He discovered that, aside from the advantages of its situation, it is militarily useless; it owed its long survival in the siege chiefly to human factors. He pointed out that in 1204, when the château was rebuilt, the heretics did not need a refuge, and had no reason to expect such a need. Further, Montségur, which is certainly the work of master craftsmen,[101] has no defensive or stylistic features in common with any other castle of Languedoc or Roussillon. Unlike almost any other mediaeval castle, it has not one but two main gates, each of which is far too wide and has no defensive structures. No stone or permanent fireproof buildings were constructed inside the main wall. The castle leaves unnecessary standing-ground on its peak for attackers, and incorporates in its wall a rock on which one could climb to within ten feet of the parapet. No permanent communication, defensible or otherwise, was provided between the 'keep' and the main enclosure; what look like archery-slits in the 'keep', covering the enclosure, are so placed as to cover nothing. The 'keep' itself has not living room for more than three or four persons. From archaeological evidence, it seems that the original construction had no water tank. Almost uniquely for a stone building of this period, no use was made of previous buildings on the site.[102]

The obvious deduction is that Montségur was some kind of temple, and Niel has been able to confirm this in an unexpected manner. In his many books and articles published since 1954, he has demonstrated that lines between the various points of the building are aligned accurately with the sun at sunrise, not only at the solstices and equinoxes, but at all the Zodiac dates between them.[103] Four parallel lines between major points in the structure — corners, mid-points of walls, and so on — align with sunrise at the winter solstice alone. Other points align exactly with the points of the compass; one of the walls incorporates a bend of six degrees to make this possible. The complexity of the whole structure, and the fact that its shape is not dictated by the terrain but rather goes against it, rule out any possibility that the alignments are accidental or a passing whim of the builders. There is no trace of any apparatus designed to let people observe the sunrise along these alignments; perhaps if there had been, the Church would have got wind of the proceedings. Presumably, most of the alignments were made just to give the building a permanently sacred character. But one central rite was possible: in the 'keep' itself, a very few people could observe the sun-rise at the summer solstice as it struck through the narrow slits in the masonry.

Niel has found no sun-worship among the heretics: 'On the contrary, sometimes it seems as if the Cathars held the sun and the moon to be the work of the devil. We would need, for example, to find a text implying an obligation for them to pray facing the sun at dawn. As far as we know, nothing of this kind has been found.'[104] He refers to the theology of Manes, with its sun-cult; but he has to admit that the name of Manes is mentioned by no known document in connection with the 'Provencal' heresies.[105] The building is there; it was the centre of an intense non-Catholic religious activity; its construction is laboriously and ingeniously shaped to involve it with the life of the sun. No theory so far propounded about the heretics will explain these facts; Manes will not do, first because his name is notably absent from contemporary texts, and second because the people of this Southern culture were, as Pound said, not 'openly famed as ascetics'.[106] Montségur is therefore a 'gristly fact'[107] which Pound can legitimately take into his myth of the 'Provencal' cult.

THE DEVELOPMENT OF POUND'S MYTH

Pound's myth always assumed something 'behind' the troubadours. Let us follow this myth chronologically as it grew. Through most of its development Pound was struggling with two opposing approaches. First was the view which was easiest: that these poets in 'Provence' and in Tuscany were writing secrets into their works in the form of A = B, or 'the Lady' really means 'the Sect', and so on. This view was easiest because it meant that one only had to explain the reasons for the secrecy, the mechanism of it, and the nature of the sect it hid. The other view was far more difficult, but was more natural to Pound's temperament: that the *psychology* of the poetry represented a world-view which could quite naturally be acted out in the form of a ritual; so that the terms of the poetry were not code-words, but represented actual specific personal situations — 'my lady's face radiates beauty' meant exactly that — yet they both pointed to a world-view and reflected the nature of a secret ritual. We can call the first view the 'code-book for Nirvana', and the second 'natural esotericism'; for the first you just have to know the codes and you have penetrated the whole secret, but for the second you have to understand, aesthetically and psychologically, the relation between personal situation, world-view, and ritual. This understanding requires the highest general human wisdom.[108]

Pound tackled the 'code-book' view in one of his very earliest writing. In 1906 he reviewed *Le Secret des Troubadours* by Péladan, which described 'four centuries of troubadours singing allegories in praise of a mystic extra-church philosophy or religion, practiced by the Albigensians'.[109] He was rightly sceptical — *Le Secret* is full of specious etymologising, and the results of its literal allegories are often farcical. But the aesthetic that Péladan saw in the troubadours was one of 'the revelation of the divine in beauty' (to borrow the phrase of Zielinski, whom Pound read much later), and Péladan made the mediaeval artist into a kind of alternative priest *through his art;* ideas which must have set Pound thinking.[110]

As is well known, G. R. S. Mead was a strong influence on Pound when he wrote 'Psychology and Troubadours' in 1912.[111] Mead was a friend of Yeats, like Pound, and Yeats in fact had met Péladan; Péladan called himself a Magus, and was a follower of the Rosicrucian Eliphas Levi; to Yeats, 'the tree of the [Hermetic] "tradition" triumphed in Rosicrucianism.'[112] Pound's own reading of Péladan and his contact with Mead and Yeats were behind 'Psychology and Troubadours', a highly important synthesis which contains most of Pound's mature thought on the troubadour esotericism. This is its structure:

The arts must 'interpret'; they must interpret something hidden to the wider public, which at this stage Pound figures as the 'vital universe', or the 'universe of fluid force'. We find this 'interpreted' in the poetry of the difficult school, from Arnaut Daniel to Dante; in particular, we find certain obscurities in Arnaut which suggest a sect. Pound does not elaborate, but the ' "lady" ' (Pound uses inverted commas) who 'made me a shield, extending over me her fair mantle of indigo, so that the slanderers might not see this' is clearly for him either a physical lady initiating the poet into a mystery, or a personification of a sect doing so.[113] The sect, like the poetry, was probably based on the two poles of sex and the heightened awareness that the poet reaches when he makes the effort towards bridging them. This on the one hand is reflected in various polarities in the

cosmic order; and on the other hand was at the time of the troubadours reflected in a sexual rite.[114] In the twelfth and thirteenth centuries the officially accepted cult of the Virgin Mary was often expressed by the poets in ways that recall worship of 'Our Lady of
Cyprus' — Venus. This gives a hint of the origin of the sect: a paganism inherited from Greece in 'Provence' because 'Provence was less
disturbed than the rest of Europe by invasion from the North in the
darker ages.'[115] We can see the ecstatic origins in the way that 'the
birth of Provençal song hovers about the Pagan rites of May Day';
we can suppose that such a cult 'of orgy and of ecstasy' declines
when a neophyte who is not properly prepared is admitted.[116] This is
the synthesis that Pound had already achieved in 1912.

It was obviously the contact with Mead's circle, and their interest
in neo-Platonism, *phantastika,* immanences, and the world of spirit
in general which freed Pound from mere mechanism and allowed
him to speak of something he 'knew', despite the lack of proof: that
the troubadour poetry contained at times a religious awareness.
Péladan perhaps gave him the idea of an esotericism and a sect. The
'evidence' of paganism in Southern Gaul probably came from the
theories of Fauriel, of whom Pound no doubt heard at college; that
of the connection with May Day festivals certainly came from a famous article published by Gaston Paris in 1891-92, either directly or
through Pound's teachers.[117] But for Pound the real evidence was
the 'weight' of the troubadours' words, which few people had been
able to evaluate as precisely as he, and which no one before him had
collocated with all these other elements.

The esotericism of the 'Psychology' theory is what I have called
'natural'; it does not particularly depend on knowing the key to
code-words or phrases in the troubadours. But in the late twenties
Pound came up against another representative of the 'code-book'
variety, and it temporarily led him astray. He was at this time devot-
ing an intense concentration to examining Cavalcanti's terms,
which he believed to be precise and profound both in their psychology and in their use of mediaeval philosophy.[118] In 1928 Luigi Valli
published a book called *Il Linguaggio Segreto di Dante,* which
'proved' that Dante and his friends were writing into their poems a
cipher concerning Manichaeist 'secret conspiracies, mystic brother-
hoods', and so on.[119] Pound devoted a great deal of thought to it.

Valli's book was derived from a work by Dante Gabriel Rossetti, published in 1840 and called *Il mistero dell' amor platonico nel Medioevo*. Rossetti believed that the *Fedeli d'amore*, the 'loyal servants of love' as these Tuscan poets called themselves, were adepts of a secret doctrine which they referred to variously as 'Rosa', 'Beatrice', 'Giovanna', 'Lagia', 'Selvaggia', and so on, by an obvious trick: these are all supposed to be the names of their ladies, but the ladies are all identical. Rossetti, as Valli says, came to consider the *Fedeli d'amore* as 'the continuers of a secret Pythagorean worship of an initiatory Wisdom, and haters of the Church and its doctrine'.[120]

Rossetti of course was a prime mover behind a tradition of culture that had been very important to Pound as a young poet. Further, he was a Rosicrucian and must have been mentioned in Mead's circle. Péladan refers to *Il mistero dell' amor platonico*, as does in fact Remy de Gourmont.[121] Pound in 1942 wrote that a reprint of this book 'would be useful'; but already in 1928 Valli wrote that it was very rare, and it is possible that Pound never read it.[122] Rossetti had another descendant, called Eugène Aroux, who published *Dante, hérétique, révolutionnaire et socialiste* in 1854, proving what its title suggests; as well as a Dante Dictionary in 1856, according to which of course the 'Whore of Babylon' in Dante is the Roman Church, and the idea of the Albigensians is 'present everywhere' in the *Divine Comedy*.[123] Rossetti was anti-Church and Aroux was pro-Church, but the method was the same; however, it is unlikely that Pound read Aroux.[124]

Pound tackled this Rossetti-inspired tradition, as it surfaced in Valli, in his famous essay 'Cavalcanti'.[125] He was sympathetic; Valli had provoked useful thought. But Valli was wrong. He had tried to suggest Cavalcanti's poetry was full of code-messages; but Pound pointed out that the *Donna mi prega* was a masterpiece of clear exposition, not a maze of dark corners. For Valli, the 'Lady' was the sect, but even conceding that possibility, Pound could see no secret in what Cavalcanti was saying to the lady. What technical and unorthodox terms might be there, were in no way coloured with the kind of 'violent and dangerous heresy' that Valli perceived, which in any case was nowhere near so strong in Cavalcanti's period as Valli suggested.[126] Cavalcanti's commentator Egidio Colonna, Pound went on, was a highly orthodox Thomist, yet he appears to have suspected nothing. Valli postulated a dualist and ascetic sect, but Colonna brought Ovid into his exegesis. Further, Cavalcanti was not hiding his lack of orthodoxy, but blasphemed openly. If we tried to imagine exactly what kind of mysticism was behind these poets, we had to remember that 'neither Frederick II nor Cavalcanti were openly famed as ascetics.'[127] Rather, 'perhaps Guido was enamoured as Dante has remarked of a certain Madonna Primavera [Lady Spring], who, as Dante does not remark, had set the dance in Langue d'Oc and in Lemosi.'[128]

But though Pound throws out Valli's code he does not throw out the idea of a code. He offers his own:

Arnaut would be perhaps better ground for him than Guido. What for example is 'Mantle of Indigo'? Is 'doma', in 'cils de doma', an equivalent to the Italian word *domma,* meaning dogma?

If Arnaut says 'I love her more than god does her of the dogma', does he speak of a secret doctrine more precious to its followers than the orthodox? Does the illegible 'di noigandres' boggle a Greek 'ennoia' or 'dianoia'? At least it is open ground, and if Valli chose to assert these things no one could bring proof against him.[129]

The 'mantle of indigo' suggestion is repeated from 'Psychology and Troubadours', where it seems to signify reception into a sect (Pound talks of entering a visionary castle); and the *cils de doma* suggestion is clearly explained here simply as a reference to a secret doctrine. The *di noigandres* suggestion must be explained by reference to mediaeval philosophy.[130] Obviously Pound has fallen into the trap of the code-book.

But Pound very quickly got himself out of this trap; in the article 'Terra Italica' of 1931-32 he returned to the fundamental structure of his 'Psychology and Troubadours' synthesis, this time with a knowledge of mediaeval philosophy and of religious anthropology to back it up. This essay can be taken as the shape of his whole myth of the 'Provencal' cult in his later years.

As before, the psychological shape of the troubadour love-situation was genuine and lived, but it was reflected in a world-view and in a central religious rite. This rite was the one that had given 'the light of Eleusis'.[131] Pound's idea of the rite at Eleusis, one of the main centres of Greek religious life, was obviously taken from Cornford and Harrison and the other scholars who had rewritten the history of Greek religion in the wake of the Frazerian revolution.[132] In this rite, they held, a priest and a priestess accomplished a sexual act in mimetic representation of the annual refertilisation of the seed in the enriched soil.[133] In 'Terra Italica' Pound does not elaborate as he did earlier on how this cult might have reached 'Provence', but we can refer to his *Guide to Kulchur* of 1938 for an explanation:

Civilization went on. I reiterate that the cultural level is the determinant. Civilization had been in Italy. It had hung on in Provence and the Exarchate after Romulus Augustulus.
A conspiracy of intelligence outlasted the hash of the political map. Avicenna, Scotus Erigena in Provence, Grosseteste in Lincoln . . . .[134]

Pound is certainly right that Roman civilisation remained undisturbed in Provence longer than elsewhere, though that only takes us as far as about AD 536;[135] we can cite the influence of Roman remains on the architecture of the area, and point out that the first Christian church in France was established in the area of Languedoc before the Roman civilisation was well out of there, but a continuity is on the face of it unlikely.[136] However, it is quite clear from the texts of this period in Pound that we have already cited that he is thinking of a sect whose leadership was tiny in number.[137]

Both he and Valli, he says, have been groping in the dark.[138] The solution is not in a code but a simple psychological fact that has endless reverberations in rite and in philosophy: that the sexual phenomenon is a source of wisdom and a source of understanding of the world. He takes this key from Eduardo Tinto:

'Paganism, which at the base of its cosmogonic philosophy set the sexual phenomena whereby Life perpetuates itself mysteriously throughout the universe, not only did not disdain the erotic factor in its religious institutions but celebrated and exalted it, precisely because it encountered in it the marvellous vital principle infused by invisible Divinity into manifest nature'.[139]

We can apply this to the rites in the following manner:

'and it was natural that the woman should have in the various rites the feminine role that holy nature had given her'.[140]

In coitu inluminatio;[141] the rite was love-making and the result was illumination. 'For certain people the *pecten cteis* is the gate of wisdom':[142] the rite exists in the lives of some people in that for them all understanding comes from the female genitals, or a ritual enactment of contact with them.[143]

Now as far as the troubadours are concerned, 'the cult of Eleusis will explain not only general phenomena but particular beauties in Arnaut Daniel or in Guido Cavalcanti.'[144] This is because the ritual is not hidden as a code in their works but is reflected in their psychology. Their psychology is explained in 'Psychology and Troubadours': the lady is a *mantram,* the equivalent of a goddess; she is the source of all wisdom. This is the view of the Provençal lyric that I have expounded in an earlier chapter. In particular, as I have explained, already by the time of Arnaut Daniel the lady is being figured as the source of light-as-wisdom, which is the central philosophical metaphor of the whole *Duecento* period in Italy. This is the explanation that Pound means of the 'beauties' that he himself has already picked up: the lady as a vision bringing peace ('I've both my eyes cankered when they're not looking at her'), and as an ecstatic vision (*e quel remir*), and of sunlight falling like rain as a holy illumination.[145]

The lady has a very precise philosophical function as the Lady Sapientia in a whole body of mediaeval writing behind these poets. She is the 'active intellect' that pours light into the 'passive intellect', which is shared by all men; which is why Pound says that the cult of Eleusis 'will also shed a good deal of light on various passages of theology or of natural philosophy re the active and passive intellect (*possibile intelletto,* etc.).'[146] This concept of course is very important in Cavalcanti. Pound further remarks, much later, that familiarity with the idea of Philosophy as a woman 'would have saved several barrels of speculation re Dante's visions'[147] — because it can be applied both to religious anthropology and to personal sexual relations.

The mediaeval philosophers in fact themselves applied it to human sexuality, no doubt both consciously and otherwise. The fundamental idea is that activating wisdom is a divine irradiating force which is female; and that its relation to activatable wisdom is always that of lady to lover.[148] It follows that, as Alexander of Aphrodisias believed, our 'suprasensible knowledge' comes about 'by the *copulatio* of the possible and the active intellect'.[149] There is a parallel among the early Fathers in the union of Sophia with Logos, which Peter Dronke calls 'the christianized equivalent of the

Neoplatonic union of Nous and Anima Mundi, of the divine Mind
with "the soul at its divinest" (Plotinus, Enn. III. 5. 2). This became
a favourite interpretation applied to the Song of Songs, which was
often read as the mystic marriage of Nous and Anima Mundi.'[150]

The Lady receives Wisdom from God; the lover receives Wisdom
from the Lady. The troubadours saw the Lady as the source of all
wisdom, and Arnaut already saw this wisdom as the universal 'pour-
ing light'. Hence it was natural that Pound should see 'behind' the
troubadours a rite of mystic marriage. This rite would be a parallel
to the rites of fertilisation which Frazerian anthropology was finding
all over the world: the sun is the source of life, the earth receives and
is fertilised, and the priest and priestess yearly enact a mystical representation of this as love-making. And it was natural that Pound
should place this rite at Montségur.

When he published Canto XXIII, in 1928, Pound had not apparently formulated the rite, but Montségur was already the centre of a
civilisation as Troy had been:

> And went after it all to Mount Segur,
>   after the end of all things,
> And they hadn't even left the stair,
> And Simone [de Montfort] was dead by that time,
> And they called us the Manichaeans
> Wotever the hellsarse that is.
>
> And that was when Troy was down, all right,
>   superbo Ilion.... [151]

But by 1919 Pound had already decided that Montsegur was a sun-
temple; and in 1947, seven years before Fernand Niel's findings
were made known, Pound had written of sun-rites in Canto LXXVI.
In an elegaic tone he recalled from the depths of his memory (*dove
sta memoria*) a certain spectacular sunburst, and with it a friend's
remark about the way Mussolini's economic structure would survive
the wreckage of Italy. Then a throng of nymphs, goddesses, and
Pound-beatified women enters the poem, and Pound asks why this
sudden vision:

> that they suddenly stand in my room here
>   between me and the olive tree
>   or nel clivo ed al triedro?

and answered: the sun in his great periplum
leads in his fleet here
            sotto le nostre scoglie
under our craggy cliffs
            alevel their mast-tops
            Sigismundo by the Aurelia to Genova
                by la vecchia sotto S. Pantaleone
Cunizza qua al triedro,
e la scalza, and she who said: I still have the mould,
and the rain fell all the night long at Ussel
cette mauvaiseh venggg blew over Tolosa
and in Mt Segur there is wind space and rain space
            no more an altar to Mithras

from il triedro to the Castellaro
            the olives grey over grey holding walls
and their leaves turn under Scirocco

            la scalza 'Io son' la luna
            and they have broken my house'

the huntress in broken plaster keeps watch no longer[152]

Most of this geography is in Italy, but Montségur is woven into it.
'Here', whether in Italy or in Languedoc, 'the sun in his great periplum / leads in his fleet': the life of the sun for men is a series of encounters making possible other encounters, a *periplous,* not a fore-
known course on a drawing-board.[153] According to Niel, the sun's
arrival at Montségur at the two solstices is a major event. At the
winter solstice, Mithras's birthday, the building is in 'overall' align-
ment with the sun's rays at sunrise; at the summer solstice, sunrise is
pinpointed by the 'archery' slits in the 'keep'.[154] In Egyptian mythology, Anubis presided at the two solstitial points, and two jackals, living images of the god, were supposed to guard the tropics along
which the sun rises to the north or descends towards the south. So in
Canto XCII Anubis guards Montségur:

And from this Mount were blown
                            seed
[. . .]
Ra-Set in her barge now

> over deep sapphire
> but the child played under wave . . .
>   e piove d'amor
>   in nui
>   a great river, the ghosts dipping in crystal
> & to Pinella. . . .
> But 'Her love' sd / Hewlett
>   'like a cage hath bars
> that break my head, seeking to touch the stars.'
> To another the rain fell as of silver.
>   La Luna Regina.
> Not gold as in Ecbatan
> O Anubis, guard this portal
>   as the cellula, Mont Ségur.
> Sanctus
>   that no blood sully this altar
> ex aquis nata
>   τά ἐκ τῶν ὑδάτων γενόμενα
> 'in questa lumera appresso'
>   Folquet, nel terzo cielo.
> 'And if I see her not,
>   no sight is worth the beauty of my thought.'[155]

The rite is a rite of pouring and fertilising light: *E' piove / gioco d'amore in nui,* 'it is raining the joy of love on us', is sung by the two peasant girls in Cavalcanti's ballad. At Ecbatan, as Pound wrote in Canto IV, 'upon the gilded tower'

Lay the god's bride, lay ever, waiting the golden rain[156]

We should expect the goddess of a rite of copulation to be Venus, and Pound refers to her with *ex aquis nata / ta ek ton hudaton genomena,* 'wave-born', as in Botticelli's painting.[157] But in the passages surrounding Montségur in the later Cantos, Pound fuses ecstatic copulation with its opposite, virginity. 'Golden rain' is obviously the sun's light, but here 'To another the rain fell as of silver', the light of the moon — 'La Luna Regina'. Pound asks 'that no blood sully this altar'; it is obviously the altar of Diana, who appeared as 'la scalza' in one of the other landscapes associated with Montségur.[158] There she said

> 'Io son' la luna [I am the moon]
> and they have broken my house'

and Pound said

> the huntress in broken plaster keeps watch no longer

Yet a few lines earlier she had been placed right next to Cunizza, who in Dante and in Pound is another incarnation of Venus. Cunizza appears again in this second passage, by association with Folquet de Marseille, and by direct quotation a few lines further on.[159] The universal rite of regeneration seems to have been modified in accordance with his idea of the troubadour ethic by Pound, who had always believed that the sexual impulse must be controlled and channelled, and that 'there is some proportion between the fine thing held in the mind, and the inferior thing ready for instant consumption.'[160] The rite must not be profaned by misuse; this is the whole theme of the troubadours. Everything that Pound wrote about them can be summed up in the lines from Bernart de Ventadorn,

> 'And if I see her not,
>   no sight is worth the beauty of my thought.'

IN CONCLUSION

One can now sum up the reasons why Pound chose Provence, and why Provence stayed with him when Camoens and Lope de Vega disappeared. First of course is the tone of the Provençal sexuality. 'The necessary restraint'[161] is an important phrase with Pound's troubadours. Love-making is at the centre of his Provence, but it is the opposite of dissipated. Throughout, Pound comes back to the idea that the troubadour ethos was a keeping back of the sexual impulse until the point when it might be released with maximum effect, which would reach to mental and even spiritual planes. Ritual unchastity is maximum energy under maximum directing control. One must have the courage not to deny the energy, and to be in contact with the great human and chthonic forces, like William IX of Aquitaine in his battles with elemental 'cunt'; but one must direct them, never floating like the Freudian on the wave of circumstance. Pound probably seemed very American, of the Pennsylvanian *grand siècle,* to some of the orgiasts and fellow-artists in the Paris 1920s; this vein of chastity was suited to the Pre-Raphaelite approach to the troubadours that he had inherited, and though it faded, it never ceased to make Pound feel that sex was the chiefest of the treasures in relation to which one must always be 'at a kind of moral attention', in Fitzgerald's phrase. So the emparadised troubadour in the later Cantos not infrequently resembles a monk, quietly celebrating the unreachable, the 'fine thing held in the mind', an altar higher than any transient pleasure:

> Alas, and what are my eyes doing to me,
> for they do not see what I wish. [162]

Pound's character made him insist that the individual could have a powerful and durable effect on his surroundings by putting the clearly felt impulse into operation as directly as possible; hence the early identification with the bull-like aspects of Bertran de Born. So his strongest emotions were always with feudal periods of history: Confucian China, the Italy of Sigismondo Malatesta, and the Aquitainian and Plantagenet dynasties. He defended mediaeval feudalism on the grounds that the obligations between a responsible lord and his people were mutual; [163] but it was still a question of the untrammelled, independent lord's personal sense of his responsibility, even if (perhaps) reinforced by collective expectations. Pound was aware of the possible sufferings at the bottom end of the scale, and after the First World War, for instance, he began to realise what the high chivalric vision of Bertran de Born had missed out. But he was not interested in democracy; for him the collective will gave rise to a political expression which was the ultimate degradation of language, permitting the highest level of deceit and exploitation, and was also (perhaps more importantly) a cushion between the maximum directed energy of the sensitive ruler and its efficient use. The Confucian ruler listened to vibrations, not to votes. In Provence, his grand exemplum of the efficient use of this personal energy was the influence of the dynasty of Aquitaine. Begun by the 'complete man' William IX, radiating out, picked up within his own family and reradiated by Eleanor his granddaughter, flowering in the great trou-

badours of Bernart de Ventadorn's period and crossing by its own
impetus (though harried at its source by the forces of the Capetian
dynasty and of Rome) into Italy—it was finally renewed there by
Sordello and his lesser colleagues, and went on via Cavalcanti to
feed the great stream of Dante, in which it contributed to a cultural
level of world significance. All this is a myth of the direct influential
(and feudal) action of the sage-ruler, fertilising, as I have said, on
sexual, cultural, and economic planes.[164]

Pound's sage cultivates silence, or listening to 'the inarticulate
heart's tone';[165] which is what the artist also does, since he has only
his insides to consult, and no one can tell him what is 'right' in his
work. As I have argued, 'in this sense, art is private.'[166] Periods of
patronage by feudal rulers were, for Pound, periods of intense devotion to craft, but not of aesthetic discussion. Arnaut Daniel achieved
his level of excellence by listening to the products of his compeers, to
'the tone of things',[167] and to his heart; the treatises on the methodology of courtly-love-lyric-writing came later. Because art does not
consist of the 'extra ingredient' but merely of an extremely clear
reflection in some form of a pre-existing state, whether internal or
external, the artist who can focus his perception on the supra-
human order becomes a celebrant of that order and thus a priest;
and so the lark and its enveloping light in Bernart de Ventadorn
become one of the epiphanies in Pound's Paradiso. Woman is in
Pound's troubadours both the 'magnet' that focuses the troubadour's perception on the divine order, and a pre-eminent example
of that order; and thus we return to the 'cult of orgy and of ecstasy'
that Pound implies behind the whole troubadour culture.

It is typical of the Pound ideogram that it returns eventually to its
starting-point. By the time of his maturity he had built up his picture of Provence into a giant ideogram, constantly chewing over it
and finding new parallels and details. An ideogram in his conception is like a multiple metaphor, and we could state some aspects of
the Provence ideogram simply like this:

<pre>
                : lady = saint : Virgin
                : lady = Eleusinian hierophant : priestess
troubadour   : light of nature = Mithraists : sun
                : house of Aquitaine = Pisanello : Malatesta
                : emotional distinctions = Coke : law
</pre>

In fact Pound thought of most of these relations not as continuities of pattern, but as historical causalities: he would assert causal links between the most distant of these components. To provide these links he would go to material like the Provencal *vidas* and *razos*—written long enough after the event to permit of sufficient 'beautiful lies'.[168] This material had a minimum relation to historicity, but a maximum relation to the 'recurrent' and the 'permanent' in human existence.[169] Lawyer Coke had, according to Pound, 'the clearest mind ever in England',[170] and was the basis of Pound's attempt at the epic of English law;[171] but it is clear that Coke chose among precedents for those most suiting his beautiful, one might say Confucian, conception of a supra-human law, and then borrowed the flimsiest fictions to persuade himself that it had existed 'time out of mind'.[172] Agassiz, whom Pound in late life wondered if he should have used as 'the top flight of the mind' instead of Confucius, stuck to an argument from design rather than accept the theories of Darwin.[173] Pound would indeed speak of 'myth',[174] but if a scholar challenged the historicity of his details—as Långfors did on the story of Cabestanh and the heart-eating—he would lash out angrily at the academic mind.[175] But how Pound thought of his work with Provence does not matter so long as we realise that it is myth, and that his typical sources, whether *vidas* or stories from Frobenius, organise the presentation of recurrent or permanent human patterns with the greatest possible intensity.

One cannot treat Pound's Provencal constructs in a straightforward way as history. The suggestions they involve are very often quite unprovable: that William IX 'brought the song up out of Spain', that Eleanor was personally close to Bernart de Ventadorn, Bertran de Born, and Arnaut Daniel, that the heretics of Languedoc were the final casting-up of a long underground wave that began at Eleusis. The Provence elements of the Cantos occupy a middle ground between the usury Cantos and the Adams and China work. The usury Cantos, as I have said elsewhere, simply cannot be related directly to any period that we know; the weavers and the brides in them would be at home in an *Annunciation* of Fra Angelico, nowhere else.[176] When Pound gets down to the exhaustive detail of history, as in the Adams and China Cantos, he loses all intensity at the same time as all convincing presentation of enduring pattern.[177] His Provence matter has both enduring pattern and historical detail, and I have tried to show that he generally gets the tones of its history right. The Cantos are what I have called complexes of aesthetic compatibilities and incompatibilities;[178] they show which ways of life and states of mind can go together, and which cannot. When Pound says that X artifact or way of life (for example, the troubadour product and the attitudes that Pound deduces from it) is incompatible with Y (the alleged 'Cathar' ethic and aesthetic), I believe that one can trust him. A sane study of the period must agree with Pound that the troubadour culture could not have developed or lived under the Capetians ('said they wd. not be under Paris').[179] All this depends on Pound's absolute sense of the tonal quality of language. The writing was what he always began from, and with the writing I believe he was always reliable. We have seen throughout that Pound might have the haziest idea of the literal meaning of individual phrases in Provencal, but I do not believe he can be faulted on his sense of the specific quality of mind behind poems. Another poet — like Eliot, for example — might have a far superior ability in formal language study, without in his lifetime making one-tenth of the discoveries of genuine new and ancient talent in writing that Pound made. 'I believe in an ultimate and absolute rhythm',[180] Pound said, and his work with Provence as elsewhere shows that he was a fit judge of it.

The epic, as Pound practised it, sharpens one's perception of what is possible. Pound got much of his history from verse, and propagated it in verse — 'British bores tried to study history from historians, being, for the most part, pompous and prosy asses they were incapable of reading verse (though Macaulay wrote it).'[181] This method can be a valuable corrective to the more usual ones. Compare, for example, the Cantos' vision of the shift of Provencal culture into Italy with that of the literary historian Santangelo.[182] Santangelo in effect asserts that Dante, author of the *Divine Comedy,* in his *De Vulgari Eloquentia* had simply waited for chance to thrust under his nose some verse to waffle about; that the Italian poets of his era had waited passively for pre-digested remnants of Provencal culture to reach them through the channels of rich men's coffee-table editions. Surfacing from the morass of Santangelo's details to the brief vision projected in the Cantos, one sees that his assumptions are preposterous; the human being is not thus but otherwise. Pound's dynastic vision of Provence may be a distortion in that it leaves out the mass of imitators and diluters, as well as many talented troubadours of Toulouse and of Provence proper. But it is perhaps a worse distortion when a respected 'doyen of Provencal studies' uses a statistically accurate survey to suggest that the troubadour lyric as a whole was a mediocre and imitative culture, with no visible lines of dynamic development beyond those dictated by fashion and accident.[183] Pound will be accused of writing bad history; but there are times when the emotional naivety, the sentimental crudity of scholars causes them simply to write bad novels — like the conjectures of Bezzola and Koehler on the love-lives of William IX and Bernart de Ventadorn.[184] There are times when history and poetry must be judged by the same criteria. In various parts of this book I have found myself defending Pound against the authority of various scholars; and if there is a common defect in these scholars' approaches to the human animal, it is a desire to deny the possibility of constructive energy in him. For them, the Good is not maximum energy under maximum directing control; it is control, for the sake of which they are willing to deny the energy at its source. Pound may have erred the other way, but I believe that his long-term effect on the study of Provencal verse will be beneficial.

APPENDIX TO PART THREE:
TABLE OF CORROBORATION FOR
THE 'EASTERN HERESIARCHS'

I have shown at some length that the 'heretic council' of Saint-Félix-de-Caraman is a kingpin in historians' convictions that the heresies of twelfth-century Languedoc were unified, and that they were a dualism imported from the East. I have been at some pains to show that this council is probably a fiction. But I have also noted (Chapter 10, n. 39) that the 'Antipope' said to have presided at this council is spoken of elsewhere, as are two Eastern heresiarchs visiting the West who are not mentioned in the 'Acts of the Council'. Examination of the sources for these three Eastern heresiarchs provides a useful example of the state of our information on twelfth-century heretic activities.

For too long any citation of an item in another quasi-contemporary document has been accepted as valid corroboration of authenticity. It has not been sufficiently considered that the documents cited come from Catholic milieux in close communication with each other, and that we are probably dealing with simple repetition, of 'information' that need have come from very few original sources indeed. Obviously what is required is a full critical analysis of the texts of the Catholic controversialists and the 'Cathar' sources, gradually eliminating all those which derive from earlier ones, until we are left with those which appear to have independent sources of information. This will be difficult, because so many stem from such a short period. As Raffaello Morghen has pointed out, many of the Catholic polemic texts that should be available for study are still unpublished (see Chapter 10, n. 79). I have attempted a small contribution by drawing up a table for the corroborations of the most-emphasised link with the East: the three Eastern 'heresiarchs', Niquinta, Petracus, and Nazarius. It will be seen that the corroborations supporting the general authority of each document speaking of these men are found in the works of thirteenth-century Catholic polemicists, supported only by the *Liber de Duobus Principiis* and the *Interrogatio* notes. The latter of these two comes to us from Inquisitorial sources, while the former was known only to the Inquisitor Raynier Sacchoni, and appears to have been written in complete ignorance of the doctrines and facts in all the other supposed 'Cathar texts' (see Chapter 10, n. 82).

The first column of my table lists the 'heresiarchs'. The second column lists the documents that mention these men, with the specific reading of the name in brackets. The third lists the documents which, by referring to some item mentioned in one of the first set of documents, support its general authority; the specific item is given in parentheses.

(A) 'Eastern Heresiarch'	(B) Document in which he is found	(C) Other item repeated elsewhere from document in (B), thus supporting its general authority
Nicetas/ Niquinta:	(as 'Niquinta') in 'Acts of the heretic Council of Saint-Félix', published by Besse in 1660 from an original 'of 1232', now lost.[1]	(Bernard Raymond, R. de Baumiac, Sicard Cellerier, Petrus Pollanus, Petrus Isarn) —notorious heretics, knowledge of whom therefore is no indication of an independent source.[3]
		(Marc de Lombardie) Vignier, *Recueil,* 1601 (see below).[4]
	(as 'Nicetas') in a document published by Vignier in 1601 from an original 'of 1023' (!), now lost.[2]	(Garatus) a fragment of a 13th-century Catholic treatise on heretics.[5]
		(Garatus) *Liber Supra Stella,* a 13-century Catholic treatise on heretics.[6]

(Garatus ['Garatenses']) *Liber de Duobus Principiis,* a 'Cathar text',[7] and (?) source for Sacchoni, who alone knew of it.[8]

(Caloianus ['Cascianus']) *Brevis Summula,* a 13th-century Catholic treatise on heretics.[9]

(Cathar schisms) Sacchoni's *Summa; Brevis Summula; Liber Supra Stella;* all 13th-century Catholic treatises on heretics.[10]

Petracus: a document published by Vignier in 1601 (see above).

Nazarius: Sacchoni, *Summa de Catharis,* a 13th-century Catholic treatise on heretics (see above).[11]

other Catholic treatises on heretics.[13]

notes added to the Lyons version of the *Interrogatio Johannis,* a 'Cathar text' from the Inquisition archives at Carcassonne (Doat coll.); the notes are not in the Vienna version.[12]

(Concorezzo) Sacchoni, *Summa de Catharis,* a 13th-century Catholic treatise on heretics (see above).[14]

(Concorezzo ['Corezium']) a document published by Vignier, 1601 (see above).[15]

(Concorezzo ['Concorenses']) *Liber Supra Stella,* a 13th-century Catholic treatise on heretics (see above).[16]

(Concorezzo) Pseudo-Bonacursius, *Manifestatio,* a late 12th-century Catholic treatise on heretics.[17]

(Concorezzo) *Summa Auctori-
tatis,* a 13th-century Catholic
treatise on heretics.[18]

(Concorezzo) *Summa contra
Haereticos,* a 13th-century
Catholic treatise on heretics.[19]

[1]Dondaine, 'Actes,' p. 327.
[2]Ibid., p. 343.
[3]Ibid., pp. 335-338.
[4]Ibid., p. 339.
[5]Ibid., p. 342.
[6]Dondaine, *Liber,* p. 28.
[7]Ibid., pp. 132-138.
[8]Cf. ibid., p. 21.
[9]Dondaine, 'Actes,' pp. 341-342.
[10]Ibid., p. 341.
[11]Dondaine, *Liber,* p. 76.
[12]Dondaine, 'Actes,' p. 345, note; Runciman, *Manichee,* p. 86, Nelli, *Ecritures,*
p. 32; cf. Chapter 10, n. 82.
[13]I have not been able to follow up the corroboration of Sacchoni's general information. However, it is clear that it is from within the circle of the Catholic polemicists; cf. Dondaine, *Liber,* pp. 7-8: 'S. Schmidt [*Cathares,* 2, p. 227] and C. Molinier [*Un traité inédit,* p. 15] have shown that the concordance of the *Summa* with
the information of the other sources from the farthest countries and different
periods can not leave room for doubt. To the witness of these *Catholic* sources' (my
italics), Father Dondaine says, we can now add witness from the Cathars themselves, thanks to the discovery of the *Liber de Duobus Principiis,* for 'the doctrinal
information brought by the Catholic polemicists in general, but more particularly
that brought by Raynier Sacchoni. . . .' Note that at first it was the other polemicists who were bringing support for Sacchoni's *Summa;* now it is the other polemicists themselves who are in need of support from the *Liber*—which was known only
to Sacchoni (Dondaine, *Liber,* p. 21). The mutual borrowing is quite circular.
　　M. A. E. Nickson, ed., 'Pseudo-Reinerius', does not discuss in detail the corroboration for the authentic part of the treatise, simply asserting that it contains 'first-
hand information', is 'clear, concise and accurate, and it immediately became one
of the most used of all inquisitorial handbooks.' Ibid., p. lxii.
[14]Dondaine, *Liber,* p. 87; Runciman, *Manichee,* p. 124.
[15]Dondaine, 'Actes,' p. 340.
[16]Dondaine, *Liber,* p. 28.
[17]Thouzellier, *Catharisme,* p. 107.
[18]Dondaine, *Liber,* p. 17.
[19]Ibid., p. 28; Guiraud, *Inquisition,* 1, pp. xxix, 198.

APPENDIX 1: SOURCES FOR CANTO VI (INCLUDING SOME FOR THE EARLIER VERSION)

TEXT A: Vanel, *Intrigues galantes de la Cour de France,*
1, pp. 91-101.

Eleonor d'Aquitaine femme de Loüis le Ieune.

Le Roi Loüis le Jeune avoit épousé Eleonor fille de Guillaume V.
Duc d'Aquitaine, Princesse d'une beautê distinguée, & d'un esprit
vif et brillant, mais d'une humeur extrémement coquette. Le Roi
qui n'avoit pas encore connu ce défaut en elle l'aima si tendrement
qu'il ne put se résoudre à la laisser en France, lors qu'l fit le voyage
de la terre Sainte, & l'engagea à le suivre dans cette expedition. Ils
s'embarquérent ensemble à Ayguemorte, & aprés plusieurs traver-
ses, ils arriverent enfin à Antioche, dont Hugues Raymond oncle de
la Reine, & frere du Duc Guillaume avoit obtenu la Principauté. Il
fit au Roi une reception magnifique, & n'oublia rien pour l'obliger à
s'y aréter. Il lui representa que Noradin Soudan de Damas faisoit
souvent des courses jusqu'aux portes de la Ville, & qu'il étoit à crain-
dre que cette place ne tombât entre les mains des infidéles, s'il
n'étoit puissamment assisté par sa Majesté. Ce n'étoit pas le seul
interêt de l'Etat, & de la Religion qui portoit Raymond à soühaitter
que la Cour de France fit quelque séjour à Antioche. Il avoit été
élevé avec Eleonor, & quoi qu'il fût son oncle, il n'avoit guéres plus
d'âge qu'elle. Cette grande frequentation avoit fait naître entre'eux
une passion plus tendre que n'en devoient avoir deux personnes si
proches; & Raymond n'avoit fait le voyage de la Palestine que pour
se guerir de cette passion, lors qu'il avoit vû sa niéce mariée avec le
Roi de France. La presence de l'objet aimé raluma ses premiers
feux, & comme il trouva la Reine aussi favorable à ses desirs qu'elle

avoit été à Bordeaux, il ne put se resoudre à s'en separer si promte-
ment. Cependant tous ces artifices furent inutiles, il ne put retenir le
Roi que peu de jours à Antioche. Ce prince qui avoit impatience de
se rendre à Jerusalem poursuivit son voyage malgré toutes les raisons
qu'on put luy aleguer, & Eleonor n'en fut pas aussi afligée que Raymond. Elle n'aimoit que les objets presens, & oublia le Prince
d'Antioche, aussi tôt qu'elle l'eut perdu de veüe. Plusieurs autres la
consolérent de son absence, & comme elle ne rebutoit aucun de tous
ceux qui soupiroient pour elle, sa Cour étoit toûjour fort grosse. Les
ocasions de la guerre faisoient la matiere la plus ordinaire de leur
conversation; & comme on parloit de tous ceux qui se faisoient dis-
tinguer entre les Turcs par leur naissance ou par leur valeur, on ne
manqua pas de l'en-tretenir des grandes qualitez de Saladin neveu
du Soudan de Damas. On lui dit que ce Prince étoit bien fait de sa
personne, adroit dans tous les éxercices, vaillant, genereux, liberal,
galant; enfin qu'il avoit toutes les maniéres Françoises. Il y en eut
meme qui ajoûtérent qu'il étoit décendu du Comte de Ponthieu
dont la fille ayant été prise sur mer avoit été presentée au Soudan
d'Alep frere de Moradin, qui l'ayant mise au nombre de ses femmes
en avoit eu ce Prince. Quoi que cette histoire fût fabuleuse, elle ne
laissa pas d'augmenter la curiosité que la Reine avoit déja de voir
Saladin. Elle en chercha les ocasions, & pour commencer d'entrer
en commerce avec lui, elle lui écrivit pour luy demander la liberté
de Sandebreüil Seigneur de Sauzay, qui avoit été pris depuis quelques jours par un parti que ce Prince Mahometan commandoit.
Saladin acorda à la Reine tout ce qu'elle demandoit, & renvoya ce
prisonnier sans rançon. Eleonor eut plusieurs conversations avec
Sandebreüil pour s'informer du plusieurs circonstances qu'elle désiroit scavoir touchant la personne de Saladin. Elle se servit méme de
luy, pour avoir une entrevue avec ce Prince. Elle fit pour cet efet
une partie de chasse à deux lieues de Jerusalem, où Saladin se rendit
à la tête de trente Maîtres seulement. Dés qu'il vit paroître la Reine
il se détacha de sa troupe, & s'étant avancé vers elle au petit galop il
mit pied à terre pour la saluer. Il lui fit un compliment en langue
Italienne que cette Princesse entendoit fort bien, & d'une maniere
qui ne ressentoit point la barbarie de la nation. Elle ne fut pas moins
satisfaite de son esprit que de sa bonne mine; elle l'obligea à remon-
ter à cheval, & ils passérent ensemble dans un bois de palmiers, où
ils eurent une longue conversation. Eleonor la remercia d'une

maniere fort obligeante de ce qu'il avoit fait pour Sandebreüil à sa priére, & détachant une écharpe en broderie qui luy servoit de ceinture la luy donna, le priant de la garder comme une marque de son estime & de sa re-connoissance. Saladin la porta toûjours depuis dans des ocasions les plus perilleuses. Elle fut reconnüe par quelques courtisans qui le raportérent au Roy, & méme d'autres luy assurérent que la Reine avoit donné plusieurs autres rendez vous à Saladin. Quoi que dans ce commerce il y eut plus de vanité de part & d'autre que de passion, le Roy ne laissa pas d'en avoir de l'inquiétude, & ne voulut plus demeurer à Jerusalem. Aprés avoir pris congé au Roi Baudoüin, il se mit à la voile avec toute sa flote, & il fut obligé de relâcher en Sicile pour faire radouber ses Vaisseaux, qui avoient été fort mal traitez par l'armée navale de Manuel Empereur de Constantinople. Il y a aparence que la Reine y fit la paix; parce qu'elle devint grosse, & acoucha, lors qu'elle fut de retour en France, d'une fille nommée Alix, & qui depuis fut mariée avec Thibault Comte de Blois. Quelque tems aprés le Roy ayant été informé de toutes les galanteries d'Eleonor, résolut de faire déclarer nul son mariage avec elle. Il convoqua pour cet éfet une assemblée du Clergé de France à Boisgency ou Alegrin:son Chancelier exposa les raisons qu'il avoit de demander cette séparation, & il obtint aisément tout ce que son maître désiroit, parce ce que la Reine ne s'y oposa pas: Louïs pour s'en tirer avec honneur, lui abandonna le Duché d'Aquitaine, & la Comté de Poitou qu'elle lui avoit aportée en dot, & retint auprés de luy les deux filles qu'il en avoit eües.

Eleonor aprés ce divorce se retira à Poictiers, où elle fut visitée par Henry Duc de Normandie fils du Roy d'Angleterre, qui demeura charmé de sa beauté & de son esprit. Quoi que ce Prince n'eût aucun agrément dans sa personne, & qu'il eût les cheveux d'une fort vilaine couleur, elle ne laissa pas de recevoir ses soins, & d'écouter les propositions de mariage qu'il lui fit, parce qu'il étoit héritier presomptif de la couronne d'Angleterre. Henry étoit informé de tous les désordres de sa vie passée, mais l'envie de joindre la Guyenne & le Poitou aux autres Etats dont il devoit hériter, le fit passer par dessus cette consideration. Il épousa cette Princesse; dequoi Louïs eut un si grand dépit qu'il ne laissa échaper aucune ocasion de s'en vanger: la guerre s'aluma entre ces deux Princes, aprés qu'Henry fut parvenue à la Couronne, & ne se termina que par le mariage d'Henry fils aîné du Roy d'Angleterre avec Marguerite fille de Louïs, & d'Elisabeth de Castille sa seconde femme. Et quoi que cette Princesse n'eût pas plus de cinq ans elle fut remise entre les mains du Roy d'Angleterre pour assurance de cette aliance. Lors qu'elle fut paruenüe à l'âge de consommer le mariage, le Roy d'Angleterre refusa sous divers prétextes de la remettre entre les mains de son fils, dans la crainte qu'il ne devint trop puissant, & qu'il ne luy prît envie de le détrôner avec le secours de la France. Le Prince Henry impatient de posseder son épouse qui devint luy assurer la succession de l'Angleterre, cette Princesse étant destinée à l'heritier de la Couronne, l'enleva, & se retira en France auprés du Roy son beaupere. Dela il écrivit à son pere pour luy demander le Royaume d'Angleterre ou la Duché de Normandie en avancement de succession, & sur le refus qu'on lui en fit, il résolut d'obtenir ses prétentions par les armes. La Reine Eleonor engagea dans le parti du Prince, Richard Duc d'Aquitaine & Geoffroy Duc de Bretagne ses freres, & Louïs obligea Guillaume Roy d'Ecosse à ataquer l'Angleterre d'un côté pendant qu'il envoyoit dans cette Isle Robert Comte de Lincestre avec une puissante armée. Il sembloit que le Roy d'Angleterre deût étre acablé par une si grande puissance, mais Dieu protégea son bon droit, & luy donna moyen de vaincre ses ennemis. Son fils Henry mourut peu de temps aprés, & la paix fut conclüe entre la France, & l'Angleterre. Le mariage de Richard qui étoit devenu l'heritier présomptif de la Couronne par la mort de son frere Henry avec Alix fille de Louïs fut le sceau de cette union. Comme la Princesse étoit encore fort jeune, elle fut remise entre les mains du Roy d'Angleterre, ainsi que l'avoit été sa soeur, en atendant qu'elle fut en âge de se marier, & la Reine Eleonor fut enfermée dans une étroite prison pour l'empêcher d'éxciter de nouveaux troubles à la Cour. Le Roy Henry eut de si grandes complaisances pour la Princesse Alix, qu'on les atribua à l'amour; cette Princesse y répondait avec une ingénuité pardonnable à son âge: Cependant Richard ne laissa pas d'en prendre ombrage, & ne put se resoudre à l'épouser, lors qu'il fut parvenu à la Couronne. La Reine Eleonor qu'il avoit mise en liberté dés qu'il s'étoit veu sur le trône, le confirma dans cette aversion, & méme négotia son mariage avec Beranguelle fille de D. Garcie Roy de Navarre qu'elle emmena à Richard dans la Palestine, où il l'épousa. Philipe Auguste Roi de France qui avoit fait aussi dans le méme tems le voyage de la terre Sainte, ne voulut témoigner aucun ressentiment de l'outrage fait à sa soeur, de peur de donner moyen aux infidéles de profiter de la division des Chrétiens; mais lors qu'il fut de retour en France, il porta la guerre dans les Etats du Roy d'Angleterre pour s'en vanger. Enfin Eleonor aprés avoir causé de grands maux dans lex deux Royaumes, finit ses jours à Poictiers âgée de quatre vints quatre ans.

TEXT B: Zeller and Luchaire, *Philippe Auguste et Louis VIII*, pp. 10-33.

B(i)

... *les plus grands ennemis de Philippe-Auguste étaient le roi d'Angleterre Henri II et ses fils, Henri Court-Mantel, Geoffroi de Bretagne et Richard d'Aquitaine, dit Coeur de Lion, parce qu'ils étaient les plus grands seigneurs de France. C'est contre eux qu'il fallait diriger maintenant les forces naissantes de cette jeune et vigoureuse royauté capétienne. Aussi verrons-nous Philippe toujours à l'affût, toujours prêt à profiter de la mort ou de l'absence d'un prince angevin, pour élever des prétentions sur une des nombreuses seigneuries qui constituaient le vaste domaine des Plantagenets. Pendant les quarante-trois ans que dura son règne, il ne laissa jamais passer deux printemps sans guerroyer contre les rois d'Angleterre ou leurs barons. Ce fut la grande affaire de toute sa vie.*

6. — GUERRE ENTRE PHILIPPE-AUGUSTE ET HENRI II, ROI D'ANGLETERRE (1187-1189).
(Rigord, *Vie de Philippe-Auguste*.)

Une querelle naquit cette même année (1187) entre le roi Très Chrétien Philippe et le roi d'Angleterre Henri. Philippe voulait que le fils du roi d'Angleterre, Richard, comte de Poitiers, lui fît hommage pour tout le comté de Poitou, et Henri II conseillait secrètement à Richard de remettre de jour en jour cette cérémonie. D'autre part, Philippe réclamait du roi d'Angleterre le château de Gisors et autres places avoisinantes que sa soeur Marguerite avait recues en dot du roi Louis, son père, à l'occasion de son mariage

avec le roi Henri, fils aîné de Henri le Grand. Or on avait stipulé à
ce sujet les clauses suivantes: Le jeune roi Henri devait posséder cette
dot durant sa vie avec retour à ses héritiers, s'il en provenait de son
mariage; dans le cas où Marguerite ne laisserait pas d'enfants à la
mort du roi Henri, sa dot devait rentrer sans débats en la possession
du roi de France. Plusieurs fois déjà le roi d'Angleterre avait été
sommé de comparaître pour ce motif devant le cour, mais il avait
toujours trouvé le moyen de produire quelque excuse pour éviter de
comparaître devant ce tribunal. . . .

[Philippe attempts to get back the territories by force, but settles
for a judgement by his court. A footnote on p. 14 says that this sudden understanding is probably explained by the Provencal razos:
'Les arguments en langue provencale qui accompagnent les chants
de Bertrand de Born . . . nous apprennent que Philippe fut trahi par
les troupes du comte de Champagne, qu'avait gagné l'or de Henri
II.']

B(ii)
7. — ÉLOGE DE LA GUERRE.
(Extrait des poésies de Bertrand de Born.)

[A translation of Bertran's *Be·m platz lo gais* (in e.g. Bertran,
Lieder, no. 40; see part translation in Chapter 2, text before n. 4).
This song was of course well known to Pound, who translated it in
Spirit, pp. 47-48. A footnote (p. 14) to Zeller and Luchaire's translation says that Bertran's songs are important in these wars because
it was his *sirventes* that stirred up the barons of Aquitaine and Poitou against the Plantagenets.]

B(iii)
8. — COMPLAINTE DE BERTRAND DE BORN SUR LA MORT DE HENRI COURT-MANTEL, FILS AÎNÉ DU ROI D'ANGLETERRE HENRI II.
(Extrait des poésies de Bertrand de Born.)

[A translation of Bertran's *Si tuit li dol* (in e.g. Bertran, *Lieder,*
no. 43; a part translation is given in Chapter 3, text before n. 21,

and Appel's text is given in Chapter 3, n. 20). This song was also well known to Pound, who translated it as *Planh for the Young English King*.]

B(iv)
[Part 2] 2. — LES DEUX ARMÉES SE RÉUNISSENT À VÉZELAI (1190).
(Benoît de Peterborough, *Vie de Richard Ier*.)

[The armies of Richard and Philippe join to begin the journey to the Holy Land.]

B(v)
3. — DUEL DE RICHARD COEUR DE LION ET DE GUILLAUME DES BARRES (1190).
(Benoît de Peterborough, *Vie de Richard Ier*.)

Le roi Richard, plusieurs chevaliers de sa maison et de la maison du roi de France se réunissaient, comme c'était l'habitude, près des murs de Messine pour se livrer à plusieurs jeux; ils revenaient au logis, traversant le milieu de la ville, lorsqu'ils rencontrèrent un paysan avec un âne chargé de ces longs roseaux qu'ils appellent des *cannes*. Le roi d'Angleterre et les chevaliers de sa suite en saisissent et se mettent à se battre entre eux. Or il arriva que le roi d'Angleterre et Guillaume des Barres, un des plus vaillants soldats du roi de France, joutant l'un contre l'autre, brisèrent leurs cannes, et que la cape du roi en fut déchirée. Le roi, furieux, se jeta sur Guillaume, qu'il fit chanceler, lui et son cheval, cherchant à le jeter à terre, mais sans pouvoir y parvenir. Guillaume se tint au cou de son cheval et menaça le roi; aussitôt Robert de Breteuil, fils du feu comte de Leicester, Robert, à qui le roi venait de donner la terre paternelle, mit la main sur Guillaume pour venir en aide à son roi. "Arrête, s'écrie le roi, et laisse-nous seuls." La lutte recommença plus vive de la voix et de geste, jusqu'à ce que le roi, éclatant, dit à son adversaire: "Va-t'en, et prends garde de reparaître en ma présence, car je deviendrai l'ennemi éternel de toi et des tiens."

[Philippe and then his great barons intervene on behalf of Guillaume des Barres, but Richard refuses to listen to them; Guillaume departs temporarily, and then the entire leadership of the French army finally succeeds in winning Richard's pardon.]

B(vi)

4. — PHILIPPE-AUGUSTE EST ACCUSÉ DE VOULOIR BROUILLER RICHARD AVEC LE ROI DE SICILE ET D'ACCABLER LES ANGLAIS SOUS LE POIDS DES FORCES SICILIENNES ET FRANCAISES COALISÉES (1191).

(Benoît de Peterborough, *Vie de Richard Ier.*)

En mars 1191, sur le conseil du roi de France, Richard quitta Messine pour aller s'entretenir avec Tancrède, roi de Sicile, à Catane. Ce dernier le recut magnifiquement, lui offrit des vases d'or et d'argent, des chevaux, des étoffes de soie; mais Richard, qui possédait de toutes ces choses, ne voulut accepter qu'un petit anneau en signe de leur mutuelle affection. Au moment de la séparation, le roi Tancrède dit à Richard: "Je sais maintenant, et par de sûrs indices, que ce que le roi de France m'a dit sur vous, par l'organe du duc de Bourgogne et par ses lettres, provient beaucoup plus d'un mauvais sentiment à votre égard que de l'amour qu'il a pour moi. Car il a voulu me persuader que vous ne m'aviez gardé ni paix ni foi et que vous aviez violé les conventions faites entre nous; que, si vous étiez venu dans ce royaume, c'était uniquement pour me l'enlever; et il m'a offert, si je voulais marcher contre vous avec mon armée, de m'aider de tout son pouvoir pour vous détruire vous et les vôtres." A quoi le roi d'Angleterre répondit avec une égale fermeté d'esprit et de parole: "Je ne suis point un traître, ne l'ai jamais été et ne le serai jamais: la paix que j'ai faite avec vous, je ne l'ai enfreinte en rien et ne l'enfreindrai point tant que je vivrai. Du reste, je ne puis croire que le roi de France ait pu vous parler ainsi de moi, lui qui est mon seigneur et mon compagnon en ce pèlerinage." Le roi Tancrède répliqua: "Voici les lettres qu'il m'a fait remettre par le duc de Bourgogne; si le duc nie m'avoir apporté ces lettres de la part de son seigneur le roi de France, je suis prêt à le combattre en duel par l'intermédiaire d'un de mes chefs." Ayant recu ces lettres de la main du roi Tancrède, le roi d'Angleterre revint à Messine. Le même jour, le roi de France vint s'entretenir avec le roi Tancrède, demeura avec lui une nuit et le matin revint à Messine.

Cependant le roi d'Angleterre, très irrité contre le roi de France, lui faisait mauvaise figure, montrait des dispositions peu pacifiques et cherchait une occasion favorable pour le quitter avec les siens. Le roi de France demanda ce que signifiait ce changement. Richard lui fit rapporter par Philippe, comte de Flandre, tout ce qu'il avait appris de la bouche du roi de Sicile et, en témoignage du fait, montra les susdites lettres. Quand le roi de France eut recu cette réponse, il resta quelque temps sans rien dire, sachant bien ce que lui reprochait là-dessus sa conscience; ensuite il revint à lui et dit: "Je vois maintenant que le roi d'Angleterre cherche tous les moyens de me nuire, car tout ceci n'est qu'invention et mensonge. Mais je suis convaincu qu'il a inventé contre moi toutes ces méchancetés parce qu'il veut renvoyer ma soeur Alix, qu'il avait pourtant juré d'épouser. Qu'il sache cependant que, s'il la refuse pour en prendre une autre, je resterai toute ma vie son ennemi et celui de sa maison." Richard répliqua qu'il ne pouvait en aucune manière épouser la soeur de Philippe, parce que le roi d'Angleterre son père l'avait déshonorée et avait eu d'elle un fils, ce qu'il se déclara prêt à prouver par toute espèce de témoignages.

B(vii)
5. — CONVENTION CONCLUE À MESSINE ENTRE PHILIPPE-AUGUSTE ET RICHARD COEUR DE LION
(mars 1191).
(Rigord, *Vie de Philippe-Auguste*.)

Au nom de la Trinité sainte et indivisible, ainsi soit-il! Philippe, par la grâce de Dieu roi des Francais.

Faisons savoir à tous les hommes présents et à venir qu'une paix solide vient d'être établie entre nous et notre ami, notre fidèle, notre frère, Richard, illustre roi d'Angleterre, qui s'est engagé lui-même par serment à la paix dont voici les clauses:

Nous permettons de bon coeur et de notre pleine volonté audit roi d'epouser librement qui il voudra, nonobstant la convention faite entre nous et lui relativement à notre soeur Alix, qu'il devait prendre pour épouse.

De plus, nous lui cédons, ainsi qu'aux héritiers mâles qui naîtront de lui et de son épouse et qui tiendront sa terre après lui, Gisors, Néauphle, Neuchâtel et le Vexin normand avec ses appartenances.

De son côté, il est convenu que, s'il vient à mourir sans héritier mâle né de son épouse et de lui, Gisors, Néauphle, Neuchâtel et le Vexin normand avec ses appartenances reviendront aussitôt à nous et aux héritiers mâles nés de notre épouse et de nous.

Si nous mourions sans héritier mâle né de notre épouse et de nous pour nous remplacer et tenir notre terre après nous, nous voulons que Gisors, Néauphle, Neuchâtel et le Vexin normand avec ses appartenances reviennent au domaine de Normandie.

Si le roi d'Angleterre avait deux héritiers mâles au moins, il est convenu que l'aîné tiendra de nous en chef tout ce qu'il doit tenir de nous en deçà de la mer d'Angleterre, et que l'autre tiendra de nous en chef l'une des trois baronnies suivantes, le domaine de Normandie, ou celui de l'Anjou et du Maine, ou celui de l'Aquitaine et du Poitou.

[Two clauses then specify Richard's payments to Philippe, and that the suzerainty shall remain as before; a third cedes certain lands to Philippe.]

Nous lui avons aussi cédé Cahors et le Querci tout entier avec ses appartenances, excepté les deux abbayes royales de Figeac et de Souillac, avec leurs appartenances, qui sont à nous et nous restent.

Il s'engage à ne plus rien prendre de la terre de Saint-Gilles, hormis ce qui a été stipulé plus haut, tant que le comte de Saint-Gilles voudra ou pourra recevoir justice en notre cour. Mais, si le comte de Saint-Gilles faisait défaut de justice en notre cour, dès lors nous cesserions de défendre le comte de Saint-Gilles contre le roi d'Angleterre, ou du moins notre secours ne serait point obligatoire.

[The next clause confirms the *status quo* for Richard, and the following determines a hostage from Philippe for execution of the treaty.]

Le roi d'Angleterre promet encore de renvoyer en France dans le premier mois de son retour et sans aucune contradiction, sans aucun délai, notre soeur Alix, soit que nous vivions ou non.

Nous voulons encore qu'il nous rende les services et justices qu'il tient de nous, comme ses ancêtres les rendaient aux nôtres, sauf les conventions arrêtées plus haut. Le tout confirmé de l'autorité de notre sceau, en gage d'une éternelle durée.

Fait à Messine, l'an 1190 de l'Incarnation du Verbe, au mois de mars.

B(viii)

6. — CHANSON DE BERTRAND DE BORN RELATIVE À LA TROISIÈME CROISADE.

(Extrait des poésies de Bertrand de Born.)

Je sais maintenant qui mérite le plus parmi ceux qui se levèrent matin; sans mentir, c'est le seigneur Conrad, celui qui se défend contre Saladin et sa bande cruelle. Que Dieu lui donne son secours! Car celui des hommes est bien lent. Seul il aura la récompense, puisque seul il supporte la peine.

[Bertran explains why he is staying at home, and curses Richard and Philippe for delaying because they fear each other.]

Seigneur Conrad, l'affection que je vous porte inspire mes vers, et je ne considère ni ami ni ennemi; mais je chante pour blâmer les croisés de ce qu'ils ont mis le passage et leurs serments en oubli: ils ne pensent pas que Dieu voit avec peine qu'ils vivent dans les orgies et dans les délices, et que vous endurez la faim et la soif, quand ils reposent tranquillement. Seigneur Conrad, la roue tourne toujours en ce monde, et enfin tourne mal. J'en connais peu qui ne se repentent d'avoir trompé leurs voisins ou tout autre; mais celui qui perd ne montre pas de joie; or sachent bien ces hommes que j'accuse d'agir ainsi, que Dieu note ce qu'ils ont dit et ce qu'ils ont fait.

[Bertran finally hopes that the two kings will set off with great armies, and conquer.]

TEXT C: Zamboni, *Gli Ezzelini,* pp. 383-385.

[I place in brackets Pound's borrowings for Cantos VI and XXIX.]

Hoc Exemplum Unius Exempli Cuiusdam instrumenti huius tenoris hoc est exemplum cuiusdam Instrumenti tenor quar / talis est Anno domini millesimo ducentesimo sexagessimo quinto Inditione octava Die mercurj primo Intrante Aprilli Inflorentia In domo domini Chavalcantis de de Cavalchantis ['In the house of the Cavalcanti / anno 1265' — *Cantos,* 29/142:147] testibus ad hec rogatis et Specialiter convocatis silicet dominus Nisi pichinus de farinatis de florentia dnus Elinus et dnus lipus ejus frater filijs q dni farinati de

farinatis de florentia ['witness / Picus de Farinatis / and Don Elinus
and Don Lipus / sons of Farinato de' Farinati' — 6/22:26-27] Pucius
de eodem loco dnus Guitus et dnus Bertaldus de cologna de ale-
mania Jacobinus q garsedi de Verona petrus Azalus de cegia phili-
pus de Imolla Et allys ibique Domina Cuniza filia quondam domini
. . . . . aci de romano pro Amore onipotentis dei et pro remissione
anime patris sui predicti ['Cunizza for God's love, for remitting the
soul of her father' — 29/141:146] et fratrum suorum dominorum
Eccellini et albrici de romano et matris sue quondam domine
Adeleyte suarumque animarum parentum atque Sue et Intuytu pie-
tatis dimisit adque relaxavit omnes homines adque mulieres que
quondam fuerunt domini Ecelli eius patris predicti ['All serfs of
Eccelin my father da Romano' — 29/142:147] et fratrum suorum
dominorum Eccellini et Aubrici predicti de masnata [cf. 'Masnatas
et servos' — 6/22:26; also 'masnatosque liberavit' — 89/596:631, and
'liberavit masnatos' — 90/606:640; for 'liberavit' see below] secun-
dum quod ad eam pertinet de ratione p̄ t illos qui steterunt cum
domino Aubrico In castro et turim Sancti Zenonis ['Save who were
at Castra San Zeno . . .' — 29/141:146; 'Save those who were with
Alberic at Castra San Zeno' — 29/142:147] qui de eo fecerunt felo-
niam in dicto castro et turim illos dimixit centum Diabollis de Inferno In anima et corpore ['May hell take the traitors of Zeno' — 29/
141:146; 'And let them go also / The devils of hell in their body' —
29/142:147] et omnes alios cum omnibus suis heredibus quos modo
habent et decetero ex eis existent exsient liberans et liberas et ab
omni vinculo ['Liberans et vinculo ab omni liberatos' — 29/141:146]
et condithione servitutis absolutos eos dimisit Sicut illi qui in quad-
rivio in quarta manu Traditi facti sunt liberi ['As who with four
hands at the cross roads'; 'are given their freedom' — 29/141:146] vel
sicut illi qui per manum regis vel Sacerdotis circa Sacratum sanctum
Altare Ducti et facti sunt liberi ['By king's hand or sacerdos' / are
given their freedom' — 29/141:146] vel sicut de libero patre et de
libera matre nati vel geniti fuissent Sicut quilibet civis romani aper-
tis portis eat in quancumque parte habitare sue anbulare voluerint
permissa potestate habeat et vitam semper integram et incoruptam
Deducant liberas personas liberos arbitrios vendendi Emendi tes-
tandi testificandi [' "free of person, free of will / "free to buy, witness, sell, testate." ' — 6/23:27] judicium existendi possideant et per-

petua libertate consistant et nulum servitio eius servitutis de cetero ei neque suis heredibus faciant nisi soli Deo cui omnia subyeta sunt peculium quoque quod nunc habent et de cetero quirent Inrevocabileliter eis donavit et cedit et omne jus patronatus eis remisit et relaxavit ita ut ab hac die in antea tam ipsi quam heredes qui de cetero ex eis exient tam de peculio suo quam de pecunia quicquid voluerint faciant sine omni sua suorumque heredum contraditione vel repititione vel alterius persone et non liceat ei aliquo tempore nolle quod modo vult sed quod per ipsam semel factum est vel scriptum semper inviolatum servetur quam libertatem pro se et suis heredibus . . . . . [ending sic]

TEXT D: Chabaneau, *Biographies,* p. 108, quoting Rolandino, *Chronica,* lib. V, cap. 3, from Muratori, ed., *Scriptores rerum italicarum,* VIII, 173:

[Ecelinus tertius] sexto genuit dominam Cunizam, vitae cujus series talis fuit. Primo namque data est in uxorem comiti Rizardo de Sancto Bonifacio; sed tempore procedente, mandato Ecelini sui patris, Sordellus de ipsius familia dominam ipsam latenter a marito subtraxit, cum qua in patris curia permanente, dictum fuit ipsum Sordellum concubuisse. Et ipse expulso ab Ecelino, miles quidam, nomine Bonius de Tarvisio, dominam ipsam amavit, eamdemque a patris curia separavit occulte, & ipsa nimium amorata in eum, cum ipso mundi partes plurimas circuivit, multa habendo solatia, & maximas faciendo expensas. Demum ambo reversi sunt ad Albericum de Romano, fratrem ipsius dominae, regentem & dominantem in Tarvisio, contra voluntatem Ecelini, ejus fratris, ut dicebatur, & apparebat; & illic stabat idem Bonius cum dicta domina Cuniza, tamen vivente adhuc uxore ipsius Bonii & in Tarvisio permanente. Occisus est demum Bonius gladio in quodam sabato sancto, cum Ecelinus civitatem Tarvisii de dominio fratris velle videretur eripere. Haec autem domina Cuniza cum post omnia haec declinasset ad fratrem suum Ecelinum, ipse maritavit eam domino Aymerio, vel Rainerio, de Bragantio, viro nobili. Sed postea, cum guerra exarsit in Marchia, Ecelinus ipsum cognatum suum, cum ceteris nobilibus de Braganzo & aliunde per Marchiam fecit occidi. Adhuc iterum ipsa Cuniza, post mortem fratris sui Ecelini, maritata est in Verona.

[Chabaneau notes (ibid.) that 'Ecelini sui patris' should read '. . . fratris'. Sordello, *Poesie,* ed. Boni, pp. XXVIII, XXX, notes that Chabaneau's brackets should read '[Ecelinus secundus]', and that his footnote on the other Ezzelino is accordingly wrong.]

APPENDIX 2: ELEANOR, BERNART, BERTRAN, AND ARNAUT

In Canto VI, Pound presents a Provencal 'Vortex' around Eleanor of Aquitaine. The detail of the connections that he sets up is strictly mythopoeic: there is no point in trying to prove that Bernart de Ventadorn met Eleanor at Malemort, that Bertran's 'Audiart' was Eleanor, that Arnaut Daniel's song of nails and uncles had anything to do with Eleanor, or that (as in Canto VII) she somehow substituted herself for the wife of William of Bouvila and thus was loved by Arnaut. But we can at least examine the known relations between Eleanor and these three, and the communications of the three troubadours with each other.

Pound asserted a friendship between Arnaut Daniel and Bertran de Born in both his verse and his prose. Where Arnaut wrote (Pound's translation):

> Sir Bertran, sure no pleasure's won
> Like this freedom naught so merry
> Twixt Nile 'n' where the suns miscarry
> To where the rain falls from the sun

Pound added a footnote to 'Bertran': 'Presumably De Born'.[1] Perhaps Pound, who made a great deal of this striking image, had noticed that Bertran borrows it also.[2]

In *Near Perigord,* developed from Bertran's song of the 'borrowed lady', Pound imagined an epilogue in the form of a discussion between Richard Lionheart and Arnaut Daniel:

> Richard shall die to-morrow — leave him there
> Talking of *trobar clus* with Daniel.

> And the 'best craftsman' sings out his friend's song,
> Envies its vigor. . . .

Pound knew about the relations between Bertran de Born and the sons of Henry II, especially Richard Lionheart; also the *razo* to a song by Arnaut, in which the 'best craftsman' is to be found at Richard's court.[3] When Pound imagines Bertran, in *Near Perigord,*

> Scribbling, swearing between his teeth, by his left hand
> Lie little strips of parchment covered over,
> Scratched and erased with *al* and *ochaisos*

he may well be alluding to a song by Bertran where the rhyme-endings take on a life of their own just like this, and he may well have observed that the song appeared to make fun of Arnaut's technique.[4] Finally, as one well acquainted with the by-roads of this part of the troubadour territory, Pound had observed that 'En Ar. Daniel was of Ribeyrac in Perigord, under Lemosi, near to Hautfort', Hautefort being the castle of Bertran de Born.[5]

Those are the limits of what Pound claimed about the relations between Arnaut Daniel and Bertran de Born, though he may well have observed other points that I shall mention. As for the relations of these two with Bernart de Ventadorn, he had observed that Bernart is usually thought of as belonging to an older generation, for he dated the encounter with Eleanor thus:

> Eleanor, domna jauzionda, mother of Richard,
> Turning on thirty years (wd have been years before this)[6]

'this' being the business of Richard's de-betrothal, which was almost at the beginning of his reign and therefore most probably before Arnaut's visit to his court.[7] But when he spoke of Arnaut's birthplace, near to Bertran de Born's, Pound also noted how near was Bernart de Ventadorn's place of origin: 'under Lemosi'. Bernart's *vida* says that he 'was from Limousin'.[8] Pound must have thought of a lingering influence via Eleanor.

We can pass in review the points of the problem in this order: relations of Bernart, Bertran, and Arnaut with Eleanor; relations of these three troubadours with each other. We can begin each time with the details offered by Pound.

BERNART AND ELEANOR

Pound suggests that the troubadour met the lady at Malemort, and this is important for Pound because of Bertran de Born's Audiart, whom the *razos* and Pound insist was of Malemort but whose identity is quite uncertain.[9] I have found no trace of evidence that this was the meeting-place, or that Eleanor frequented Malemort. But the main assertion, that Bernart met Eleanor, is most likely to be true. The evidence is all in Bernart's songs, since there is nothing in the *vidas* which could not have come from the songs. In one of Bernart's songs, apparently written in autumn, he says

> If the English King and the Norman Duke
> so wishes, I shall see her before winter surprises us.
> For the King I am English and Norman,
> and if it weren't for my Lodestone,
>   I would stay till past Christmas.[10]

The 'English King' and the 'Norman Duke' are Henry II. Bernart is 'English and Norman': he is with the King. The preceding strophe shows where the King is:

> The poem is constructed right to the end,
> so that not a word is defective in it,
> beyond the Norman territory,
>   on the other side of the wild deep sea;
> and if I am getting further from my Lady,
> the beautiful one whom God protect
>   pulls me to herself like a Lodestone.

'Beyond the Norman territory, on the other side of the wild deep sea' can only mean England. If this seems a little hyperbolic as a description of the Channel, one should remember that in those days, if a storm blew up, ships often took several days to make the crossing—if they arrived at all.[11] Appel has carefully shown that in only a few years of Henry's agitated reign was he in England in late autumn and expecting to return to France in the near future. To Appel, the most likely date seemed to be 1155, the year after Henry's coronation. From an allusion in Chrétien de Troyes' *Cligès,* he showed that Chrétien was probably also with Henry's court in

England that year. Bernart's famous song of the lark has left clear traces in Chrétien's work.[12]

In another song by Bernart, it is certain that the 'Queen of the Normans' is Eleanor of Aquitaine, and that the song is addressed to her:

> I don't know when I shall ever see you again;
> but I leave sad and cast down.
> I have left the King for you,
> and I beg you it may not go against me,
> because I shall be well-mannered in court. . . .
>
> Huguet, my well-bred messenger,
> sing my song willingly
> to the Queen of the Normans.[13]

The only thing that we do not know, and which Pound probably accepted as he accepted so much in the *vidas,* is what Bernart's *vida* tells us: that they fell in love, or rather had fallen in love before Eleanor was Henry's Queen.[14] The *vida* at this point is extremely unreliable, because it has Eleanor as 'Duchess of Normandy' before she has married the Duke (later Henry II), and appears to know nothing of her previous marriage to Louis VII of France.[15] But there is no particular reason for disbelieving the *vida* on this essential.

BERTRAN AND ELEANOR

As I have noted, this affair between Bernart de Ventadorn and Eleanor depends in Pound on having Malemort as Eleanor's place, to which the suffering Bernart comes in Canto VI. Pound makes great play with Malemort in his translation of the song of the borrowed lady, by Bertran de Born, and in *Near Perigord,* having first identified it in *Na Audiart* as the castle of Bertran de Born's lady, Audiart. 'Audiart of Malemort', Pound seems to have thought, would be Bertran's poetic name for Eleanor. Pound probably also thought that this fitted the better because, according to the *razos,* Audiart was the friend of Maria de Ventadorn. He doubtless thought that Maria was that wife of the Lord of Ventadorn with whom Bernart de Ventadorn had fallen in love, so that it would be natural for Bernart to appeal concerning her to her 'friend' Audiart/Eleanor, as in the *vida* she seems to appeal to her.[16]

The chronology does not make this impossible. Presumably Pound has Bertran de Born addressing his strophe to Eleanor/Audiart after (considerably after) the liaison with Bernart de Ventadorn, since at that period Bertran de Born would be impossibly young. But there are great improbabilities.[17]

We have very little idea who the 'Audiart' in Bertran de Born's song of the borrowed lady might have been.[18] She appears in the prose of the Provencal biographers, but only in the contexts that we know to be the least reliable: the love-stories attached to the various poems. Thus she plays a part in the saga of Gaucelm Faidit, which is constructed from various themes standard to these writings—and also, I have noted, to the supposed 'judgements' of the 'courts of love'. In the *razo* to a poem by Pons de Capdoill, she is identified as the 'wife of the lord of Marseilles', whom one manuscript identifies further as Roncelin, brother of the famous Barral. This is unsupported. As for Malemort, it exists, but it is not mentioned either in the song of the borrowed lady or in any other song by Bertran de Born or Bernart de Ventadorn.[19]

The supporting idea that Pound may have had—that Bernart de Ventadorn went to Eleanor/Audiart to seek help concerning his lady who was being guarded close, because the lady was Audiart's friend—is unlikely. The wife of the Viscount of Ventadorn who 'fell in love with [Bernart] and he with her' would not have been Maria, because Maria married Eble V de Ventadorn in about 1190; that is, forty-two years after Henry II took Eleanor away from Bernart, an event that the *vida* places after the Ventadour affair.[20]

So one cannot prove that Bertran de Born gave the name 'Audiart' to Eleanor of Aquitaine. On the other hand, the old battle-axe may well have been close to Eleanor. I have discussed at some length a song that he addressed to her daughter, Matilda of Saxony, making intimate allusions to Matilda's beauties. He appears to have owed the introduction to his overlord, Richard Lionheart, the lady's brother—with whom, as I have argued, Bertran de Born was probably involved politically for many years. Richard, of course, was Eleanor's favourite son, and it was for aiding and abetting her sons in their rebellions that Henry II imprisoned her. She could hardly not have known Bertran.

ARNAUT AND ELEANOR

Pound connects Arnaut with Eleanor when he refers to Arnaut's song of nails and uncles in the middle of Eleanor's affair with her uncle in Antioch (Pound's Acre), in Canto VI. Arnaut's song is a strange one, and it is the first known sestina. Pound had said of it in 1913: 'nor do I translate the sestina, for it is a poor one'; but many of his opinions on the troubadours had changed since then.[21] In the song, Arnaut says that he will seduce the lady under the nose of her uncle, as here in Pound's erroneous translation:

> Firm desire that doth enter
> My heart will not be hid by bolts or nailing....
> Yea, by some jest, there where no uncle enters
> I'll have my joy in garden or in chamber.
>
> I remember oft that chamber
> Where, to my loss, I know that no man enters
> But leaves me free as would a brother or uncle....[22]

I know of nothing specific to suggest that this song is about Eleanor and Raymond of Antioch.

I have noted the lines in Canto VII that weave Arnaut Daniel in with Eleanor, going from Helen of Troy ('helenaus') to Odysseus and his beach-groove, to Eleanor, to Arnaut/Ovid's 'scarlet curtain', to

> Lamplight at Buovilla, e quel remir

and back to Poe's Helen. William of Bouvila's wife is said by the Provencal *vida* to have been Arnaut's lady, but the vida says that he never had joy of her.[23] *E quel remir* is a piece of Arnaut's writing on which Pound played many variations in his ideograms of clear outline; one of the parallels is the 'scarlet curtain' which 'throws a less scarlet shadow' in the previous line.[24] What is Eleanor doing at Bouvila? Perhaps I am wrong to think that she is there in Pound. At any rate, I know of no evidence to connect Eleanor with this place.

If Arnaut Daniel knew Eleanor of Aquitaine, we know it from Eleanor's very close relationship with her son Richard (certain) and from Arnaut's relations with Richard (not so certain). Arnaut's relations with Richard are known only from a *razo* to one of Arnaut's songs, telling of a poetic competition between Arnaut and another *jongleur* under the genial chairmanship of King Richard. I think Toja is right to call this *razo* an anecdote.[25] I would point out that the whole thing is probably expanded from a misreading of the *envoi* to the song, where, thought the *razoiste,* Arnaut speaks of a 'song that Arnaut doesn't forget'—the point of the story being that he learns the other *jongleur's* song off by heart because he can't invent one for himself.[26] It is very interesting to note that Pound made exactly the same error: in his essay 'Arnaut Daniel', he excludes the song from the Arnaut canon on the grounds that 'he learnt this song from a jongleur, and he says as much in his coda: —...."Give thanks my song, to Miells-de-ben that Arnaut has not forgotten thee." '[27] Thus not only did Pound construct his Provençal myth from the Provençal *vidas* (used in so many Cantos); he also checked it from the songs, thus reinforcing his belief in the *vidas,* as did scholars through most of the nineteenth century. Gaston Paris, whom Pound respected, was one of the first to point out that there was no point in checking *vidas* against songs, because many *vidas* were cooked up from the songs.[28] None the less I would not reject the information in the *razo* that Arnaut knew Richard. Stories in this material are often invented; connections of persons and places are usually correct.[29]

BERTRAN AND ARNAUT

First there is the 'Bertran' addressed by Arnaut in the striking image, 'from the Nile to the setting sun'—an image that Bertran uses, though Giraut de Bornelh does also.[30] This piece of Pound's evidence stands. Then there is the common relationship with Richard Lionheart, which can be judged on the evidence I have already cited; to me it seems likely.[31] There is the '*al* and *ochaisos*' in *Near Perigord,* which, as I have said, may allude to a song in which Bertran clearly makes fun of Arnaut.[32] Bertran obviously takes on its form to prove that he can equal the great master of the 'closed style', and at the end he wipes his brow in mock weariness now that the test is passed.[33] It happens that Bertran's song is addressed to the barons, to bring them onto Richard's side against Philippe-Auguste of

France; Arnaut Daniel was in contact with Philippe at least and, as we have seen, probably with Richard.[34]

The final point in Pound is that Bertran and Arnaut came from very near each other. This is valid; Bertran's castle is documented by a chronicler (a relative of his), and Arnaut's birthplace, Ribérac, is not the kind of place that the Provencal biographers chose to name when they were inventing.[35] Bernart de Ventadorn comes into this point. Bernart was from the castle of Ventadorn, near Egletons (again the *vida* is the authority but is probably right).[36] Ventadorn (modern Ventadour) is about 140 kilometres east of Ribérac, and Hautefort (Bertran's castle) and Excideuil (Bertran's final retreat) are close together about half-way between them. And finally, just as Arnaut addresses a 'Bertran' in his song, so Bertran addresses 'Arnaut the *jongleur*' in a *sirventes* aimed at Richard.[37] It seems certain that Arnaut and Bertran knew each other.

BERNART, ARNAUT, AND BERTRAN

Bernart de Ventadorn was probably about thirty years older than Arnaut, and twenty years older than Bertran. But there is the geographical proximity; and there is also the fact that Bernart and Bertran both retired to the Cistercian abbey of Dalon, about six kilometres from Hautefort.[38] Clearly there is no strong connection between Bernart de Ventadorn and the other two, nor does Pound make any, beyond what we can infer from their having known Eleanor.

To conclude, hard evidence for this central 'Vortex' in Pound is lacking, but on the other hand the evidence does not rule it out. Given the cultural currents that I have described in Eleanor's time, not to mention the shared poetic awareness, Pound's myth is representative of interactions between these people.

NOTES

✣✣✣✣✣✣✣✣✣

INTRODUCTION

1. 'Provence' is, geographically, the part of Southern France that lies East of the Rhône. But the traditional name for the language of Southern France as a whole is 'Provençal' (though sometimes the *langue d'oc* or hence *Occitan*), and 'Provence' is a traditional name for the whole linguistic area and its mediaeval troubadour culture.

2. See Chapter 5, text before n. 41.

3. Cf. Chambers, 'Imitation of Form in the Old Provencal Lyric', p. 114, and passim; Dante, *De Vulgari Eloquentia*, II.III.

4. See Chambers, 'Imitation of Form in the Old Provencal Lyric', pp. 112 ff., and Chapter 9, text before n. 55.

5. For the 'first troubadour' see Chapter 5, text before n. 1 ff. Richard I of England, a patron of troubadours, was an accomplished versifier in French; Savaric de Mauléon was both baron and troubadour (Chaytor, *Savaric de Mauléon,* passim), as was the Dalfi d'Alvergne (Boutière and Schutz, *Biographies,* pp. 284-285). For Bertran de Born and Raimbaut d'Orange, poor knights, see Chapter 2, text before n. 20.

6. Among troubadours who appear to have lived by singing are Bernart de Ventadorn (Boutière and Schutz, *Biographies,* p. 20), Marcabrun (ibid., p. 10), Peire d'Auvergne (pp. 263-264), and Giraut de Bornelh (pp. 39-40). Arnaut de Maroill is said to have been unable to earn a living by his letters, and so to have taken to wandering as a singer (p. 32); Gaucelm Faidit lost everything at dice and so became a singer (p. 167); and Peirol was thrown out by his patron, and so forced to live as a wandering singer (p. 303). Although much of this information is not supported by sources other than the *vidas* I have cited, this material is reliable in such areas to a considerable degree (see Appendix 2, nn. 35, 29).

7. Cf. Raimon de Miraval, *Poésies,* no. XL, *Bajona, per sirventes:* 'Bajona, I know for certain that it is for a sirventes you have come among us, and counting this one there will be three, for I have already made you two, from which you have earned much gold and silver, Bajona! and many a worn outfit and clothes bad and good....'

8. See Chapter 8, text before n. 8, Chapter 9, text before n. 37, Chapter 6, text before n. 5.

9. See Chapter 9, n. 26, text before nn. 25 ff.; Chapter 3, text before n. 49; above, n. 7.

10. For this process cf. Chapter 9, text before n. 108.

11. For the history of interest in the Provencal lyric see especially Jeanroy, *Poésie,* 1, pp. 1-30.

12. Kenner, *Pound Era,* pp. 109-112.

13. Among those writing in the decades before and after the turn of the century, Paul Meyer, Gaston Paris, and Carl Appel remain as readable as when they were first published, since their deeper humanity and genuine enthusiasm for the subject triumphs over these impulses.

14. See Chapter 8, nn. 52, 98, 106, and Makin, *Ezra Pound and Mediaeval Provençal Poetry,* pp. 399ff.

15. *Spirit,* p. 5.

16. Frank's figure, in *Répertoire métrique,* I, p. xvi, note.

17. The order of troubadours treated in the 'Proenca' chapter of *The Spirit of Romance* (1910) is taken from Farnell, *Lives of the Troubadours,* with interpolations from Dante, *De Vulgari Eloquentia,* and Appel, *Chrestomathie.* Cf. Chapter 4, n. 13, and Makin, *Ezra Pound and Mediaeval Provencal Poetry,* pp. 699ff., on some of Pound's early sources.

18. Cf. Makin, *Ezra Pound and Mediaeval Provencal Poetry,* pp. 62-98, and below, n. 22.

19. The only professional Provençal scholar to have assessed Pound's handling of the language is A. H. Schutz, co-editor of the standard edition of the *vidas* and *razos.* His skimpy article, 'Pound as Provençalist', is misconceived and ill-executed. It restricts itself to questions of scholarly accuracy in Pound's treatment of the Provencal prose, on the theory that translation or adaptation 'is a poet's privilege' (p. 60) — and therefore, we are to take it, entirely unamenable to scholarly comment, while prose is entirely a matter for scholarly comment and has nothing to do with poetic abilities. Such a distinction will not work with anything more complex than 'The cat sat on the mat.' Even within the limitations that it permits, Schutz deals only with the more obvious essays in *Spirit* and *Essays.*

The article's sense of the scope and priorities of scholarly concern is remarkable. Of the sixteen points it makes, one is in Pound's favour: that the reference 'R71 superiore' (sic in Schutz) in *Cantos,* 20/98:93, shows that 'Either Pound utilized the manuscript itself or the reference to it in *Herrig's Archiv*' (p. 61). (It is in fact quite clear from the Canto's narrative that Pound was bringing copies he had made from the MS. in Milan.) Schutz is not concerned with any particular gain that Pound may have made by using the manuscript; only, it is unscholarly to use printed editions. Of the other fifteen points, eight concern mis-spellings, mis-declinings or mis-conjugatings of Provencal words or phrases, and in none of these eight cases does Schutz bother to claim that the mistake was at all material to Pound's understanding of the original. Accuracy of spelling is taken as an end in itself, and carelessness dealt with in appropriate rhetoric: 'This conflict is eternal and to be expected when the poet meets the academic, but does that justify the change in spelling of *A. de Mareuill* de *Marvois?*' (p. 62, ref. to 'Troubadours', p. 430 [*Essays,* p. 98]).

The remaining points are either trivial or, which is less excusable in an attack based on scholarly accuracy, wrong in point of fact. Pound, Schutz observes, uses the word *razo* to cover the 'lives' as well as the commentaries (p. 59, ref. to 'Troubadours', p. 427 [*Essays,* p. 95], etc.). Further, Pound permits himself to translate words meaning 'let herself be abducted by him' as 'let herself go gay' (p. 60, ref. to

'Troubadours', p. 429 [*Essays*, p. 97]). Then Pound's misreading of an MS. leads him to translate 'gave candles at church for his recovery' instead of, perhaps, 'put herself in a heretic convent' (p. 60, ref. to 'Troubadours', p. 432 [*Essays*, p. 100]); but here, instead of making clear to Pound what he has done (he has read something like French *cierges*, 'candles', for Provencal *eretges*, 'heretics'), Schutz instigates this futile exchange: 'When I pointed out to him that there were no candles in the *razo* version, Mr. Pound came back with the incontrovertible question: "Any evidence against candles?" What is to be done with this situation? The matter of academic accuracy obviously did not enter the picture.' I note also that even in the matter of spellings, Schutz is willing to exercise very little acumen on Pound's behalf: he says that '*Boetand of Beanon* should be *Boet e Beanon*' (p. 62), when it is simply a printer's error for 'Boet and of Beanon' (*Essays*, p. 99; 'Troubadours', p. 432, has 'Boet and of Benaon').

Pound, Schutz goes on to complain, read a MS. *Uzerna* as 'the Palux Lerna', when 'the most respectable authority' says it refers to a place called *Uzercha* (ibid., ref. to 'Arnaut Daniel', p. 44 [*Essays*, p. 109]); true, but that 'authority' was not sure of itself on this point: Canello changed his mind, later proposing to accept the inferior manuscripts' readings *p[a]lus [plutz] de [da] lerna;* and the latest edition prefers *Ugernum* (Beaucaire), another place altogether (see Arnaut, *Canzoni*, p. 354, nn. 27-28). Further, Schutz objects, Pound refers us to a 'manuscript of Miquel de la Tour' in Paris, when la Tor's original collection has certainly disappeared (p. 61, ref. to 'Troubadours', p. 427 [*Essays*, p. 95]); true, but it is hardly a grievous mistake for Pound to have been misled by the Paris MS. that says la Tor wrote it, not realising that it is a partial copy made only a few years later than the original (cf. Peire Cardenal, *Poésies*, pp. 608-609). Then comes the criticism of Pound that in *Cantos*, 20/89-90:93-94, he has Emil Levy telling him that he, Levy, does not know the meaning of *noigandres*, when in fact Levy had published the meaning of it years before (ibid.). This is quite wrong; in the poor English that Pound has Levy using, the great man is clearly intended to be referring to *past* bewilderment (see Chapter 8, text before n. 86). All that this incident shows is that Pound had not by then noticed the solution in Levy's dictionary or in Lavaud's edition of Arnaut, but had to ask the professor in person (cf. Chapter 8, n. 91). Finally, in *Spirit*, p. 53, Pound does not, despite Schutz (p. 63), wonder what has happened to the rest of the Aimeric de Belenoi; he simply says 'I have not come upon the rest of the stanzas.'

I go over Schutz's article thus exhaustively (I have included all the concrete points it makes) to show to the reader — Provençalist, Poundian and impartial — the quality of attention that Pound has received from the world of Provençal scholarship. In all this there is no mention of Pound's wider aims, or of the qualifications that Schutz actually considers necessary to fulfil them. For this kind of approach by scholars to translation, and for a discussion of criticism of Pound's work with Provencal in general, see my article, 'Ezra Pound's Abilities as a Translator of Provencal', pp. 39ff.; and for an estimation of his early competence in the language see ibid., pp. 29-38.

20. Like Eliot, Pound believed that, cut off from the past culture, life becomes meaningless; but while Eliot tended to think that he himself as a function of that

past culture could hardly even presume to choose between the relative values of its different elements, Pound was American enough to think that his single, Midwestern soul could confront the entire past culture of the world and pronounce on its relative utility for modern man. The results were not so different: both poets effectively made a choice from past cultures, Pound's based on what might be called a 'Specific Fulfilment-level', Eliot's on what had actually constituted the core and direction of the past culture itself, whose coherence it was his duty to preserve.

21. Jeanroy's phrase describing the troubadours around Eleanor of Aquitaine, in *Poésie*, 1, p. 151 (see Chapter 6, n. 65).

22. For valuable treatments of the early work with Provençal, see Kenner, 'The Broken Mirrors and the Mirror of Memory'; Quinn, 'The Metamorphoses of Ezra Pound'; Baumann, *The Rose in the Steel Dust*. See discussions of these and other critical works in Makin, *Ezra Pound and Mediaeval Provencal Poetry*, pp. 62-98, and discussions of Pound's metamorphosis-Cantos and related poems, ibid., pp. 37-47.

Surviving information about the troubadours can be divided into three categories: (a) songs or other versified material; (b) *vidas* and *razos;* (c) historical material (non-literary documentation, archaeological remains, possible spoken tradition and indeed all material that does not come within the first two categories).

Until about 1913, Pound had at his disposal, broadly speaking, only the first two categories; but by the time he had ceased to write short poems and to translate the troubadours, that is by about 1920, his sources of information had greatly expanded, and it becomes difficult to identify them in every instance (see Chapter 4, nn. 14ff.). He had studied the songs of Arnaut Daniel in great detail, and had considered the troubadour culture so deeply that adequate explication of his work on it requires the whole second section of this book.

Three possible manners of studying Pound's work on the troubadours would be: (a) to use only that information on the troubadours that Pound himself gives in his various works; (b) to use the information that Pound gives, with the addition of the relevant songs, *vidas,* and *razos*—in other words, to be generally in the same position as Pound's up to about 1913; (c) to use all information of whatever kind, and in particular all that discovered by researchers into the troubadour culture, so as to be in a position to assess Pound's work from an independent standpoint.

The relative value of these methods is not as straightforward as it might seem. In certain areas—because Pound only went to a certain depth of a study, because that depth is possessed of its own mythic reality, and because Pound's writings cross-refer so extensively—it is possible to do no research at all on the troubadours themselves, and yet to deal with them in an entirely adequate manner in a very profound study of Pound's poetry. Baumann has done this in *The Rose in the Steel Dust*. By contrast, it is possible to adduce the texts of the *vidas* and the songs in a study of Pound's early troubadour-inspired poetry, without in the least adding to the reader's understanding of Pound. In this case the text is given in the Provencal, to impress the unlearned, but the unlearned cannot read it and the learned learn nothing that would not have been clear from a translation—and probably knew the text anyway. This has been practised extensively by Nagy, and less so by others.

There are various positions between the two. Stock, for instance, carries an air of great learning in this field as in others, though he adduces no Provençal texts; yet he follows all Pound's mistakes. The *Annotated Index* of Edwards and Vasse attempts to solve the problems posed by the Cantos in the Provençal field by recourse to the texts of the songs and the *vidas*, but simply does not know enough to avoid misinforming as much as it informs. Until recently the sole venture into my third category of information (with the exception of isolated citations of Jeanroy's general study) was by Ruthven in his *Guide to Ezra Pound's 'Personae' (1926)*; Ruthven had read Stronski's work on Bertran de Born and Farnell's *Lives of the Troubadours,* and referred to Hatto *Eos.* However, his Provençal scholarship was not reliable. Despite its title, McDougal's *Ezra Pound and the Troubadour Tradition* added nothing to these sources, though it followed up the reference to Hatto, and even muddied waters that had been clear in Ruthven (see my review, cited in the Bibliography). Hugh Kenner in *The Pound Era* makes an independent, valuable, and generally reliable use of other sources, but his treatment is necessarily very brief.

23. *Hugh Selwyn Mauberley: 'The Age Demanded'.*

CHAPTER 1. GLAMOUR AND POLITICS

1. Smith, *Troubadours,* 2, p. 50; cf. Boutière and Schutz, *Biographies,* p. 280. For more 'drama' see Smith, *Troubadours,* e.g. 1, p. 7. Cf. Pound's much later remarks on nineteenth-century culture in *Essays,* p. 340; 'there was the Mephistopheles period, morals of the opera left over from the Spanish seventeenth-century plays of "capa y espada".'

2. Quoted in Norman, *Ezra Pound,* pp. 17-18.

3. Cf. Stock, *Life,* pp. 41-43.

4. Cf. *Letters,* to William Carlos Williams, 21 Oct 1908.

5. Paige's footnote to *Letters,* to Harriet Monroe, 1 Jan 1918.

6. 'Note' to *Na Audiart;* for the dating of *Na Audiart* see Stock, *Life,* pp. 37-38.

7. Appel, *Chrestomathie,* no. 20 (Bertran, *Dompna, puois*) (Bertran, *Lieder,* no. 5). None of the texts of the *Dompna puois* available to Pound differs significantly.

8. A 'germ' (Henry James's term) is not a literally read and historically placed event, but a psychological interaction whose force happens to be felt particularly by the writer. All his poetic life, Pound found 'germs' in the interstices of the most accidental phrases, as well as in mistranslations; see, for example, his Chinese work, discussed in Dembo, *The Confucian Odes of Ezra Pound,* pp. 28-32, Kennedy, 'Fenollosa, Pound and the Chinese Character', pp. 28ff., and Kenner, *Pound Era.* For the way Pound picked up things that a native speaker might not be aware of, cf. Kennedy, ibid., p. 35. Of course, it goes without saying that these things are usually present in the native speaker's mind at some sub-conscious level, and may legitimately be brought out by the translator to buttress what he feels is the general direction of the original.

9. Published in *Personae* (1909).

10. Pound's *'Dompna pois de me no'us cal'* was published in 1914, as *A Translation from the Provençal of En Bertrans de Born*.

11. See below, text before n. 45, and for Provençal prose based on misreadings, below, text before n. 47.

12. *The Garden* (published in 1913) describes a girl who

> is dying piece-meal
> of a sort of emotional anaemia.

13. Cf. *Spirit*, p. 128, on Dante's myth of justice by prolongation of states of mind after death. Pound's own hell-Cantos seem to have a similar intention; there is no threat of a real after-life in them; in *Cantos*, 13/59:63, Confucius firmly says 'nothing of the "life after death"', and in *Cantos*, 29/145:150, Pound records his antipathy to the fear of an after-life expressed by Arnaut/Eliot (cf. Kenner, *Pound Era*, pp. 336-337, and Chapter 10, n. 156).

14. *Essays*, p. 342.

15. Published June 1908 in *A Lume Spento;* one of the poems in the manuscript 'Hilda's Book' of 1905-07 (cf. Stock, *Life*, pp. 23-24).

16. *Piere Vidal Old* says

> Green was her mantle, close, and wrought
> Of some thin silk stuff that's scarce stuff at all,
> But like a mist wherethrough her white form fought

and

> God! how the swiftest hind's blood spurted hot
> Over the sharpened teeth and purpling lips!

For such reasons I find the neo-Platonic interpretation of these poems, e.g. in McDougal, *Ezra Pound and the Troubadour Tradition*, p. 38 and passim, superfluous.

17. For Pound's comments on the original see *Spirit*, p. 47. His translation, eventually called *'Dompna pois de me no'us cal'*, was published in *Poetry and Drama* in 1914; when Pound reprinted it as part of a footnote to *Near Perigord* (his reconstruction from Bertran's poem, published in *Poetry* in 1914), he added the envoi that he had omitted: see below, n. 44. The praise that Pound gave to Bertran's poem is in 'Arnaut Daniel', p. 48 (*Essays*, p. 114).

18. Cf. Kenner, 'The Broken Mirrors and the Mirror of Memory', p. 9: 'Maent herself, like the lady in the canzone, *was* a collection of fragments. Perhaps it was a love-poem. Perhaps it sang of war. . . . But preeminently, it was imitation in the Aristotelian sense: an arrangement of words and images corresponding to the mode of being possessed by the subject.'

19. *Three Cantos of a Poem of Some Length: I*, p. 182.

20. Cf. ibid; this meditation is more extended in the slightly earlier *Three Cantos: I*, pp. 114-115, where Pound notes that the point is the poet's self-projection into these figures, but gives the process the same sense of 'evasion' and contrivance. *Three Cantos of a Poem of Some Length: I*, p. 184, seems to suggest that Arnaut

and Uc de St.-Circ are too real, for Pound, to allow him to subject them to the same process (the sense is slightly clearer in *Three Cantos: I*, p. 117).

21. *Three Cantos of a Poem of Some Length: III*, p. 196 (cf. *Three Cantos: III*, p. 250).

22. Ruthven (*Guide*, p. 178) notes that Pound told T. E. Connolly that this Cino was fictional, and that some of Pound's early poems reprinted in the 1965 *A Lume Spento* are signed 'Cino'. Pound cites part of Browning's *Sordello*, about 'Cino at the fountain', in *Spirit*, p. 132.

23. *Cantos*, 2/6:10.

24. *Confucius to Cummings*, p. 8.

25. Cf. *Essays*, p. 267, attacking the Browning conception of 'thought', and comparing 'ideas' unfavorably to the direct apprehension and articulation of particulars. Cf. also Pound's description of the Mauberley as 'a mere surface. Again a study in form, an attempt to condense the James novel' (*Letters*, to Felix E. Schelling, 9 July 1922). Note further Louis Zukofsky's remarks in 1929 (*Prepositions* p. 69), describing the self-conscious, gesturing operatics of Pound's philosophising in the 1917 *Three Cantos of a Poem of Some Length*. Zukofsky says that Pound has now moved towards the method of the *Divine Comedy*, 'directed towards inclusiveness, setting down one's extant world and other existing worlds'.

26. See Pound's Note 'On "Near Perigord" ', p. 146. The *razo* says that Henry II took Bertran's castle, and then taunted the troubadour with his poem in which he had said he would never need more than half his wits; didn't he need them now? Bertran replied that he had lost his wits the day that the Young King died; and Henry, moved to tears, thereupon gave him back his castle, with the royal favour and 500 marks (Boutière and Schutz, *Biographies*, pp. 107-108). This is apocryphal; cf. Chapter 3, n. 53.

In *Three Cantos of a Poem of Some Length: I*, p. 182, Pound seems to say that Browning's historical errors are not important:

> half your dates are out; you mix your eras;
> For that great font, Sordello sat beside—
> 'Tis an immortal passage, but the font
> Is some two centuries outside the picture—
> And no matter.

But they contribute to the general sense of dissatisfaction that makes Pound conclude, as we have seen (above, n. 20), that he cannot do a *Sordello* with the troubadours:

> what's left?
> Pre-Daun-Chaucer, Pre-Boccaccio? Not Arnaut,
> Not Uc St Circ.

27. 'On "Near Perigord" ', pp. 145-146; though Pound pointed out that 'When [Bertran] did not keep them busy fighting each other they most certainly did close in upon him—at least once' (ibid., p. 146).

28. Compare the description of Chalais in *Near Perigord* with Smith, *Troubadours*, 2, p. 228: '. . . poor Born crossed the hills, and rode on till the woody mead-

ows of the Teude grew narrow, and the highlands thrust a wedge between the river and its confluent [the Dronne]. At the point of the wedge stood Chalais. A comfortable chateau is there now, looking down comfortably upon the marshes and poplars.' Pound refers to Smith's book for the meeting between Bertran and Henry II in his note 'On "Near Perigord" ', p. 146.

29. For *Provincia Deserta* see Stock, *Life*, p. 177; cf. also *The Gypsy*, stemming from the same summer. For the holiday with Eliot in 1919 see Kenner, *Pound Era*, pp. 333-338. The architectural education is described in *Kulchur*, p. 111; cf. Pound's disagreement with James in *Essays*, p. 330. For the *Pisan Cantos* see Peck, 'Landscape', p. 27.

30. Cf. Chapter 3, n. 62.

31. Quoted Appel, *Bertran*, p. 37; see Chapter 3, n. 53.

32. Ibid., p. 30ff.

33. Clédat, *Bertran*, was published in 1879; it placed *Un sirventes on motz no falh* in 1176; cf. Appel *Bertran*, p. 28, note, and Bertran, *Lieder*, no. 13. This song is discussed in Chapter 3, n. 43.

34. It is true that the song which is Pound's epigraph, *Un sirventes on motz no falh*, is impossible to date with any certainty (cf. Appel, *Bertran*, p. 28, note). Pound might therefore legitimately take it to be of the period of the 1176 revolt, as did Clédat (*Bertran*, pp. 29ff.). But this plea, and my point about misinterpreting the song as implying that Périgueux is in the enemy's camp, may be misplaced, for Pound probably lumped all these songs together. He quotes *Be·m platz lo gais temps de pascor* (Bertran, *Lieder*, no. 40): ' "Pawn your castles, lords!" '—and the *razo* to *Puois lo gens terminis floritz* (cf. ibid., no. 21):

> Beaten at last,
> Before the hard old king

These songs are, respectively, undatable (cf. Appel, *Bertran*, p. 80) and of the period when Bertran was with Richard against his barons, that is 1184 (cf. ibid., p. 44, note). But even this cannot reconcile history with the abortive 'compact' that Pound has Bertran setting up with the surrounding castles against both Périgord, one of the principal barons, and Richard. At no time was Bertran against both Richard and the barons, as is suggested by the lines where Sir Arrimon sends word to Coeur de Lion:

> The compact, de Born smoked out, trees felled

Until the barons betrayed him, Bertran was with them and against Richard; and after, vice versa. For the historical alliances see Chapter 3, text before n. 9; cf. especially 'Since Ventadorn and Comborn and Segur', quoted in Chapter 3, text before n. 14, and Appel, *Bertran*, p. 23.

35. Chabaneau, *Biographies*, pp. 18, 24; (cf. Boutière and Schutz *Biographies*, pp. 75, 91) (*razos* to Bertran's *Domna, puois* and *Puois lo gens terminis*, *Lieder* no. 5, 21).

36. The form *Maenz* was used by editors up to and including Stimming; but it is ruled out by manuscript and linguistic considerations (cf. Stronski, *Bertran*, p. 9, note). Appel, *Bertran*, p. 16, note, gives up the attempt to find out who the real 'Bel Senher' was.

37. Stronski, *Bertran*, p. 33.

38. Ibid., pp. 20ff.

39. It is quite possible that the historical prototype of 'Maeut/Maent', 'Beautiful-Lord', is the third daughter of Turenne (cf. Chapter 3, text before n. 61, and Stronski, *Bertran*, p. 95). But Contors de Turenne did not marry Hélias de Comborn until about 1184 (Stronski, *Bertran*, p. 41), so that the key castle would have to be that of her father, Raimon II, situated about forty kilometres south-east of Hautefort and, again, not outflanking it. However, as a mere daughter of the house, she might not have much sway over its politics.

40. Stronski, *Bertran*, pp. 60-61.

41. Bertran, *Poésies*, p. xiv, and cf. Chapter 3, n. 53. Connolly, 'Ezra Pound's "Near Perigord"', pp. 112-113, says that the 'four brothers' are the Plantagenet princes, and Ruthven, *Guide*, p. 179, makes them the sons of the Count of Perigord; but cf. 'I Gather the Limbs of Osiris V: Four Early Poems of Arnaut Daniel', p. 201: 'En Bertrans de Born, fourth holder in the tower of Altaforte.'

42. Appel, *Chrestomathie*, no. 35, *Ieu m'escondisc*.

43. For Wagadu see e.g. *Cantos*, 74/430:457, 77/465:494; for the Hautefort story see *Cantos*, 105/749:774, and Stock, *Reading the Cantos*, p. 112.

44. Appel, *Chrestomathie*, no. 20; Pound added his version of this coda when he cited the poem in the note 'In "Near Perigord"', p. 145; it contains his mistake:

> Papiol, my lodestone, go, through all the courts sing this canzon,
> how love fareth ill of late; is fallen from his high estate.

45. *Kulchur*, p. 127.

46. Pound's terms, describing the *Cantos* in 1932: 'Best div. prob. the permanent, the recurrent, the casual' (*Letters*, to John Drummond, 18 Feb 1932).

47. Cf. Appendix 2, text before n. 25. The classic study of the way *vidas* and *razos* were built out of misreadings of the songs is Paris, *Mélanges* (his article, 'Jaufre Rudel'), pp. 498-533: Jaufre's death at the feet of the Countess of Tripoli was built out of various metaphors in his songs, pp. 529-530, and Richaut de Berbézieux's complicated romance was built out of another metaphorical hyperbole, p. 509. Note also that the story of Peire Vidal and the 'She-Wolf' of Pennautier was built out of a wish and a pun in the troubadour's works; cf. Stronski, *Folquet*, p. VIII. The unidentifiable 'Bernart de Cornilh', whom the Arnaut Daniel *razo* takes as a genuine person, was probably invented by Arnaut out of the word *cornar* (Chapter 8, n. 13); cf. Paden's similar suggestion for the origin of 'William of Bouvila' (ibid.).

48. There is no phrase corresponding to 'lust of travel' in the original (cf. Chabaneau, *Biographies*, p. 49, Appel, *Chrestomathie*, p. 191, Boutière and Schutz, *Biographies*, pp. 229-230, and Pound's translation in 'Troubadours', pp. 427-428 [*Essays*, pp. 95-96], which is largely accurate). But in 'Troubadours', p. 430 (*Essays*, p. 98), translating the *vida* of Elias Cairel (Chabaneau, *Biographies*, p. 50; cf. Boutière and Schutz, *Biographies*, p. 252), Pound misreads the phrase *en Romania*, 'in Romania', as 'wandering'—presumably something like *en romerya*. This passage in *Cantos*, 5/18:22, also has the line

> *Lei fassa furar a del,* put glamour upon her. . . .

This is a combination of Pound's idea that such was the way the English knight won the lady, and his translation of this into Provençal. It should read *Fes la furar ad el*, 'had her carried off to him', and is modified from the *vida* of Peire de Maensac (Boutière and Schutz, *Biographies*, p. 301: *se laisset furar ad el*), which Pound translates in the same essay, giving his misreading of this phrase in brackets ('Troubadours', p. 429 [*Essays*, p. 97]). Chabaneau, *Biographies*, p. 58, has *se laisset envolar ad el*, so that this is clearly one of the mistakes arising from Pound's own work with the manuscripts; see Chapter 4, n. 16, and Introduction, n. 19.

49. See Chapter 8, text before n. 98.

50. First published in the *English Review* (June 1909).

51. 'How I Began', p. 707 (facsimile in Stock, *Perspectives*, p. 1).

52. 'Ezra Pound', p. 258 (in Russell, *An Examination*).

53. *Gaudier-Brzeska*, p. 44; *Letters*, to William Carlos Williams, 19 Dec 1913.

54. The solidity of the structure (cf. e.g. photograph in Davenson, *Troubadours*, p. 55) may well have added to Pound's impressions, though it had been completely rebuilt (Clédat, *Bertran*, p. 24).

55. Hutchins, *Pound's Kensington*, p. 129.

56. Ruthven, *Guide*, s.v. *Sestina: Altaforte*.

57. *Cantos*, 80/509:543; cf. Edwards and Vasse, *Annotated Index*, s.v. *Altaforte*.

58. For a gloss on the Velasquez see *Kulchur* p. 110, where Pound is describing the Prado; also 'Pastiche. The Regional. IX', p. 284. For the encounter at Born see *Impact*, p. 77. Edwards and Vasse, *Annotated Index*, s.v. *c'est nôtre comune*, gloss this as 'it's our bailiwick', but given Pound's French, the context of the story, and the circumflex in *nôtre*, it seems more likely that it means 'It belongs to all of us', i.e. the omelette that the peasant was sharing out. For the *cavals armatz* see Bertran, *Lieder*, no. 40, *Be·m platz lo gais*, and Chapter 2, text before n. 4.

59. Kenner, *Pound Era*, p. 256; cf. Pound's description in *Gaudier-Brzeska*, p. 49.

60. 'Vortex. Pound', p. 153.

61. Gourmont, *The Natural Philosophy of Love*, pp. viii, xvi. For the date of the 'Postscript' see Gallup, *A Bibliography of Ezra Pound*, A22.

62. For 'direction of the will' see Dante, *De Vulgari Eloquentia*, ed. Meozzi, II.II, and Pound, in *Impact*, pp. 136, 122, 129, *Confucius/Analects*, pp. 243 (11.XXV, cf. *Cantos*, 13/58:62), 268 (15.XXXVI), *Cantos*, 77/467:497, 87/572: 608, 87/576:612, and *Jefferson and/or Mussolini*, p. 17, etc. In *Impact*, p. 136, Pound glosses it with a phrase from Mencius: two characters, the first of which he translates as 'raise' and the second as 'will'. He divides the 'will' character into a scholar-officer on top and a heart beneath: the raising action is built-in. This 'direction' prepares for the intuitive leap, as Brancusi says in *Cantos*, 97/677:708: 'mais *nous*, de nous mettre en état DE les faire', 'But *ourselves*, to get ourselves ready TO make them.' The 'First Classic' passage is *Cantos*, 99/702:732 (cf. 99/697:727); its source is given in Terrell, 'The Sacred Edict of K'ang-Hsi', p. 87 (cf. p. 99).

63. *Kulchur*, p. 194; *Essays*, p. 83, cf. below, n. 67.

64. 'Psychology', pp. 45-46, 50 (*Spirit*, pp. 92, 97).

65. *Essays*, p. 151.

66. Cf. 'Psychology', pp. 37-53 passim (*Spirit*, pp. 87-100), *Selected Prose*, pp. 55-60, and Chapter 10, text before n. 131.

67. *Cantos*, 53/263:273; cf. *Kulchur*, p. 106, referring to Mussolini and others: '"Human Greatness" is an unusual energy coupled with straightness, the direct shooting mind, it is incompatible with a man's lying to himself, it does not indulge in petty pretences.'

68. *Essays*, pp. 150-151.

69. *Letters*, to Felix E. Schelling, 9 July 1922.

70. *Cantos*, 45/230:240; *Gold and Labour*, p. 12; *Letters*, to Carlo Izzo, 8 Jan 1938. Cf. *Social Credit*, p. 6: 'Usury and sodomy, the Church condemned as a pair, to one hell, the same for one reason, namely that they are both against natural increase.' See also *Impact*, p. 233, where Pound repeats the phrase *contra natura*, 'against nature', that is the climax of the usury-Canto cited above, 45/230:240. (The New Directions has the correct 'CONTRA NATURAM'.) Banks of discount were for Pound 'hell banks' (*Social Credit*, p. 8); cf. also the 'buggering bank' quoted from *Cantos*, 77/468:497, by Hugh Kenner in *Pound Era*, p. 426, note.

71. Bertran, *Lieder*, no. 35; see Chapter 2, text before n. 14.

72. *Impact*, p. 13; cf. *Cantos*, 17/78:82: 'In the gloom the gold / Gathers the light about it.'

73. *Cantos*, 14/63:67.

74. *Cantos*, 107/762:787; cf. Bowen, *The Lion and the Throne*, p. 360. Elizabeth I translated Horace; 'the buggar' is James I.

75. For the clean line see *Letters*, to Carlo Izzo, 8 Jan 1938; for 'Hoggers of harvest' see *Gold and Labour*, p. 13. I cannot recall the location of the phrase 'facile abnegation' in Pound; it refers to an over-readiness to give up hope in the human faculties and to see virtue in denying them. Cf. *Cantos*, 99/702:731: 'Bhud: Man by negation.' For static harmonics see *Patria Mia*, p. 80; for 'sharp song' see *Cantos*, 74/439:466, and Chapter 8, nn. 97, 81. Though I refer to the distinction between genital and anal, and the connection between money-hoarding and anality, as 'Freudian', I should not wish to imply that Freudian analysis accounted for or invalidated Pound's aesthetic. My formulations would probably not have been reached without the stimulus of Norman O. Brown's *Life Against Death* in particular, but there is a great deal in Brown that I would not accept. I am willing only to show psychological *groupings* and their possible consequences, on the basis of characteristics visible in Pound's writing, of image and tone; and having done that, I will judge the value of particular groupings by my own sensibility. I will not, as Freudians do, speculate on the possible *origins*, in an unknowable individual or universal childhood, of these groupings. Such speculation seems to me to belong to pure metaphysics, though for example Brown is not loth to acknowledge this: ibid., p. 84. Pursued relentlessly, it gives rise to categorisations that are radically cruder than the more empiric groupings of poetry (see Pirandello on Cocteau and Freud, *Cantos*, 77/469:498, cited in Chapter 5, n. 64). This rationalistic machinery is then used to judge the value of particular image-groups — according to whether they are associated with the death-wish, etc.

It is clear that Brown's favoured groupings do not tally with those of Pound. Brown is a little vague on desirable states for the human being; he speaks of the resurrection of childhood polymorphous perversity, and the way that this can express itself in art, but we see few examples—perhaps they belong to the area of the millenium. Brown's speculations, like Freud's, make him connect 'phallic organization' to the death-instinct (p. 27), and though he may convince himself that this death-wish is necessary, we are by now in the realm of pure talk. For Brown, all civilisation is anal (p. 295); capitalism is merely a limiting emphasis on the anal, in the same way that the phallic emphasis of adult sexuality is too limiting.

My groupings of Pound's images show that Pound allowed for areas of adult, phallic, and beneficent constructivity, which partly took their ethic-aesthetic value from their difficulty. The reader must decide for himself whether the groupings represent accurately the content of Pound's work; whether Pound was making valid connections between these images; and which of the two groupings he himself finds the more admirable, if either.

76. For the relation of these qualities to Pound's Provence see especially Chapter 8, text before n. 79. For Malatesta 'as illustration of intelligent constructivity' see letter quoted by Myles Slatin in 'A History of Pound's *Cantos* I-XVI, 1915-1925', p. 194.

77. Cf. *Cantos*, 39/196:204, 47/238-239:249, 29/145:150.

78. Dick, *Writers at Work*, p. 112.

79. *Cantos*, 99/702:732. See also the attack on 'sissified fussiness' and 'slovenly sloppiness' in *Cantos*, 99/705:734, and Terrell, 'The Sacred Edict of K'ang-Hsi', p. 79. Eliot describes Pound's 'increasing defect of communication', 'as if the author was so irritated with his readers for not knowing all about anybody so important as Van Buren, that he refused to enlighten them', in 'Ezra Pound', p. 23. For Pound's struggle of the will see also Olson's remark: 'Ep's poems are—after the early Guido's—one long extrapolation, canzone, on WILL: how, to get it, up' (*Letters for Origin*, p. 129).

80. Norman, *The Case of Ezra Pound*, p. 55.

81. *Spirit*, p. 178.

82. Ibid., p. 46.

83. 'Troubadours', p. 440 (*Essays*, p. 107). *Gai saber*, 'gay wisdom/learning', is a term for the later institutionalised poetry of the troubadours' successors (see Lafont and Anatole, *Littérature occitane*, 1, pp. 229ff.), but here Pound obviously means that of the troubadours themselves.

84. *Hugh Selwyn Mauberley: E.P. Ode Pour l'Election de son Sépulcre*, IV; Bertran *Lieder*, no. 9, *Lo coms m'a mandat*, quoted in Chapter 2, text before n. 2. Bertran's phrases seem to fuse with those of a 1918 anti-war pamphlet: see Griffin, ' "E.P. Ode Pour L'Election de Son Sepulchre" and Max Plowman's Pamphlet'.

85. *Gaudier-Brzeska*, p. 63.

86. *Essays*, p. 296.

87. *Spirit*, p. 48, note.

88. *Kulchur*, pp. 205-206.

89. *Essays*, p. 296.

90. *Cantos*, 7/24:28.

91. 'I Gather the Limbs of Osiris VI: On Virtue', p. 224 (*Selected Prose*, pp. 229-230); *Letters*, to W.H.D. Rouse Jan 1937.

92. For similarly badly invented Old French see Chapter 4, text before n. 22. For the idea of 'listening to one's craft' cf. *Cantos*, 85/546:582, where one shuttles between *techne*, 'craft', and *seauton*, 'self'. John E. Hankins's suggestion in *Paideuma*, 2.1, p. 141, based on a rare meaning of the Old French *mestiers*, that it means ' "and the listened-to needs" ' referring to the prayers which are uttered by celebrants in the religious procession which E. Hesse thinks is suggested by the beginning of the line', does not seem to me to fit any possible context. Eva Hesse (*Paideuma*, 1.2, p. 272) points out that the text appears to have been changed at this point; and I think she is right to refer to the connection between *métier* ('craft') and 'mystery' (which gave rise to a confusion between the two roots in older English, as she does not mention). But I think her suggestion of a religious procession for 'To file and candles' is unlikely, given the words of Horace, Arnaut Daniel, and Dante on poetry as a business of filing down, and the English cliché 'burning the midnight oil'.

93. Dante, *Paradiso*, 18.100-101; Edwards and Vasse, *Annotated Index*, s.v. *ciocco*, seems unaware of this source.

94. *Cantos*, 5/17:21.

95. See *ABC of Reading*, pp. 51-52 relating ideogram to the saga narratives' ability to convey the moving image.

96. *Kulchur*, p. 261.

97. *Cantos*, 85/548:584.

98. *Confucius*, p. 21; see also *Cantos*, 85/546:582, 87/574:610.

CHAPTER 2: BERTRAN'S PROPAGANDA

1. *Confucius/Analects*, pp. 203 (3.XIV), 226 (8.XI); cf. *Cantos*, 53/268:278-279.

2. Bertran, *Lieder*, no. 9, *Lo coms m'a mandat*.

3. Ibid., no. 28, *No puosc mudar, un chantar*.

4. Ibid., no. 40, *Be·m platz lo gais*. Appel places this with 'Songs of which Bertran's authorship is doubtful'. I see no troubadour other than Bertran whose tone of mind corresponds to that shown in this song.

5. Bertran, *Lieder*, no. 22, *Quan vei pels vergiers*.

6. The *razo* at least (to ibid., no. 7, *Ges de disnar no*) tells us that this poem was written on campaign, to the sister of Richard Lionheart and mother of the Emperor Otto, and though it takes the complimentary epithet 'Helen' to be her real name, there seems no reason to doubt the situation it suggests; cf. Appel, *Bertran*, pp. 6-10.

7. Bertran, *Lieder*, no. 7, *Ges de disnar no*. Compare the sound and image play in Bunting's *Briggflatts*, in *Collected Poems*, p. 53, describing tea in a Dales farmhouse.

8. Bertran, *Lieder*, no. 11, *Puois Ventadorns*.

9. Ibid., no. 40, *Be·m platz lo gais*.

10. Ibid., no. 24, *Mout m'es deissendre*.

11. Ibid., no. 29, *S'ieu fos aissi senher*.

12. Ibid., no. 13, *Un sirventes on motz*.

13. Ibid., no. 35, *Be·m platz quar trega*.

14. Ibid., no. 19, *Rassa, mes si son*.

15. Ibid., no. 10, *Cortz e guerras*.

16. Ibid., no. 35, *Be·m platz quar trega*.

17. Ibid., no. 37, *Miei-sirventes vuolh far*. Cf. also below, text before n. 55, for what Pound takes to be a trick on usurers.

18. 20/92:96.

19. Bertran, *Lieder*, no. 39, *Bel m'es, quan vei*. Bertran does not think that only the young have courage (ibid.):

> A man is young when he puts his goods at risk,
> and when he is impecunious;
> he stays young, when hospitality costs him a lot,
> and when he makes extravagant gifts;
> he keeps himself young when he burns up coffer and jar
> and when he wants to hold a court and enter lists;
> he stays young when he likes gaming
> and is expert at womanising.

20. Cf. Bloch, *Feudal Society*, p. 169.

21. Raimbaut, *Works*, p. 16.

22. Ibid., pp. 14, 13.

23. See Chapter 3, n. 53, Chapter 1, text before n. 41, and Bloch, *Feudal Society*, p. 131: 'Many petty lords, however, particularly in central France and in Tuscany, practised parcenary just as the peasants did, exploiting their inheritance in common, living all together in the ancestral castle or at least sharing in its defence. These were the "parceners of the ragged cloak", whom the troubadour, Bertrand de Born, makes the very type of poor knights.'

24. See Raimbaut, *Works*, p. 16.

25. The rise of the communes in Languedoc closely parallels that of the city-states of North Italy, with which they had strong economic links: ibid., p. 17.

26. *Girart de Roussillon*, tr. Meyer, p. lxxvii, referring to laisse 637.

27. Cf. Bloch, *Feudal Society*, p. 238.

28. Cf. Raimbaut, *Works*, p. 18, and Bertran, *Lieder*, no. 36, *Ar ve la coindeta*.

29. Raimbaut, *Works*, p. 18.

30. *The Seafarer*, p. 44.

31. Pound's phrase, *Essays*, p. 343.

32. Bertran, *Lieder*, no. 28, *No puosc mudar, un chantar*.

33. Ibid.:

> No puosc mudar, un chantar non esparja,
> Puois n'Oc-e-No a mes fuoc e trach sanc,
> Quar grans guerra fai d'eschars senhor larc,
> Per que·m platz be dels reis vezer la bomba,
> Que n'aian ops paisso, cordas e pom,
> E·n sian trap tendut per fors jazer,
> E·ns encontrem a miliers et a cens,
> Si qu'apres nos en chan hom de la gesta.

34. Ibid., no. 33, *Anc no·s poc.* Appel has

E si tolia e donava,
No·s biais
Dels afans!

But he notes that Stimming, Thomas and all the MSS. have

E sai tolia

which is the reading that I follow.

35. Ibid., no. 25, *A totz dic;* cf. Chapter 3, text before n. 60 for the lament on the Young King. See also Lefèvre, 'Bertran', pp. 603, 606, for Bertran's epic heroes and use of the 'epic list'.

36. *Girart de Roussillon,* tr. Meyer, p. lxxii.

37. Bertran, *Lieder,* no. 37, *Miei-sirventes vuolh far.*

38. *Roland,* laisse CIV, where Bédier strangely translates 'Trenchet le cors [?]' as 'tranche la coiffe (?)'. Compare also the mashing of brains in Bertran, *Lieder,* no. 13, *Un sirventes on motz,* and *Roland,* laisse CVI.

39. Owen makes the soldier into a modern St. Sebastian in his 'Preface', in *Fragment: 'It is not Death',* in *The Parable of the Old Men and the Young,* etc., and especially in *Arms and the Boy* and *Greater Love:* a laughing, supple, lithe, blond youth twisted in exquisite agonies of death. The Darwinian mode is in *The Show, Asleep, Sonnet: On Seeing a Piece of Our Artillery Brought Into Action,* etc.: man as worm, universe as machine.

40. Lejeune and Stiennon, *La légende de Roland dans l'art du moyen âge,* I, p. 405.

41. Ibid., I, p. 325.

42. Ibid., I, p. 235.

43. *Roland,* laisse CIII. Cf. Bertran, *Lieder,* no. 34, *Volontiers feira,* where Bertran urges Philippe-Auguste to attack Richard (Bertran's own lord).

44. Cf. Bloch, *Feudal Society,* p. 102: '. . . from the very earliest period of the French *gestes*—before 1100—noblemen took to giving their sons the names of Oliver and Roland, while that of Ganelon, branded with a mark of infamy, was never used again.' Bloch notes (ibid.) how Glanville, Henry II's justiciar, seems to cite *Gormont* and *Raoul de Cambrai* as history.

45. Ibid., p. 99; cf. Adams, *Mont-Saint-Michel,* pp. 19-23.

46. *Girart de Roussillon,* tr. Meyer, p. lxxxv.

47. It was hard to inflict decisive defeats in the field, and until the tactical innovations of Henry II and Richard, castles were extremely difficult to reduce; so that, unable to 'knock out' his enemy, the attacking leader would use strategic devastation to punish or demoralise. Cf. ibid., p. lxxv; Warren, *Henry II,* p. 102, for the power of castle-holders in the south-west, and pp. 231-237 for Henry II and Richard's new methods of warfare. For examples of strategic devastation by Stephen, Richard, and others, see Warren, *Henry II,* pp. 37, 87, 106, 108, 571, and the advice given to Philip of Flanders: 'First waste the land, deal after with the foe' (ibid., p. 231).

48. Bertran, *Lieder*, no. 13, *Un sirventes on motz.* Cf. ibid., no. 19, *Rassa, mes si son,* second strophe.

49. Bloch, *Feudal Society*, pp. 290-291; *Girart de Roussillon*, tr. Meyer, p. lxxii; Warren, *Henry II*, p. 232; above, n. 47. For the horrors inflicted by mercenaries, cf. Ramsay, *Empire*, p. 212, and *Chanson de la Croisade*, laisses 20-22.

50. Bertran, *Lieder*, no. 17, *Mon chan fenisc.*

51. Ibid., no. 15, *Ieu chan que·l reis.*

52. *Girart de Roussillon*, tr. Meyer, pp. lxxxvii-lxxxviii. Raimbaut, *Works*, p. 16, note Peire Rogier urging Raimbaut d'Orange to live up to the image of noble munificence.

53. Ibid., pp. 13-14.

54. Ibid., p. 17. In Raimbaut's case the lenders were mostly related to him, but the chiefest of them, Guilhem VII of Montpellier, was connected with the wealth of that great new trading town (see ibid.).

55. Bertran, *Lieder*, no. 40, *Be·m platz lo gais.*

56. *Essays*, p. 94. This was not in the original of 1913: 'Troubadours: Their Sorts and Conditions', p. 426, being added at a time when Pound was more interested in economics: it first appears in the revision for *Pavannes and Divisions* (1918), p. 166. Cf. *Near Perigord:* ' "Pawn your castles, lords! / Let the Jews pay." ' This is almost undoubtedly more Pound than Bertran (the mistranslation of these lines in *Spirit*, p. 48 [cf. above, text before n. 55], is, however, not material here). Probably all that Bertran meant was 'put money in your purse', as Iago says to Roderigo: he was telling the barons to put everything into cash for arms and supplies: in other words, to risk everything on the fortunes of war, and not to feel tied down by the vulnerability of real property. Cf. above, n. 19: 'A man is young when he puts his goods at risk....' Raising money on real property was probably much riskier than Pound thought, since it was more like an actual pawning than a mortgage: there was no tenure during the period of the loan, no enjoyment of the income from the holdings, and every chance of not getting the property back. This was Raimbaut d'Orange's situation; cf. Raimbaut, *Works*, pp. 13-14. Meyer notes borrowing *sur nantissement* ('pawning') in *Girart de Roussillon*, Meyer, p. lxxxviii, note.

57. Warren, *Henry II*, pp. 33, 49, 58; Guillaume le Maréchal, *Histoire*, vv. 2223ff.

58. Cipolla, *Money*, p. 64. Hence it was probably not the Jews, as Pound hoped in *Near Perigord* (cf. above, n. 56), who paid for the warfaring, but the people at large, through exactions by their rulers.

59. See Warren, *Henry II*, pp. 582-583.

60. Guillaume le Maréchal, *Histoire*, vv. 6805ff.

61. Cf. especially Cipolla, *Money*, p. 56; and compare Bloch, *Feudal Society*, pp. 64-65, on the dangers to merchants from local lords, somewhat before Bertran's time, with Bertran, *Lieder*, no. 37, 13 (quoted above, text before n. 17, and Chapter 3, text before n. 14).

62. Bloch, *Feudal Society*, p. 332, says Bertran was a man of 'begging habits'. Bloch sets out most vividly the physical delights of warfare for a knight of Bertran's time, and illustrates with a long quotation from Bertran himself, with his 'accurate

observation and fine verve' (p. 293). Then he feels that he must look for more solid motives. War 'offered a remedy for boredom' for 'these men whose culture long remained rudimentary' (p. 295). 'But fighting was also, and perhaps above all, a source of profit — in fact, the nobleman's chief industry' (p. 296). It seems to be the hallmark of the post-Marxist historian that he must refuse to believe his own perceptions, unable to rest until he has traced all action to that most bourgeois of motivations, desire for wealth. Only such an urge could make one implicitly include Bertran and his peers among the 'uncultured'. Warren, in *Henry II,* pp. 577-579, takes some of his approach from Bloch, but his views also stem from O. H. Moore, for whom see Chapter 3, text before n. 36. Karen Wilk Klein in 'The Political Message of Bertran de Born', p. 614, says that Bertran was 'very much concerned for his own skin'; she persuades herself that it was safer for Bertran to live under the suzerainty of Richard than under that of Henry II or Philippe-Auguste: 'He supported Richard in his wars with Henry II and Philip Augustus, always exhorting Richard to stand up and fight for his domains — which also meant fighting for the safety of Hautefort' (p. 615). First she argues that Bertran was chiefly interested in *terra,* 'land', then that he wanted to vindicate *dreit,* 'right(s)', and finally that he fought for *pretz,* 'reputation'; but since she then says that *pretz* is not simply based on the amount of land acquired, but is specifically distinguished by Bertran from acquisition motivated by greed for wealth and is dependent on *pro* 'inherent nobility', one wonders what has happened to her initial argument that Bertran only cared about property (pp. 614-630). Cf. Chapter 3, n. 39.

63. Cf. Bloch, *Feudal Society,* pp. 154, 157, 158, 163-164, etc.

64. Cf. ibid., pp. 171, 191-197.

65. Cf. ibid., pp. 224-238, 195.

66. See Chapter 1, text before n. 96, quoting from *Kulchur,* p. 261.

67. Cf. Bloch, *Feudal Society,* p. 202.

68. Cf. ibid., pp. 213, 219, 222, 223.

69. Ibid., p. 210.

70. Ibid., pp. 68-69, 71.

71. *Kulchur,* pp. 348-349.

72. Bloch, *Feudal Society,* p. 238.

73. Dante, *De Vulgari Eloquentia,* I.XVII-XIX.

74. For a definition of 'courtly love' see Chapter 5, text before n. 42. Peter Dronke (in *European Love-Lyric,* pp. 4-46) has shown that, thus defined, 'courtly love' can be found in many places outside the traditions connected with Provence and in many un-courtly situations. Why then do we call it 'courtly'? Because of the Provencal tradition, which was given a powerful secondary impulse by the Italians, and which is unthinkable without the vocabulary of the court and of nobility. Dronke says (pp. 2-3):

> Like Dante in the fourth book of the *Convivio,* I hold that here is a *gentilezza* which is not confined to any court or privileged class, but springs from an inherent *virtù;* that the feelings of *courtoisie* are elemental, not the product of a particular chivalric nurture. In the poets' terms, they allow even the most *vilain* to be *gentil.*

Admittedly Dante also wrote in the second book of the *Convivio* that *cortesia* derives from *corte*, for once virtù and *belli costumi* were in use there (though now, he says, the opposite is true).

Even in arguing that fineness of spirit is democratic in distribution, both Dante and Dronke are forced to use *gentile, cortese,* and so forth; which shows that their (our) myth is the Provençal one of the court, the myth without which we are unable to think of such qualities.

75. Cf. Davidsohn, *Firenze ai Tempi di Dante,* pp. 315, 318.

CHAPTER 3. HISTORY AND BERTRAN'S POETRY

1. For Dante's probable knowledge of the Provençal background, see Chapter 9, text before n. 94.

2. Stock, *Life,* p. 113, referring to 'Psychology and Troubadours': 'As a survey it is' useless because he did not know the subject beyond its literary surface. . . .'

3. Dante, *Inferno,* 28.112ff. and note.

4. Dante, *De Vulgari Eloquentia,* II.II.

5. Bertran, *Lieder,* no. 28.

6. The story of the struggle is concisely narrated in Higounet, 'La rivalité des maisons de Toulouse et de Barcelone'; cf. especially Raimbaut, *Works,* pp. 7ff.

7. Appel, *Bertran,* p. 19; cf. Higounet, 'La rivalité des maisons de Toulouse et de Barcelone', pp. 319-320.

8. Raimbaut, *Works,* p. 7; cf. Bloch, *Feudal Society,* pp. 211-214.

9. Cf. Warren, *Henry II,* pp. 560-561.

10. Cf. ibid., pp. 110-111; Ramsay, *Empire,* pp. 119ff.; Eyton, *Itinerary,* pp. 118-119. John received no land, hence his name 'Lackland'.

11. Cf. Warren, *Henry II,* pp. 117-118, 587-588 (Henry II required homage to the Young King from all of them, but Richard refused it); Ramsay, *Empire,* p. 183; Warren, *Henry II,* pp. 117-138.

12. The excuse was Richard's cruelty, but the barons may simply have disliked his interference in their affairs: cf. Benoît de Peterborough, quoted in Clédat, *Bertran,* p. 41; Warren, *Henry II,* pp. 564-565, 575-576, and on Richard's cruelty, p. 593.

13. Gervais de Canterbury, quoted in Clédat, *Bertran,* p. 41; Robert de Torigni, quoted in Ramsay, *Empire,* p. 212, note; Roger of Howden, quoted in Warren, *Henry II,* p. 587; for the rebellion as a whole cf. ibid., pp. 575-587.

14. The Provençal commentator explains that here Bertran is 'reproaching the Young King, because he was not more valiant in war, reminding him how Sir Richard had taken from him the revenue from the carts' (Boutière and Schutz, *Biographies,* p. 98). In other words, presumably, Henry II had allotted to the impecunious Young King the tolls on the roads in some of his territories, including Richard's Poitou and Aquitaine; or, perhaps, as Kate Norgate took it (*Angevin Kings,* II, p. 222), these revenues should have gone, in Bertran's eyes, to anyone calling himself a 'King'; but Richard, who as we know had effective power in his territories, was taking them for himself. Stimming said outright that the Provençal commentator

had this from a misreading of Bertran's text, which was really only a comparison (Bertran, *Bertran,* p. 159); and Moore followed him in this (*Young King,* p. 38). But Stimming gave no evidence for his view, and in particular no proverbs such as might give some significance to an otherwise bathetic simile. Appel leaves the case open (*Bertran,* p. 25). Lefèvre in 'Bertran', pp. 606-607, argues that Bertran was mocking the Young King by comparing him to the Chevalier de la Charrette in the work by Chrétien de Troyes composed a few years earlier. The Chevalier had to ride in a cart and endure public humiliation to deliver Guinevere; the Young King, by contrast, shamefully 'quit the cart'.

15. Bertran, *Lieder,* no. 11, *Puois Ventadorns.*

16. Ibid.

17. For this rebellion and earlier covert alliances see Ramsay, *Empire,* pp. 214-215, and Warren, *Henry II,* pp. 587, 589ff.

18. Bertran, *Lieder,* no. 14, *D'un sirventes no·m chal.* 'Broceliande', in Brittany, is Arthurian territory.

19. Warren, *Henry II,* p. 591.

20. Bertran, *Lieder,* no. 43 (among those that Appel considers of doubtful authorship; but the only other serious possibility as author is Peire Vidal). This is Appel's text:

> Si tuit li dol e·lh plor e·lh marrimen
> E las dolors e·lh dan e·lh chaitivier
> Qu' om anc auzis en est segle dolen
> Fossen ensems, sembleran tot leugier
> Contra la mort del jove rei engles,
> Don rema pretz e jovens doloros
> E·l mons oscurs e teintz e tenebros,
> Sems de tot joi, ples de tristor e d'ira.
>
> Dolen e trist e ple de marrimen
> Son remasut li cortes soudadier
> E·lh trobador e·lh joglar avinen....

21. The complaint to Geoffrey is in Bertran, *Lieder,* no. 19, *Rassa, mes si son;* for the taking of Hautefort see Geoffroy de Vigeois, quoted in Appel, *Bertran,* p. 37 (see below, n. 53).

22. Cf. Appel, *Bertran,* pp. 6ff., and below, text before n. 59.

23. Bertran, *Lieder,* no. 18, *Ges no mi desconort.*

24. Ibid., no. 20, *Ges de far sirventes.*

25. Ibid., no. 26, *Al doutz nuou,* no. 27, *Puois als baros enoia.*

26. It appears that Richard thought his father meant to pass him over for the succession to the throne; cf. Appel, *Bertran,* p. 54, and Ramsay, *Empire,* p. 240.

27. Ibid., p. 244, quoting Henry's no doubt apocryphal exclamation from Gerald of Wales; Appel, *Bertran,* p. 54.

28. Bertran, *Lieder,* no. 31, *Ara sai ieu,* lines 17-18.

29. Appel, *Bertran,* pp. 58-60; Bertran, *Lieder,* no. 42, *Quan mi perpens* (Appel is uncertain of the authorship).

30. Dante, *Inferno,* 28.35.

31. Cf. Clédat, *Bertran,* p. 22, quoting the Cartulary of Dalon; Raimbaut, *Works,* pp. 13-17.

32. Warren, *Henry II,* pp. 321-324, 571, and cf. Chapter 2, text before n. 49; Geoffrey of Vigeois called the castle *valde inexpugnabile* (below, n. 53).

33. For Constantine de Born see below, n. 53.

34. This is demonstrated quite clearly in Moore, *Young King,* pp. 48-61.

35. Bertran, *Lieder,* no. 13, *Un sirventes on motz.*

36. See Chapter 1, n. 47.

37. Moore, *Young King,* p. 38.

38. Ibid., p. 47.

39. Warren, *Henry II,* cites Moore as authoritative, concluding that Bertran was a composer of 'vocal graffiti' and without influence (pp. 577-578). He says (ibid.), 'It is significant that none of the major chroniclers of the time appears even to have heard of Bertrand de Born'; he omits to mention that Geoffrey of Vigeois, whom he calls 'the best' of the Aquitainian chroniclers (p. 576), speaks of Bertran (see below, n. 53). Klein, *Partisan Voice,* also accepts Moore as a basis for its section on Bertran (pp. 127-152; cf. p. 45), based on her 'The Political Message of Bertran de Born', for which see Chapter 2, n. 62.

40. Though one should not take Bertran at his (literal) word, one should certainly consider the tone of his language. Moore is sceptical, among other reasons, because Bertran claims to 'melt and temper' the barons of his neighbourhood (*Young King,* p. 39); Moore feels this to be a ridiculous claim. This shows a great insensitivity to the context: a certain hyperbole would be very natural to someone with Bertran's aims.

41. Moore alleges that Bertran's nickname for Richard Lionheart, 'Yes-and-No', was inappropriate because — historians tell us — Richard was a brilliant and very decisive warrior (*Young King,* p. 40); and that Bertran's compliments to Geoffrey were inappropriate because — Kate Norgate tells us — when he died 'No one regretted him....', and — as Ramsay tells us — for him no writer 'had a word of praise'. For a typical character-summary by Ramsay, one of Moore's standard sources, see Ramsay, *Empire,* p. 247, on Henry II: 'a clever, plausible, self-confident, assiduous man of business; industrious and prompt in action, subtle, tricky, and unscrupulous'.

42. Moore, *Young King,* pp. 44, 45; Moore also claims (ibid., p. 46) that Bertran made mistakes about the appearances of the three princes. Cf. Aston, 'The Provencal *planh:* I, The lament for a prince', p. 28: in the eleven laments considered, 'no attempt is made at a physical description of the departed prince beyond one cursory reference to his *bella faisso* and *humil semblan...* and to the fact that the poet weeps for *son cors e sa faysso e.l avinent aculhir e.l parlar.'* — references to personal appearance in this literature are so generalised as to be unidentifiable.

43. The song is Bertran, *Lieder,* no. 13, *Un sirventes on motz.* It belongs to the period of the 1182-83 uprising that Bertran had helped to stir up with his song about the new castle at Clairvaux. At this point he was trying to persuade William of Gourdon to join two (unnamed) Viscounts in the alliance, and to get Talairan of Périgord to stir himself (cf. Appel, *Bertran,* pp. 27ff., and Chapter 1, text before

n. 33). Since the first strophe concerns Bertran's brother, and since the second concerns his brother's old allies Adémar of Limoges and Richard (now fighting each other), we may assume that the song is some sort of agitation about Bertran's private struggle over the possession of Hautefort; though, as Appel says (*Bertran*, p. 26), many things in it are unclear. At any rate, this is the relevant stanza:

> I've got all my wits in my strongbox,
> even though, between them, Adémar and Richard
> gave me a fright;
> they've had me worried for a long time,
> but they've got such a brawl on now
> that their children (if the King doesn't separate them)
> will have a bellyful.

The King in question is clearly Henry II, the only person who could possibly be in a position to separate Adémar and Richard. Cf. Appel's remarks, *Bertran*, p. 65, with translation.

44. Moore, *Young King*, p. 42.

45. Ramsay, *Empire*, p. 65, note; Guillaume le Marechal, *Histoire*, vv. 2223ff. In the treaty of 1174 the Young King has been given only 'two castles in Normandy (of his father's choosing), with £15,000, Angevin (£3,750 sterling) *per annum*'. In the middle of the 1182-83 troubles Henry II raised the Young King's allowance to £100 Angevin per day, with trimmings; but this would still hardly compare with his brother Richard's rights over the whole of Poitou and Aquitaine, with legal use of half Poitou's revenue (cf. Ramsay, *Empire*, p. 183, and Warren, *Henry II*, pp. 138, 584). It was still, after all, 'living completely off allowances by number and by measure', which is what Bertran reproached him with, as a way of life unfit for a 'crowned king' (see above, text before n. 18).

46. There is further error in Moore's argument, and part of his attack on Bertran's credibility is based on obscurity. In Bertran, *Lieder*, no. 13, *Un sirventes on motz*, lines 3-7 can be translated:

> ...I have acquired such a manner
> that, if I have a brother, a cousin or a second cousin,
> I share with him egg and groat [i.e. everything],
> and if he then wants my share,
> I throw him out of the partnership.

Moore (*Young King*, pp. 49-50) takes the last line to mean 'I throw him some, out of good fellowship', tracing Bertran's name for largesse partly to this. But this misreading, made by Raynouard (1817-19), was corrected by Clédat in 1879, and the phrase was glossed clearly as '[aus der] Gemeinschaft' by Stimming in 1913. Cf. Clédat, *Bertran*, p. 30, note, Bertran, *Bertran*, p. 227, and Appel, *Bertran*, p. 29.

Further, Moore says that the name *senher de Niort*, 'lord of Niort', that Bertran uses for Richard when he asks for the return of his castle (*Lieder*, no. 18, *Ges no mi desconort*), is respectful in tone; hence, he claims, it is inconsistent with the supposed implications of the nickname 'Yes-and-No' (*Young King*, p. 40, note). One may reply that, first, a respectful tone in such a situation would hardly be surprising; but that, secondly, it is impossible to be sure of the tone of *senher de Niort*.

The turn of phrase is a common one; one suspects irony when Arnaut Daniel calls Philippe-Auguste of France the *bon rei d'Estampa*, the 'good King of Etampes', or Henry II the *reis de Dobra*, 'King of Dover' (Arnaut, *Canzoni*, no. XII, p. 310, and no. XII again). One suspects a pun when Bertran calls Richard *senher de Bordel*, either 'lord of Bordeaux' or 'lord of the brothel' (Bertran, *Lieder*, no. 23; cf. no. 24); for Bertran's taste for punning see Appel, *Bertran*, p. 44. It is conceivable that the *senher de Niort* has some connection with the famous abbey of prostitutes that William IX set up at Niort, according to legend current in Richard's time (see Chapter 5, text before n. 31). Richard was a notorious womaniser; see Benoît de Peterborough, quoted in Clédat, *Bertran*, p. 41.

For Moore's doubtful position on another crux, see above, n. 14.

47. Appel, *Bertran*, p. iii, noted that modern philology had examined Bertran's songs more than those of any other troubadour; William IX has by now probably caught up.

48. Bertran, *Lieder*, no. 9, *Lo coms m'a mandat*.

49. Chaytor, *Script*, pp. 130ff. For the subsistence of singers cf. Bloch, *Feudal Society*, p. 94.

50. Compare the *chanson de geste* behaviour of William the Marshal, noted by Paul Meyer in Guillaume le Maréchal, *Histoire*, p. xlvii, referring to vv. 5715ff.; Richard in his turn behaved in the same manner towards William (Appel, *Bertran*, p. 70, note; Guillaume le Maréchal, *Histoire*, vv. 9291ff.), who, though of humbler origins than Bertran, was considered the paragon of chivalry.

51. Moore, *Young King*, p. 41, referring to Bertran, *Lieder*, no. 14, *D'un sirventes no·m chal*.

52. Bertran, *Lieder*, no. 32, *Folheta, vos mi prejatz*.

53. Geoffrey of Vigeois, in Bouquet, *Recueil*, 18, p. 218:

Duke Richard and the King of Aragon, Alfonso, who had come to help the older King, came to Autafort and laid siege to the castle in strength, . . . and, to make it short, on the seventh day, on the octave of the day of the Apostles Peter and Paul (i.e. the 6th July), the Duke took the apparently untakeable castle by right of battle and gave it back to Constantine de Born, the son-in-law of Olivier de Lastours, whom his brother Bertran de Born had kicked out therefrom with treachery. . . .

54. Cf. Warren, *Henry II*, pp. 141-142, 234-235, 570-571.

55. Ibid., p. 593.

56. Geoffrey of Vigeois, in Appel, *Bertran*, p. 37 (see above, n. 53).

57. Cf. *Translations*, pp. 23-24, *Gaudier-Brzeska*, p. 84, and *Confucius/Digest*, p. 47 ('Tseng's Comment', VI.1), on 'absolute rhythm' and 'the precise word'.

58. Appel, *Bertran*, pp. 18-19; Chapter 6, text before n. 50. Appel, *Bertran*, p. 19, notes that Bertran had written political verses before the Plantagenet contact, but that only one song from among them has survived.

59. Bertran, *Lieder*, no. 7, *Ges de disnar no*; cf. Appel, *Bertran*, pp. 6, 7, 8, note, on the flattering address to Matilda as 'Helen'.

60. Bertran, *Lieder*, no. 8, *Chazutz sui de mal*.

61. Ibid., no. 7, *Ges de disnar no*; 'Beautiful-Lord' and 'Beautiful-Cembeli' are also mentioned in the song of the borrowed lady (ibid., no. 5; cf. Chapter 1, text

before n. 16) along with an Elis who could well be the third of the 'three of Turenne', Hélis (cf. also Stronski, *Bertran*, p. 96).

62. Whichever songs we take to be concerned with 'Beautiful-Lord' must be from before 1182, since in that year, as we have seen, Bertran says that she is as sand to Matilda's gold. Stronski appears not to have noticed this, since he places the *Dompna puois* after the arrival in Limousin of Guicharde de Beaujeu, and therefore after 1185 (*Bertran*, p. 96). But this event itself is difficult to date. Stronski bases himself on the fact that Geoffroy de Vigeois, whose chronicle stops on 26 February 1184, does not mention the marriage of Guicharde to Archambaut VI de Comborn, though he mentions that of Archambaut's brother; and that sometime between 1190 and 1195, when Guicharde's cousin made his will, the lady already had two sons; Stronski, *Bertran*, pp. 67-68 (cf. Clédat, *Bertran*, p. 11). But this dating is rather vague, and so Appel (*Bertran*, p. 14) takes it that we may well accept what the *razos* say: that the *Dompna puois* and the *Ieu m'escondisc* (Bertran, *Lieder*, no. 4) were composed by Bertran to excuse himself towards 'Beautiful-Lord' for his over-enthusiastic reception of Guicharde. Cf. Boutière and Schutz, *Biographies*, pp. 78, 81; *razos* to Bertran, *Lieder*, no. 4, 5. All this action would therefore take place before 1182, when Bertran was praising Matilda at Argentan; for if the *Dompna puois* must antedate the songs to Matilda, since Bertran there takes leave of the 'Beautiful-Lord' to whom the *Dompna puois* was addressed, the songs to Guicharde also antedate the *Dompna puois* according to the story in the *razos*.

63. The welcome to Guicharde is in Bertran, *Lieder*, no. 2, *Ai! Lemozis*, no. 3, *Cel qui chamja bo*.

64. Stronski, *Folquet*, p. 68*. Appel's argument (*Bertran*, p. 14) that Bertran's women are individually recognisable seems to me misconceived.

65. Bertran, *Lieder*, no. 8, *Chazutz sui de mal*.

66. Appel, *Bertran*, pp. 8, 10.

67. Giraldus Cambrensis, quoted in Bezzola, *Origines*, 3.1, p. 84; Warren, *Henry II*, p. 42, and note; Chapter 6, text before n. 20.

68. Cf. Chapter 6, text before n. 31; Bezzola, *Origines*, 3.1, p. 15, and note; Ramsay, *Empire*, pp. 97, 289; Warren, *Henry II*, pp. 119, 601.

69. Ibid., p. 575.

70. Bloch, *Feudal Society*, p. 308.

71. Bertran, *Lieder*, no. 33, *Anc no·s poc*; Appel, *Bertran*, p. 16.

72. Eyton, *Itinerary*, p. 248.

73. Bertran, *Lieder*, no. 3, *Cel qui chamja bo*; cf. Appel, *Bertran*, p. 12.

74. Appel, *Bertran*, p. 15.

75. Bertran, *Lieder*, no. 1, *Rassa, tan creis*. I think that Appel interpreted the term *entendedor*, 'confidant', correctly in the poem where it occurs: cf. *Bertran*, p. 12.

76. Villon, *Oeuvres*, 'Testament', lines 501ff.:

> 'Ces gentes espaulles menues,
> Ces bras longs et ces mains traictisses,
> Petiz tetins, hanches charnues,
> Eslevees, propres, faictisses
> A tenir amoureuses lisses: . . .'

Bertran:

> Rassa, domn' ai qu'es frescha e fina,
> Coinda e gaia e mesquina:
> Pel saur, ab color de robina,
> Blancha pel cors com flors d'espina,
> Coude mol ab dura tetina,
> E sembla conil de l'esquina.

77. Appel, *Bertran*, p. 14.

CHAPTER 4. FROM WILLIAM IX TO DANTE

1. *Kulchur*, p. 217: 'THE CULTURE OF AN AGE / is what you can pick up and / or get in touch with, by talk with the most intelligent men of the period?'; Eliot, 'Ezra Pound', p. 19: 'the ideal intellectual and artistic milieu which he was always trying to find or to found'; *Cantos*, 13/60:64: 'And Kung said, "Without character you will / be unable to play on that instrument" '; Pound, in Dick, *Writers at Work*, p. 102: 'I went to London because I thought Yeats knew more about poetry than anybody else.' Cf. Pound's interest in quality of conversation, *Cantos*, 82/525:560, 83/528:563.

2. *Impact*, p. 50, says that the ruling class rules because it communicates most quickly and uses information most efficiently; *Cantos*, 98/685:715: 'But Gemisto: 'Are Gods by hilaritas'; / and their speed in communication' (cf. 98/690:720).

3. Hutchins, *Pound's Kensington*, p. 31; cf. *Letters*, to Hubert Creekmore, Feb 1939:

> Literature rises in racial process. No need of letting off steam about process. You belong to the human species, you don't have to *do* anything about that; you can't become a kangaroo or an ostrich. Take all known family stocks from about 1630 via N. Eng. or Quaker whalers, landing I believe in N.J. Could write the whole U.S. history (American hist) along line of family migration; from the landing of *The Lion*, via Conn., N.Y., Wisconsin (vide *Impact*), to Idaho.

4. On his own 'frontier aristocracy' as race see *Impact*, p. 27; on its continuity of interest, pp. 65, 33; p. 247 says that made of government should suit racial character, so that fascism for example is wrong for the Anglo-Saxons. Radio broadcast quoted in Mullins, *This Difficult Individual*, p. 218: immigrant Americans had battened on a 'sort of carcass that can support the greatest number of lice, namely, parasites, subhuman or other'; Rachewiltz, *Discretions*, p. 167: 'his good friend Ubaldo degli Uberti, also mentioned for is likeness with the ancestor mentioned by Dante: ". . . Farinata, kneeling in the cortile, built like Ubaldo, that's race. . . ." ' —a reference to *Cantos*, 78/480:512 (cf. 95/644:677, 89/599:634, for the necessary 'Firm taste for good company', Kenner, 'D. P. Remembered', p. 490, and Chapter 9, text before n. 88).

5. *Confucius/Digest*, p. 59 ('Tseng's Comment', IX.3): 'One humane family can humanize a whole state. . . . Such are the seeds of movement.' For these 'seeds' working through history and producing the troubadours see Chapter 10, text be-

fore nn. 115, 134; for the Adamses as such a family see *Impact,* pp. 24, 59; *Cantos,* 37/186:192 (cf. *Impact,* p. 169). For the good/evil opposition see *Visiting Card,* p. 7: 'We find two forced in history: one that divides, shatters, and kills, and one that contemplates the unity of the mystery' (cf. *Cantos,* 'Addendum for Canto C', 798-799:28-29). For the chains working through history on the side of light see Chapter 10, n. 160, and Makin, 'Ezra Pound and Scotus Erigena', pp. 60-65.

6. *Cantos,* 95/647:679.

7. Pound, in Dick, *Writers at Work,* p. 109: 'My method of opposing tyranny was wrong over a thirty-year period; it had nothing to do with the Second World War in particular.' His remarks in this interview concede not that his perception of tyranny was wrong, but that having to construct his whole approach to it on his own had enmeshed him in errors of method.

8. *Cantos,* 40/199:207.

9. *Cantos,* 6/21:25. For William's life see following chapter.

10. See below, n. 13.

11. For the idea that William IX learned from Moorish culture, see Chapter 5, text before n. 57.

12. *Cantos,* 8/32:36.

13. There are two separate, but probably related, stories here. If 'ground rents' are Pound's modern equivalent for feudal dues and services, his line is closest to the story that William sold his wife's rights in the County of Toulouse, which is in the chronicle of Robert de Torigni (Robert de Torigni, *Chronique de Robert de Torigni,* 1, p. 320). If Pound's wording can be interpreted more generally, it could fit the story that William tried to pawn all his lands to William Rufus, King of England, but was thwarted when the king was killed; this is related by Orderic Vitalis (*Ecclesiastical History,* X.13, in e.g., Orderic Vitalis, *Ecclesiastical History,* ed. Chibnall, 5 p. 280, and Bouquet, *Recueil,* 12, pp. 677-678). Martindale, in *Duchy of Aquitaine,* pp. 139-140, raises not altogether conclusive doubts about both stories. I have not been able to identify Pound's immediate source, but cf. Richard, *Comtes de Poitou,* 1, pp. 424-428.

14. I translate this song, *Farai un vers, pos mi sonelh,* in its entirety, in Chapter 5, text before n. 85. The text is in Appel, *Chrestomathie,* no. 60, which Pound possessed, and from which he may have remembered it; but his reading is closest to Guillaume IX, *Chansons,* no. V:

> Tant las fotei com auzirets:
> Cen e quatre vint et ueit vetz

15. I have not identified Pound's immediate source. Any history would do; cf. e.g. Richard, *Comtes de Poitou,* 2, p. 59.

16. Boutière and Schutz, in *Biographies,* p. 8 (cf. Chabaneau, *Biographies,* p. 4), observe that the wife of William IX's son was not called 'Duchess of Normandy', this title being acquired by *her* daughter (Eleanor of Aquitaine) when she married Henry II of England. In thus showing himself unaware of the way in which the title was acquired, the biographer also seems to show that he did not know that Eleanor was first married to Louis VII of France. For a translation of this *vida* see Chapter 5, text before n. 32.

It is not possible to be sure of Pound's immediate text for the Provencal biographies, since in at least one case (see below, n. 33), and Chapter 1, n. 48) he was clearly still using his notes made in the Bibliothèque Nationale in May 1912 (cf. Stock, *Life*, p. 117) for the essay 'Troubadours: Their Sorts and Conditions'. For that essay, Pound did not use the available collection of *vidas* and *razos* (Chabaneau, *Biographies*), but copied all his material—except that referred to in passing —from the B.N. manuscripts. There are wide disagreements with Chabaneau's readings, and Pound's readings are very idiosyncratic. The essay, furthermore, contains material that was only available in Paris manuscripts at the time, and all the material was in Paris manuscripts IKCE; Pound did not even refer to sources he had used earlier, such as Farnell, *Lives*, and Appel, *Chrestomathie*. But Pound seems to have referred both to Chabaneau and to Jeanroy's edition of William IX for material other than the Provençal prose at certain points in this Canto. Jeanroy follows Chabaneau's text for this *vida* (Chabaneau, *Biographies*, p. 6; Guillaume IX, *Chansons*, p. 30):

17. *Cantos*, 1/3:7: 'Thus with stretched sail, we went over sea till day's end.'

18. Eleanor's uncle, Raymond of Antioch, 'commanded' and met them in Antioch, not in Acre: cf. Setton, *Crusades*, 1, pp. 503-504, Kelly, *Eleanor*, pp. 52, 67, 69, and Richard, *Comtes de Poitou*, 2, pp. 92-94; their port of entry was St.-Simeon, the port of Antioch, but their port of exit was Acre (Labande, 'Aliénor', pp. 184, 188). In *Cantos*, 94/640-641:673, Pound has

> Acre, again,
>   with an Eleanor

(referring to Eleanor of Castile, Queen to Edward I of England)—an obvious reminiscence of Canto VI. Pound's source, Vanel, *Intrigues galantes*, 1, p. 92, has 'Antioche' correctly. For the story see Chapter 6, text before n. 20.

The contemporary sources for the strong suspicions about the Queen's behaviour with Raymond include John of Salisbury, whose account seems reliable; see especially Labande, 'Aliénor', pp. 184-186, and also Pacaut, *Louis VII*, pp. 59-60, and Richard, *Comtes de Poitou*, 2, p. 93, note.

Pound's immediate source for this and for most of Eleanor's life with Louis was Vanel, *Intrigues galantes de la Cour de France*, of 1694, as is clear from the *New Age* article quoted in this chapter (text before n. 73). Vanel's work contains a large element of fiction: see below, n. 19. It relates (1, pp. 91-93) how Louis had married Eleanor in ignorance of her 'humeur extrémement coquette', and loved her so dearly that he insisted she accompany him to the Holy Land. At Antioch, Raymond tried to make them stay instead of pressing on for Jerusalem. Raymond had been brought up with Eleanor, and was of almost the same age as her, so that an illicit passion had grown up between them: Raymond had only gone to the Holy Land in order to forget Eleanor. Now his passion burned once more, and Eleanor was as complaisant as she had been at home. But the King insisted on reaching Jerusalem, and Eleanor soon forgot about Raymond, for she only loved what was in front of her, and there were many to console her. For the text, see Appendix 1, Text A.

19. Like the childhood affair with her uncle, Eleanor's affair with Saladin is impossible: in 1148, Saladin was ten years old (Labande, 'Aliénor', p. 187). According

to Paris, 'La Légende de Saladin', pp. 434-435, the Saladin story first surfaces in the *Récits d'un Ménestrel de Reims,* a fictionalised history written a little more than 100 years after the Second Crusade (cf. Chaytor, *Script,* p. 84). The *Récits* (like Vanel, *Intrigues galantes,* 400 years later) see Eleanor's life as one long interlude of jousts and dalliances. They recount how Saladin say Louis's 'flabbiness and foolishness' and therefore challenged him to battle, but Louis would not respond. 'And when Queen Eleanor saw the lack that the King had in him', she informed Saladin secretly that she would allow him to carry her off and be her lord. Saladin brought a galley at midnight, and Eleanor slipped out by a hidden entrance; but a chambermaid warned the King, who pounced on them at the port. See *La Chronique de Rains,* pp. 4-7; *Récits d'un Ménestrel de Reims,* pp. 1-7. The story may have arisen from the way that Louis carried Eleanor off by night to get her away from Raymond; later writers altered the legend in many ways, substituting the wife of Philippe-Auguste for Eleanor, for instance (see Paris, 'La Légende de Saladin', pp. 436, 434-435).

Pound's immediate source, as is quite clear from the earlier published version (see e.g. *The Sixth Canto,* p. 83), is Vanel, *Intrigues galantes.* In Vanel's account, having forgotten Raymond, Eleanor is fascinated by stories of Saladin, hearing that he is 'vaillant, genereux, liberal, galant; enfin qu'il avoit toutes les maniéres Francoises': a romantic descent from a French noblewoman taken into a Sultan's harem is attributed to him. Eleanor finds occasions to have dealings with Saladin, notably concerning the ransom of one Sandebreuil, captured by the Mohammedans. They rendezvous; Eleanor is greatly impressed by Saladin's compliments in perfect Italian; they retire for a long conversation in a bosque of palm trees, where Eleanor gives Saladin a scarf that she uses as a belt, which he wears ever afterwards (though not specifically in his helmet, despite Pound), thus giving rise to gossip which reaches the King. 'Though there was more vanity than passion on both sides in this commerce', the King is disturbed, and they leave the Holy Land. 'It seems that [in Sicily] she made peace with him; for she became pregnant...' (Vanel, *Intrigues galantes,* 1, pp. 94-96). For the text see Appendix 1, Text A.

20. The song says that Arnaut will seduce the lady despite her uncle; but I know of nothing to link it with Eleanor. For this and other possible links between Eleanor and Arnaut in Pound's thinking, see Appendix 2 and text before n. 21.

Arnaut's poem is *Lo ferm voler,* which I translate in its entirety, Chapter 8, n. 18. The text was available to Pound in Arnaut, *Opere,* no. XVIII, Arnaut, *Poésies,* no. XVIII, and Appel, *Chrestomathie,* no. 26, the latter of which he possessed, and all three of which he used at different times; the differences of reading do not seem to explain anything about this passage.

21. See above, n. 18, and Walker, *Eleanor,* p. 75.

22. Louis divorced Eleanor in March 1152, that is, three years after they left the Holy Land (Labande, 'Aliénor', p. 195); so Pound's 'Divorced her in that year' is wrong.

The continuity of the events that followed follows quite closely the brief account in Vanel, *Intrigues galantes,* 1, pp. 96-98. This, however, does not even mention the two high-ranking and importunate suitors who beseiged Eleanor on her way to Poitou before Henry met her, and who obviously gave rise to Pound's hyperbole in '(that had dodged past 17 suitors)'. Nor does Vanel's account give Pound's dating, or the several details in the earlier version (e.g. *The Sixth Canto,* p. 83), such as Louis's new queen (Pound has 'Adelaide', confusing her with Louis's third wife, Alais or Adèle, while Vanel has 'Elisabeth', and the right answer is 'Constance'); the time that Eleanor was free (Pound has five months; read, two); or the description of Henry (taken ultimately from Giraldus Cambrensis, *De Principis Instructione,* p. 214 [II.XXIX]). In view of the errors, Pound is unlikely to have used any of the standard histories available to him; cf. e.g. Richard, *Comtes de Poitou,* 2, pp. 106-110, Ramsay, *Foundations of England,* pp. 444-445, Lavisse, *Histoire de France,* III.I, pp. 28-29; he may have used the schoolbook that he speaks of (see this chapter, text before n. 73).

I have not been able to trace the Old French quotation, and in view of its peculiarities one might well conclude that it is Pound's invention in the style of one of the late French chronicles, such as the *Chronique de Normandie* in Bouquet, *Recueil,* 13, pp. 221ff., a thirteenth-century versification of Wace's *Roman de Rou.* Put into the French of the *Récits d'un Ménestrel de Rheims,* for example, it would come out perhaps as 'Et quand li rois Loeys l'oï, si en fu moult coureciés' (cf. *La Chronique de Rains,* e.g. pp. 6, 95). The earliest citation of *fascher* in Bloch and Wartburg, *Dictionnaire étymologique,* is for 1442. Pound did not invent Louis's general reaction: cf. e.g. the *Fragmentum genealogicum . . .* in Bouquet, *Recueil,* 18, p. 242, etc. But it is probable that Pound made a similar mis-invention in *Cantos,* 7/24:28; see Chapter 1, text before n. 92.

23. Henry II was laying a very dubious claim to the County of Nantes, as part of his general Continental expansion. To have any chance of succeeding in this, he needed the neutrality or the support of Louis VII, who of course should have seen the scope of Henry's designs and have put a stop to them. Henry sent the accomplished diplomat Thomas Becket to pave the way, offering the bait of marriage with his son Henry for Louis's daughter Margaret. Louis not only conceded a treaty of peace, but threw in as dowry the Vexin, which he, Louis, was to keep until the wedding; if the Young King died before the marriage, Margaret could marry elsewhere, and her future husband would receive Lincoln, Avranches, two castles, and various monies from Henry II (Bouquet, *Recueil,* 13, p. 300, note; cf. Robert de Torigni, *Chronique,* 2, pp. 167-168). But there were problems: Henry II wanted the lands immediately, without waiting for a marriage; and it was agreed that these lands should be held by the Templars. A second treaty was signed, to this effect, in 1160. The text of this treaty exists; it is printed in Bouquet, *Recueil,* 16, pp. 21-23, Delisle, *Recueil des Actes de Henri II,* 1, pp. 251-253, and so forth. It gave the Vexin to the Young King by way of dowry, to be taken by him in three years' time; but if the children married before then, with the Church's consent, Henry II could take the land immediately for his son. If the girl died, the Vexin and the castles would return to Louis; meanwhile, the Templars were to hold them.

This treaty of 1160 still does not name the places Pound specifies. However, as Bouquet, *Recueil,* 16, p. 21, note, points out, the castles mentioned in the treaty must be those the Templars handed over to Henry II as soon as the marriage was celebrated, as in Robert de Torigni's account of the year 1160 (Bouquet, *Recueil,* 13, p. 305): 'Without delay Margaret daughter of Louis King of the French was married off to Henry the son of Henry King of England . . . and Henry King of the English took three well-fortified castles, *Gisorz, Neafliam, Novum-Castellum*. . . .'

But the fact remains that the four lines in Pound are in the form of a quotation from a treaty, and that the treaty of 1160 does not give the details he mentions, while the formulae he uses (even ignoring the point that the *joven* is Provencal) are not in it or in any of the sources I have mentioned. (The treaty of 1160, it is true, gets somewhere near to Pound's 'But if no issue Gisors shall revert . . .', when it says that if Margaret dies before the marriage, 'the castles and the Vexin will go back to the hand of the King of France.')

Pound in fact probably never saw the treaty of 1160 or heard that there had been an earlier agreement in 1158. What he apparently did was to put together a chronicler's account of what had been agreed in 1158-60, with the text of the treaty of 1191, thus cooking up a 'text' for the 1158-60 agreements. The chronicler's account and the later treaty are both given (translated into French) in Zeller and Luchaire, *Philippe Auguste et Louis VIII*, which Pound used (see this chapter, text before n. 73). The former told Pound that Margaret had, by the earlier pacts, received 'the castle of Gisors and other neighbouring places' from her father Louis as dowry when she married the Young King, and that 'The Young King Henry was to hold this dowry for his life with reversion to his heirs, if any issued from his marriage; if Margaret left no children at the death of King Henry [the Young King], her dowry was to revert without dispute into the possession of the King of France.' (Zeller and Luchaire, *Philippe Auguste et Louis VIII*, pp. 11-12.) It only remained for Pound to take the names and the phrases from the much later treaty of 1191, which is given (again translated into French) in the same collection of documents, seven documents further on (ibid., pp. 29-32). He thus created something that appears to be excerpts from a treaty when no treaty in this wording exists.

This transfer of wording from 1191 to the document of 1158-60 seems to express Pound's sense of the continuity of this haggling over marriage alliances, as pretexts for settlements of the same territorial disputes, over a period of more than thirty years. Such a sense is stated very strongly in the earlier published version of Canto VI (cf. e.g. *The Sixth Canto*, p. 84), where Henry II and then Richard are shown hanging on to Gisors and the other places, against Louis and then against Philippe, using new marriage pairings as pretexts, and constantly embroiled in war: 'and never two years go by / but come new forays'. This latter line, repeated with variations, is taken from the brief introductory paragraph in Zeller and Luchaire, *Philippe Auguste et Louis VIII*, p. 11, which describes Philippe's constant attempts to increase his strength at the expense of the Plantagenets: 'During the 43 years that his reign lasted, he never allowed two springs to pass without warring against the Kings of England or their barons.'

For the texts, see Appendix 1, Texts B(i) and B(vii).

24. This treaty is still extant: see Chaplais, *Diplomatic Documents Preserved in the Public Record Office*, pp. 14-16, Bouquet, *Recueil*, 17, pp. 32-33, etc. Pound's source is the translation into French in Zeller and Luchaire, *Philippe Auguste et Louis VIII*, pp. 29-32, the text of which is given in Appendix 1, Text B(vii). Pound has added only 'once is father's ward and . . .', for the reasons given in the following note.

25. This treaty between Richard Lionheart (now King) and Philippe-Auguste came as the conclusion of a great deal of manoeuvring, recorded in French in Zeller and Luchaire's documents and taken into the text of the earlier version of Canto VI, but dropped by Pound from the final version. As we have seen in looking at Bertran de Born's career, Richard and Philippe, mutual and hereditary enemies, both wanted to go on crusade, and in order to protect their territories from each other, they agreed to go together. After a great deal of delay as each tried to be the last to go, they set off. Reaching Sicily, they ran into further disputes as Richard quarrelled violently with one of Philippe's knights over a game of tilting with reeds (Benedict of Peterborough, *Gesta Regis*, ed. Stubbs, 2, pp. 155-157). Then Tancred of Sicily told Richard that Philippe had claimed that Richard was plotting against Tancred, and had offered to join with Tancred in attacking Richard; but Tancred mistrusted Philippe's intentions. Philippe, confronted with his letters to Tancred, denied everything and claimed that Richard was trying to invent an excuse finally to get rid of Philippe's sister Alix/Aelis, though he had sworn to marry her. Richard's reply was that he could not marry the girl anyway: she had been tampered with by his father and had had a son by him. Philippe appears somewhat to have been taken aback by this; at any rate, on the receipt of large sums of money, he agreed to take back his sister and to let Richard marry as he wished (ibid., pp. 159-161).

A rather confusing agreement was reached concerning Gisors and the other territories: the treaty itself says that Richard and his heirs male by his new betrothed, Berengaria of Navarre, are to have these territories, but if Richard dies without heirs male, they are to revert to Philippe's male descent, and if Philippe has none, to whoever shall be Duke of Normandy at the operative time (Bouquet, *Recueil*, 17, pp. 32-33, Chaplais, *Diplomatic Documents Preserved in the Public Record Office*, pp. 14-16, etc., cf. Ramsay, *Empire*, pp. 289-290).

Pound takes the whole of this business into the earlier version of the Canto, along with Bertran's lament on the death of the Young King and his complaint at the delays of Richard and Philippe in setting off for the crusade; for all these documents are given in French translation in Zeller and Luchaire, *Philippe Auguste et Louis VIII*, pp. 15-34 — see Appendix 1, Texts B(iv)-(viii) — and the sense of their chronological evolution is compelling; Zeller and Luchaire, furthermore, are quite definite on the point that it was Bertran's songs that caused the barons of Aquitaine and Poitou to rise against Henry and his sons (ibid., p. 14, note). The whole narrative is dropped, except for the four lines of extract from the treaty of 1191, in the final version of Canto VI; it amounted to an excess of energetic *faits divers*, and Pound probably betrayed his feeling that this was so by the sub-Shakespearian metric and diction into which he had put it all.

Of all these events between the two treaties, only one trace remains: it is Pound's altering of the 1191 wording, when he has 'Need not wed Alix, once his father's ward and . . . .' The 'once his father's ward and . . .' is not there in the treaty, and the ambiguous hiatus at the end is no doubt intended by Pound to suggest what more the girl was to Henry II besides.

(The *Annotated Index* of Edwards and Vasse [s.v. Alix], like some historians [e.g. Pacaut, *Louis VII*, p. 200], gives Alix simply as Louis's second daughter, thereby possibly confusing her with his second daughter by his first wife [Eleanor of Aquitaine], called Aélith/Aaliz/Alix. She would then be uterine sister to Richard, her betrothed. In fact the Alix/Aélis/Alais/Adelais in question here is Louis's second daughter by Constance of Castille [Richard, *Comtes de Poitou*, 2, p. 146].)

26. This *vida*, like the *vida* of William IX, makes Eleanor Duchess of Normandy before her marriage to Henry Plantagenet, and ignores Louis VII (see above, n. 16, and Appendix 2, text before n. 15). Its scenario is remarkably similar to that of Sordello's *vida*, but that *vida* turns out to have a great deal of historical corroboration, as we shall see. Relations of some kind between Eleanor and Bernart seem to me probable (see Appendix 2, text before n. 9); it is even possible that Eleanor was the 'Aziman' who occurs in Bernart's songs, though this is rejected by Appel in Bernart, *Lieder*, p. xxxviii, on the doubtful grounds that humble troubadours do not address erotic songs to the wives of noble patrons, an argument we have dealt with for Bertran de Born. For a translation of the three versions of the *vida* combined into one, see Chapter 7, text before n. 1.

It is not possible to ascertain whether Pound's text was his own notes, or one of the many editions of this *vida* that were available, such as Chabaneau, *Biographies*, pp. 10-11, Appel, *Chrestomathie*, no. 122b, or Bernart, *Lieder*, pp. xi-xv (though the dating might make this latter unlikely).

27. Pound's identification of 'Audiart' in Bertran as being the Audiart of Malemort to whom the *vidas* refer is unverifiable (see Appendix 2, n. 9); no doubt he was encouraged to make it by Bertran, *Poésies*, p. 112, note, which confidently asserts that they were 'probably' the same woman. For the historical identity of Bertran's Audiart (which is not known) and of Maria de Ventadorn, see Appendix 2, text before n. 16. For a translation and part text of the Bertran poem in which Audiart appears, see Chapter 1, text before n. 16, and for other references to Audiart of Malemort in the *vidas* cf. Boutière and Schutz, *Biographies*, pp. 170, 171, 172, 180, 314, 315.

28. The song is Bernart's *Tant ai mo cor ple de ioya*. It is not in the first (1895) edition of Appel, *Chrestomathie*, but Pound may have had one of the later editions that I have not seen. The song does appear in Appel, *Chrestomathie*, 6th ed. (1930), no. 18a:

> bona domna iauzionda,
> mor se·l vostr' amaire!

> Good, happy lady,
> your lover is dying!

See also *Cantos*, 93/624:657, which uses the same song. Eleanor was born in 1122 (?) (Labande, 'Aliénor', p. 176) and married in 1152 to Henry II, so that in placing the Bernart-Eleanor encounter when she was 'Turning on thirty years', Pound placed it at about the time of this second marriage. This accords with Appel's chronology for the contacts between Bernart and the Plantagenets in Bernart, *Lieder*, pp. lvii-lix.

29. *Letters*, to Carlo Izzo, 8 Jan 1938.

30. Appel, *Chrestomathie*, no. 17:

> Quant vei la lauzeta mover
> de ioi sas alas contral ray,
> que s'oblida e·s laissa cazer. . . .

> When I see the lark move
> for joy its wings against the light,
> so that it forgets itself and lets itself fall
> for the sweetness that comes to its heart,
> oh! such a great envy comes to me
> of anyone I see happy,
> I am surprised that on the spot
> my heart does not melt with desire.

Eva Hesse, in *Paideuma,* 1.2 (Fall and Winter 1972), p. 272, refers baldly to 'the famous lark song that Bernart of Ventadour composed for Eleanor'. Pound no doubt thought it was composed for Eleanor, but we have no way whatsoever of knowing. Appel, in Bernart, *Lieder,* pp. xxxi-lix, draws on all possible internal and external evidences to relate the songs to a biographical structure, with some success; but as far as this song is concerned, he succeeds (p. xl) only in a speculative linking to a cycle of songs for an unknown beloved of Vienne, all putatively written after the end of Bernart's involvement with the Plantagenets.

The *razo* to this song gives the first stanza a biographical interpretation: Bernart calls Eleanor *Alauzeta,* 'skylark', and she names a certain knight how loves her *Rai,* 'ray'; one day the knight comes to her, and she lifts her cloak and puts it around his neck, and falls back on the bed, observed secretly by Bernart; whence this song (see Boutière and Schutz, *Biographies,* p. 29). I know of no evidence that Pound saw this *razo,* which is only in a Barcelona manuscript and is not given by Chabaneau.

31. Cf. Cavalcanti, *Rime,* no. IV, lines 1-2:

> Chi e questa che ven, ch'ogn'om la mira,
> che fa tremar di claritate l'âre

> Who is this lady who comes, for all men gaze at her,
> for she makes the air tremble with clarity

But for Pound's text see *Translations,* p. 38:

> Che fai di clarità l'aer tremare

and especially the footnote. Cf. also *Cantos,* 74/444:472, 74/448:476.

32. See Chapter 9, text before n. 115.

33. Both versions of the *vida* have been verified in many details; see translation of this version, and discussion, in Chapter 9, text before n. 23. Pound writes into it the names of Rizzardo di San Bonifacio and of Cunizza, which he could find in Benson (see following note), de Lollis, or Chabaneau. Editions of the *vidas* were available in Chabaneau, *Biographies,* p. 106, and in Sordello, *Poesie,* ed. de Lollis, pp. 147-148; but the spelling 'Escort' (which Pound first gave in 'Troubadours: Their Sorts and Conditions', p. 429 [*Essays,* p. 97]) is not given by editors for any of the manuscripts, which indicates a misreading on Pound's part, and certainly shows that he was still using his own copies from the manuscripts (see above, n. 16).

34. For the story, and for Pound's use of the document, see Chapter 9, text before nn. 44, 56. Though it is known only from a poor thirteenth-century copy (MS. 2120 from the 'ospital di Treviso'), the act of emancipation appears to be quite genuine: cf. Sordello, *Poesie,* ed. Boni, p. XCII, note. Pound's immediate source was probably Zamboni, *Gli Ezzelini, Dante e gli schiavi* (1902), pp. 383-384, or the edition of 1906; the document may also be in the editions of 1862-64 and 1897. It seems likely that Pound was led to Zamboni by the reference to him in Benson, *Sordello and Cunizza,* pp. 50-53, a passage which clearly provided the structure of thought that Pound centres around Cunizza in Canto VI and that he asserts explicitly in *Kulchur,* p. 107 (for which see Chapter 9, text before n. 64). Thus Benson:

> Cunizza's was one of those rich and complete organisations to which the ordinary restrictions of married life are not only oppressive, but insufferable. Sordello and other Provencal poets praised her, or alluded to her wilful and joyous life; but it was left for Dante's earliest commentator to degrade her as a *magna meretrix,* in contradiction to the infallible judgment of Dante himself who honoured her memory as a woman, and exalted her to the dazzling sphere of Paradise—to a place there only lower than the place of Beatrice.

Benson then observes that scholars had been puzzled by Dante's praise for Cunizza, and that Zamboni thought he had solved this problem when he discovered the document freeing the slaves. He notes that such documents have since been found to be not so uncommon, but that Cunizza's was unusually generous in scope. He points out that Cunizza was living

> at the house of the celebrated Cavalcante, father of Guido Cavalcante, Dante's poet-friend; and there Dante, as a boy, must have seen and heard her and been impressed by the story of her life, her misfortunes, her goodness and strength of soul.

The *Kulchur* passage contains clear verbal reminiscences of this. Benson continues with a long description of the stature that Cunizza's past passions and sufferings at the hands of her family and its enemies must have seemed to give her in her old age, where she still asserted her courage:

> Instead of seeking the shelter of a convent like a benumbed and frightened soul, she sought the companionship of one of the most remarkable men of his time, Cavalcante the elder, the philosophic Epicurean sceptic. Ghibelline as she was, no religious house would have harboured her.

Benson then (p. 54) points to the 'unusual energy of her expression' in the part of the emancipation document where Cunizza curses those who betrayed her brother Alberico, a part which Pound inserts from the original into *Cantos,* 29/141-142: 147, along with the lines from Dante that Benson cites on the same page.

Benson's book, published in 1903, is a fine example of nineties English scholar-dilettante presentation of mediaeval Italy, in the post-Rossetti tradition, with luxurious untrimmed paper, wide margins and quasi-Venetian typography. It incorporates a large amount of original reading, including most of the principal sources (cf. especially pp. 59ff.), but is too generous in interpreting mere fantasists like

Nostredame. There is a very great deal of the glamorous chiaroscuro of mediaeval passions, more in adjective than in fact, a point that the mature Pound would have wanted to correct; but I think that otherwise he would have agreed wholeheartedly with almost every sentiment in the book. At one point Benson chides the scholar de Lollis for lowering rather than raising his subject, Sordello, who is 'to be rightly interpreted only by a poet. The historic critic but shows us what fagots were consumed in a great and ardent life' (pp. 90-91). If one compares the passages quoted above with the *Kulchur* passage, it becomes clear that all Pound has done is to remove rhapsodic adjective and add the toughness of his own blunt idiom.

By contrast, Zamboni, *Gli Ezzelini,* probably gave Pound nothing beyond the essential text of the emancipation document, being a cantankerous and egotistical ramble about slavery and about the author himself.

For the text of the emancipation, see Appendix 1, Text C. Pound's 'That freed her slaves on a Wednesday' is not in it, but cf. perhaps 'in quodam sabato sancto', in Text D.

35. The story of Cunizza's life and amours as given by this chronicler, Rolandino, appears to be quite reliable, though the facts were certainly embroidered upon by the Dante commentators; see Chapter 9, text before nn. 31, 63. It seems most likely that Pound's immediate source was Chabaneau, *Biographies,* p. 108; this text is not in Sordello, *Poesie,* ed. de Lollis. I translate the whole passage in Chapter 9, text before n. 31, and give the text in Appendix 1, Text D.

36. It is not known for certain who the beloved is in this song; it is possible that she is Guida of Rodez (cf. Sordello, *Poesie* ed. Boni, pp. LXIII, LIX). She is unlikely to be Cunizza. Pound's text was probably Sordello, *Poesie,* ed. de Lollis, no. XXI, lines 1-8 (the song is not in Appel, *Chrestomathie*):

> Atretan deu ben chantar finamen
> d'invern com fatz d'estiu, segon rason,
> per c'ab lo freitz voill far gaja canson,
> que sen pascor de chantar cor mi pren,
> quar la rosa senbla lei de cui chan,
> aultresi es la neus del sieu senblan:
> per qu'en andos deu per s'amor chantar;
> tant fort mi fai la rosa el neu menbrar.

> I must sing as finely
> in winter as I do in summer, according to reason,
> for with the cold I want to make a gay song,
> since if the desire to sing takes me at Easter,
> because the rose resembles the lady I sing of,
> equally the snow is like her;
> so that in each season I must sing for her love;
> so much does the rose make me remember the snow.

For Boni's more recent text see Chapter 9, n. 22; and for a translation based on it, Chapter 9, text before n. 22.

37. *Kulchur,* p. 134.

38. There seems no reason to doubt the account in this *vida* except perhaps for

the order of Elias's travels: cf. Boutière and Schutz, *Biographies,* p. 253, note. Pound's text in this case is particularly likely to have been his own copy from the manuscript (see above, n. 16, and especially my remarks on his translation of the *vida* in Chapter 1, n. 48). The *vida* was also available in e.g. Chabaneau, *Biographies,* p. 50, the text from which I translate here.

39. *Cantos,* 13/60:64.

40. *Impact,* p. 215; see Chapter 1, n. 83.

41. See above, n. 2.

42. *Cantos,* 7/24:28.

43. These remarks owe much to the chapter, 'Small Ritual Truths', in Kenner, *A Homemade World,* pp. 133ff. In Hemingway, the sexual part of the scheme is often complicated by the hero's physical inability (an 'accidental' escape route that is not necessary to Pound's psychology); it is the 'cad' who is actually able to make love, but there is a suggestion that it is not quite the real thing, that perhaps it is contrived by cheating, like the temporary triumphs of the evil genius in Ian Fleming.

44. Cf. especially *The Eyes* and *The Flame; Essays,* p. 9.

45. *Cantos,* 18/83:87.

46. The best critique of this persona is by Wyndham Lewis in *Time and Western Man,* as quoted in Stock, *Life,* p. 271.

47. *Cantos,* 80/498-499:532.

48. Pound had often been involved in 'The hunt for a subject, etc.' (*ABC of Reading,* p. 102); but he would not handle any subject unless he knew it was important to his psyche, and then he would try to create a new vocabulary to fit it, so that in effect subject still came before forms.

49. Pound must have noted that Louis VII was, all his life, priest-ridden; nationalist historians like Luchaire were not slow to point out that France was only set on the road to unity when Philippe, Louis's son, followed the example of Henry II Plantagenet in curbing Papal attempts to rule his affairs.

But at this stage, Pound did not respond to the great politically constructive themes implicit in this material. As a post-Romantic, all he required in his heroes was energy, and he was content to let this energy seem quite miscellaneous, provided that it had a cultural aspect. Pound's chief source for the Plantagenet-Capetian territorial haggling, Zeller and Luchaire, devoted space to this haggling because it had a concrete result: where Louis VII had let his power be eroded by the energy of Henry II, Philippe's insistent attacks on the Plantagenets, and his rejection of Papal interference, finally increased the Capetian territorial base so significantly that it paved the way for the ejection of the English from the Continent, and became a solid foundation for the French nation-state. Nothing of this is noted by Pound, except marginally in his prose. For Pound, the voice of the anticlerical nationalist French historians must have been too close to that of the state-worshipping, practical, sceptic, Bouvard and Pécuchet-like 'citoyen' lampooned in his quotations from Gourmont (*Essays,* p. 347, etc.). In much later years, Pound worked his way back from Edward Coke to Magna Carta, and thus perhaps to some glimpse of the way in which Henry II had made that document possible, by laying the foundations of communal legal responsibility, by working against arbitrary administration, and by excluding arbitrary interference from Rome. But before that, Pound had to work through not only his own post-Romantic heritage but also the sophistications of Dada and later movements, which held any concern with constructive politics to be beneath the artist.

50. *Cantos,* 10/44:48.

51. Cf. *Essays,* pp. 357-358, *Cantos,* 15/65:69.

52. Definitely used for Canto VI: see above, nn. 16, 33.

53. It is not absolutely certain that Pound used any one of these, though in each case it is highly probable. After each title in the following list I refer to the notes, above, which support this probability most strongly: Guillaume IX, *Chansons:* n. 14, Appel, *Chrestomathie:* nn. 20, 28, Sordello, *Poesie,* ed. de Lollis: n. 36, Zamboni, *Gli Ezzelini:* n. 34, Chabaneau, *Biographies:* n. 35.

54. Zeller and Luchaire, *Philippe Auguste et Louis VIII* (certainly used: cf. this Chapter, text before nn. 59, 73, and above, nn. 23, 25).

55. Vanel, *Intrigues galantes de la Cour de France* (certainly used: see this Chapter, text before nn. 60, 73, and above, nn. 18, 19).

56. I have not been able to discover where Pound read about William IX's raising of money in order to go crusading (see above, n. 13); it is conceivable that his source was Richard, *Comtes de Poitou.*

57. See this Chapter, text before n. 73, for Pound's remarks about this schoolbook. For places where it may have been used, see above, n. 22.

58. See above, n. 34, for Benson, *Sordello and Cunizza,* a literary history. The scholarly Michaud, *Histoire des Croisades,* 3, pp. 17-20, was Pound's source for the story of Frederick II and Malek Kamel in *The Sixth Canto,* p. 84; see 'Pastiche. The Regional. XVIII', p. 48. For indications of some further reading in Provençal-related history see 'Pastiche. The Regional. IX', p. 284.

59. These are numbered as Part I, no. 6, 8; Part II, no. 3, 4, 5, 6. For the publishing history of Canto VI, see below, n. 61.

60. Vanel, *Intrigues galantes,* seems to have been written in imitation of the many precursors by Gatien de Courtilz de Sandras.

61. Eleanor's illicit amours from the *Intrigues galantes* have dropped to seven lines, and are patched with allusions to literary texts. The haggling over the Vexin has fallen to eight lines, and all the other material from Zeller and Luchaire's translated documents, about Bertran, Richard, and Philippe, has disappeared. The Sordello matter has appeared from new sources, and new material has developed the connection between Eleanor and her grandfather. Though Pound's immediate source-books are only seven in number, in the seventy-seven lines of the final Canto there are twenty separate source-attributable sections, some of these subdivided by pieces from other sources.

The earlier version of Canto VI, called *The Sixth Canto,* was published in *Dial* in August 1921, in *Poems 1918-21* in December 1921, and in *A Draft of XVI. Cantos* in January 1925; all these drafts are substantially similar, and the last is reprinted in Bush, *The Genesis of Ezra Pound's Cantos,* pp. 310-313. The final Canto VI was first published in *A Draft of XXX Cantos* in August 1930; thus the Sordello material was added between 1925 and 1930, which makes it contemporaneous with the Sordello material in Canto XXIX, first published in April-June 1930. It is therefore one of the few instances, after the first years of organising the Cantos, in which an early piece was reworked for architectonic purposes — that is, in order to alter its relationship to a later element.

62. Attacking American academics after the war, Pound accused them of being unable to absorb anything they had not been taught as students: 'None of them had noticed either the method of historiography followed in the Malatesta cantos, or the methodology in the Genova palaeographic edition of the Cavalcanti *Rime.…*' The above is from the dustjacket to the New Directions (1952) edition of *Kulchur*, quoted in Stock, *Life*, p. 432. The Malatesta Cantos use substantially the same methods as Canto VI.

63. Compare the way in which European kings might sonorously assert their absolute sovereignty in mediaeval grants of charters, as a prelude to wholesale concessions of privilege forced by their economic or other needs: Holt, *Magna Carta*, pp. 73-74.

64. Fearful of being thought unscientific, mediaeval historians have often avoided with horror anything that obviously contains mythic elements (songs and *vidas*, for example), while believing the distortions of superficially rational prose chroniclers. See the use of Roger of Wendover discussed in Warren, *King John*, pp. 25-27, and that of Guibert de Nogent, discussed in Chapter 10, text before nn. 68, 70, 71.

65. *ABC of Reading*, pp. 17-18: Agassiz insists that the student not merely name the fish according to a pre-established set of coordinates, but describe it as an organic whole.

66. Pound had finished *The Sixth Canto* by 22 November 1919 (Slatin, 'A History of Pound's *Cantos* I-XVI, 1915-1925', p. 188); in the summer of 1919 he had visited Montségur (Stock, *Life*, p. 224), and it seems from 'Pastiche. The Regional. IX', p. 284, that he had been told something of the history of Montségur by local people. He referred (ibid.) flatly to the building as 'a Cantabrian sun-temple with a Roman superstructure' (the Cantabrians lived to the south-west of the Pyrenees, and were subjugated with great difficulty by the Romans in 25 BC). From this it is not clear whether the idea that Montségur had been a sun-temple was suggested to Pound by local legend or by his own observation of the ruins, or both; but both methods are those he later praised in Frobenius (see especially *Letters*, to T. S. Eliot, 1 Feb 1940).

Pound may well have been led to Montségur in the first place by the discussion of it in the section of the *Chanson de la Croisade Albigeoise* that is printed in Appel, *Chrestomathie*, no. 7, which of course he possessed. It is clear from 'Pastiche. The Regional. IX', p. 284, that by 1919 he had read more extensively in the *Chanson*. For Montségur and the heretics, see Chapter 10, text before nn. 96, 151ff.

67. Cf. the citing of 'Miquel de la Tour' as author of *razos* in 'Troubadours: Their Sorts and Conditions', p. 427 (*Essays*, p. 95).

68. The tone of a quotation *as it appears in the poem* may survive distinct after any amount of rereading the quotation and registering its tone *in its original context*.

69. Compare the way in which Pound calls our attention to his Renaissance Latin source for the *Odyssey* in *Cantos*, 1/5:9.

70. Pound's misquotation from Bernart de Ventadorn in Canto VI, 'Que la lauzeta mover', would make no sense if fitted back into Bernart's poem as it stands; it
means something like 'That the lark (to) move'. The shift in 'e quel remir' (see
Chapter 8, n. 98) may also be due to a kind of carelessness, but it has more point as
a reshaping of the poem.

71. However, Joyce's elaborate half-historicity is something distinct from Nabokov's elaborately punning anti-history; the shift of the relation to 'reality' has its
effect.

72. See above, n. 25.

73. 'Pastiche. The Regional. VIII', p. 300. There are many errors in the *Intrigues galantes* which naturally run counter to Zeller and Luchaire's accounts, but
the sequence and emphases of the Capetian-Plantagenet struggle are remarkably
similar in both works.

74. Cf. the comparison between James and Gourmont in *Essays,* pp. 339-340.

75. Pound headed for the British Museum almost as soon as he reached London
(Stock, *Life,* p. 54); he used it constantly (e.g. 'How I Began', p. 707), and saw such
libraries as a necessity for the modern writer (e.g. *Letters,* to Harriet Monroe, 21
Aug 1917), but later came to see their enormous resources as a threat (cf. *Kulchur,*
pp. 53-54).

76. Pound's term describing the work that Binyon put into condensing the enormous Dante commentaries into the pithy canto headings in his translation: *Essays,*
p. 208. Cf. also *ABC of Reading,* p. 92.

CHAPTER 5. WILLIAM IX OF AQUITAINE

1. Cf. *Letters,* to Homer L. Pound, 11 Apr 1927; Kenner, *Pound Era,* especially
pp. 365-381.

2. Cf. *Letters,* to Homer L. Pound, 11 Apr 1927, to W. H. D. Rouse, Feb 1935;
Kulchur, p. 146.

3. Pound's phrase for Bertrand Russell in *Kulchur,* p. 166.

4. Cf e.g. *Ta Hio,* pp. 19-20.

5. Franklin's exemplum is in *Cantos,* 31/155-156:159-160, taken from John
Adams (Adams and Jefferson, *Adams-Jefferson Letters,* p. 399).

6. *Cantos,* 8/30-32:34-36.

7. Jones, *The Malatesta of Rimini,* pp. 176-177.

8. Bezzola, *Origines,* 2.2, p. 273; Martindale, 'Duchy of Aquitaine', p. 129. His
father and his grandfather had been highly influential in Church matters: Bezzola,
Origines, 2.2, pp. 258, 260; Martindale, 'Duchy of Aquitaine', pp. 108-109.

9. Cf. especially ibid., p. 1, and Higounet, *Aquitaine,* pp. 136-138.

10. Martindale, 'Duchy of Aquitaine', pp. 142ff.

11. Cf. ibid., pp. 73, 75-76, 87, 79, 80, 108-109, 87-88, and Bloch, *Feudal
Society,* p. 176.

12. Martindale, 'Duchy of Aquitaine', p. 133, note.

13. One of these was William *Fredelamus,* lord of Blaye, great-grandfather of
the troubadour Jaufre Rudel: Bezzola, *Origines,* 2.2, p. 263; Paris, *Mélanges,* p.
500, notes.

14. For the risks and crises of this tutelage see Martindale, 'Duchy of Aquitaine', pp. 7, 8, 216ff., 133, 135, and Bezzola, *Origines*, 2.2, p. 262.

15. Martindale, 'Duchy of Aquitaine', p. 136; Bezzola, *Origines*, 2.2, p. 263; cf. Bouquet, *Recueil*, 12, p. 403, for the Chronicle of St. Maxence.

16. Cf. Peters, *First Crusade*, pp. xvi-xvii.

17. *Cantos*, 6/21:25.

18. Martindale, 'Duchy of Aquitaine', p. 139, doubts the first story, refuting the opinion of Richard in *Comtes de Poitou*, 1, pp. 424-428 (followed by Bezzola, *Origines*, 2.2, p. 265). The second is in Orderic Vitalis, *Ecclesiastic History*, ed. Chibnall, 5, p. 280 (X.13), but see discrepancies noted ibid.; Martindale, 'Duchy of Aquitaine', pp. 140-142, finds that Orderic was unaware of material facts. See Chapter 4, n. 13.

19. Cf. William of Newburgh, quoted in Bezzola, *Origines*, 2.2, p. 270, note.

20. Orderic Vitalis, *Ecclesiastical History*, ed. Chibnall, 5, p. 324 (X.20); Geoffrey of Vigeois, quoted in Bezzola, *Origines*, 2.2, p. 271, note.

21. Quoted ibid., p. 268, note.

22. Orderic Vitalis, *Ecclesiastical History*, ed. Chibnall, 5, pp. 334-340 (X.20), and Martindale, 'Duchy of Aquitaine', pp. 141-142. Geoffrey of Vigeois (see n. 20 above), saying that William was a Don Juan and therefore unstable, concludes simply: 'Tunc trucidatus est exercitus ejus a Sarracenis....'

23. Orderic Vitalis, *Ecclesiastical History*, ed. Chibnall, 5, p. 342 (X.21).

24. Martindale, 'Duchy of Aquitaine', pp. 142-143, 147-150; and cf. p. 80.

25. Ibid., pp. 129, 108, 113.

26. Ibid., pp. 154, 131; cf. Bezzola, *Origines*, 2.2, p. 267.

27. Quoted in Bezzola, *Origines*, 2.2, p. 272, note. Before the Crusade, William had antagonised the clergy by defending Philip of France for keeping a mistress: ibid., 2.2, pp. 265-266.

28. Ibid., 2.2, p. 271; Rajna, 'Guglielmo', p. 352.

29. Quoted in Bezzola, *Origines*, 2.2, p. 272, note.

30. Quoted ibid., 2.2, p. 273, note; cf. the memorable excommunication of Malatesta, in *Cantos*, 10/44:48. Orderic Vitalis (*Ecclesiastical History*, tr. Forester, 4, p. 7; cf. Bezzola, *Origines*, 2.2, p. 263, and note) has William's *first* wife turning up at a Church council at Rheims in 1119 to claim her rights against the usurping Viscountess.

31. William of Malmesbury quoted in Rajna, 'La Badia di Niort', p. 250; Etienne de Bourbon, quoted in Bezzola, *Origines*, 2.2, p. 271, note.

32. Boutière and Schutz, *Biographies*, p. 7; for the errors cf. Chapter 4, n. 16.

33. As is frequently the case with troubadour material, manuscripts attribute some of the songs to other authors; for William's case see Dumitrescu, 'Eble et Guillaume', p. 397.

34. Guillaume IX, *Chansons*, no. XI, *Pos de chantar m'es pres talentz*. I have left the reference of 'that gives me sorrow' and of 'in great fear, in great danger' (lines 2, 6) ambiguous, to reflect the ambiguity of the original. Despite Roncaglia, 'Obediens', passim, I do not think the third line can be pinned down to the single meaning, 'I shall cease to exercise my (feudal) functions', 'I shall die'; 'in Poitou or Limousin' seems to be the part standing for the whole, in the territories of his amours or of his vassalage. In line 14 ('and the King I hold my honour from') *onor*

can mean 'fief', so that King and honour can both be territorial and spiritual.

35. The discussions are summarised in Roncaglia, 'Obediens', pp. 597-599, based on Storost; but cf. Martindale, 'Duchy of Aquitaine', p. 143, note.

36. Roncaglia, 'Obediens', pp. 598-599, cites Diez, Vossler, and Battaglia; cf. e.g. Bec, *Petite Anthologie*, p. 67. This song is in more of the manuscripts than any other by William: Dumitrescu, 'Eble et Guillaume', p. 396. It was imitated in a song that Cercamon wrote on the death of William's son (Cercamon, *Poésies*, no. VI, *Lo plaing comenz iradamen;* cf. ibid., p. 37).

37. See above, n. 34.

38. Cf. the rhythms of Villon's *neiges d'antan* ballad.

39. Cf. Pearlman, *Barb of Time*, p. 247, note: this is the fulfilment of Tiresias' prophecy that Odysseus/Pound would 'return through spiteful Neptune, over dark seas, / 'Lose all companions' (*Cantos*, 1/5:9). 'Lordly men are to earth o'ergiven / these the companions:' (74/432:459) is from *The Seafarer* (Pound's version). 'Si tuit li dolh elh planh el marrimen' (80/516:550) and 'Si tuit li dolh el plor [. . .] tuit lo pro, tuit lo bes' (84/537:572) are from Bertran de Born's lament for the Young King (cf. Chapter 3, text before n. 21). (The 'leopards and broom plants' are for Richard Lionheart and the Plantagenets — cf. *Sestina: Altaforte*, and 'I Gather the Limbs of Osiris IV: A Beginning', p. 179 [*Selected Prose*, p. 26].) 'Tout dit que pas ne dure la fortune' (*Cantos*, 76/456:484) and 'Les moeurs passent et la douleur reste' (80/504:538) are a borrowing and an adaptation from Froissart; 'Que tous les mois avons nouvelle lune' (80/510:544, in the same passage as the reference to William IX) is also from Froissart (cf. *Essays*, p. 113). 'Où sont les heurs of that year' (*Cantos*, 74/433:460) and 'Où sont?' (79/484:516) are from Villon's song of the snows of yesteryear.

40. *Cantos*, 80/510:544. Nancy Cunard is suggested by Edwards and Vasse, *Annotated Index*. These lines are obviously also built on Villon; *vair* is a slight reminiscence of William IX. The whole line, with its *cisclatons*, recalls Pound's conclusion to his essay 'Troubadours: Their Sorts and Conditions', p. 440 (*Essays*, p. 107): Peire Cardenal's stanza 'may well serve as a final epitaph on all that remained of silk thread and *cisclatons*, of viol and *gai saber*', which is a lament for the chivalric aspect of troubadour culture. A *cisclaton* was a garment of silk brocade worn over chain mail, or the fabric itself (cf. *Chanson de la Croisade*, I, p. 269, note); Pound had no doubt been struck by a glittering passage in Bertran de Born:

> And it cannot be otherwise
> than that splinters should fly into the sky
> and that silk and *cisclaton*
> and samite should be ripped there. . . .

(Bertran, *Lieder*, no. 9, *Lo coms m'a mandat*). *Vair and gris* is a common enough mediaeval phrase, but in this case Pound was probably thinking of Provence, and, since it is a lament, of William IX's song. Another occurrence of *vair* (in *Cantos*, 76/455:483: ' "in heaven have I to make?" / but all the vair and fair women') is from *Aucassin et Nicolette*, VI.24-39, as Hugh Kenner has pointed out to me; but the sense of the passage is different.

41. The term 'courtly love' (*amour courtois*) was first used by Gaston Paris in

1883 ('Etudes sur les romans de la table ronde. Lancelot du Lac. II. Le *Conte de la Charrette*', p. 519); though Dronke has shown that this relationship is not essentially 'courtly' (see below, text before n. 61, and Chapter 2, text before n. 74), the term is so widely accepted that it would waste time to invent another.

42. Dronke, *European Love-Lyric*, 1, p. 4, cites a similar definition by Joseph Bédier: 'What is peculiar [to courtly love poetry] is to have conceived of love as a cult which is addressed to an excellent object and is based, like Christian love, on the infinite disproportion of merit to desire....'

43. Guillaume IX, *Chansons*, no. IX, *Mout jauzens me prenc en amar*. In the fifth stanza there is an ambiguity in the *del penr'* and the following infinitives, giving as an alternative 'I am ready to accept *it* (her love)', and so forth.

44. 'Psychology', p. 43 (*Spirit*, p. 92). Cf. also Lejeune, 'Formules féodales', pp. 231-232.

45. Cf. Hackett, ' "midons" ', p. 289.

46. Schultz-Gora, *Elementarbuch*, p. 75, suggested that the *mi* recalled the Latin vocative; but Hackett, ' "midons" ', p. 286, points out that *midons* is never used as a term of direct address, and suggests that the *mi* was perhaps borrowed from fixed forms like *mi moiller,* of which traces exist (pp. 293-294). Paden, 'The Troubadour's Lady', p. 33, points out that even if the *-i* were a Latin vocative, it would not agree with the invariable *s* ending, which suggests Latin nominative *dominus* (note that the normal Provencal *don* is naturally without the *s* when used vocatively: Guillaume IX, *Chansons,* no. VI, V). Paden suggests that the *dons* of *midons* is simply the normal Provencal *don,* which was used so frequently for address (he should say: as the subject of propositions concerning the lady) that it became invariably nominative. The masculine gender was used as a 'verbal caress', like the French *mon petit* for one's girlfriend. Paden also suggests (p. 35) that the *-i* participates in 'the analogical feminine *i* of demonstrative flexion . . . which eventually produced the feminine definite article *li;* the personal pronoun *ilh;* and, in series with *ilh* the demonstratives *cilh, aquilh, cist* and *aquist.'*

The pronoun corresponding to *midons* is 'she' in the penultimate strophe of the above-quoted poem, and in the last two lines of the final strophe of Bertran's *Dompna puois* (see Chapter 1, text before n. 16).

47. Hackett, ' "midons" ', pp. 289-292, shows that the etymon *dominus* was not the dominant term for 'feudal lord' in the troubadour period, though it could have that sense; *don* is found in the charters only once with that meaning, and in literature it has perhaps a wider and more absolute sense. The troubadours used *midons* as semantically distinct from images of feudal lordship. Paden, 'The Troubadour's Lady', pp. 32-33, supports Hackett: we cannot simply claim that *midons = mi dominus* = 'my feudal lord'. He gives ample documentation for usages of *domina* and *domna* in Classical and Mediaeval Latin and in Provencal that do not connote superiority of social rank, but merely affection; and suggests that *dominus* or *don* (whichever is behind *midons*) would likewise simply suggest an amorous bond. I think that this de-metaphorises words one degree too much. The application of *domina* to their sweethearts by Tibullus, Propertius, and Catullus no more proves that it had no (however subliminal) connotation of social superiority than the average French lover's application of *mon cheri* to his girl proves that this phrase has no

connotation of masculinity. See also below, n. 51.

48. *Dominus,* for 'God', is incorporated into Marcabrun's famous Provençal song with its Latin first line (*Poésies,* no. XXXV, *Pax in nomine Domini!*). The *Chanson de Sainte Foy* addresses God as *nostre don* (Hackett, ' "midons" ', p. 291). It is worth noting that *don* seems to be felt as equivalent to *seigner* in the sense of 'God': William IX in his lament (cf. above, text before n. 34) speaks of *nostre Seigner*. When Bertran de Born and Guiraut de Borneil use *Bels Senher* as a poetic name for their lady, it is hard to know whether the religious or the feudal association is dominant; Bertran twice uses it in the same poem with *senhor* for 'feudal lord', which once denotes the epic hero Aigar, and once Richard Lionheart (Bertran, *Lieder,* no. 1, 7; cf. Chapter 3, text before n. 59; also cf. Appel, *Bertran,* p. 16, note). Finally, *Domna* was a normal term for the Virgin Mary in Provençal; it was used by the troubadours for their ladies; it was used to render the Lady Philosophy in Boethius, and also for the spouse of the Emperor of Constantine in the *Chanson de Sainte Foy* (cf. Lejeune, 'Formules féodales', pp. 229-230). Its connection with *domina* would have been obvious to the troubadours.

49. Cf. *Philippians,* 2.10.

50. For this device of repetition see e.g. the *Te Deum* and the Psalm *Confitemini Domini* from the Vulgate (Brittain, *The Medieval Latin and Romance Lyric,* pp. 63, 67).

51. Compare the feudal language in Guillaume IX, *Chansons,* no. VIII, *Farai chansoneta nueva,* lines 7, 26, 24, 5; cf. Lejeune, 'Formules féodales', pp. 228, 235, 242, 250. (Though I consider this song to be unserious [see below, text before n. 80], the introduction of these metaphors means that they were being used seriously somewhere.) Rita Lejeune (ibid., passim) starting from Wechssler's work, has picked up many reminiscences of feudal language and situation. In the song I have translated above, the penultimate stanza follows almost exactly the statement of feudal duties that Fulbert of Chartres gave to William's grandfather; Lejeune says that William 'promises to the lady he loves everything that, in the oath of fidelity to the suzerain, the *fides,* constitutes the obligations of the vassal' (ibid., p. 237; cf. pp. 238, 236). The later troubadours took into the courtly-love imagery the chief formal act in homage, the clasping of the man's hands between those of his lord; cf. Bernart de Ventadorn, Chapter 7, text before n. 34, and especially Bernard, *Chansons,* no. 18, line 48, no. 4, line 58, etc.; also Bloch, *Feudal Society,* p. 233. Paden, 'The Troubadour's Lady', p. 36, notes that feudal language is used to express the lover's humility in 24 per cent of the samples taken; cf. excellent examples, ibid., p. 37. Of course this implies nothing about the relative social status of poet and lady, as the article carefully points out; the lady's elevation was all talk, as Gui d'Ussel implies in the lines quoted, ibid., p. 38.

52. Bloch, *Feudal Society,* p. 233, gives significant parallels: the normal posture of praying in Christian countries was borrowed during the Middle Ages from the feudal act of 'commendation'; for Cynewulf, angels were the 'thegns' or retainers of God, and for Bishop Eberhard of Bamberg, Christ was the vassal of the Lord. As the man was the *dru* or lover of his lady, and the Church (or the believer) was—following allegories based on the *Song of Songs*—the Bride of Christ, so the vassal, when the ties of feudalism were close, was the *dru* of his lord. For *drudaria* in

courtly love see e.g. Bernard, *Chansons,* no. 11, *Ges de chantar no· m pren talans,*
line 6, where it clearly means 'courtly love in general':

> mas era no vei ni non au
> c'om parle de drudaria,
> per que pretz e cortezia
> e solatz torn' en no-chaler

though ibid., no. 40, *En cossirer et en esmai,* line 15, and no. 38, *Lancan vei la
folha,* line 49, seem to mean 'love-making' (physical). Arnaut, *Canzoni,* no. III,
line 25, is ambiguous, despite Toja's translation. For the believer as Bride of Christ,
cf. the sequence from Gottschalk, quoted in 'Psychology', p. 52 (*Spirit,* p. 99) from
Gourmont's *Latin mystique* (see Makin, 'Pound's Provence and the Mediaeval Paideuma', p. 42). For the vassal and lord as *dru,* cf. Bloch, *Feudal Society,* p. 231.

53. Bloch, ibid., pp. 309-310, makes a great confusion of these things.

54. Erich Koehler in 'Observations historiques' suggests that poor knights could
thus bypass economic humiliations by appealing to courtly-love values not dependent on wealth. This is valid except in so far as it is then somehow taken to be an
economic motivation, and to be a possible historical origin of the courtly-love phenomenon. Koehler's close reading of Bernart de Ventadorn's song of the lark makes
it mean something like 'When I see the skylark move its wings with joy. . . . Ah! how
I desire to be a baron of the next rank up!' (cf. ibid., p. 48), and the whole study
ignores any psychology of the sexual relationship.

55. See Paden, 'The Troubadour's Lady', passim, and above, n. 51.

56. For Réto Bezzola the ascetic religious movement of Robert d'Arbrissel, which
drew large numbers of ladies of rank into the great monastery founded at Fontevrault — among them William IX's first wife — was a symptom of a new independence among women. William IX found that his bawdy verse no longer attracted
them, underwent a crisis registered in his song of negations (see below, n. 81), and
came up with the new idealism, of a nature perfectly suited to interesting leisured
and noble ladies (*Origines,* 2.2, pp. 278ff., especially pp. 295-297). This idea implies that William simply had a random need to attract the interest of women,
which if it could not be accomplished by singing bawdy songs might as well be
achieved with idealistic ones.

There are traces of Bezzola's idea in Topsfield's *Troubadours and Love,* for
example, p. 39, where it is suggested that William was beginning to use terms of
courtly love that were already current, particularly in the song that I have quoted
above, either for reasons of fashion or because of pressure from his lady. Here and
elsewhere, the book tends to resolve emotional states into sets of concepts, preferably in opposing pairs. These concepts are identified with various words taken from
the troubadours' verses, which are left in Provencal and treated as technical terms.
Isolated thus, the words *joven, joi, domna,* and so forth, are radically vaguer — that
is, semantically much more crude — than the movement of image and breath; but
they are then taken as keys on which whole poems depend. When William IX's
verse is read in this manner there is no way in which anything could change in its
author except by the ditching of one set of cardboard concepts in favour of another,
for some suitably external reason such as fashion; so that William's sensibility and

those of his successors can tend to become battlegrounds of *idées reçues* dressed in allegorical armour.

57. Cf. bibliography in Bezzola, *Origines*, 2.1, pp. 183-203.

58. 'Arnaut Daniel', p. 44 (*Essays*, p. 109): Arnaut 'may, in the ending "piula," have had in mind some sort of Arabic singing: for he knew well letters. . . . So it is as like as not he knew Arabic music. . . .' As we have seen, *Cantos*, 8/32:36, has William IX bringing 'the song up out of Spain'. In *Kulchur*, pp. 108-109, Pound connects the fineness of line in the troubadours' work with that in the stonework coming out of Byzantium to the Romanesque in Southern France, and with the buildings of Moorish Spain. Ibid., p. 152: he brings 'The Persian hunting scene, the Arabian ribibi' into the tradition of clarity in Arnaut Daniel, Janequin, and so forth (see Chapter 8, text before n. 84).

59. Cf. also Dronke, *European Love-Lyric*, 1, p. 50.

60. For William's possible borrowings see especially ibid., pp. 51-56. Istvan Frank, in ' "Babariol-babarian" ', has made it clear that the compiler of the anthology known as *C* (written in the fourteenth century in South-Western France: Arnaut, *Canzoni*, p. 151) was a *litteratus* (p. 232) who altered verses throughout to make them more polished and added erroneous toponymics to troubadours' names (pp. 233-234). He 'polished' the diction of William's song of the two women and the cat throughout, removed the first two stanzas, omitted an essential narrative stanza, and reworked the following stanza (stanza five as I translate it, in Chapter 5, text before n. 86) with the rhymes of the abandoned one (pp. 231-232). Yet it is this stanza of this song as it appears in this anthology only that has been taken by Lévi-Provençal and others to contain lines of Syrian-Turkish, with or without African elements, or Hispano-Arabic (pp. 229-230). Frank observes that the version in the better manuscripts fulfils what was clearly the intention of these phrases, that is, to mean nothing (p. 229). Dronke (in *European Love-Lyric*, I, pp. 50-51, and note perhaps had not seen Frank's article.

61. Ibid., pp. 2, 50.

62. Ibid., pp. 9-46.

63. See Chapter 8, text before n. 61.

64. 'Sexuality' taken as mere random drive-to-make-love will not explain the particular tone or direction taken by our involvement with another person, and by memory's handling of it. It cannot explain why we focus on one individual rather than another, and why sometimes the image of a person to whom we never got very close will recur with extraordinary intensity year after year, or why a random face (as Nabokov describes in *Lolita*) will cause a pang because of its half-resemblance to that Person. No doubt this has to do with images powerful in our infancy; and perhaps their power then was partly sexual. At any rate, one should recall the anecdote in the *Cantos*, where Pirandello remarks that Cocteau is 'too good a poet' to get involved with Freud as he tackles the Oedipus myth (77/469:498). 'Too good a poet' because for him these forces could not be reduced from their capacity to call forth our most subtle and lasting emotions merely by calling them sexual and conditioned by infancy, as is the tendency with Freudian writing (see also Chapter 1, n. 75).

65. Guiraut von Calanso, *Lieder*, pp. 305-307, *Los grieus dezirs;* text quoted and translated in Goldin, *Mirror of Narcissus*, pp. 71-74.

66. *Essays*, p. 152. First published March 1928.

67. 'Psychology', p. 48 (*Spirit*, p. 96). First published October 1912.

68. See discussion ibid., and Chapter 10, text before n. 128.

69. See Chapter 10, text before n. 116, where all Pound's suggestions as to origins are discussed.

70. Seeking for the origins of this fusion, one will not find it in the occurrence of merely *one* of its elements, the celebration of spring, in a certain number of lyrics in earlier Latin. James J. Wilhelm, in *The Cruelest Month*, seems to imply that this is possible when he tries to show that the spring-element in the Provençal lyric simply grew out of a classical and Christian Latin tradition. As is natural, since in these Latin lyrics the spring-element is still unfused with the woman-cult, its tone is (at least to the present writer) quite different from that of the troubadour *Natureingang*, for which see Chapter 7, text before n. 49. For theories, including Pound's, relating troubadour lyrics to May dances, see Chapter 10, n. 117.

71. Here I disagree with Dronke, *European Love-Lyric*, 1, pp. 50-56. William IX was among the first of the powerful men of Europe to be super-literate in this period; cf. Bloch, *Feudal Society*, p. 307. Poetry was important in the circle he dominated: Eble II de Ventadorn owed William's favour to his skill in poetry (cf. Dumitrescu, '"L'escola N'Eblon"', p. 114). He was imitated by Cercamon (above, n. 36), and probably in the *devinalh* genre in general (see Pasero, '*Devinalh*', passim, and below, n. 81 on *Farai un vers de dreyt nien*), and one of his melodies lasted long enough to be used for the fourteenth-century *Jeu de Sainte Agnes* (Guillaume IX, *Chansons*, p. 43). These surviving indications should be enough to show that his personal influence was out of the ordinary, and not merely as a symptom of his times.

72. See quotation below, text before n. 104, and Chapter 4, passim.

73. Pound's phrase, not for the troubadour aesthetic in particular, but for the religious attitudes he saw behind it; see Chapter 10, nn. 115, 134.

74. See Chapter 3, n. 64.

75. See discussion and references in Chapter 7, text before n. 39.

76. Guillaume IX, *Chansons*, no. X, *Ab la dolchor.*

77. Dante, *Inferno*, 2.127-30.

78. 'Psychology', p. 51 (*Spirit*, p. 98).

Discussing this poem in *Lyrics of the Troubadours*, p. 17, Frederick Goldin seeks to make a separation between courtly love and the sexual interest. Having described (see below, n. 89) the songs of 'cunt', as scurrilous but pointing to a universal doubt, and then the songs of woman-adoration as a process of self-identification as a member of the courtly class, he enumerates William's other voices. The voice of *Ab la dolchor*, he says, is placed by William higher than either the lust or the vassalage of love that he has sung of; the love here is shared, and the quarrel itself is evidence of this. By comparison with this love, courtly love is clearly intended to be seen as the gibberish that the last words of the poem refer to.

I would suggest that the mutuality is clear enough, as is the sexuality; but that this song also contains perfectly clear elements of the 'vassalage' of courtly love. It is 'our love', and thus clearly when they are both loving each other everything is fine; but it is *the lady* who is currently withholding her love, and *the poet* who is expressing himself as completely lost until she restores it to him: no messages from her, sleepless nights until he hears whether she—or perhaps 'the truce' (which is clearly dependent on her)—is 'how I wish'. When they made peace, it was *she* who *gave him* 'such a great gift, / Her loving and her ring'—and if it is relevant here that the giving of the ring is a symbol of feudal investiture (see Lejeune, 'Formules féodales', pp. 229, 244), then the lady is clearly in the position of *seigneur*. Whatever scorn the last stanza appears to express for love-talk—talk of dependence on her, which is what the poem consists of—is merely part of a wish, that *she* will *permit* him to get on with it (cf. Bernard, *Chansons*, no. 20, *Can l'erba fresch'*, lines 45-46). Once more, the temperature-guage of their relationship is imagery of nature blossoming, which I have argued connotes sexual atmospheres, and it should be observed that the most striking example of this in the poem—the hawthorn-branch stanza—is placed directly between two stanzas that express the poet's doubts and dependence on the lady: so that it is clearly *her* frowns that are frost, and her smiles, sun. Here is a poem, such as we find also in Bertran de Born, where in that fusion between sexual and other elements of dependence on and enlightenment by the lady, the sexual element is stronger and more obvious than usual; so that ideological interpretations such as Goldin's, which can only admit sex as desire-immediately-to-go-to-bed-with and courtly love as entirely desexualised communal image-making, have to assign it to the former, since it is impossible to fit it to the latter. But like all courtly-love poems it fuses a type of sexuality with the other emotional-intellectual attitudes I have described.

79. See below, text before n. 101.

80. Guillaume IX, *Chansons*, no. VIII (this song is only in MS. *C*, for which see above, n. 60). Here is a literal translation:

> I shall make a new song
> before the wind blows, or it freezes or rains;
> my lady is trying me out and testing me,
> to see how I love her;
> and never for any accusations that she makes
> shall I release myself from her bond.
>
> For instead I hand myself over and deliver myself to her,
> so that she can write me down on her charter.
> And don't consider me drunk for this,
> if I love my fine lady,
> for I cannot live without her,
> I am stricken with such a hunger for her love.
>
> For she is whiter than ivory,
> so that I adore no other lady.
> If I don't have help soon,
> so that my fine lady loves me,

I shall die, by St Gregory's head,
if she does not kiss me in chamber or under branches.

What will you gain, pretty lady,
if your love sends me away?
It seems that you want to become a nun.
Know this: because I love you so,
I am afraid that the pain will hurt me deeply,
if you do not put right the wrongs I allege of you.

What will you gain, if I enter a monastery
and you do not accept me as your own?
All the joy of the world is ours,
lady, if we love each other.
Over there, to my friend Daurostre,
I order and command that he sing and do not bray.

For this lady I shiver and tremble,
for I love her with such true love;
for I do not believe that there was ever born one similar to her
in the image of the great lineage of Adam.

81. My remarks refer also to *Pus vezem de novelh florir* (ibid., no. VII), whose voice is so pat, circular, and self-serving that it seems almost, but not quite, a persona, that of an Osric of the art of courtly love. Compare the pious banalities of Arnaut Daniel's *Lancan son passat li giure* (*Canzoni,* no. IV). Ignoring these problems of tone and immediate reference, critics have read closed-system technicalities into particular phrases, in order to hang on to them large gobbets of mediaeval philosophy or history. See especially Roger Dragonetti's *'Aizi* et *aizimen'* for some complicated spatial allegories of love-doctrine in *Pus vezem* and other songs. But if we take odd phrases on a technical level, then we must stand ready to explain all the other phrases in relation to that level; and further, once we have cut the cable of the human weight of the words, the number of possible allegorical or technical levels of interpretation becomes limitless, and criticism is self-perpetuating.

Farai un vers de dreyt nien (Guillaume, IX, *Chansons,* no. IV, but see Pasero's text in his *'Devinalh',* pp. 113-115) is a somewhat different case. William announces: 'I shall make a song about nothing at all', and then denies a series of possible subjects, states, and motivations. However, all these are connected with love, happiness, madness, illness, and their opposites, and the poem is clearly about the extreme states involved in courtly love. It is also clearly a *jeu d'esprit,* as Gaston Paris said (*Mélanges,* p. 522) of its close parallel, *No sap chantar qui so no di* by Jaufre Rudel. It has tripping rhythms, with throw-away half-lines that take a sideswipe at any sensible idea the reader may have been building on what has been said:

> Bos metges er si m pot guerir,
> Mas non, si amau

whose metric is thus:

He'll be a good quack if I cure,
But not if not.

The idea of William's having been 'witched by a fairy at night / on a high peak'
(lines 11-12) is quite unserious, and there is a delighted panache in the fast play of
contradiction and convoluted logic in the last stanza. But Lynne Lawner in *'vers de
dreyt nien'* has argued that William was actually calling on the kind of scholastic
argument on nothing and unknowables with which he was in all probability familiar; and Réto Bezzola has claimed that the poem expresses William's state of crisis
when he was just about to invent courtly love—which was to be the 'doctor' mentioned above (Bezzola, *Origines,* 2.2, p. 297; cf. above, n. 56).

82. Guillaume IX, *Chansons,* no. I, *Companho, faray un vers. . . covinen.* The
allegorical interpretation in Camproux's 'Farai un vers *tot* covinen' presupposes
(especially p. 162) a hermetic group of *fedeli d'amore,* in the manner of Rossetti
and his followers, and follows (pp. 163ff.) the mediaeval-etymology method of
choosing among all the true and false cognates of every single word for clues, in the
manner of Péladan; for such approaches see Chapter 10, text before nn. 118, 109.

83. Guillaume IX, *Chansons,* no. II, III (for a text and translation see also
Pasero, *'Companho',* passim). Pasero's interpretation (ibid., p. 27), taking the
point to be that when there is a great deal of 'cunt' its price goes up rather than
down, seems at variance with his own translation (ibid., p. 26).

84. The solemnity of William's rhythms is ironic in these songs, but it is a pon-
derous irony.

85. Dragonetti, in *'Aizi* et *aizimen',* p. 137, translates this to mean that the pilgrim seems well situated in Love's domains; cf. above, n. 81.

86. For 'Hispano-Arabic' in these lines, cf. above, n. 60.

87. Guillaume IX, *Chansons,* no. V, *Farai un vers, pos mi sonelh.* The other success in this field seems to me to be ibid., no. VI, *Ben vuelh que sapchon li pluzor,*
where the rhythms are also sufficiently light.

88. Lines 41-42; cf. lines 39-40, 47-48, and Bertran de Born's similar effects,
Chapter 2, text before n. 6.

89. See above, nn. 82, 83. Frederick Goldin, in *Lyrics of the Troubadours,* pp.
6-8, describes with great acuteness the way in which the *leis de con,* the 'law of
cunt', has people stumbling through a world of accidents until they recognise each
other as sexual objects, and realise the limitless possibilities of lust. But since this
blind turbulence is ultimately disturbing, each encounter has some kind of sour
ending, as in the dice-game song, when the throw of the dice obliterates all the
poet's vaunted skill and leaves him at the mercy of a universe of chance. I would
suggest, however, that William's is more of an ironic smile than the horror that is
implied by this. I do not see any particular reason for connecting the 'song of nothing' with the arena of lust, rather than that of courtly love, in William's concerns;
see above, n. 81.

90. See Chapter 4, text before n. 14.

91. The 'two-faced' idea was put forward in 1928 by Rajna in *'Guglielmo',* pp.
356-357, etc. It is behind Jeanroy's interpretation (*Poésie,* 2, p. 7), Bezzola's theory
of the origins of courtly-love poetry (*Origines,* 2.2, p. 307, etc.; cf. above, n. 58),
and the views of Errante and Viscardi, that William experienced some kind of 'con-

version' (*Marcabru*, p. 170; *Letterature d'Oc e d'Oil*, p. 127). It should be noted that we have no evidence other than this psychologising for any relative dating of William's poems (cf. Dumitrescu, 'Eble et Guillaume', p. 380, Guillaume IX, *Chansons*, pp. viii-ix, and Camproux, 'Faray un vers *tot* covinen', p. 159); this does not prevent Errante, in *Marcabru*, p. 167, for example, from talking confidently of 'last poems'.

92. Pio Rajna had suggested this in 'Guglielmo', p. 357. Maria Dumitrescu has taken it up: she starts from a reading of William's works which is almost identical in its vocabulary to Jeanroy's cited above (cf. 'Eble et Guillaume', p. 379). For her, the courtly songs must have been written by Eble II de Ventadorn.

93. These terms are used throughout by the critics in the passages cited above, nn. 91, 92. They are taken up by Fiedler, *Love and Death in the American Novel*, p. 47: '... William of Poitou, with whom courtly love as we know it begins, was a king, not a dependent knight. He is a strange double-faced figure: the author of phallic poems full of male arrogance ("and so I screwed them eighteen times so hard I broke my belt and armor") and contempt for women, and, at the same time, the first of the poets of domnei — the service of ladies.' (William IX was not a king; he did not screw the women eighteen but 188 times; and if there is 'male arrogance' in him, it is certainly not in the poem Fiedler cites [cf. above, text before n. 77].)

94. Lot-Borodine's phrase, in '*Service d'Amour*', p. 223.

95. In Bezzola's psychic biography of William (*Origines*, 2.2, p. 307; cf. above, n. 56), the hawthorn-flower image is

a passing phase. In this period filled with violent passions and with brutal desire on the one hand and with mystical flights and fervour on the other, there was no room, on a durable basis, for such a balanced mental state. It had to be paradise or hell, cynicism or ethereal exaltation. It is in the famous song of 'joy' [cf. above, text before n. 43] that the Count succeeds in formulating, with an impressive intensity, this paradise of the courtly society of the time, this new idea of profane love....

96. Gourmont, *Lettres à l'Amazone*, p. 124.

97. *Spirit*, p. 41 (which should be corrected: William was IX of Aquitaine, but only VII of Poitiers; 1086 was the date of his accession to the dukedom, and 1071 the date of his birth; eleven songs are attributed to him (cf. Dumitrescu, above, n. 91); 'Troubadours', p. 426 (*Essays*, p. 94), with which cf. my translation of the *vida*, above, text before n. 32.

98. See Chapter 4, text before n. 12.

99. The translation is *Avril*, first published as part of *Homage à la langue d'or* in 1918 (Gallup, *A Bibliography of Ezra Pound*, C354). The *Homage* was reprinted in the same year in the *New Age*, with *or* corrected to *oc* but *Homage* unchanged (C367), and in 1919 in *Quia Pauper Amavi* as *Langue d'Oc* (A17). The parenthesis is on p. 39 of *Spirit*, and was added for the To Publishers' edition of *How to Read* with Part I of *Spirit* (A33b).

100. See above, text before n. 76.

101. It is possible that Pound's lines, 'Defeat / Or luck, I must have my fill' (for lines 10-12 in Jeanroy) come from a misreading, since I cannot see how they follow the sense of the original (see above, text before n. 76, stanza 2). His last line is a

legitimate conjecture for the obscure *Nos n'avem la pessa e·l coutel,* which Jeanroy renders with the previous line as 'tels autres peuvent se vanter d'amour; nous, nous en avons la pièce et le couteau (*c.* -à-d. nous pouvons jouir du nôtre).' *Mon bon vezi* need not be, despite McDougal (*Pound and the Troubadour Tradition,* p. 132), a *senhal* or poetic name.

102. In *Quia Pauper Amavi* (see above, n. 91).

103. *Letters,* to Felix E. Schelling, 9 July 1922.

104. See above, n. 99. This is a mere half-paragraph, compared with the whole chapters and repeated translations Pound devoted to Arnaut Daniel. But it compares William with Arnaut — with whom the chapter begins — and was written at a time when Pound felt he had a right to present conclusions, not detailed arguments. Cf. the remarks in *Kulchur* (1938), especially pp. 284-287, on Hardy, and the implicit comparison with men Pound had long boosted, like Eliot.

105. Gourmont, *Lettres à l'Amazone,* pp. 35-36.

106. Gourmont, *Physique de l'Amour,* translated by Pound in 1922 as *The Natural Philosophy of Love,* passim; e.g. *Natural Philosophy,* pp. 93-94.

107. Íbid., p. xvii.

108. *Essays,* p. 343; 'Diomède' is Gourmont's *Les Chevaux de Diomède.*

109. *Essays,* pp. 343-344. F. S. Flint appears to have put Pound on to Gourmont at some time between March 1911 and February 1912 (Stock, *Life,* pp. 96, 112); Hutchins, 'Ezra Pound's "Approach to Paris"', p. 350, gives 1910 as Pound's first mention of him, but the part of *Spirit* that she cites ('Psychology and Troubadours') was first given as a lecture in 1912 (Stock, *Life,* p. 113; Gallup, *A Bibliography of Ezra Pound,* C55). By 1913 Pound was 'booming' Gourmont's verse ('The Approach to Paris...II', in *New Age,* 11 Sept 1913, pp. 577-579), and getting a translation of him published (Hutchins, 'Ezra Pound's "Approach to Paris"', pp. 351-352). Gourmont's influence is strong in the *Contemporania* of 1913 and in other poems that went into the *Lustra* of 1916; cf. also *The Alchemist* of 1912, Chapter 8, text before n. 47.

110. What follows this passage is also important. Cf. Gourmont, *Lettres d'un Satyre,* p. 72, on the movement between sexuality and intelligence; also *Natural Philosophy,* pp. 153-154. It is this kind of 'intelligence' that, Pound tried to convince Santayana, moves the growth of the cherry tree from its stone (Kenner, *Pound Era,* pp. 103, 568, references), and without which the body politic begins to die from the neck down (cf. Rome broadcast, 24 Apr 1942, quoted in Mullins, *This Difficult Individual,* p. 214). What some might call 'mere instinct' is part of it: cf. *Kulchur,* p. 195, and especially *Jefferson and/or Mussolini,* pp. 18-19. For Gourmont on 'the physicality of Christian metaphysics', see *Lettres à l'Amazone,* pp. 281-282.

111. *Essays,* p. 339.

112. Hugh Kenner's phrase: *Pound Era,* p. 29.

113. Ibid.

114. *Moeurs Contemporaines,* IV: *Sketch b. 11;* the *Moeurs* were published in the *Little Review* (May 1918) and then in *Quia Pauper Amavi* (1919), each time with the *Homage à la Langue d'Oc* poems (see above, n. 91).

115. See Chapter 7, text before n. 7, Chapter 9, text before n. 8.

116. Cf. Dronke, *European Love-Lyric*, 1, pp. 52-53, for this source in general.

117. Cf. e.g. Cavalcanti's pastourelle, *Era in penser d'amor* (*Rime*, no. XXX), and for the pastourelle in general: Paris, *Mélanges*, pp. 556ff.

118. *Cantos*, 11/51:55.

119. Sophocles, *Women of Trachis*, tr. Pound, p. 62.

120. Rochester, *Gyldenstolpe Manuscript*, p. 132. For similar themes cf. *A Ramble in St James's Park* ('Much wine had past'), and *On Mrs Willis* ('Against the Charms our B-llox have'), ibid., pp. 77ff., 157-158. On the authenticity of these songs cf. Vieth, *Attribution in Restoration Poetry*, pp. 436, etc.

121. Rochester, *Complete Poems*, pp. 88-89; cf. e.g. 'The Mistress', ibid., pp. 87-88.

CHAPTER 6. ELEANOR OF AQUITAINE

1. Cf. Cercamon, *Poésies*, p. vi; Marcabru, *Poésies*, p. 38.

2. Bezzola, *Origines*, 2.2, p. 316.

3. Dumitrescu, 'Eble II et Guillaume', p. 384; Bernard, *Chansons*, no. 44, *Lo tems vai e ven e vire*, lines 22-25.

4. Cercamon, *Poésies*, no. VI, *Lo plaing comenz iradamen*, lines 49-50.

5. Bernart, *Lieder*, p. ix.

6. Jeanroy, *Poésie*, 1, p. 85.

7. Bernart, *Lieder*, p. xvii.

8. Stronski, *Bertran*, pp. 34, 41-44.

9. *Kulchur*, p. 107; cf. ibid., p. 194, on Malatesta as a 'factive personality'.

10. *Cantos*, 27/132:137.

11. Richard, *Comtes de Poitou*, 1, p. 488; Bezzola, *Origines*, 3.1, p. 255.

12. Labande, 'Aliénor', p. 176, note; cf. Bezzola, *Origines*, 3.1, p. 84.

13. Discussions as to whether William X wanted to 'centralise' the kingdom (Martindale, 'Duchy of Aquitaine', pp. 162-163) or keep his patrimony separate (Warren, *Henry II*, p. 44) should bear in mind that the king would in any case exercise feudal wardship over the eldest daughter of a vassal deceased without heirs male, if he could (cf. Labande, 'Aliénor', p. 176, note).

14. Labande, 'Aliénor', p. 178.

15. Ibid., pp. 177, note, 180, note.

16. Ibid., p. 181. Berger, followed by Labande (cf. p. 178, and note), speculates that the erratic nature of Louis's actions in these years stemmed from the contradictory influences of his clerical adviser Suger on the one hand, and on the other of Eleanor's retinue, to whom he wanted to show his manhood.

17. Ibid., p. 181, and note.

18. Lejeune, 'Rôle littéraire d'Aliénor', p. 12, note, referring to Marcabru, *Poésies*, no. XLIV, *Soudadier, per cui es Jovens*. That the 'paid soldiers' addressed are those on crusade is made more probable by Marcabru's close interest in the crusade, urging men to join it (ibid., no. XXXV, *Pax in nomine Domini!*) and having

a shepherdess curse it for taking her friend (ibid., no. I, *A la fontana del vergier*). Cf. also ibid., p. 238, note to no. XLIV. The chronicler is Vincent of Prague, cited in Labande, 'Aliénor', p. 181, note.

19. Ibid., p. 182; cf. Kelly, *Eleanor*, p. 42, etc.

20. Labande, 'Alienor', pp. 184-185; the treatment of this episode in Kelly, *Eleanor*, pp. 52-60, may well give the correct tone of the events.

21. Cf. Labande, 'Alienor', p. 194; Labande observes (p. 192) that the tension between Louis and Eleanor came to the breaking-point when the young Henry Plantagenet was a visitor at their court.

22. Ibid., p. 196.

23. A memorable account of this episode is in Ramsay, *Foundations of England*, 2, pp. 444-445, which Pound may well have read. For the political considerations cf. also Warren, *Henry II*, p. 44: Eleanor should not have remarried without the consent of her suzerain, Louis.

24. Ibid., pp. 44-53.

25. Labande, 'Aliénor', pp. 192, 176.

26. Ibid., p. 199.

27. Ibid., pp. 199-200.

28. Ibid., p. 203.

29. Ibid.

30. Cf. ibid.

31. For all this see ibid., pp. 205-210, and above, Chapter 3, text before nn. 9ff.

32. Cf. the anonymous writer quoted in Labande, 'Aliénor', pp. 213-214.

33. Ibid., pp. 215-217.

34. Ibid., pp. 217-225; cf. Ramsay, *Empire*, p. 289, and for a strongly written version of her last years, ibid., p. 334. Lejeune, 'Rôle littéraire d'Aliénor', p. 48, note, observes that she does not call herself Duchess of Aquitaine 'by the wrath of God'.

35. Labande, 'Aliénor', pp. 226-233. Labande notes (pp. 229-230) that it was apparently Eleanor who chose her granddaughter Blanche to be the wife of Philippe-Auguste's heir, and that it was Blanche who brought about the end of the Plantagenet dynasty. Cf. her role in urging on her husband Louis VIII to the conquest of Languedoc in the aftermath of the Albigensian Crusade (Chapter 10, text below n. 15).

The fact that Eleanor's tomb in Fontevrault lies beside Richard's rather than her husband's (cf. Warren, *Henry II*, p. 600, and ibid., plate 25) is probably not of significance, since the tombs were originally elsewhere in the building: Boase, 'Fontevrault and the Plantagenets', p. 8.

36. Warren, *Henry II*, passim, is the best source for these aspects of Henry's reign.

37. See Labande, 'La civilisation de l'Aquitaine', p. 17.

38. Cf. Labande, 'Aliénor', pp. 198-204; Warren, *Henry II*, p. 121.

39. Ibid., pp. 38-39, 208; cf. Bezzola, *Origines*, 3.1, pp. 84, 16-18. The spleen of the clerical chroniclers over the Becket affair has damaged Henry's standing, as Warren notes (*Henry II*, pp. 214-215).

40. Labande, 'Aliénor', p. 208; Lejeune, 'Rôle littéraire d'Aliénor', p. 45.

41. See below, text before nn. 55ff.

42. Cf. Chapter 10, n. 70.

43. Labande, 'Aliénor', pp. 187-188.

44. She tried at every opportunity to return to Aquitaine, and attempted to perpetuate its dynasty at least in name by calling her son 'William': ibid., p. 199.

45. Labande, 'La civilisation de l'Aquitaine', p. 26.

46. Appel, *Bertran,* pp. 5-6, and see Appendix 2, text before n. 11. Lejeune, 'Rôle littéraire de la famille d'Aliénor', p. 323, says that in the romance of *Erec et Enide* by Chrétien de Troyes, 'The final episode of the coronation celebrations at Nantes uses data probably picked up at the place itself, at the brilliant Christmas court that Henry II and Eleanor held at Nantes in 1169 for the betrothal of their son Geoffrey.'

47. Lejeune, 'Rôle littéraire d'Aliénor', pp. 20-22.

48. Labande, 'Aliénor', pp. 213-214 (and p. 207 citing the same source).

49. Cf. Lejeune, 'Rôle littéraire d'Aliénor', p. 12; Appel, *Chrestomathie,* no. 48, *A l'entrade del tens clar;* Pound, *La Regina Avrillouse* and *A Rouse* in *A Lume Spento* (orig. publ. 1908: Gallup, *A Bibliography of Ezra Pound,* A1). Cf. Pound, *Hesternae Rosae,* no. IX, *A l'entrade.*

50. Appel, *Bertran,* pp. 18-19.

51. Lejeune, 'Rôle littéraire d'Aliénor', p. 25; but her proofs often tend to be very circumstantial: as for example that since Henry cannot have commissioned the work, because he was only nineteen and fighting for his prospective throne, Eleanor must have. Perhaps neither of them in fact commissioned it.

52. Ibid., p. 32; but the same criticism as above can be made: it is mere speculation to date the *Tristan* of Thomas between 1154 and 1158 simply because by the time Eleanor was in her second phase of patronage (1163-73) she was forty years old and no longer (according to Lejeune) identifiable with the 'rayonnante' Iseut.

53. Ibid., p. 24. The chronicler Jordan de Fantosme appears to have been in Eleanor's entourage (p. 27).

54. Ibid., p. 39, but again Lejeune's argument seems weak: that though the *Lais* were dedicated to the King, they look like work intended for a female audience, and therefore were probably written for Eleanor's circle. This weakness extends to another type of argument used here and elsewhere by Lejeune: that the places named in the writings fit Eleanor's movements. Since Lejeune seems to be willing to accept any place named within a hundred miles of Eleanor's movements as evidence of a connection, her net could sweep in everything written in the whole kingdom.

55. Lejeune, 'Rôle littéraire de la famille d'Aliénor', p. 329.

56. Ibid., pp. 320-321.

57. Appendix 2, text before n. 25.

58. Gennrich, *Die altfranzösische Rotruenge,* p. 20:

> . . . Moult ai d'amis, mès povre sont li don;
> Honte en avront, se por ma reancon
> Sui ces deus yvers pris.

> . . . Je nel di pas por nule retracon,
> Mes encor sui ge pris.

> . . . I have many friends, but small gifts;
> it will be a shame to them, if for my ransom
> I stay captive these two winters.
>
> . . . I don't say it to blame anyone,
> but I am still captive.

59. See above, Chapter 3, passim, and Lejeune, 'Rôle littéraire de la famille d'Aliénor', p. 320, and note; though cf. Lejeune, 'Rôle littéraire d'Aliénor', p. 39.

60. Cf. Lejeune, 'Rôle littéraire de la famille d'Aliénor', p. 323.

61. Cf. ibid., pp. 325-327. For the influence of Marie de Champagne at least, there is a very useful check on Rita Lejeune's conclusions, in John F. Benton's 'The Court of Champagne as a Literary Center', which is based on a more rigorous approach to historical evidence. Where Lejeune suggests that contact took place in Marie's entourage between French poets (Chrétien, Conon de Béthune, and Gace Brulé) and troubadours, Benton points out that Marie is merely mentioned as being present at the royal court, not her own, by Conon (pp. 577-578), and that there is no evidence of Southerners at the court of Champagne (p. 589). Benton also suggests (p. 590) that there is unlikely to have been important personal contact between these writers at court, because no writers seem to have spent much time there. However, we know that there was very rapid communication between the troubadours and *trouvères* in general (cf. Introduction, text before n. 4), and intelligent patronage by the politically powerful must certainly have patterned these lines of communication. Benton also suggests at length that Marie is unlikely to have been a propagandist in herself of the ethic of courtly love as Andreas Capellanus conceived it; a point which I would accept (see below, n. 66), without accepting that it has any bearing on her influence on artistic currents.

62. Lejeune, 'Rôle littéraire de la famille d'Aliénor', pp. 328, 330.

63. Cf. ibid., pp. 321, 324.

64. See above, nn. 51, 52, 54, and below, n. 66.

65. Jeanroy said that the patronage offered to poets by the Plantagenets was 'banal' and 'distant'; none of Henry II's three sons was an 'enlightened Maecenas, putting his wits into discovering or encouraging real talent'. He said of Eleanor herself, and in the next sentence implied of Henry (*Poésie*, 1, pp. 161, 153, 151): 'The daughter of [William X], the frivolous and vain Eleanor, could only have a welcome for the distributors of glory that the troubadours were. Although we only know one of her protégés, we can affirm that poets and *jongleurs* pullulated around her.' But for the far more sensitive judgement of Appel, see above, text before nn. 46, 50.

66. The treatise *De arte (honeste) amandi* by Andreas, 'Francorum aulae regiae capellanus', purports to give the judgements on love-problems rendered by, among others, Eleanor of Aquitaine, her daughter Marie de Champagne, and the Viscountess Ermengarde of Narbonne. For a long time scholars believed that these judgements had actually been rendered at 'courts of love' to which lovers submitted their problems, as Andreas describes. The treatise does date from within about forty years of Eleanor's death in 1204 (cf. Paris, *Mélanges*, pp. 478-480, 481-482; the composition can be dated about 1196, and must be from before 1238: cf.

Andrea Capellano, *Trattato d'Amore,* p. vi, note). Gaston Paris considered that the 'judgements of love' grew out of the verse-debates commonly held between troubadours which came to be submitted to ladies thought wise in love; but he thought that the problems were invented for the occasion (*Mélanges,* pp. 492-494).

But there is no historically reliable evidence connecting this work or its author or the events it describes with either Eleanor or Marie de Champagne (or anyone else, for that matter). Andreas was tentatively identified with a chaplain at Marie's court, but this Andreas seems to have ceased to have been attached to her court before the book was written, and there is no historical evidence of her patronage of the work (see Benton, 'The Court of Champagne as a Literary Center', pp. 579-580). The only evidence connecting the *Treatise* with Eleanor of Aquitaine is the fact that Andreas ascribes judgements to her. To some, that is sufficient; thus Lafitte-Houssat, *Cours d'Amour,* p. 37, who dismisses all questions of date and authorship like this: 'It is enough for us to know that this methodical exposé of courtliness . . . is the one that was in use at the end of the twelfth century. This is sufficiently proved by the mention of the great ladies whose judgements are given: the Queen of France, Alice, Eleanor of Poitou, the Countess of Champagne, etc.' It was of course the habit of all late fictionalisers of the Provençal culture, like the *vida* writers, to sprinkle their works liberally with great names.

It should be noted that the term 'court of love', in the sense of a tribunal handing down judgements, was unknown to the Middle Ages; the *Treatise* itself receives no surviving mention in the Middle Ages, being discovered at the beginning of the nineteenth century (Lafitte-Houssat, *Cours d'Amour,* pp. 24, 31-32).

Rita Lejeune's excess of optimism is nowhere clearer than in her handling of Andreas Capellanus, whose scenarios involving Eleanor she takes as perfectly historical. Observing that their spirit owes much to the Provençal *ensenhamen,* which is true, she then attempts to tie the *ensenhamen* to Eleanor by saying that its first authors came from her territories ('Rôle littéraire d'Aliénor', pp. 42-44). But John F. Benton, in 'The Court of Champagne as a Literary Center', after demonstrating the absence of any evidence relating the treatise to Eleanor and to Marie, notes that particular judgements in it would have been taken by a contemporary audience as quite clearly scandalous references to Eleanor's own marital affairs (p. 581), and that if Marie had literally propagated the doctrines it credits her with uttering, she would instantly have become a social outcast (pp. 587-588).

One must consider the tones of the work, as compared with those of works that we can historically connect with Eleanor and Marie. This paraphrase of one of the judgements by Gaston Paris (see the original in Andrea Capellano, *Trattato d'Amore,* pp. 332-333) gives an idea (*Mélanges,* p. 488): 'A confidant reveals secrets of love entrusted to him. All the 'knights of love' (*omnes in castris militantes amoris*) demand a punishment. A court of ladies assembled in Gascony decides that the babbler shall be deprived of all hope in love and despised in every court of knights and ladies; any woman loving him in spite of this decision should share his punishment and would henceforth be the enemy of all noble ladies.' It comes from the same kind of mental world as produced the more elaborately pompous *vidas* and *razos,* which come from a moment when the Provençal culture falls in love with itself. In the story of Rigaut de Barbézieux, reworked in those of Gaucelm

Faidit, Maria de Ventadorn, and the lady of Malemort (cf. ibid., pp. 509-511, 509, note), the apparatus of salon games, assembling ladies in judgement, and so forth, is very similar to that of the *Treatise*.

The tones of the *Treatise* have been much debated. Robertson in *A Preface to Chaucer*, pp. 391-418, suggests that Andreas's laborious fun is ironical and therefore moral in intent. But if there is a moral intention, it is strongly subordinate to a quasi-pornographic one. I would tend to follow Donaldson's argument in *Speaking of Chaucer*, that the first two parts of the treatise are a playful attempt to push rationalist argument on love as far as it will go; but I doubt whether this can apply to the retraction, which Donaldson argues (p. 161) is just as deliberately outrageous. Neville Coghill's sensitive reading in 'Love and "Foul Delight"' suggests that having toyed with the forbidden sexual areas in a pornographic manner in the first two parts, Andreas shows his true psychological colours in the violent (but morally safe) antisensualism and antifeminism of the last; and it seems to me that this pornographic intent is what one should emphasise in Donaldson's argument about rationalist fantasy.

Whatever discussions of ethics or aesthetics went on between ladies and poets at the courts of Eleanor and her connections, they are unlikely to have had the form or content given them by the banal Andreas.

Pound associated Andreas's production with Eleanor in 'Psychology', p. 50 (*Spirit*, p. 97), but this was written before Pound had any more than second-hand information about Eleanor herself. He could already see that the treatise had not much to do with the troubadour aesthetic.

67. See Chapter 8, text before n. 98.

68. *Cantos*, 7/25-26:29-30.

69. Ibid., 2/6:10.

70. Ibid., 20/90-95:94-99, where '(Epi purgo) peur de la haule' is from the old men talking about Helen (cf. *Essays*, p. 254), 'HO BIOS' is 'life', and 'cosi Elena vedi' means 'thus see Helen', at least if Pound is following his source (cf. Dante, *Inferno*, 5.64), and not 'thus Helen sees' as in the *Annotated Index*, s.v.

71. *Cantos*, 8/32-33:36-37.

72. See Chapter 9, text before n. 126.

73. *Cantos*, 29/144:146.

74. Ibid., 24/111-112:116; cf. e.g. Noyes, *Story of Ferrara*, p. 68, and especially Hugen, '"Small Birds of Cyprus"', passim.

75. *Cantos*, 20/90-91:94-96 (the Este), 5/18-22 (Maensac), 29/109:113 (Montsegur).

76. See Appendix.

77. In the Cantos, Malatesta is the ideal patron for Pier della Francesca (8/29: 33): he is reticent but open-handed. The example of John Quinn is also to the point: Pound, Joyce, and Eliot all acknowledged that his help had been crucial to them; yet Pound had to defend him against charges that he was ungenerous, and unable to talk about art (*Letters*, to Margaret C. Anderson, [ca. May] 1917; cf. ibid., to John Quinn, 24 Jan 1917).

78. *Kulchur*, p. 59.

79. *Letters*, to James Vogel, 23 Jan 1929.

CHAPTER 7. BERNART DE VENTADORN

1. Bernard, *Chansons*, pp. 54-58. Following Lazar, I put in parentheses those passages that are only in N^2. For the errors, cf. Chapter 4, n. 26. For Bernart's life, see Appendix 2, text before n. 9.

2. *ABC of Reading*, p. 55.

3. Cf. *Spirit*, p. 166, note, quoted below, text before n. 66.

4. Cf. *Letters*, to Felix E. Schelling, 9 July 1922: 'I can't count six people whom I have succeeded in interesting in XIIth Century Provence.'

5. 'Psychology', p. 40 (*Spirit*, p. 89).

6. Cf. *Kulchur*, p. 108.

7. Bernard, *Chansons*, no. 16, 13, 37, 36, 34, 23, 21, 20.

8. Ibid., no. 36, *Ja mos chantars no m'er onors.*

9. Ibid., no. 37, *Gent estera que chantes.*

10. Ibid., no. 20, *Can l'erba fresch' e·lh folha par.*

11. Ibid., no. 37, *Gent estera que chantes.*

12. Ibid., no. 38, *Lancan vei la folha.*

13. Ibid.

14. Ibid., no. 10, *Pel doutz chan que·l rossinhols fai.*

15. Ibid., no. 23, *Lo·rossinhols s'esbaudeya.*

16. Ibid., no. 19, *Lonc tems a qu'eu no chantei mai.*

17. Ibid., no. 20, *Can l'erba fresch' e·lh folha par.*

18. Ibid., no. 40, *En cossirer et en esmai.*

19. Ibid., no. 13, *Be·m cuidei de chantar sofrir.*

20. Ibid., no. 38, *Lancan vei la folha.*

21. Ibid., no. 13, *Be·m cuidei de chantar sofrir.*

22. Ibid., no. 41, *Bel m'es qu'eu chan en aquel mes.*

23. Ibid., no. 13, *Be·m cuidei de chantar sofrir.*

24. Ibid., no. 32, *Bernart de Ventadorn, del chan.*

25. Ibid., no. 30, *Estat ai com om esperdutz.*

26. Cf. the similar situation of Arnaut Daniel, Chapter 8, text before n. 1.

27. See Paden, 'The Troubadour's Lady', passim, especially p. 29.

28. Bernard, *Chansons*, no. 18, *Pois preyatz me, senhor.*

29. Ibid., no. 7, *Can vei la flor, l'erba vert e la folha.* On the Greeks, cf. Kenner, *Pound Era*, pp. 259, 577.

30. Bernard, *Chansons*, no. 29, *Lancan vei per mei la landa;* cf. the way he mingles his longing and his own nakedness, ibid., no. 24, *Can par la flors josta·l vert folh:*

> I know well that at night, when I undress,
> I shan't sleep in my bed.

and no. 4, *Tant ai mo cor ple de joya:*

> I can go without clothing,
> naked in my shirt,
> because fine love makes me safe
> from the cold wind.

31. Ibid., no. 31, *Can vei la lauzeta mover.*

32. Fiedler, *Love and Death in the American Novel,* pp. 49-50.

33. Bernard, *Chansons,* no. 29, *Lancan vei per mei la landa.*

34. Ibid., no. 30, *Estat ai com om esperdutz.*

35. See Chapter 5, text before nn. 42, 62.

36. See Chapter 5, text before n. 76.

37. See Chapter 5, text before n. 42.

38. Bernard, *Chansons,* no. 17, *Lo gens tems de pascor,* lines 23-24, no. 31, *Can vei la lauzeta mover,* lines 25-32, etc.

39. For what follows see especially Goldin, *Mirror of Narcissus,* pp. 74-81, 252-255, 97-101; 'Array of Perspectives', passim; *Lyrics of the Troubadours,* pp. 108-125.

40. To say that the lady exists, as a person, in the poem, is not to say that such a person existed historically at one particular moment we could name, such as the moment of composition, or the moment of first singing. At the moment when Bernart writes

> deceiving heartless flatterers
> have sent me away from her country

he need not just have arrived in exile (Bernard, *Chansons,* no. 37; cf. above, text before n. 9). Some of the experience may be 'second-hand', vicarious; but in so far as the creation of the poem's situation works, all of it must have been intimately 'known' and highly important to the poet, whether acquired by a grain of experience and a mountain of intuition, or however. Henry James in 'The Art of Fiction' said he thought a good lady novelist could write a novel about soldiers on the basis of a snatch of talk heard through a barrack-room window (see especially *The House of Fiction,* p. 31); but even when every word and phrase in Eliot's poetry shall have been proved to have been borrowed from a literary source, the whole is undeniably 'his', and that is because his emotions predisposed him to select and arrange this information. Bernart de Ventadorn's process may be more like that of Matisse: a lifetime's struggle towards the perfect assembly of that ideal composite out of their experience that haunts them most strongly, producing on the way what looks to the insensitive like an endless series of identical women. The result in Bernart, as in most troubadour poetry, is an art relatively little concerned with personality in its external forms, but suffused with very personal emotion.

Many theories have been built on the fact that the ladies of the troubadours are more or less anonymous. Positivist critics tended to say that since they are not identified personally in the songs, the troubadours cannot have been in love with them, and so either they did not exist but were invented as material for poetising (cf. e.g. Stronski, Chapter 3, text before n. 64), or they were simply the object of fashionable exercises (e.g. Jeanroy, *Poésie,* 2, pp. 94, 175, laying great stress on repetitiveness among the troubadours). There are the theories that since the ladies are blanks to which the same qualities are frequently attributed, either they are digits representing entities in a secret code (cf. Chapter 10, text before n. 118) or they represent concepts (but see Chapter 8, text before n. 63, and especially Chapter 8, n. 66). This type of theory has been developed more with reference to the Italians of Cavalcanti's period. Recent critics have often accepted the idea that the songs bear little relation to experience, but have said that this does not diminish their value; one should admit that the text is built of clichés, but follow the artistry with which these clichés are patterned, counterpointed, etc., as in the construction of music. Robert Guiette is a leading exponent of this view, and has been followed for example by Koehler (cf. 'Observations historiques', p. 42) and Zumthor (*Langue et techniques poétiques à l'époque romane*, p. 9). But this kind of argument never finally claims that the poetry is the play of absolutely blank counters on a board; it always includes caveats about not neglecting the interest of the theme and 'the expressive quality of the moves' (Guiette, quoted by Koehler, 'Observations historiques', p. 42), and thus admits that the changes of pattern have their interest because the counters have intrinsic weights for us, derived from their human connotations, and carried by rhythm, tone, and image. A poetry which should succeed in extricating itself from all emotional association with the things it names (impossible, but perhaps some of Gertrude Stein's comes closest) would have removed from itself the largest possibility of structure. Since we are therefore back in the realm of felt human situation, a cliché remains a cliché, and is felt as such, though no doubt it is right to point out that permutation has its interest.

41. Goldin, *Mirror of Narcissus*, pp. 258, 81.

42. Cf. Chapter 5, n. 54, and Koehler, 'Observations historiques', pp. 37-39.

43. Though homosexuality has been alleged in Provencal culture, I am not aware that it has been shown convincingly to be the basis of any of the love-lyrics; cf. Lavaud, cited in Arnaut, *Canzoni,* p. 9, and Appendix 2, n. 37. For Sappho see Chapter 5, text before n. 63.

44. This question cannot be avoided by immediately referring to the theological plane, to Augustine on self-love; if we do that, we must be able to explain the bed, the feet, the kisses, the *drudaria* on the same level, and there is no suggestion that the troubadours intended their works to be interpreted in the same way as St. Bernard interpreted the *Song of Songs,* for which see my 'Pound's Provence and the Mediaeval Paideuma', p. 49.

45. See especially Goldin, *Lyrics of the Troubadours,* pp. 9-13.

46. On p. 92 of his *Mirror of Narcissus,* Goldin observes: 'Before it is possible to call [the real physical lady] a mirror, a great psychic event has taken place: the courtly ideal and all the doctrines that define it have been translated into a visible form in the immediate image of the lady.' If 'the courtly ideal' means the general ideal self-images of knights and lords in the troubadour period in areas *other* than that of sexual relations, there is still lacking an account of their choice particularly to fuse them into the area of sexual relationships rather than another. If 'the courtly ideal' includes self-images in the sexual area, then the observation is circular: these self-images, sexual included, are being fused into the sexual area. I suspect a confusion: that it is being supposed that 'the courtly ideal and all the doctrines that define it' existed before any one of these troubadours fell in love with their ladies in the courtly-love manner, that is to say before there existed that psycho-sexual relation between man and woman which alone could produce 'the courtly ideal and all the doctrines that define it'. In any case, I would emphasise that this 'ideal' is only secondarily a group phenomenon.

47. Bernard, *Chansons,* no. 16, *A! Tantas bonas chansos,* is a good example of this; roughly following its metric, one might translate the first stanza thus:

> Ah me! how much worthy song
> and good verse I shall have made,
> with which I'd not pained myself,
> lady, if I'd thought of you
> that you'd act to me so harshly.
> Now I know that I have lost you!
> But at least you are not stolen
> from me by my proper failing. . . .

The rest might be paraphrased like this: 'I had thought it low to love one-sidedly, but who can defend himself against Love? Now I'm happy, for her eyes have given me a potion that fills me with joy at the same time as it takes away all moderation. Whatever complaint I had against Love, this arrival in the nick of time makes it right. Anyone who sees her face will know (I'm only inferring this!) that her naked body makes snow seem muddy. If these jealous ones try to find out how it is with us, don't be lost by them; I shall never say a word about our love.'

48. Cf. Carl Rakosi, 'A Note on the "Objectivists" ', p. 37, on the lack of strongly felt experience in certain modern poetry, covered over by new intellectual procedures: 'the name of the game is still *game.*' It may be valid with such after-comers to say that the whole apparatus of subject-matter is so standardised that it is clearly only being used to project a self-image; but one will have to allow for such a category in many literatures. Turning from the poems that Fenollosa and Pound translated for *Cathay,* which are by and large masterpieces universally acknowledged among the Chinese, one finds the same *topoi* in less concentrated form throughout the lyrics of the classic Chinese eras: exile, loss of friends, and so forth. If more Anglo-Saxon poetry had survived, no doubt one would find *The Seafarer's* images everywhere in it. In the blues, the 'mama' is always 'treatin' him mean', and so on.

49. 'Preface: *Discrete Series* by George Oppen', p. 21.

50. 'I Gather the Limbs of Osiris VI: On Virtue', p. 224 (*Selected Prose,* pp. 28-29).

51. Bernard, *Chansons,* no. 20, *Can l'erba fresch' e·lh folha par.*

52. Zukofsky, 'Sincerity and Objectification', p. 278, describing an effect in Charles Reznikoff.

53. See Paterson, *Troubadours and Eloquence,* pp. 183, 138-139, and Chapter 8, n. 19.

54. As the literary image is not visual in a simple sense — one could not draw Bernart's lark — so this kind of sound-effect comes out of onomatopoeia somehow but is not simply onomatopoeia in any easily describable way. For the way in which mediaeval writers did *not* present us with detailed and realistic landscapes, see Pearsall and Salter, *Landscapes and Seasons of the Medieval World,* pp. 41ff. On musical invention in Pound, cf. Zukofsky, *Prepositions,* pp. 133-134.

55. It is easy enough to say that this invention is there, but very difficult to say what it consists of. One must make an attempt, bearing in mind that the things I point out will only have effect if one looks out for them *in rereading Bernart's lines.*

The chief stresses in the first line, *Ai las! com mor de cossirar,* are *mor* and *-rar.* The second line does not repeat them but establishes new ones with *-etz* and *tan,* though cleverly inserting a repeat of the *cossir* element; then the third line manages an echo of the *Ai* and *las* vowels of the first line, with *lairo* and *-an* (which also echoes the *tan/fan* rhyme), while also alluding to the *mor* with *por,* and reminding one of the *Ai* again with *poir-.* The last of these four lines achieves a further counterplay against these expectations with the *sab-* against *manh-* and *tan,* which we then expect to find repeated when the *s* of *que's* comes up, only to find that the poet is introducing a new consonant: *fan.* Thus:

> Ai las! com mor de cossirar!
> Que manhtas vetz en cossir tan:
> lairo m'en poirian portar,
> que re no sabria que's fan.

56. *Essays,* p. 197.

57. See below, text before n. 63.

58. Bernard, *Chansons,* no. 31.

59. Goldin, *Mirror of Narcissus,* pp. 96-99.

60. Ibid., p. 97.

61. See Chapter 5, text before n. 76, Chapter 9, text before n. 22.

62. 'I Gather the Limbs of Osiris IV: A Beginning', p. 179 (*Selected Prose,* p. 27).

63. *Spirit,* p. 31; cf. his letter to William Carlos Williams satirising the modern product of this tradition (*Letters,* 21 Oct 1908):

> 1. Spring is a pleasant season. The flowers, etc. etc.
>   sprout, bloom etc. etc.
> 2. Young man's fancy. Lightly, heavily, gaily etc. etc.
> 3. Love, a delightsome tickling. Indefinable etc. . . .

64. See also above, n. 54.

65. *Kulchur,* p. 28.

66. *Spirit,* p. 166, note.

67. Bernard, *Chansons,* no. 14, *Anc no gardei sazo ni mes.*

68. Villon, *Oeuvres,* 'Testament', lines 333-334.

69. Bernard, *Chansons,* no. 29, *Lancan vei per mei la landa.*

70. Ibid., no. 31, *Can vei la lauzeta mover.*

71. Bertran, *Lieder,* no. 40, *Be'm platz lo gais.*

72. Bernard, *Chansons,* no. 24, *Can par la flors josta'l vert folh.* For the last of these lines, Lazar has 'et me ranime', which seems to me less accurate.

73. Arnaut, *Canzoni,* no. V, *Lanquan vei fueill' e flor e frug.* There are also very similar feelings and sounds in Bernard, *Chansons,* no. 42, *Can lo boschatges es floritz:*

> e vei lo tems renovelar
> a chascus auzels quer sa par
> e·l rossinhols fai chans e critz

> and I see the season renewing itself
> and each bird seeking its mate
> and the nightingale makes songs and cries

and in Arnaut, *Canzoni,* no. XII, *Doutz brais e critz:*

> Doutz brais e critz,
> lais e cantars e voutas
> aug dels auzels q'en lur latin fant precs
> qecs ab sa par, atressi cum nos fam

> The sweet noises and cries
> lays and songs and trills
> I hear, of the birds that in their language make pleadings
> each with his mate, just as we do

74. Bernard, *Chansons,* no. 44, *Lo tems vai e ven e vire.*

75. *Cantos,* 7/26:30.

76. 'I Gather the Limbs of Osiris IX: On Technique', p. 298 (*Selected Prose,* p. 34).

77. Bertran, *Lieder,* no. 6, *S'abrils e fuolhas.*

78. Arnaut, *Canzoni,* no. IX, *L'aur' amara.*

79. *Spirit,* p. 150; see Dante, *Paradiso,* 26.85-88:

> Come la fronda, che flette la cima
> Nel transito del vento, e poi si leva
> Per la propria virtù che la sublima,
> Fec'io in tanto in quanto ella diceva,
> Stupendo

80. *Cantos,* 20/90:94; cf. Chapter 8, text before n. 86.

81. Pound wrote of William Carlos Williams's 'lack of form' that, while major form mattered, many indispensable writings were completely lacking in it. He listed the plotless *Iliad,* the constructionless *Prometheus,* the formless Montaigne and Rabelais, and the endingless *Bouvard et Pécuchet* as examples (*Essays,* p. 394).

82. Pound identified the key images in Noh plays and the key phrases in *Women of Trachis, Elektra,* Cocteau's *Antigone,* and other pieces (see *Translations,* p. 237; Sophocles, *Women of Trachis,* p. 66; *Kulchur,* p. 93).

83. *Letters,* to Agnes Bedford, Oct 1920.

84. Bernard, *Chansons,* no. 24, *Can par la flors josta· l vert folh.*

85. *Cantos,* 95/645:678 (cf. 92/619:652); the original Provencal is quoted at 20/89:93. Cf. Chapter 8, text before n. 121, Chapter 10, text before n. 160.

86. See Chapter 8, text before n. 115, from Bernard, *Chansons,* no. 31 (see above, text before n. 58), which Pound adapts in *Cantos,* 91/610:644, to 'ab lo dolchor qu'al cor mi vai', probably conflating it with the first line of William IX's *Ab la dolchor del temps novel* (Guillaume IX, *Chansons,* no. X), 'With the sweetness of the new season'. This point has been noted by Dekker in *Sailing After Knowledge,* p. 200, by Eva Hesse in *Paideuma,* 1.2 (Fall and Winter 1972), p. 272, and by James J. Wilhelm in *Paideuma,* 2.2 (Fall 1973), pp. 333-335, who also discussed the source of the music and the logic of Pound's adaptation of it and of the words.

87. *Cantos,* 74/430-431:457.

88. The legend of the city of Wagadu, four times destroyed by evil motivations and one day finally to rise indestructibly in the mind, is translated from Frobenius in Emery, *Ideas into Action,* p. 130. Italy's betrayal is mentioned two lines earlier in the Canto.

89. Dante, *Purgatorio,* 8.2. *A sinistra la Torre,* 'on the left the Tower', refers to the tower in which Ugolino and his sons starved: Dante, *Inferno,* 33.1-75.

90. Pound has escaped between the Scylla of the land of the dead (Nekuia, the Evocation of the Dead in the *Odyssey*) and the Charybdis of action, to find himself a lone survivor. For the sun 'in periplum' see Chapter 10, text before n. 153. Bernart's lark song also appears in Canto VI, as we have seen (Chapter 4, text before n. 30), and in a final fragment in 'Notes for Canto CXVII et seq.' (802:32), where the mood is sad again, as of Pound's own thwarted aspirations. Bernouard, referred to in this passage, was a publisher of good writing whose bankruptcy Pound much regretted. *Es laissa cader* is 'and lets itself fall', and *de joi sas alas* is 'for joy its wings' (see the Provençal text, above, text before n. 58).

CHAPTER 8. ARNAUT DANIEL

1. Arnaut, *Canzoni,* pp. 7-11.
2. Ibid., p. 165.
3. Ibid. (MSS. *EIKN²*).
4. Bertran, *Lieder,* no. 39, *Bel m'es, quan vei.*
5. Cf. Appendix 2, text before nn. 29, 35.
6. Cf. e.g. Sordello, *Poesie,* ed. Boni, pp. XXXV-XXXVI.
7. Arnaut, *Canzoni,* p. 19, note; cf. 'Arnaut Daniel', p. 44 (*Essays,* p. 109).
8. Raimbaut de Vaqueiras, *Poems,* pp. 13ff., and Chapter 9, text before n. 37; though Raimbaut and Sordello were also warriors.
9. Boutière and Schutz, *Biographies,* p. 147.
10. Critics have hinted at sodomy (cf. Arnaut, *Canzoni,* p. 182), but ibid., no. I, *Pois Raimons e·n Trucs Malecs,* refers to

> he who takes his mouth to the horn

says that the action

> would completely scald his neck and cheeks

and that

> it is not right for a lady to kiss
> a man who blows a smelly horn

which indicates 'cunt-lapping', in Ed Sanders's phrase. The *cul* referred to (ibid.) is probably no more precise than Modern French *cul* or American 'ass'.

11. Ibid. The song is the one that Pound says he does not print 'for reasons clear to all who have read it' ('Arnaut Daniel', p. 45 [*Essays,* p. 110]), and compares to Villon (*Spirit,* p. 167). In 'Arnaut Daniel', p. 46 (*Essays,* p. 111), he says, 'It is like

that men slandered Arnaut for Dante's putting him in his *Purgatorio,* but the Trucs Malecs poem is against this.' (Arnaut is in fact with the bisexuals in Purgatory: cf. Santangelo, *Trovatori,* p. 181.) Pound seems to have taken Arnaut's poem as a straightforward denunciation of these goings-on; to me it is a *jeu d'esprit,* the mock vice-crusader deliberately throwing mud around.

12. Arnaut, *Canzoni,* p. 190, with Toja's translation, p. 13 (P-C 447, 1, attributed to Truc Malec).

13. Cf. discussion, ibid., pp. 167-168, note; see also Appendix 2, text before n. 21. Paden, 'The Troubadour's Lady', p. 46, makes the excellent suggestion that 'William of Bouvila' was invented by the *razoist* from Arnaut's song (*Canzoni,* no. X) in which he says, 'I am Arnaut who gather the wind and hunt the hare with the ox and swim against the undertow.' Because in Provencal the hare is feminine and the ox masculine, the commentator read something like: 'I . . . pursue my (hare-like) lady in rivalry with her (ox-like) husband', and hence called this 'ox' (*bou*) 'Guillem de *Bou*vila'. (Compare the 'knight of Cornil' mentioned above, text before n. 9, whose name probably came from *cornar,* 'to play the horn': cf. Arnaut, *Canzoni,* p. 183, n. 39.) Paden's other suggestions about this *razo* seem eminently sound. None the less Pound takes up the 'Bouvila' name in *Cantos,* 7/26:30: see below, text before n. 98, Appendix 2, text before n. 23.

14. Arnaut, *Canzoni,* p. 166.

15. See Chapter 10, text before n. 108.

16. Guillaume IX, *Chansons,* no. IV, *Farai un vers de dreyt nien;* see Chapter 5, n. 81.

17. Arnaut, *Canzoni,* no. XIV, *Amors e iois.*

18. Ibid., no. XVI, *Ans qe·l cim;* ibid., no. XVIII, *Lo ferm voler.* An excellent text, translation, and analysis of *Lo ferm voler* are given in Paterson, *Troubadours and Eloquence,* pp. 193-201. Paterson's suggestion is that the movement of the poem is from physical to courtly love and perhaps to a spiritual love. I would doubt whether such a split between spiritual and physical qualities can be made in this poem. Paterson suggests that the spiritual element is first introduced in line 12, reading it 'I so fear that I may be hers too much in soul', but if so its entry is abrupt and unexplained; it seems just as likely that Lavaud's translation is right, and in fact that one could read it without such a specific emphasis, as meaning 'I am so afraid of being too much hers'—that is, 'of being overwhelmed by her.' The imagery of stanza IV is, as Paterson says, both violent and self-abandoning; it provides no basis for the sudden transition that, Paterson suggests, then occurs with stanza V and the appearance of *Fin'amors,* a fusion of the physical and spiritual. (To suggest that being attached to the lady both out in public and in chamber means the same as being hers spiritually and physically, seems to me to stretch the images.) The emphasis in *fin'Amors* may fall on the *fina,* which would thus not be a categoriser of the type of love, but simply an intensifier of the love. The entry into Paradise in the final stanza seems to be to be hyperbole for what Arnaut's love was from the beginning: a sexual-emotional-intellectual adoration, for the giddiness of whose prostration the poem gives unusually powerful concrete images. But I think it unlikely that we shall ever find a literal explanation for some of these images.

Like Paterson's, Topsfield's interpretation in *Troubadours and Love,* pp. 213-

218, seems to me to make too much of a very elusive debate between body and soul. Charles Jernigan's sexually anatomical interpretation of the rhyme-words in 'Song of Nail and Uncle', pp. 132-135, seems to me not to work out. In the following translation I underline the rhyme-words:

Firm desiring that *enters* my heart
cannot ever be torn by the beak or *nail*
of a flatterer, who loses his *soul* for having spoken ill;
and because I dare not strike him with branch or *rod,*
at least secretly, where I shall have no *uncle,*
I shall enjoy delight, in orchard or in *chamber.*

When I remember the *chamber*
where I know no man *enters* (to my loss)
but all are more than brother or *uncle* to me,
I have no limb that does not tremble, not even the *nail,*
as a child does before the *rod;*
such a fear I have that I shall be too much hers in my *soul.*

Would I were hers with my body, not in my *soul,*
and by her consent she hid me in her *chamber.*
And it wounds my heart more than *rod*-strokes
that her servant doesn't *enter* where she is;
as flesh and *nail* I shall always be with her,
and I shall not listen to advice from friend or *uncle.*

The sister of my *uncle*
I never loved more or as much, by this *soul!*
And as close as the finger is to the *nail,*
if she pleased, I would like to be to her *chamber,*
for the love that *enters* my heart can do more with me
as it wishes than a man strong in a weak *rod.*

Since the dry *rod* flowered
or nephew or *uncle* descended from Adam,
a love as fine as the one that *enters* my heart
was never, I think, in body, or even in *soul;*
wherever she be, outside in the square, or in her *chamber,*
my heart doesn't leave her as long as the *nail* holds.

For my heart roots and en-*nails* itself
in her as the bark does on the *rod;*
for she is for me the tower, palace and *chamber* of joy,
and I do not love brother, kin or *uncle* so much;
my *soul* will have a double joy in Paradise for this,
if ever any man *enters* there for having loved well.

Arnaut sends his song of *nail* and *uncle,*
for the pleasure of her who has his *rod's soul,*
his 'Desirat', whose worth *enters chambers.*

19. Arnaut, *Canzoni*, no. XVI, *Ans qu·l cim*, line 5. Linda Paterson (*Troubadours and Eloquence*, pp. 186-206) has an extremely useful chapter on Arnaut's use of language, including the various established styles, and on his concern with craftsmanship as an expression of love. She also gives an indispensable exposition of the troubadours' own terms for these styles, with examples of their practice. For Paterson, *ric* and *car* are both simply descriptive rather than categorising terms, indicating that the troubadour feels his style to be elevated and the work valuable (pp. 180-182). The key term is *trobar clus*. In general she defines it in terms of the way the troubadour makes clear his themes gradually as he tackles a central problem, and mediates between different levels of meaning (see p. 193), rather than giving variations on a theme immediately clear to the reader. There might be an intention deliberately to mislead the stupid by 'cunning meanings' in Marcabru, who wrote before the term *trobar clus* was actually coined, but used most of the style's elements (see p. 42); and Raimbaut d'Orange might be scornful of any attempt to simplify his meaning for the benefit of a wide audience (p. 147); but generally speaking, the difficulty was held to come from the difficulty of the content itself, and the foolishness of sections of the audience, and there was no deliberate intention to be hermetic (see pp. 131, 98, 147). Paterson assigns only one of Arnaut's songs, *Lo ferm voler*, to *trobar clus*, on the grounds of its gradual unfolding of meaning and its shifting from literal to figurative uses of the rhyme-words (p. 193); but see my previous note for doubts about this interpretation. And though she tends to deny *trobar ric* or *car* as a category, she shows very effectively how in Arnaut's poetry '*ric* or *car trobar* reaches its culmination' (p. 202) with a brilliant exposition of the way in which alliteration, assonance, antithesis, dense rhyming, and rare vocabulary combine with sound-qualities to produce 'compactness, intensity, concentration' (p. 203).

The chief elements in these sound-qualities are the *trobar prim* and the *trobar braus*, which are sound-textures, well exemplified elsewhere in the book. *Trobar prim* combines images of small and light things with 'tight, small, smooth sounds' to produce 'a finely detailed texture' (p. 183; cf. pp. 138-139); *trobar braus* puts together harsh, rough sounds to produce violent effects (pp. 52-54, 183-184). The former can be seen in parts of Arnaut's *L'aura amara* (see below, text before n. 36), and the latter in his *En breu brisara·l temps braus* (*Canzoni*, no. XI):

> En breu brisara·l temps braus,
> e·ill bisa busin' els brancs
> qui s'entreseignon trastuich
> de sobre rams claus de fuoilla

for which see Pound's remarks in *Essays*, p. 134.

20. Arnaut, *Canzoni*, p. 41; see also Paterson, *Troubadours and Eloquence*, Appendices I-III.

21. Stronski, *Folquet*, no. XXI.

22. *ABC of Reading*, p. 104, referring to Villon, *Oeuvres*, 'Testament', line 524.

23. Jeanroy, *Poésie*, 2, p. 49, and note.

24. Ibid., and pp. 50-51. As part of his attempt to diminish the effect of Dante's praise of the troubadour, Jeanroy rewrites the *miglior fabbro*, 'best smith': ' "carver" (*ciseleur*) is even more exact; the instrument that Arnaut handles is not the

hammer, but, as he has told us, the file; what comes out of his workshop is not majestic ironwork but brilliant and fragile "Emaux et Camées".' Jeanroy's image is quite confused, unlike either Dante's (which simply means 'artificer', not necessarily 'blacksmith') or Arnaut's (Arnaut has *capuig*, from *capuzar*, 'to work' (wood), *doli*, from *dolar*, 'to plane', and *lima*, 'file', in *Canzoni*, no. X, *En cest sonet*, all of which have to do with carpentry). Jeanroy's *ciseleur* could have to do with carpentry, but has nothing to do with the making of either enamels or cameos. None the less the Gautier comparison is reasonable.

25. F. S. Flint, quoted in Hutchins, *Pound's Kensington,* p. 56, compared Pound's reading of Arnaut to 'Bantu clicks'.

26. *Spirit,* p. 30: 'Dr. Ker's objection that the harmony of this song is not obtained by the rules of thumb which Dante prescribes for obtaining harmony in another language, does not seem to me valid.' W. P. Ker, in *Dante, Guinicelli and Daniel,* had said that he was unable to make out Dante's division of word-sounds into *pexa* and *hirsuta* ('combed' and 'shaggy') in connection with the examples given, but 'it is plain that there is, somewhere in his theory, a principle of verbal euphony; and it is plain that no force or persuasion can make Arnaut's syllables agree with any such law' (pp. 148-149). He referred to Dante's rule that 'shaggy' words should be kept down to those which, mixed judiciously with the 'combed' ones, will create a harmony of structure (*De Vulgari Eloquentia,* II.vii); and he claimed that a passage like Arnaut's (*Canzoni,* no. IX, *L'aur' amara*)

> E·ls letz
> becs
> dels auzels ramencs
> ten balps e mutz

was impossible to reconcile with this.

27. Ibid., no. IX. Arnaut, *Opere,* Arnaut, *Poésies,* and Arnaut, *Canzoni,* have all used the same numbering for the songs.

28. *Antheil and the Treatise on Harmony,* pp. 95-96.

29. But cf. Kenner, *Pound Era,* p. 88, for a very similar aesthetic in Marianne Moore.

30. Schafer, 'Ezra Pound and Music', p. 132.

31. Arnaut, *Canzoni,* no. V, *Lancan vei.*

32. *Essays,* p. 123.

33. Ibid., p. 193 (section published in 1929).

34. Ibid., p. 116.

35. Bunting, *Briggflatts,* in *Collected Poems,* p. 54.

36. Arnaut, *Canzoni,* no. IX, *L'aur' amara.*

37. Ibid., no. XII, *Doutz brais e critz.*

38. 'Arnaut Daniel', p. 44 (*Essays,* p. 109).

39. *ABC of Reading,* pp. 199-200.

40. I am here echoing Zukofsky, in *Prepositions,* p. 17, based on Dante's *De Vulgari Eloquentia.*

41. 'Psychology', p. 40 (*Spirit,* p. 89).

42. *Selected Prose,* p. 49 ('Axiomata', published 1921).

43. Cf. Gourmont, *Natural Philosophy,* p. vii.

44. 'Psychology', pp. 49-50 (*Spirit*, p. 96).

45. *Impact*, p. 200; for Richard of St. Victor's possible relevance to Arnaut see below, n. 92.

46. The *Litanies de la Rose* are quoted in *Make It New*, pp. 188-192.

47. *The Alchemist*, published in *Umbra* (1920) but written considerably earlier (cf. Gallup, *A Bibliography of Ezra Pound*, A20).

48. Pound's 'Introduction' to his versions of Cavalcanti (*Translations*, pp. 18-19), which continues:

> La virtù is the potency, the efficient property of a substance or person. Thus modern science shows us radium with a noble virtue of energy. Each thing or person was held to send forth magnetisms of certain effect; in Sonnet XXXV [about the Madonna of Orsanmichele, see below, text before n. 59], the image of his lady has these powers....
>
> ...'her' presence, his Lady's, corresponds with the ascendancy of the star of that heaven which corresponds to her particular emanation or potency.

49. See Chapter 5, text before n. 44.

50. It is true that by circumstantial evidence we may eventually be able to identify all the women in the Cantos; for example the profile 'against the half-light' in *Cantos*, 74/444:472, identified by Stock, *Reading the Cantos*, pp. 87-88, and by Rachewiltz, *Discretions*, p. 150, as that of Olga Rudge. For the merging of goddesses, see Chapter 10, text before n. 157.

51. It has worried critics of the troubadours and *stilnovisti* that, for all the poets tell us about them, their ladies might not have existed; some say that they did not (cf. Chapter 3, text before n. 64). For the troubadours, see Chapter 7, text before nn. 27, 33; for the *stilnovisti*, see below, n. 66.

52. Arnaut, *Canzoni*, no. IX, *L'aur' amara*.

53. See below, n. 55.

54. *Essays*, p. 131.

55. Arnaut, *Opere*, note to no. IX, *L'aur' amara*, referring to VIII, lines 39ff. (see below, text before n. 68). Canello put this suggestion to Chabaneau, who dismissed it in favour of his own: that *cill de Doma* referred to monks at a monastery at 'Doma', so that, reversing the syntax, it would mean 'I desire you more than the monks of "Doma" desire God.' He pointed to a passage in Bertran de Born, *lo Filhs* ('the son'): *Et etz plus leials vas Joven / No son a Dieu cilh de Cadonh*, 'And you are more loyal to Youth / Than are those of Cadonh to God.' Cadouin was a famous abbey in Périgord. Chabaneau then suggested that 'Doma' was the little village in Périgord (*chef-lieu de canton, arrondissement* of Sarlat, as Lavaud specified) where there might have existed in Arnaut's time a monastery, or only a hermitage. (For the discussion with Chabaneau see Canello's note.) Toja points out (Arnaut, *Canzoni*, p. 264) that this interpretation 'finds partial confirmation also in the marginal note of H (fol. 32): *doma es us mons fort autz on es solamen una maissos d'omes spirituals forts*' — a very high mountain where there is only a house of zealous men of the spirit. Further, as Toja says, there would be a parallel in Arnaut's no. XIV, *Amors e iois*, lines 25-27: *Non sai un tan si'e Dieu frems, / ermita ni monge ni clerc, / cum ieu sui a leis de cui can*—'I do not know a man as faithful to God, / hermit or monk or religious, / as I towards her whom I sing.' The manuscripts tend to

favour Chabaneau's reading (Arnaut, *Canzoni,* p. 258): AN²KDHNUV have *dieu* or *deu* (oblique case) while only CIR have *dieus* (subject case). To sum up, both interpretations presuppose a religious establishment referred to as 'Doma', whether it be the dwelling of those who love God less than Arnaut loves his lady, or the shrine of Our Lady whom God loves less than Arnaut loves his lady. The parallel readings in Bertran de Born *lo Filhs* and in Arnaut favour the comparison with monks loving God. But in either case, Arnaut is saying that his love for his lady is greater than an orthodox religious love.

56. *Spirit,* p. 31 (cf. Gallup, *A Bibliography of Ezra Pound,* B1, note), referring to Dante's *Voi che 'ntendendo il terzo ciel movete* (in e.g. Dante, *Dante's Lyric Poetry,* 1, p. 100, no. 59).

57. 'Psychology', p. 43; in *Spirit,* p. 91, 'Cypress' is corrected to 'Cyprus'.

58. Cavalcanti, *Rime,* no. XLVIII (a).

59. Ibid.; cf. Pound's translation in 'I Gather the Limbs of Isiris III', p. 155.

60. *Essays,* p. 181.

61. 'I Gather the Limbs of Isiris XI', p. 370 (*Selected Prose,* p. 41).

62. See Chapter 5, text before n. 42.

63. For Dronke, *European Love-Lyric,* 1, pp. 98-112, this stage is first embodied in Raimbaut d'Orange, to whom Arnaut is a 'disciple' (p. 98). The following pages adapt Dronke's arguments, in that for example Dronke would probably not agree that the force of the connections with God is weakened by any lack of orthodox reverence.

64. Arnaut, *Canzoni,* no. XVI, line 21 (in that she is first after God), no. XV, lines 12-14 (see below, text before n. 69), no. XIV, lines 25-27, no. XII, lines 25-29 (see below, text before n. 96), no. VIII, lines 10-12.

65. See Dronke's brilliant exposition in *European Love-Lyric,* 1, pp. 57-97, especially pp. 91, 57, 88-90, 93, 70-73.

66. Cf. ibid., pp. 94-95:

> Behind such a way of 'mostrando la mia condizione sotto figura d'altre cose' lay, to quote Erich Auerbach's exposition of the device *figura,* 'the idea that earthly love is thoroughly real, with the reality of the flesh into which the Logos entered, but that with all its reality it is only *umbra* and *figura* of the authentic, future, ultimate truth, the real reality that will unveil and preserve the *figura*'. Thus the love-poets did not need to choose between writing to a girl of flesh and blood and writing to a more-than-human Donna. The one does not exclude the other, but necessarily presupposes her. Otherwise there could be no figura: only because and in so far as the beloved is conceived as alive and human can she figure something else.

I take it that this is the point of Pound's remark in Gourmont, *Natural Philosophy,* p. xvii that in Propertius's *Ingenium nobis ipsa puella fecit* ('the girl made my genius') 'is the whole of the twelfth century love cult . . . and for image-making . . . Fenollosa on *The Chinese Written Character*.' It is the *dynamic* of the man-woman relationship that sets up the creation of systems of metaphoric parallels (images) that are the basis of language and poetry as Fenollosa explains them (*Chinese Written Character,* e.g. pp. 12, 22-23).

67. Arnaut, *Canzoni,* no. XVIII, *Lo ferm voler,* lines 25-28; for the 'dry rod'

(*verga,* Virgin) image see Toja's parallels, ibid., p. 380.

68. Ibid., no. VIII, *Autet e bas,* lines 39-45.

69. Ibid., no. XV, *Sols sui qui sai,* lines 12-14.

70. Ibid., no. XVI, *Ans qe·l cim,* line 21.

71. In Provençal the song to the Virgin was a recognised *genre;* Jeanroy, *Poésie,* 2, pp. 310-313, cites examples. Of course Arnaut's lady has the standard powers to kill or cure; cf. *Canzoni,* no. X, lines 33-35, no. XVI, line 32, no. IX, line 64, no. VIII, line 21, and no. XIII, line 11.

72. 'Arnaut Daniel', p. 49 (*Essays,* pp. 114-115).

73. Arnaut, *Canzoni,* no. X, *En cest sonet,* lines 12-14.

74. Ibid., no. XI, *En breu brisara·l temps braus,* lines 41-43 (in Pound's translation, 'I Gather the Limbs of Osiris XI', p. 369; more correctly, read 'and may a canker take away both my eyes if I don't reserve them for looking at her'). The rest of the stanza says that Arnaut prefers her worship to the rites of the Church, which is another reason for connecting it to Cavalcanti's poem. Cf. also a similar passage from Raimbaut d'Orange, cited in Dronke, *European Love-Lyric,* 1, p. 107.

75. See above, text before n. 58.

76. Arnaut, *Canzoni,* no. VIII, *Autet e bas,* lines 10-12.

77. Ibid., no. IX, *L'aur' amara,* lines 18-21.

78. Dante, *Vita Nuova,* II.4.

79. See Chapter 7, text before nn. 66ff.

80. 'I Gather the Limbs of Osiris IV: A Beginning', p. 179 (*Selected Prose,* p. 25).

81. *Confucius/Analects,* p. 244 (12.III.).

82. *Letters,* to Mary Barnard, 23 Feb 1934; *Essays,* p. 116 (cf. p. 112).

83. 'Mediaeval Music and Yves Tinayre', p. 187.

84. *Kulchur,* p. 60; the line continued: 'Down on through Vivaldi and Couperin there is this kind of music, music of representative outline' (p. 153).

85. *Cantos,* 107/758:783.

86. Levy, *Provenzalisches Supplement-Wörterbuch,* from 1894; M. Raynouard's *Lexique Roman* was published 1836-45 in Paris.

87. *Cantos,* 20/89-90:93-94; the 'ranunculae' must be ranunculi (crowfoot).

88. See *Moeurs Contemporaines VII: I Vecchii* (sic), and Hutchins, *Pound's Kensington,* pp. 27, 111. Pound said of Levy, 'I know of at least one professor who has produced a dictionary and remained delightfully human at the age of about sixty-five' (ibid., p. 44, quoting *New Age,* 26 July 1917). Levy lived from 1855 to 1918.

89. *Confucius/Analects,* p. 267 (15.XXV); cf. *Cantos,* 13/60:64.

90. *Spirit,* p. 31.

91. Arnaut, *Canzoni,* no. XIII, *Er vei vermeills,* lines 1-7. See Kenner, *Pound Era,* pp. 114-118, for an account of the meeting and of the significance of this crux. Kenner points out (p. 116) that Pound's question about *noigandres* was not superfluous even though Levy had published his solution to the problem in 1904 in the *Supplement-Wörterbuch:* he had entered it under *gandir,* where Pound would not have known to look. The visit took place in 1911 (*Pound Era,* p. 114). The text Pound uses in *Essays,* p. 139 (1920), is Lavaud's of 1910, which uses Levy's reading;

but his work on Lavaud's text obviously post-dates his meeting with Levy.

92. *Ta Hio,* pp. 19-20 (Gallup, *A Bibliography of Ezra Pound,* A28): '1. The expression clarify and render sincere.one's own intentions, means: Don't denature your own direct tropisms; such as the tendency to escape from a disagreeable odour, or to love an agreeable and seductive object.' Pound suggested that one look for allegories when he noted under his translation of the *noigandres* passage (*Essays,* p. 139): 'The . . . cryptic allusion is to the quasi-allegorical descriptions of the tree of love in some long poem like the *Romaunt of the Rose.*' I know of no such descriptions in the *Roman* itself; but Arnaut (*Canzoni,* no. XI, *En breu brisara·l temps braus,* line 11, and no. V, *Lanquan vei fueill' e flor e frug,* line 5) has flowers of love and a tree of love.

In his discussion of Valli's codes and Arnaut Daniel (see Chapter 10, text before n. 125), Pound asks (*Essays,* p. 180), 'Does the illegible "di noigandres" boggle a Greek "ennoia" or "dianoia"?' In the same year that he published this question, Scotus Erigena appeared for the first time in the Cantos (*Cantos,* 36/179:185, Apr 1934 — Gallup, *A Bibliography of Ezra Pound,* C1048). Erigena has an interesting hierarchy of awareness (here paraphrased by Mario del Pra in *Scoto Eriugena*), of which the lowest rank is *dianoia:*

> The highest form of consciousness is the *nous* of the Greeks, or the intelligence; this constitutes the principal part of the soul and is that movement by which the spirit, purified and illuminated by action and by learning and rendered perfect by theology, turns eternally around God, known in Himself . . . [p. 207].
>
> The second [movement] is that which is contained within nature and which defines God as cause, that is to say in so far as He is the cause of all that exists. This movement impresses on the soul as far as it can the consciousness of the primordial causes of all things. . . . This second movement is the *logos,* the reason, which is born with the intelligence . . . [p. 209].
>
> The third movement refers itself to the reasons of things in their singularity in so far as they are founded in the primordial causes; it begins from the images of things announced by means of the external senses, and reaches the purest discrimination of all things by means of their own reasons, collecting them into the most general essences, both in the most general categories and in the determined forms and species. This movement, which is called *dianoia* or interior sense, proceeds from the intelligence by means of the reason [p. 210].

The hierarchy is almost exactly as in Richard of St. Victor (whom the Cantos put in the company of Erigena: *Cantos,* 85/546:582). Thus Pound's summary of Richard in the footnote to *Guillaume de Lorris Belated* in 1909:

> In cogitation the thought or attention flits aimlessly about the subject.
>
> In meditation it circles round it, that is, it views it systematically, from all sides, gaining perspective.
>
> In contemplation it radiates from a centre, that is, as light from the sun it reaches out in an infinite number of ways to things that are related to it or dependent on it. . . .

Cf. Stock, *Reading the Cantos,* p. 98: 'In a letter dated 6 June 1954, from St Elizabeths, Pound told me that he had "absorbed a lot" of Richard in 1908, but had not referred to him again until, it would appear, about the time of the letter.'

93. *Cantos,* 70/413:435; 74/434:461.

94. Opinion communicated by letter; cf. the plates of Venuses by Sandro (Botticelli) and Jacopo del Sellaio, and the Flora by Agostino di Duccio, in Kenner, *Pound Era,* pp. 364, 332.

95. Arnaut, *Canzoni,* no. XII, *Doutz brais e critz.*

96. Kenner, *Pound Era,* p. 373.

97. 'Ligur' aiode' (from the *Odyssey:* 'keen or sharp singing (sirens), song with an edge on it'— *Letters,* to Homer L. Pound, 11 Apr 1927) recurs in *Cantos,* 20/89:93, and in 74/439:466 is glossed 'the sharp song with sun under its radiance'. (This is Pound's breakdown of *Shao* 招 [see *Cantos,* 74/440:467, and Confucius, *Analects,* p. 164, note], whose constituent parts mean [clockwise] 'cut', 'mouth', 'sun', 'stand'.) Cf. also *Cantos,* 39/193:201. For the whole passage at the beginning of Canto XX see Kenner, *Pound Era,* pp. 112-113.

98. *Essays,* p. 237; *Cantos,* 7/25-26:29-30. He makes the connection in 'Arnaut Daniel', p. 46 (*Essays,* p. 111). In the original, Arnaut wishes for an agreement 'that I should gaze at' her body 'against the light of the lamp'. This may just fit with Pound's prose translation here (*Spirit,* p. 34): 'she shall disclose to me her fair body, with the glamor of the lamplight about it. (E quel remir contral lums de la lampa.)' — and his poetic version here:

> laugh and strip and stand forth in the lustre
> Where lamp-light with light limb but half engages.
> (*Essays,* p. 137)

but these are not literal enough to tell exactly how Pound read the syntax. However, the interpolation of the single word *remir* in this way in Canto XX:

> and the light falls, *remir,*
> from her breast to thighs.

makes it clear that he read the phrase *quel remir* as demonstrative subject pronoun plus verb in the indicative, meaning 'that [body] glows'. Cf. also the comparisons with Ovid and Juan de Mena, in *Spirit,* p. 34. So, for Pound, the lines probably meant:

> that kissing and laughing I uncover her pretty body
> and that glows against the light of the lamp.

However, *quel* is not a demonstrative subject pronoun (nor, as Kenner suggests, a demonstrative object pronoun giving 'and I look at that [body]'— cf. *Pound Era,* p. 118), but is *que·l:* the conjunction *que* ('that') with the masculine article in the object case *lo* ('it') contracted together (cf. Schultz-Gora, *Elementarbuch,* p. 77). Pound obviously took the verb *remir,* as Kenner implies (*Pound Era,* p. 118), to mean 're-mirrors'.

99. *Essays,* p. 184; Dante, *Paradiso,* 10.67-69.

100. *Essays,* p. 154.

101. Cavalcanti, *Rime,* no. XXVII, *Donna me prega; Essays,* pp. 155-157; *Cantos,* 36/177-179:182-185. Cf. Pound's note to *Confucius/Analects,* p. 254 (13.

XXVIII), pointing out Karlgren's remark about 'the impure light of fire that shines outward, the pure light of water that shines inward.'

102. Dante, *Paradiso*, 2.97ff.

103. *Cantos*, 25/119:124.

104. *Cantos*, 23/109:114.

105. *Cantos*, 29/145:150, etc., discussed in Chapter 10, n. 156.

106. *Cantos*, 4/15:19, Arnaut, *Canzoni*, no. IV, *Lancan son passat*, line 52. In his verse translation, *Essays*, p. 123, Pound follows Lavaud's reading in the penultimate line, *poigna*, as throughout the *Translations* print Canello's text opposite. That the last line refers to the descent of the sun in the West, 'in a rain of light' (Arnaut, *Canzoni*, p. 219, Toja's phrase), seems certain from various parallels. Toja (ibid.) cites Giraut de Bornelh, *Lieder*, 1, no. 19, lines 52-53: *De lai on s'abriva·l Nils / Tro lai on sols es colgans*, 'from where the Nile hastens to where the sun sets'. Bertran de Born (*Lieder*, no. 17) has almost exactly the same figure. Cf. Arnaut, *Canzoni*, no. XVI, line 36: *De part Nil entro c'a Sanchas*; no. VI, line 21: *don part soleils duesc'al jorn quez ajorna*, no. VII, line 26: *qan sols clau ni s'aiorna*.

107. *Cantos*, 92/618-619:651-652.

108. Rachewiltz says, in 'Pagan and Magic Elements', pp. 180-181, that the 'Ra-Set' who appears in this passage 'is a syncretic deity of the poet's invention'; 'In a microcosmic sense, i.e. *sub specie interioritatis*, the male and female components of Ra-Set would represent the full solar and lunar cycles. . . .'

109. Cavalcanti, *Rime*, no. XXX, *Era in penser d'amor quand' i' trovai*; cf. *Translations*, p. 110.

110. Cavalcanti, *Rime*, no. XLIV (b), *Ciascuna fresca e dolce fontanella* (I give Pound's version, *Translations*, p. 59).

111. See below, Chapter 10, n. 156, and above, text before n. 72.

112. *Cantos*, 99/694-695:724; the passage is glossed by David Gordon, in 'Thought Built on Sagetrieb', p. 180:

> 'all astute men of comprehensive, *chou* mind regard, *shi*, the people, *pien meng*, exactly, *cheng*, as children, *ch'ch.*' '*Chou*' 'comprehensive' also means 'catholicity,' 'encircling,' and the 'Chou Dynasty,' as well as the name of one of Confucius' favorite heroes. Pound also sees its relevance to the common store of ideas, KOINE ENNOIA, of all mankind (comparable to the Four *Tuan*) and described by Gemisthus Plethon, who tried to make a fifteenth century edict that would restore the *senso morale* of the ancient greeks. . . .

Cf. also *Confucius/Pivot*, p. 187 (26.10).

In 'Psychology and Troubadours', p. 53 (*Spirit*, pp. 99-100), Pound had thought of Arnaut's vision of his lady as a deflection, 'something short of grasping at the union with the absolute'. In saying so, he referred to what Arnaut says in Dante's *Purgatorio*, 'at almost the summit of the purifying hill, and just below the earthly paradise':

> I am Arnaut, who weep and go singing,
> For, though I see the past folly [passada folor],
> I see rejoicing the dawn that I hope for, ahead.
> (*Purgatorio*, 26.142-144)

In the late Cantos, Pound took the emphasis away from Arnaut's *passada folor* and put it more on his role as prophet:

> Some faint connection
> between criminality and calamity
> lo jorn, Der Tag
>
> that at least a few should perceive this **H** tan
>
> Arnaut spoke his own language, 26th Purgatorio,
> above the Moon there is order,
> beneath the Moon, forsitan.
> (*Cantos,* 98/677:707)

Lo jorn, 'the dawn', is what Arnaut, speaking in Provençal, foresees in Purgatory. (*Tan* is also the dawn.) Dawn is the return of the earthly paradise, such as Pound had predicted it in the coming American Renaissance, in 1913, using the Provençal word *alba* (*Patria Mia,* p. 14).

113. See above, text before n. 52.

114. See above, text before n. 72.

115. *Cantos,* 91/610:644, 91/611:645.

116. Dante, *Paradiso,* 26.34-35. For Bernart's song see Chapter 7, text before n. 58, and Chapter 4, n. 30. Pound echoes Bernart's chastity again in *Cantos,* 93/624:657, from *Chansons,* no. 4, *Tant ai mo cor ple de joya,* which can be translated:

> I suffer the pain of love more
> than Tristan the lover
> who suffered many a pain from it
> for Iseut the blonde.

Pound's text differs insignificantly. For Cavalcanti see *Cantos,* 36/177:182, from Cavalcanti, *Rime,* no. XXVII, *Donna me prega;* cf. especially *Cantos,* 76/457:485.

117. For this rite see Chapter 10, text before n. 131.

118. See Chapter 10, text before n. 141.

119. *Essays,* p. 151.

120. See Chapter 10, text before n. 157.

121. *Cantos,* 95/645:678; cf. Chapter 6, text before n. 103.

122. *Cantos,* 20/89:93.

123. *Cantos,* 92/619:642, cf. Chapter 10, text before n. 155.

124. See Chapter 9, text before nn. 75, 85; Cunizza as Venus is present together with Bernart's 'And if I see her not....' in *Cantos,* 92/619-620:652-653.

125. Arnaut, *Canzoni,* no. XVII, *Si·m fos Amors,* lines 49-50; cf. ibid., lines 5-8, and Pound's translation in *Essays,* pp. 145-147. For Propertius see Chapter 5, text before n. 99. For similar passages in Arnaut on how the lady raises him see *Canzoni,* no. III, lines 57-60, no. V, lines 22-25; on his horror at the idea of turning elsewhere, see ibid., no. III, lines 8, 36, no. V, lines 17, 40, no. VII, line 24, no. VIII, line 16, no. XV, line 4, no. XVI, line 14.

CHAPTER 9. SORDELLO

1. Cf. 'Psychology', pp. 39-40 (*Spirit*, pp. 88-89). Since the chapter 'Proença' in *The Spirit of Romance* is partly modelled on Dante's *De Vulgari Eloquentia* (see Introduction, n. 17), we may take it that in mentioning Sordello there (*Spirit*, p. 58, cf. p. 56), Pound simply follows Dante. Dante's mention is in the first part of the book (*De Vulgari Eloquentia*, I.15), where there are few troubadours, and Pound had forgotten it by 1938 when he published the *Guide to Kulchur* (see following paragraph). 'Proença' brushes over Sordello without offering a firm opinion. In 'Troubadours: Their Sorts and Conditions' (1913), pp. 429-430, Pound says nothing at all about Sordello's verse, simply translating the *vida* which explains the Cunizza story (*Essays*, p. 97).

2. *Letters*, to Katue Kitasono, 11 Mar 1937. In *Impact*, p. 61, Pound refers to Dante as his 'Baedeker in Provence', and in *Kulchur*, p. 108, he says that the next generation studying the troubadours should 'look harder at what Dante indicates.'

3. *Kulchur*, p. 108.

4. Ibid.

5. *Spirit*, p. 25, note, presumably one of the notes added in 1929 for the 1932 reissue of Part I (see Gallup, *A Bibliography of Ezra Pound*, A33b).

6. Sordello, *Poesie*, ed. Boni, no. IV, *Bel m'es ab motz leugiers a far*.

7. Ibid., no. V, *Dompna, meillz qu'om pot pensar;* cf. no. IX, lines 9ff. Sordello seems to equate respect for his lady's honour with not asking for permission to make love to her: ibid., no. IV, IX.

8. Ibid., no. XVI, *Senh' En Sordel, mandamen*.

9. Ibid., no. IV, *Bel m'es ab motz leugiers a far*.

10. Ibid., no. III, *Atretan dei ben chantar finamen;* see Chapter 7, text before n. 20.

11. Ibid., no. VI, *Er encontra l temps de mai*, no. X, *Si co l malaus qe no se sap gardar*.

12. Ibid., no. VII, *Gran esfortz fai qui ama per amor*.

13. E.g. ibid., no. IV, *Bel m'es ab motz leugiers a far*.

14. Ibid., no. IX, VI, VII, and especially X.

15. Cf. *Essays*, p. 344, quoted in Chapter 5, text before n. 109.

16. Sordello, *Poesie*, ed. Boni, no. VII, XI, VII, IV, IX.

17. Ibid., no. VI, *Er encontra l temps de mai;* for particularly striking enjambments see ibid., no. IX, X.

18. Cf. e.g. ibid., no. XI, *Tant m'abellis lo terminis novels:*

Pero per tal m'es al cor us cairels

no. II, *Aitant ses plus viu hom quan viu jauzens:*

qu'ie·l quier sirven aman ab tals turmens

and an exception to my rule, no. IV, *Bel m'es ab motz leugiers a far:*

que·m lansero siey huelh lairo

19. Ibid., no. X, *Si co l malaus qe no se sap gardar*.

20. Ibid., no. III, *Atretan dei ben chantar finamen.*

21. *Cantos,* 6/23:27; see Chapter 4, text before n. 36.

22. *Cantos,* 74/438:465, 74/443:471, 76/452:480, 78/482:514, 89/596:631, 90/606:640, 92/620:653; cf. 78/480:512, 89/599:634, 95/644:677, and Chapter 10, text before n. 55.

23. Boutière and Schutz, *Biographies,* p. 562; for the vagaries of Pound's prose translation in 'Troubadours', pp. 429-430 (*Essays,* p. 97), see Chapter 4, nn. 33, 16.

24. There is the story of falling in love with the patron's wife, and the same list of virtues making the troubadour a desirable person, in the longer version: 'and he was a handsome man as to his person, and was a good singer and a good composer of songs, and a great lover' (Boutière and Schutz, *Biographies,* p. 566). For Bernart, see Chapter 7, text before n. 1.

25. Cf. Peire Bremon Ricas Novas, quoted in Sordello, *Poesie,* ed. Boni, p. LXXV, and notes; but the other version of Sordello's *vida* says that he was a *gentils catanis,* a 'noble chatelain' (Boutière and Schutz, *Biographies,* p. 566).

26. Cf. Aimeric de Peguilhan, quoted in Sordello, *Poesie,* ed. Boni, p. XVIII:

> when there's no-one to lend him the money
> he can't do his five, two-sixes, three.

For the meaning of the last line (dice-throwing), cf. the MS. illumination mentioned by Pound in 'Troubadours', p. 431 (*Essays,* p. 98), and Bertran, *Bertran,* no. 15, and ibid., p. 180. Joan d'Albusson accuses Sordello of being a *jongleur* for reasons of poverty, and of taking clothes for pay, in a *tenson* with him: Sordello, *Poesie,* ed. Boni, no. XIII, *Digatz mi s'es vers.*

27. Azzo VII d'Este is the 'Marquis' in the *tenson* cited above, n. 26; cf. Bertoni, quoted in Sordello, *Poesie,* ed. Boni, p. XXVI.

28. Cf. ibid., p. XXVIII.

29. Ibid., no. XV, *Uns amics et un'amia.*

30. Ibid., p. XXXI; Reforzat declared (p. XXXIII):

> They think Sordello a loyal knight
> because loyally he dishonoured the lady
> whom he made to flee from her place by night
> so that she had to come and stay with us [i.e. in Provence].

Uc de Saint-Circ said (p. XXXVII, note) to a troubadour who defended Cunizza:

> ...of the lady Cunizza I know
> that she made such a triple throw last year
> as lost her eternal life.

The 'triple throw' was in moving from Rizzardo to Sordello to Bonio.

31. For the text and corrections see Appendix 1, Text D.

32. Boutière and Schutz, *Biographies,* p. 566.

33. Its rhythm is like this:

> I want to make a little dance
> playing, laughing,
> of *Ma Vida,* whom God keep

his noble wit,
with which I shall brighten up
his grieving heart.
With sweet song
dancing on
let him laugh and play along,
trafficking,
swindling,
seducing each and all the dames.

His good wisdom makes him change
lodging often,
for now he's come here to stay
and now he's off
to find another dame to trick
and one that's rich.
With sweet song....

Mantua and Verona,
I've lost him,
Treviso and Senedes
you have too,
and if Vicenza loses him
where'll we go?
With sweet song....

To Auvergne and to Forez
and to Velay,
where they don't know who he is
or care for him;
then we're off to Viennois
to Annonay.
With sweet song....

(Uc, Poésies, no. XXIV)

Peire Bremon Ricas Novas mocks Sordello's fear of staying in one place, in *Poésies,*
no. XVII. In Sordello, *Poesie,* ed. Boni, p. XLV, the editor paraphrases the song
of a troubadour who says that while Sordello is conquering Provence, England,
France, Lunel, and so forth, Cunizza is taking Byzantium, Hungary, and the rest,
so that 'they will end up taking the lot, she beneath and he on top.'

34. Cf. Peire Bremon Ricas Novas, *Poésies,* no. XVIII, and Sordello, *Poesie,* ed.
Boni, p. LI.

35. Ibid., no. XX, *Puois no·m tenc per pajat d'amor.* The entire metrical and
rhyme scheme is borrowed from Bertran de Born's *Be·m platz lo gais temps de pascor* (Bertran, *Lieder,* no. 40, cf. Chapter 2, text before n. 4). Cf. Bertran's own
twisting of the spring-opening, and Peire Cardenal's ironic twisting of Bertran's
opening, pointed out by Pound in 'Troubadours', p. 440 (*Essays,* p. 107).

36. Sordello, *Poesie,* ed. Boni, no. XXVI, *Planher vuelh en Blacatz,* translated
by Pound in *Spirit,* pp. 58-59. Pound's mistakes: *tanh qu'en manj'a rescos,* 'he had
better eat it secretly', translated as 'I wager he...'; *deia,* 'that he should', in line

25, taken as cognate with French *déjà* and translated as 'straightway'; *si*, 'if', ig-nored in line 35; *guaire*, 'scarcely', misapplied in line 38, giving 'lives hardly' instead of 'is hardly worth anything'; *a mon dan met*, 'I scorn', taken as an impera-tive in line 44.

37. Cf. Sordello, *Poesie*, ed. Boni, p. LVI, for the imitations, always a sign of success in Provençal poetry. Cf. ibid., no. XIX, *Non pueis mudar, qan luecs es*, lines 51ff., p. LXXVII, note, LXXV. Also cf. the shorter *vida*, quoted above, text before n. 23.

38. Ibid., no. XXVIII, *Ar hai proat q'el mon non ha dolor*.

39. Ibid., p. LXXI, note, LXXXIII, note; Sordello excused himself from join-ing the Seventh Crusade, on which Charles was absent for two years.

40. Ibid., p. XCIII; cf. ibid., p. XCV; Pound's source was Sordello, *Poesie*, ed. de Lollis, p. 60.

41. Sordello, *Poesie*, ed. Boni, p. XCVI; for other gifts after Tagliacozzo cf. ibid., pp. XCVIII-XCIX. On 30 June 1269 Sordello had exchanged San Silvestro, Pila, and Pagliete for the castle of Palena, a place famous for its dye-works; cf. ibid., pp. XCVIII-XCIX; Charles reminded him that all these were in effect gifts from him (ibid., no. XXXII, *Toz hom me van disen*) in reply to Sordello's com-plaints.

42. Ibid., p. CII. The document recording the grant of fiefs after Tagliacozzo calls Sordello *familiaris*, an epithet that Boni says 'was normally given only to the barons most closely connected with the court and to those of the highest lineage, and with it went special rights and particular distinctions at court' (ibid., p. XCVIII; document quoted ibid., pp. 276-277, and in Sordello, *Poesie*, ed. de Lol-lis, p. 323; for its use in Canto XXXVI see below, n. 84 and preceding text).

43. Ibid., p. CII.

44. Ibid., p. XCII. Pound, correctly, has Cunizza finally changing her mind and releasing the traitors also. The relevant part of the document (given in full in Ap-pendix 1, Text C) may be translated: 'excepting those who were with Lord Alberico in the castle and tower of San Zeno who did him treachery in the said castle and tower; she has set them free, a hundred devils from hell in their soul and body.'

45. *Spirit*, pp. 57-58; Dante, *Purgatorio*, 6.58-71.

46. *Cantos*, 7/24:28; cf. *Essays*, p. 295; altered from Dante, *Purgatorio*, 6.61-63: *O anima lombarda, . . . nel muover degli occhi onesta e tarda!*, 'Oh Lombard soul, . . . slow and honest in the moving of the eyes!' For James cf. a letter from Pound to Patricia Hutchins in 1957: 'London possible in 1908 because Browning and H. J., and a few others, HAD smacked the teak-heads with their flails/ one by one / driving some sense into 'em. There was in fact a cultural level above that of the stinkers' (quoted in Hutchins, *Pound's Kensington*, p. 141). For Eliot cf. 'Henry James', in *The Shock of Recognition*, p. 858.

47. *Cantos*, 16/68:72.

48. *Cantos*, 32/159:163, quoting Thomas Jefferson to John Adams, 1 June 1822 (*Adams-Jefferson Letters*, p. 578).

49. *Spirit*, p. 58.

50. Cf. e.g. Sordello, *Poesie*, ed. de Lollis, p. 60.

51. Ibid., pp. 68-72. I leave out of this discussion Sordello's moral songs; for

just reflections on them see Chaytor, *The Troubadours of Dante,* p. 180.

52. Raimon VII of Toulouse, James I of Aragon, and Henry III of England were particularly affected by French expansionism, and in the long list of repetitions gathered by de Lollis, we find Tomier and Palazi, Bertran de Born 'the son', Bertran de Born himself, Peire Cardenal, Duran de Carpentras, Guilhem de Montanhagout, and Bernart de Rovenac constantly attacking these princes for weakness under attack: Sordello, *Poesie,* ed. de Lollis, pp. 72-74, 68-71.

53. Note how Dante placed his hopes for a free Italy with the young Manfred of Hohenstaufen: Hauvette, *France,* pp. 74ff. There was a feeling that neither just government nor true succession was enough in itself, but there was also a strong predisposition to place hopes for just government in the rightful heir, as being the one on whom God had placed *both* his blessing *and* his expectation of justice. The young William IX of Aquitaine was able to hold his patrimony together against much stronger vassals (see Chapter 5, text before n. 12). The young Henry III was able to exploit both his true descent and his reaffirmation of the 'ancient rights' of the English to secure his inheritance (cf. G. R. C. Davis, *Magna Carta,* p. 14). A brief account of some mediaeval political expectations, with references, is found in Klein, *Partisan Voice,* pp. 49-52.

54. Cf. Chapter 10, text before nn. 13, 89.

55. Sordello, *Poesie,* ed. Boni, no. XXVI, *Planher vuelh en Blacatz;* cf. Chapter 3, text before n. 20. Aston, in 'Provençal planh: I', suggests that there is no point in looking for any real poetry in the *planh* because it is always written for an occasion (p. 23). Accordingly, he takes only the trouble to show that the poets repeat each other, and makes only one cursory reference to a basic criterion, the strength of the cadence, on p. 30.

I have noted, in relation to Bertran's *planh* for the Young King, his 'vision of the prince as chief among Rolandian "companions", under the protection of God' (see Chapter 3, text before n. 21). There is clearly an effort to invest the dead hero with as many *geste* qualities as possible. One can then take the same step as Goldin does with the courtly-love lyric (see Chapter 7, text before n. 39), and suggest that the dead hero is not perceived as an individual; and Goldin himself says that in Aimeric de Peguilhan's *planh* for Malaspina, Malaspina is a compound of qualities projected for use as a standard of class self-comparison (*Mirror of Narcissus,* p. 81, note). But see my remarks on this argument as applied to the courtly-love lyric, Chapter 7, text before n. 40ff.

56. Dante, *Paradiso,* 9.25ff.

57. Hauvette, *France,* p. 132.

58. Dante, *Paradiso,* note to 9.7-36.

59. *Spirit,* p. 146.

60. Cf. below, n. 124, and an obscene verse of Folquet's, with Stronski's comments, in Stronski, *Folquet,* p. 47*; also cf. ibid., no. XVI, where Folquet denies his relationship with 'Vermillon' by saying that it would stain his hand to touch her.

61. Dante, *Paradiso,* 9.34-35.

62. Benvenuto da Imola, quoted in Chabaneau, *Biographies,* p. 107, note.

63. Jacopo della Lana, quoted ibid.

64. *Kulchur,* p. 107; 'the most violent authority' was the tyrant Ezzelino III da

Romano. Benson, *Sordello and Cunizza*, p. 51, notes that Cunizza's act of emancipation was not as uncommon as had been supposed; but this does not much diminish its significance. It is probable that Pound saw Benson's quite moving presentation of Cunizza, ibid., especially p. 52: see Chapter 4, n. 34. *Kulchur*, p. 120, compares Cunizza's freeing of her slaves, while she lived, favourably with Aristotle's testamentary act.

65. *Kulchur*, pp. 108-109.

66. Toleration of usury 'runs concurrent with a fattening in all art forms' (ibid., p. 109); the corollary is that clear emotional perception helps the perception of economic injustice.

67. Dante, *Vita Nuova*, II.5: 'In quello punto lo spirito animale ... parlando spezialmente *a li spiriti del viso*, si disse queste parole: "Apparuit jam beatitudo vestra" ' (my italics). Cf. also Gourmont, *Dante, Béatrice*, pp. 57-58, 64-65, etc.

68. *Cantos*, 74/434:461.

69. *Cantos*, 29/141:146.

70. Cf. Chapter 6, text before n. 70.

71. Edwards and Vasse, *Annotated Index*, referring to

> From the Via Sacra
> (fleeing what band of Tritons)

say (s.v. *Via Sacra*) 'prob. a street in Verona'. But it seems likely that this refers to Propertius, *Elegies*, IV.VI, lines 61ff. (cf. *Homage to Sextus Propertius*, XI).

72. *Cantos*, 29/141:146; for the original document see Chapter 4, n. 34.

73. For Rolandino, see Chapter 4, n. 35.

74. Cf. above, text before n. 56. This line is recalled in *Cantos*, 92/620:653; cf. Chapter 10, n. 159.

75. Sordello, *Poesie*, ed. de Lollis, no. XXX, *Ailas, e que˙ m fau miey huelh*, of which these lines are the refrain.

76. *Cantos*, 36/177:182-183.

77. Cf. Makin, 'Ezra Pound and Scotus Erigena', pp. 73-77.

78. Cf. ibid., pp. 65-73.

79. *Cantos*, 36/180:185.

80. Edwards and Vasse, *Annotated Index*, s.v. *Sacrum*..., has 'a sacred thing, a sacred thing, the cognition of coition', which is impossible.

81. See above, text before n. 23.

82. For the five castles, see below, n. 84. For the dye-works cf. above, n. 41, and the exchange between Sordello and Charles of Anjou in Sordello, *Poesie*, ed. de Lollis, no. XI, *Toz hom me van disen:*

> ...how could a man [be of comfort]
> when he's poor in goods and ill every day
> and badly-off for a lord and for love and a lady? ...'

> 'Sordello speaks ill of me, and he shouldn't,
> for I hold and have held him dear and honoured always;
> I have given him cloth-works, mills and other goods,
> and a wife just like he wanted....'

For the Pope's letter, cf. above, text before n. 40. Pound's source for all this was the texts in Sordello, *Poesie,* ed. de Lollis.

83. *Cantos,* 36/180:185; punctuation sic.

84. The document from which most of this is taken is quoted in Sordello, *Poesie,* ed. de Lollis, p. 323, and Sordello, *Poesie,* ed. Boni, pp. 276-277. I translate it in part here, including the relevant pieces of Canto XXXVI in brackets:

> . . . Considering therefore the great, pleasing and fit services received that Sordellus de Godio the beloved close and faithful knight [Dilectis miles familiaris] has shown to our Serenity and that we hope he will show in the future we give
> . . . the castles of Monte Odorisio Monte San Silvestro Paglieta and Pila [castra Montis Odorisii / Montis Sancti Silvestri pallete et pile] and the hamlet of Castiglione situate in the Justiciarate of Abruzzi otherwise in the district of greater Thetis [in partibus Thetis] with their vassals possessions houses vineyards lands cultivated and uncultivated [vineland / land tilled / the land incult] plains hills meadows groves pastures [pratis nemoribus pascuis] mills waters watercourses and other rights and jurisdictions [with legal jurisdiction] and things pertaining as from domain to domain and as from servitude to servitude to the aforesaid Sordellus and his heirs of both sexes [heirs of both sexes]. . . .

Pound's 'dilectis' should read 'dilectus'. For the last line of the Canto see n. 85.

85. Sordello, *Poesie,* ed. Boni, no. III, *Atretan dei ben chantar finamen;* Pound's source, Sordello, *Poesie,* ed. de Lollis, no. XXI, line 20, has *chascun en men,* giving 'for I hold each of them in mind'.

86. *Cantos,* 29/142:147; *Kulchur,* p. 107.

87. *Cantos,* 6/22:26-27; cf. Chapter 4, text before n. 35.

88. Dante, *Inferno,* 10.35-36, 40-45.

89. See Chapter 4, n. 4.

90. Davidsohn, *Storia di Firenze,* IV, III, p. 358.

91. Carducci, *Opere,* X, pp. 48-49.

92. 'I Gather the Limbs of Osiris III', p. 155 (omitted from *Selected Prose*).

93. *Kulchur,* p. 134.

94. Avalle, *Letteratura,* pp. 44-45.

95. This book was first published in 1921, and it might seem superfluous to examine it closely at this late date. But opinions in scholarship are more durable than those in the monthly magazines, and this book is at this moment an accepted authority. It was reprinted in 1959 on the initiative of a committee of professors (see its frontispiece), and both Avalle, *Letteratura,* p. 123, and Arnaut, *Canzoni,* p. 56, note, refer to it as conclusive. It is cited without query as a source of troubadour-Dantean knowledge by Bondanella, in 'Arnaut Daniel and Dante's *Rime Petrose*', p. 416, note. Its methods, those of the traditional science of manuscript classification, are used for example in Peire Vidal, *Poesie* (1960), Cavalcanti, *Rime* (1957), and Arnaut, *Canzoni* (1960).

96. Santangelo, *Trovatori,* pp. 9ff. See n. 102 below.

97. Santangelo, *Trovatori,* pp. 29-51. See n. 102 below.

98. Ibid., pp. 59-70.

99. Ibid., p. 70.

100. Santangelo's list of items shared by Dante and the supposed manuscript-group $GQUcV^2PS$ is given in *Trovatori,* pp. 59-70.

101. See n. 100.

102. Though the intention of these pages is to show what sort of void this manuscript-genealogising is based on, it may be of interest to see some of the consequences of operating in this void.

The following are the stages of Santangelo's argument. First, he attacks the idea that Dante's sources of information were the *vidas* and *razos* by pointing out 'contradictions' (pp. 9ff.). For example, the *vida* says that Peire d'Alvernhe was the 'first good troubadour'; Dante merely names him among an unspecified number of 'more ancient sages'. However, this point only makes it clear either that Dante read the *vidas* and *razos* more intelligently than Santangelo, or that he had other sources of information, or both. It is clear from other *vidas* (cf. ibid., p. 56) that Marcabrun was of the same period or earlier than Peire, while the genealogy in the *vida* of William IX shows his antiquity, and the information in the *vida* of Bernart de Ventadorn, if placed with that of William, does likewise for Bernart. Santangelo's general and textual reasons why Dante could not have known the *vidas* of these other troubadours stand or fall together. Santangelo argues that the *vidas* say nothing that could have told Dante that Provencal was the first of the Romance poetic languages. Does the fact that I express an opinion that was not printed in yesterday's *Times* prove that I did not read yesterday's *Times?* Only if we assume that I am not only deaf and blind but also incapable of thinking for myself, i.e. an automaton; yet this type of argument from absence is one of Santangelo's commonest. For the argument from Dante's opinion of Giraut de Bornelh, see below. Of the same type are Santangelo's arguments that Dante speaks of Bertran de Born's generosity, which is not apparent in the *vidas;* that the *vidas* speak of Bertran as stirring up hatred between brothers, which Dante would have considered more important, had he known of it, than the stirring up of strife between fathers and sons that he mentions; and that Dante could not have read the *vida* which speaks of Bertran as retiring to a monastery, for he places him in hell; with similar 'contradictions' in Arnaut Daniel's case. Such entirely unwarrantable suppositions are disposed of, for example, in Moore, *Young King,* p. 74. Jeanroy, like Santangelo, had said that if Dante had known everything the *vidas* and *razos* say about Bertran he would not have put him in hell; Moore shows by obvious examples that Dante's views as to who was saved did not agree with those of the Church. The remaining supposed contradictions are of the type I describe in the case of Folquet de Marseille (see below, n. 124), and will not stand if we suppose that Dante had any other source of information, traditional or textual, with which to supplement the *vidas.* Santangelo's dismissal of the *razos* as a source for Dante is based on the same mixture of arguments from personal reaction, trivialities, and the fixed assumption that Dante could have had no other source than the relatives of the surviving *chansonniers* (*Trovatori,* especially pp. 18-21).

Santangelo then proceeds to attack Bartsch's grouping of the extant *chansonniers* (ibid., pp. 28-29). It is clear that Bartsch's reasoning was also of the kind I have described above. Then he devotes many pages (pp. 30-51) to a new grouping of the extant *chansonniers* according to supposed common ancestors; and following this he decides that Dante's source must be a hypothetical ancestor of $GQUcV^2PS$, and reorganises the classification of this supposed group (p. 57). Finally (pp. 59-70) he gives his detailed reasons for saying that Dante's source was the ancestor of $GQUcV^2PS$. In this work he does not cite the variants on which he bases his original manuscript groupings, but it is clear from the reasoning that they are of the same nature as the reasons for deciding that Dante's source was the ancestor of $GQUcV^2PS$; thus there are two stages of reasoning from the same fragile bases of difference in spelling and the like.

It is to be observed that in the table of corroborations given above, text before n. 100, the rate of actual corroboration is very low. If scribes were not human, of course, all twenty 'virgin' readings that Santangelo believes were in the original source (q^2) would have come down uncorrupted to its hypothetical descendant (q^1) and thence, still uncorrupted, to the extant manuscripts $GQUcV^2PS$ that he has grouped together. Likewise, if scribes were not human, our manuscripts of Dante would have the same readings, equally uncorrupt. We would therefore find all twenty readings in Dante reproduced exactly in all the manuscripts $GQUcV^2PS$, giving 140 corroborations. Any two scholars would find it difficult to agree on the exact number of corroborations that we actually find, since their nature varies, but out of the ideal 140 there are certainly not more than sixty — that is, less than 50 per cent. Less than half of the readings chosen by Santangelo support his contention, that Dante's source was the source of the grouped manuscripts $GQUcV^2PS$. But Santangelo used the same methods in the logical first step of his argument — that is, 'proving' that $GQUcV^2PS$ belong together because they have a common ancestor; and we must assume that he accepted as proof a similarly low rate of actual corroboration. If we multiply together the rates of error in the two processes, it is difficult to imagine the chances that Santangelo's answer is the right one. The fact is that it is as likely as not that $GQUcV^2PS$ have no particularly central common ancestor, and that their history is as complicated a story of cross-borrowings as that of any Misrahi describes; thus it is most probably impossible to form any idea as to which of the surviving *chansonniers* (if any) Dante's source (and why do we assume that he had only one source?) was nearly related.

Further, since even with his flexible tools he is unable to get a satisfactory answer, Santangelo says that Dante's source was not the source of $GQUcV^2PS$ but (*Trovatori,* p. 70) the source of that source. According to his theory, all the corruptions except the one about Bertran de Born took place in the second step of this descent (see ibid.). We then have, in the case of several of the 'shared readings', a survival rate over one generation of one-seventh — since these readings are only corroborated in one out of seven manuscripts. Had the case demanded it, no doubt Santangelo would have accepted an equal proportion of corruption over the generation q^2 - q^1, with, again, a survival rate as low as one-seventh, without letting it disturb his confidence in the genealogical connection. Over two generations this would have given a survival rate of the relevant readings as low as one-forty-ninth.

The final absurdity is that, though this methodology would probably have permitted Santangelo to give as Dante's source of information the ancestor of any group of manuscripts he chose, he has already ruled out the *vidas* and *razos* as a source, and so is obliged to suggest an entirely hypothetical source: a version of a thirteenth-century grammar which would have contained biographical notes.

And yet the use of these methods, based on the idea that the late Provençal/early Italian literary culture consisted entirely of relatives of the extant *chansonniers,* continues. Favati has recently produced an edition of the 'lives' of the troubadours, *Le Biografie trovadoriche* (1961), largely in order to attack the earlier edition of Boutière and Schutz for not describing a detailed manuscript-grouping. Boutière, in his revised edition, defends himself (Boutière and Schutz, *Biographies,* p. xxxviii) by saying that the genealogy is impossible to establish because 'the transcriptions of the *vidas* and the *razos* have been, over the course of time, so numerous; so many intermediate copies have been lost, that it is now impossible to re-establish the filiation of the twenty-odd remaining *chansonniers,* the only survivors of a considerable number.' He is driven (ibid.) to consider oral transmission; but not, apparently, ordinary sheets of ad hoc manuscript.

103. Chaytor, *Script,* p. 14.

104. See Chapter 5, n. 60.

105. In the *razo* to a song by Bertran de Born which says, 'En Richartz asega borcs e chastels e pres terras e derroca et ars et abrassa' (Boutière and Schutz, *Biographies,* p. 113), the endings are clearly taken from the song itself (Bertran, *Lieder,* no. 14, *D'un sirventes no·m chal far lonhor ganda:*

> Conselh vuolh dar el so de n'Alemanda
> Lai a'n Richart, si tot no lo·m demanda:
> Ja per so frair mais sos omes no blanda.
> Nonca·s fai el, anz assetja e·ls aranda,
> Tol lor chastels e derocha et abranda
>   Deves totz latz.
> E·l reis tornei lai ab cels de Garlanda
>   E l'autre, sos conhatz.

Boutière in his new edition of the 'lives' takes the -*a* endings in the *razo* to be Italianisms, suggesting that this 'cascade' of three in a row is highly significant and helps to prove that manuscripts *FIK* go back to an original made in the Venetian area in the thirteenth century (Boutière and Schutz, *Biographies,* p. xliii); he seems not to have considered the relationship with the text of the song, in which point precisely he differs most from the author of the *razo,* who was working with it under his nose because he considered it a magic treasure-house of story.

It is true that -*a* forms in the relevant lines of the song are in the present tense, while the -*a* forms in this part of the *razo* seem to be in the aorist; but this is probably a mixing of the past tenses with the historic present. We find such a mixing for example in ibid., pp. 20, 530, 539, 303, though it is true that these are all -*a* endings and thus could be aorists. For an historical present continuous mixed with past tenses see the Arnaut Daniel *razo* in Arnaut, *Canzoni,* p. 169, where Arnaut 'la va tota arretener'. Thomas notes of another of Bertran's *razos* that is is only 'un pitoyable délayage des vers de Bertran de Born' (Bertran, *Poésies,* notes to *Pois Ventadorns,* p. 11); in the case of the present *razo,* Moore (*Young King,* p. 37) has observed the verbal parallelisms. The other *razo* cited by Boutière in support of his hypothesis, one for a song by Raimon Jordan (Boutière and Schutz, *Biographies,* p.

162), seems a clear case of this mixing, if we remember that the historic present tends to be used at moments of critical action:

> Quant lo vescoms auzi aquels honratz plazers que la gentils valenz domna li mandava, e si li *comensa* a venir una granz dousors d'amor al cor; si qu'el *comensa* a far alegressa et a esjauzir se, e *comensa* a venir en plasa e recobrar solatz entre la bona gen, e vestir se e sos compaingnos e cobrar se en arnes et en armas et en solatz.

106. Quoted in Chaytor, *Script,* p. 129. It is not surprising that Bédier, cited ibid., p. 150, said that with many manuscripts, while it is not difficult to produce a system of groupings, it is possible to produce several, any one of which is as defensible as the others.

107. See above, n. 98.

108. Stronski, *Folquet,* pp. 44*, 77*-86*.

109. Boutière and Schutz, *Biographies,* p. xxxix; cf. e.g. Avalle, *Letteratura,* pp. 44-45. For Boutière this is a measure of desperation in cases of extreme genealogical confusion.

110. Cf. Chaytor, *Script,* pp. 115ff.

111. Arnaut, *Canzoni,* pp. 169-170. The *razo* is probably not factual, being concocted from a misreading (see Appendix 2, text before n. 25), but it shows a near-contemporary's idea of how things were done.

112. For Church-educated troubadours see Boutière and Schutz, *Biographies,* pp. 233, 255, 229, 202, 307, 335, 267, 199, 239. For the kind of education they received cf. Peire Cardenal, *Poésies,* pp. 614, 617, 618. Elias Cairel 'wrote down words and tunes well'; cf. Chapter 4, text before n. 38. Ferrarino di Ferrara 'was a better scribe than any man'; cf. below, text before n. 118. Peire Cardenal may have been a scribe; cf. Peire Cardenal, *Poésies,* p. 618. For Ovid in the troubadours cf. Stronski, *Folquet,* pp. 78*-81*; Schrötter, *Ovid,* pp. 8-9, dates French translations of Ovid from the end of the twelfth century, but notes that there is no trace of any Provençal translations of Ovid, and suggests that the troubadours were too well educated to need them.

113. Avalle, *Letteratura,* p. 56, suggests that songs could not have survived from the period of Marcabrun to that of the first surviving anthologies without some kind of written records, 'were they "manuscrits de jongleur" or enthusiasts' copies', especially in view of the sophistication of these songs.

114. Cited ibid., plate 2, and pp. 47-48. These are standard examples, taken from Avalle's recent work, which takes most of its evidence on these points from Chaytor, *Script.* To them one might add Bernard, *Chansons,* no. 40:

> mais d'una re me conort be :
> ela sap letras et enten,
> et agrada·m qu'eu escria
> los motz, e s'a leis plazia,
> legis los al meu sauvamen.

Cf. also Arnaut de Maroill's 'Amors m'a comandat escrire / so que·l boca non auza dire', which as Lazar notes (ibid., p. 284) is from Ovid. Jeanroy, in *Poésie,* 2, p.

225, cites a heretic who possessed unauthorised writings, but who also recited a poem by Guillem Figueira. Avalle, *Letteratura,* p. 47, notes that no one now doubts that the troubadours wrote or dictated their songs; but when it comes to discussing the history of the surviving manuscripts these ad hoc scribblings seem to be forgotten.

115. Cf. Jeanroy, *Poésie,* 1, p. 248, Bertoni, *Duecento,* p. 14, and below, n. 120.

116. Cf. De Bartholomaeis, in Bertoni, *Provenza,* pp. 38ff., and Bertoni, *Duecento,* pp. 61ff.

117. Cf. ibid., p. 61.

118. Bertoni, *Trovatori,* p. 125; this *vida* has been dated as late as the fourteenth century.

119. Quoted in Bertoni, *Duecento,* p. 14; cf. Jeanroy, *Poésie,* 1, p. 248, for Ezzelino's relations with Uc de Saint-Circ.

120. Bertoni, *Trovatori,* pp. 66ff., no. XIX, XX.

121. For these arguments see Santangelo, *Trovatori,* pp. 9ff.; Boutière and Schutz, *Biographies,* p. 39.

122. He said 'La parleure francaise est plus delitable et plus commune à toutes gens'—Chaytor, *Script,* p. 23.

123. Cf. Hauvette, *France,* p. 16.

124. Santangelo once more combines the peculiarity of his argument from absence with the idea that Dante's generation lived in an informational vacuum, when he says that the *vidas* could not have been Dante's source because they do not explain Sordello's high position in the *Purgatorio.* Again, he claims that Dante's source could not have been the *vidas* because they do not contain the information that Folquet de Marseille was a lecher in his youth; and the *vidas* that (according to Santangelo) Dante could have known do not say Folquet was from Marseilles. Now it happens that poems have survived which *show* just how lecherous Folquet was (see above, n. 60). If Dante did not see these, it simply confirms once more that he had sources of information not known to us. As for Folquet's origin in Marseilles, when Stronski proved in 1910 that Folquet the troubadour was one with Folquet the Bishop of Toulouse, the proofs he cited made it quite clear that at least around 1260—five years before Dante was born—it was public knowledge in France that Folquet had been a bishop and a troubadour, originally from Marseilles (Stronski, *Folquet,* pp. 105*-113*). If Brunetto Latini did not inform Dante of these things, his other contacts with France—not to mention those of his friends and antecedents —could have. Dante himself shows a close acquaintance with Paris; his youth saw the intervention of France in the affairs of Italy, so bitterly execrated by him (*Purgatorio,* 7.126, 20.43, etc.).

125. Davidsohn, *Firenze ai Tempi di Dante,* p. 138; in *Provincia Deserta* Pound exclaims ' "Riquier! Guido." ' when he sees the 'Dorata' that Cavalcanti speaks of, and in 'Troubadours', pp. 435-436 (*Essays,* p. 103), he wonders whether they met and decides that in any case Cavalcanti must have been stimulated by hearing Giraut's work. (N.B. The *Essays* text corrects 'Riquier may as easily have been in Spain at the time' to '...have not been....')

126. *Cantos,* 8/32:36-37.

127. Dante, *Inferno,* 5.73-142; cf. Chapter 6, text before n. 52.

128. *Cantos,* 24/110:115; Noyes, *Story of Ferrara,* pp. 71-72.

129. Jeanroy, *Poésie,* 1, pp. 3-4.

130. Ibid.; his passage idcirca reproduces most of the important points from S. Debenedetti, 'Tre secoli di studi provenzali (XVI-XVIII)', cited by Jeanroy, p. 57, as 'P. Debenedetti' and without mention of source. For the Gonzagas cf. *Girart de Roussillon,* ed. Hackett, 3, p. 464. I have concentrated on the houses Pound refers to.

131. Cf. Bertoni's remarks to this effect, in *Trovatori,* p. 34, note.

CHAPTER 10. THE HERETICS OF 'PROVENCE'

1. Boris de Rachewiltz, in 'Pagan and Magic Elements', pp. 174ff., connects the 'Cathars' with the Manichaeans of Persia, implying that they shared a dualist ascetic ethic. Peck, in 'Landscape as Ceremony in the Later *Cantos*', pp. 38-39, makes Pound agree with Simone Weil:

> This parallel, of Cathar Languedoc with Troy, is also Simone Weil's in her splendid lament for the destruction of Toulouse and its culture—the decisive loss, in her view, of spiritual freedom in Europe. Like Weil, Pound mourns the Cathars as martyrs in a suppressed tradition of pre-Roman spirituality, going back through the Manicheans and Gnostics to oriental roots; there is at Montségur, he says, 'no more an altar to Mithras'.

Peck refers (ibid.) to Weil's congratulatory letter to Roché in Nelli, *Cathares,* pp. 3-5; but it is certain, as we shall see, that Pound would have had no sympathy with the view of the 'Cathars' entertained by Weil, Nelli, Roché, etc., who tended and tend to respect the 'Cathars' for their independence of mind in acknowledging that the world is evil. Peck cites ('Landscape as Ceremony in the Later *Cantos*', p. 42, note) Gaussin, *L'Abbaye de la Chaise-Dieu,* but that book gives nothing relevant to Pound on the abbey's 'connections with Toulouse and their dissolution by Boniface VIII'. Peck's only other sources are Nelli, *Cathares,* and Fernand Niel. Peck claims that Pound traced the 'Cathars' back 'through the Manicheans and Gnostics to oriental roots', but in fact Pound traced them back to the Hellenic world, from which I think he was aware that Mithra 'remained forever excluded' (Cumont, *Mysteries of Mithra,* p. 33).

Such confusions are normal in this area of Pound scholarship. Christine Brooke-Rose, in *A ZBC of Ezra Pound,* p. 216, flatly states that the 'Cathars' were Manichaeans, leaving the reader to assume that Pound thought so. There is no authority for her *ipse dixit* in her Provencal scholarship (see Makin, *Ezra Pound and Mediaeval Provençal Poetry,* p. 97).

Hugh Kenner, however, is careful not to associate the Albigensians with Manichaeism, though he calls their religion a 'cosmic dualism' (*Pound Era,* p. 335). It is clear that, as Kenner suggests, Pound connected the ritual and the light-worship of the Albigensians with Manichaeism, but it is also clear that his Albigensians were not Mithraic-Manichaean dualists in any ethical or aesthetic sense. The one point that is well made in Nassar's recent *Cantos of Ezra Pound* is that Pound saw a dualism: moments where one perceived (did not construct, *pace* Nassar) an order, which stayed as a vision in the mind and was thus indestructible, amid a material flux of creation and destruction. The ecstatic passages in the Cantos show the triumph of order and light for brief moments over chaos and darkness, while admitting that chaos persisted. This is quite different from the Manichaean dualism, which is ineradicably ascetic, holding the material to be essentially degraded, evil; Pound felt that the order was not only pre-existing but only to be perceived in its material embodiment—the trees, the birds. Like the Japanese poet, he laments the fall of the plum blossom, he does not revile the blossom itself.

2. 'Terra Italica', quoted in Stock, *Exile*, p. 23 (*Selected Prose*, pp. 58-59). For Davidsohn see below, n. 135.

3. See especially *Essays*, p. 150.

4. Dante, *Paradiso*, 2.1-6; cf. *Cantos*, 109/774:798.

5. *Cantos*, 74/429:456; cf. also Makin, 'Ezra Pound and Scotus Erigena', pp. 60-65. But to speak of these mysteries is not to destroy them; see below and *Cantos*, 91/615:649.

6. *Kulchur*, pp. 144-145.

7. See below, text before n. 131.

8. Cf. Makin, 'Ezra Pound and Scotus Erigena', pp. 60-65, 73-77, and Kenner, *Pound Era*, p. 451.

9. *Kulchur*, pp. 294-295.

10. *Essays*, p. 150.

11. See below, text before n. 113.

12. *Selected Prose*, p. 58. Pound seems to take the Mithraic bull ritual into his final myth of Provence: see Kenner, *Pound Era*, p. 335.

13. Pound was correct in believing that the theology of Manichaeism was dead; see below, n. 31. He was also correct in identifying the basic structure of Manichaeism, theological and ethical, with that of Mithraism. For the theology cf. Widengren, *Mani and Manichaeism*, p. 44: 'It is perfectly clear, as Baur emphasized, that Mani took for his starting-point the ancient Iranian dualism.' This dualism is Zoroastrianism and the allied sects. For the growth of Mithraism out of Zoroastrianism, cf. Zaehner, *The Dawn and Twilight of Zoroastrianism*, and Cumont, *The Mysteries of Mithra*, pp. 1-29. For the ethic see Widengren, *Mani and Manichaeism*, p. 43:

> In a dispute with the Manichees Augustine puts the following words into the mouth of Faustus: 'I teach that there are two primary elements, God and Matter. To Matter we ascribe all maleficent, to God all beneficent potency, as is proper.' (*Contra Faustum*, XI.1.)
> Here Faustus conducts himself as a true pupil of Mani. . . .

14. Adémar of Chabannes said that certain heretics of 1015 were 'Manichaean'; the word 'Cathar' was first used of a community in Italy in 1030: Guiraud, *Inquisition*, I, p. 2; Runciman, *Manichee*, p. 117, and note. The account given in Guiraud makes the diverse and scattered manifestations of the eleventh and early twelfth centuries seem homogeneous, but it is still relied upon by scholars of all camps (see Nelli, passim; Thouzellier, *Catharisme*, Preface; Leff, *Heresy*, pp. 35-36), despite doubts about Guiraud's use of evidence (cf. Dondaine, 'Actes', p. 332).

All the relevant details of the various heresies accounted 'Cathar' will be found in Makin, *Ezra Pound and Mediaeval Provençal Poetry*, pp. 613-617.

15. This may have been with the connivance of Raymond: cf. Guiraud, *Inquisition*, I, pp. 403-407, and *Chanson de la Croisade*, ed. Martin-Chabot, I, p. 15, note. There is no definitive history of the Albigensian Crusade, as Manselli notes ('Eglises et théologies cathares', p. 173, note), but the remarkable work of scholarship by Eugène Martin-Chabot in his edition of the *Chanson de la Croisade* has provided an excellent comprehensive source. Cf. review of vol. III, by Yves Dossat, in *Annales du Midi*, lxxiv (1962), p. 337: 'Une annotation très importante. . . .'

16. *Chanson de la Croisade*, ed. Martin-Chabot, I, pp. 50, 52, 58, and note; *Chanson*, ed. Meyer, pp. xxj, xvij.

17. *Chanson de la Croisade*, ed. Martin-Chabot, I, p. 76.

18. Ibid., p. 80, and note.

19. Simon's family had been deprived of its county by John Lackland; Simon had already fought against the Moslem: cf. Dossat, 'Simon de Montfort', pp. 282-284.

20. For the strategies and politics cf. ibid., pp. 299, 295.

21. Dossat, 'La croisade vue par les chroniqueurs', p. 222. For the burnings at Minerve, the counter-massacre of Simon's garrisons, the hangings and burnings at Lavaur, and the war of the small castles in general, see *Chanson de la Croisade*, ed. Martin-Chabot, I, pp. 116, note, 117, note, 116-118, 123, note, 116, note, 138, and note, 141, note, 164, 166, and note.

22. The militant churchmen were in general less willing to make peace than the French nobles; cf. e.g. ibid., p. 200. They generally led the negotiations, cf. e.g. ibid., p. 146; they were generally more anti-Languedoc than Innocent III, and they had constantly to stiffen his resolve: cf. e.g. ibid., II, p. 48.

23. Pierre des Vaux-de-Cernay, cited in Dossat, 'La croisade vue par les chroniqueurs', pp. 226-233 (cf. below, text before n. 66).

24. *Chanson de la Croisade*, ed. Martin-Chabot, I, p. 290, II, pp. 16-32, especially 27, note, 32, note. Simon de Montfort said that Peter had only come to see a lady (ibid., p. 19, note). Peter thus effectively brought about the end of the whole fusion of chivalry and courtly love that we have seen in Bertran de Born, by not realising that it was militarily outmoded.

25. Raymond and his young son retired to England, to seek help from John Lackland, while the Crusaders entered Toulouse in 1215. Lackland was able to provide money (extorted from the Cistercians as a fine for what the Abbot of Cîteaux had done at the head of the crusaders in Languedoc!), but his power did not stretch to Languedoc as had that of his father Henry II and brother Richard Lionheart: ibid., p. 34, note.

26. Cf. Guiraud, *Inquisition*, I, pp. 335-337.

27. Ibid., p. 374, II, p. 5.

28. Ibid., I, pp. 42-44, 46, 52, 59-60, 90-91, 61, 66-67, 70-74.

29. Ibid., ch. III, passim.

30. Ibid., I, pp. 111, 137, 108, 95.

31. In *The Medieval Manichee* Runciman begins with the Gnostics, whose distinguishing doctrine was that 'the visible world was created not by God but by the Demiurge' (p. 6), and who were flourishing throughout the Roman Empire by the

middle of the second century AD. The Gnostics, Runciman thinks, were not at all influenced by Zoroastrian thought, which had of course professed a dualist solution to the problem of evil since the sixth century BC (Zaehner, *Zoroastrianism,* pp. 19, 42-43). It was in the bosom of a Zoroastrian civilisation that the next link in Runciman's chain — Manichaeism — arose (*Manichee,* pp. 183ff.), but Runciman regards Manes not only as essentially a Gnostic but even as a heterodox Christian. This is in accordance with his clear intention of justifying the Church's action against Manes's supposed descendants, the Albigensians, on the grounds that they were not believers in a religion worthy of the name, but mere heretics, and immoral anarchists to boot.

Runciman then follows the spread of certain Manichaean sects into Armenia. In the eighth century AD there arose in that country the sect known as the Paulicians, whose doctrines 'must remain largely a matter of conjecture', but are held to have had many similarities with those of the Albigensians (p. 46). The information about these doctrines stems from the Greek authorities (pp. 46-47).

Noting the activity of Paulician missionaries in Bulgaria, Runciman suggests a link with the new doctrine of Bogomilism that arose in that country in the tenth century (p. 66). His account of its doctrines shows a faith similar in most points to that of Manichaeism, though the cosmogony is described in a different way (pp. 73-77). With Bogomil missionaries active, later on, in Herzegovina and Bosnia, and with a convenient local desire for independence both from the Catholic kings of Hungary and from the Orthodox emperors, a similar doctrine arose there in about 1180 (pp. 101, 46). This doctrine, called Patarinism, lasted right through until the Turks invaded in 1463 (pp. 114-115). Finally, because 'probably missionaries from the Balkans were definitely operating in and from Italy' (p. 118), the dualist doctrine reached the Italian peninsula. Since 'it was in Italy that the first explicitly Cathar Church appeared' (Runciman refers to the heretic community at Monteforte in 1030, but he means simply that it was called 'Cathar'; see below, text before n. 78), and for other reasons that Runciman adduces, he concludes that from Italy the 'Cathars' of Languedoc received their dualism (p. 117).

Runciman's chief basis of comparison is Guiraud's picture of the Albigensian ethic and theology — Guiraud is his only source for Languedoc, though Runciman's footnotes might seem to suggest otherwise; as we shall see, Guiraud's picture is highly implausible. Even if we accept that basis of comparison, the chain of descent is largely a matter of conjecture; one scholar proposes a 'source' in the Qaraites (a Jewish sect tainted with dualism, very active around AD 800) and thus, instead of going round by Paulicians and Bogomils, takes 'Catharism' straight from an ancient Gnostic-Manichaean sect, making 'an economy of three centuries'. Another suggests that the Kabbalists of Languedoc show the survival of Gnostic texts from the early centuries. For all this see Delaruelle, 'Etudes sur le Catharisme', pp. 37-38. On other weaknesses in Runciman's chain see Russell, *Dissent,* pp. 201-202. Obviously there is no possibility of proving from a reliable chain of descent that the heresy of Languedoc must have been so-and-so; instead scholars are in the position of having to try to establish what the heresy of Languedoc was, and then grope in the murk of the centuries for antecedents. If the picture of Languedoc is wrong, then the ancestor-hunting is falsely based.

Manichaeism is in any case pretty well ruled out as an ancestor. None of the heretics or their chroniclers, not even Sacchoni the 'convert', has left a trace of the name of Manes. Morghen says, 'A Manichaeism in which the very memory of the founder has disappeared and in which the essential mythological and cosmogonic features...are completely lost, is no longer Manichaeism' (*Medioevo*, p. 251). Morghen notes that there is a profound distinction between the cosmogonic and metaphysical dualism of Manes, and the anthropological and ethical dualism of the Christian heresies (ibid.). Father Dondaine is obliged to note that the *Liber de Duobus Principiis* makes no mention of any written tradition, and that 'the Manichaean gnosis does not easily fit with sacraments that are the essential principles of salvation' (*Liber*, pp. 25, 55). Thus even if we accept the classic picture of the Albigensians, there is no reason to connect them with Manichaeism.

32. Morghen, *Medioevo*, pp. 238-240.

33. Russell, *Dissent*, pp. 196-197, 208.

34. E.g. ibid. pp. 192, 200; Manselli, in 'Eglises et théologies cathares', p. 132, finds no 'radical dualism' before the 'Council'. Chiefly because of this 'Council', most scholars take the 1160's as the beginning of 'Catharism' proper: see Russell, *Dissent*, p. 208, citing H. C. Puech and Arno Borst; Thouzellier, *Catharisme*, pp. 19-23, 33, note—though apparently she changes her mind in Le Goff, *Hérésies*, p. 109; Morghen, *Medioevo*, p. 127.

35. Dondaine, 'Actes', p. 326.

36. Ibid., p. 334.

37. Dossat, 'A propos du concile cathare de Saint-Félix: les Milingues', passim. Father Dondaine had been able to confirm that Caseneuve was Prebend at St. Etienne in Toulouse in 1652; that two of the new bishops are corroborated as heretics by Roger de Hoveden and Guillaume de Puylaurens; that another is corroborated by Puylaurens and by an anonymous Catholic polemicist; and that Petrus Isarn is in the Inquisition Registers—though he was burned in 1226—and Petrus Pollanus is there also; cf. 'Actes', pp. 334, 336-338, 347-350. On the other hand, he had been obliged to note that what appeared to be the date of copying, 11 August 1232, did not exist in the calendar, so that 11 August must have been in 1167 (the date of the Council), while 1232 was that of the copying. That not only leaves an awkward syntax, but eliminates the copyist, Peter Isarn. For a summary of the situation and comments, see Wolff, *Documents de l'Histoire du Languedoc*, pp. 104-105.

38. Dossat, 'A propos du concile cathare de Saint-Félix: les Milingues', p. 202.

39. Cf. ibid., p. 213. Though the 'Cathar bishops' and 'Antipope' might seem to be left intact even if this document is a fake, the Appendix to this chapter will show how much their existence depends on the word of the Catholic polemicists, who read of it in each other's works.

40. Russell, *Dissent*, pp. 216-217.

41. Ibid.

42. Thouzellier, *Catharisme*, p. 27, and note.

43. Russell, *Dissent*, pp. 220-224.

44. E.g. Dondaine, 'Actes', p. 354.

45. Dondaine, *Liber*, p. 49.

46. Cf. e.g. Guiraud, *Inquisition,* I, pp. 385-392.

47. Russell supports three of these four cases; as well as their dates, he cites their names (*catti, Piphili, Publicani*) and in the case of the Oxford heretics the fact that they came from Germany. Yet Russell himself in other cases provides reasons for setting no store by the names (*Dissent,* pp. 217-227).

48. Cf. her summary of discussions, Thouzellier, *Catharisme,* p. 58. Christine Thouzellier also accepts the 'Council' as a turning-point; for her the heretics before about 1140 had nothing to do with the 'Cathars', but 'Cathars' were present in strength by 1177; see above, n. 34.

49. Ibid., p. 21.

50. *Chanson de la Croisade,* ed. Martin-Chabot, I, p. 10. The anonymous continuer of the *Chanson* makes a distinction between *crezens,* 'believers', and *vestitz,* 'enrobed ones', ibid., II, p. 50.

51. The most coherent witness is Peire Garsias, who is one of Guiraud's main props, being cited by him in *Inquisition,* I, pp. 42, 47, 61, 64, 102. The only other coherent witness cited by Guiraud is Limosus Negre (pp. 40-41) who said that

> God the sovereign creator first of all made and created the Archangels who are truly the sons of God; they, through a power which they held of God their Father and their Creator, created in their turn the angels of lesser virtue and value; these angels of second rank are all called Virgin Mary and in their turn they created abstinence and chastity which live above the sun and the moon ...everything beneath the sun and beneath the moon is mere corruption and confusion.

Yves Dossat in his researches into the Inquisition Registers found only the repeated statement that *Deus non fecit visibilia,* 'God did not make the visible things', together with two statements that the Devil created the human body, one inference to the same effect, and one remark that 'there were two gods, one good and the other evil' (Les Cathares d'après les documents de l'Inquisition', pp. 77, 78).

52. Confused and inconclusive witness by various speakers is cited by Guiraud, *Inquisition,* I, pp. 46, 49, 53, 68. Together with various ambiguities, Dossat, in 'Les Cathares d'après les documents de l'Inquisition', p. 78, cites the following:

> The wife of a knight of Montgiscard, in the Lauragais, had heard the heretics say that the things which were visible had been made by the will and with the consent of God, though He did not intervene directly. A woman from Toulouse, the wife of a carpenter, declared that Lucifer had made man, but had not been able to make him speak; God breathed on man's face and he began to speak. An even more divergent point of view is expressed by an inhabitant of Cordes. The Devil having made man's body, God gave him a soul, and when he had received this soul, man jumped to one side and said 'I don't belong to you'.

Dossat explains these statements by referring to the idea of 'mitigated dualism' that has been so convenient to Catharologists; but he notes (p. 79) that there is no sign of rival sects among the Languedoc heretics in these Registers, and these statements represent the exact opposite of any dualism worthy of the name. When the Registers record that two heretics said they did not teach that the Devil created the human body, Dossat ascribes this to 'prudence', since the *perfecti* then turned the conversation to other things (p. 88).

53. Ibid., p. 77.

54. Cf. especially ibid., pp. 79-92.

55. Leff, *Heresy,* p. 14.

56. Ibid., p. 22.

57. See especially the account of the Lateran Council in 1215, in *Chanson de la Croisade,* ed. Martin-Chabot, II, pp. 40-88. When Innocent preached the Albigensian Crusade, even Philippe-Auguste declared that he could not legally march against his vassal Raymond of Toulouse until the latter was declared a heretic. The legate Peter of Castelnau formed a league for the repression of heresy among Raymond's vassals in Provence, with the intention of turning the league against Raymond if he would not co-operate. See Guiraud, *Inquisition,* I, pp. 403-409.

58. The indulgences offered in return for crusading were a chief reason why men undertook it (*Chanson de la Croisade,* ed. Martin-Chabot, I, pp. 23, note, 24, 38); when the required forty days were over, many men quit immediately (cf. e.g. p. 280). Excommunication could be purely tactical: it was threatened and used against crusaders for misappropriation of booty (p. 82, and note).

59. Manselli, 'De la "Persuasio" à la "Coercitio" ', p. 192, says that Innocent III was disturbed by the rise of heresies in the lands that he intended to be the basis of the Church's State. His decretal *Vergentis in senium,* appealing to Roman law and assimilating heresy to lese-majesty, influenced the introduction of the death penalty for heresy.

60. Ibid., p. 195.

61. The terms and the concept are Donald Schon's, in his Reith Lecture, 'Dynamic Conservatism', p. 724. For the mishandling of Peter Valdès's reforming zeal, turning it into outright heresy, cf. Thouzellier, *Catharisme,* pp. 16-18, 24-38.

62. Leff, *Heresy,* pp. 21, 15-16.

63. Guiraud, *Inquisition,* II, p. 7; Lea, *Inquisition,* pp. 123, 202, 162, 164.

64. Ibid., pp. 175, 145, 310, 240-242, 139-141, 153; Thouzellier, *Catharisme,* p. 55.

65. Cf. e.g. St. Bernard, *Letters,* p. 8, where the fear of hell seems to be the only reason that St. Bernard can suggest for enduring monastic hardships. Russell, in *Dissent,* p. 209, notes that St. Bernard lived on bread and water, with boiled vegetables twice a week, and suffered eternal stomach-pains.

66. Dossat, 'La croisade vue par les chroniqueurs', p. 227.

67. Ibid.

68. Guibert de Nogent, *Memoirs,* pp. 212-213.

69. Guiraud, *Inquisition,* I, p. 44.

70. Guibert de Nogent castigated himself for his interest in erotic verse in the past (*Memoirs,* p. 87), as did Bishop Folquet of Toulouse, once the troubadour Folquet de Marseille (see Stronski, *Folquet,* p. 89*). On Guibert's fears of his own body see *Memoirs,* pp. 13-14.

71. Ibid., p. 10, and cf. e.g. Bordonove, *Templiers,* pp. 205-206. Guibert is obsessed with excrement, which is associated for him with sin and punishment and forms a large part of his fantasies; cf. *Memoirs,* pp. 14-15. He is highly credulous

about all sorts of doubtful material (pp. 28-33). Yet he has been used as a source of information on the ethos of the Albigensians, in which area, Henri Maisonneuve said, 'it would be an injustice to suspect his honesty' (quoted, p. 31). Similarly Father Dondaine said of Raynier Sacchoni, the Inquisitor, that to reject his testimony on the beliefs of the Albigensians is to question his sincerity (Dondaine, *Liber*, p. 7).

72. Morghen, *Medioevo*, pp. 232-233.

73. Dondaine, *Liber*, p. 58; see below, n. 79.

74. Quoted in Morghen, *Medioevo*, p. 234.

75. Cf. ibid., pp. 252-259; Thouzellier, *Catharisme*, pp. 16-18, etc.

76. Morghen, *Medioevo*, pp. 233, 227-228, points out that Etienne de Bourbon and Eckbert of Schönau explicitly refer to St. Augustine for information on the nature of the heresy; we have seen Guibert de Nogent doing so (above, text before n. 68). Cf. also Dondaine, *Liber*, p. 53: 'The Catholic polemicists certainly recognised Manichaean doctrines in the Cathar heresy, but it was thanks to their knowledge of St. Augustine.' For the absence of any genuine Manichaeism at the time they were writing, see above, n. 31. Cf. Pound in *Essays*, p. 176: 'For centuries if you disliked a man you called him a Manichaean, as in some circles today you call him a Bolshevic to damage his earning capacity.'

77. Russell, *Dissent*, pp. 213-214, where Russell mentions that the heretics in question bear no traceable resemblance to Arians.

78. Ibid., p. 194; Runciman, *Manichee*, p. 118, for example, thought that the term came from the depths of the sect's supposed past.

79. Father Dondaine (*Liber*, pp. 7-8) observes that the corroboration of the information in Raynier Sacchoni's *Summa* comes from (a) Catholic sources and (b) the 'Book of the Two Principles'. For the latter, see below, n. 82. My Appendix to this chapter gives part of the Catholic corroboration, which is probably in fact simply repetition. On the failure to publish these minor texts see Morghen, *Medioevo*, p. 259.

80. See Dondaine, *Liber*, p. 60, and Nickson, ed., 'Pseudo-Reinerius', p. lxii.

81. Thus Dossat, in 'La croisade vue par les chroniqueurs', p. 225, says that the chronicler Pierre des Vaux-de-Cernay was to some extent a witness of the crusade he described; but when it came to describing the heresies he used the *Manifestatio heresis albigensium et lugdunensium*, the work of a twelfth-century churchman, and had a solid grounding in the anti-heretic works of St. Augustine, Isidore of Seville, and St. Bernard, 'among many others'. Father Vicaire, in 'Les Cathares albigeois vus par les polémistes', pp. 110-111, notes that the Cistercian archives that Pierre des Vaux-de-Cernay had at his disposal already contained such items as the letter of Ebroin of Steinfeld on the heretics of Cologne and the correspondance of St. Bernard on his 'Arians' and Henry the Monk. Thus the works of a churchman putting down what he thinks are the ideas of heretics in the North of Europe as far back as 1143 (Ebroin of Steinfeld) — already no doubt heavily influenced by the writings of St. Augustine many centuries before — are subsumed into the Church's 'knowledge' of what is happening in early thirteenth-century Languedoc.

82. On the abundance of clerical forgeries see Bloch, *Feudal Society*, p. 91. On the significance of the 'Book of the Two Principles' see Dondaine, *Liber*, p. 50:

Certain Inquisition documents held that among the books known by the Cathars were Biblical apocrypha, the Vision of Isaiah, and the False Gospel of St. John (Secret Supper); and more recent discoveries have also led to the belief that they used works like the *Capitula* of Faustus of Milève, the romance of Barlaam and Josaphat in a Romance translation, etc. The Florence collection [containing the 'Book of the Two Principles'] seems completely unaware of these various works; so that great reserve should be exercised in using them to explain Latin neo-Manichaeism. The 'Book of the Two Principles' was composed for Cathars; how can one explain the silence of its author on these writings if they are held to be authentic? Perhaps certain groups possessed them, but great care must be exercised in generalising.

Father Dondaine seems to point to the obvious corollary when he says that the 'Book' itself 'only gives the witness of one group among the multiple splittings of Cathar sects'. On another text held to be 'Cathar', the *Interrogatio Johannis,* and one which is involved in the web of Catholic 'corroboration' of Cathar facts (see the Appendix to this chapter), see Dando, 'Hell, Purgatory and Paradise in Mediaeval Provençal Literature', p. 248, where it is noted that both the language of the original and the place of translation are in dispute. Manselli, in 'Eglises et théologies cathares', p. 135, says that the witness of the *Interrogatio,* the *Visio,* and so forth for Cathar doctrines is worthless.

Father Vicaire ('Les Cathares albigeois vus par les polémistes', p. 106) has perhaps unintentionally pointed out the way in which these texts depend on the support of the churchmen:

When it was desired to show the authenticity of a rare Cathar document, the protocol of the council of 1167 (or 1172) at St.-Félix-de-Caraman, it was at the same time noticed that most of the persons or churches mentioned were already known through the writings of the polemicists, either Catholic, or Valdensian, or Poor Catholic. It is thanks to the same polemicists that the two Cathar doctrinal works known today have been preserved: the *tractatus* reproduced by Durand de Huesca at the head of his refutation and the collection of opuscules of the school of John of Lugio, preserved by an inquisitor, and published by Dondaine under the name *De duobus principiis*. Above all, it is only through them that one can know at what moment of the evolution of Catharism and in what region one should place these two precious sources and to what extent one can use them to know the particular Catharism of Languedoc.

83. Dondaine, *Liber,* p. 51.

84. Ibid.

85. *Selected Prose,* p. 62.

86. It seems quite probable that they also practised chastity in some form; see Vicaire, 'Les Cathares albigeois vus par les polémistes', pp. 124-125.

87. We find for instance among the nobles and knights variously associated with the heresy no trace of *contemptus mundi;* they delighted in *chanson de geste* splendours (cf. Bagley, '*Paratge* in the Anonymous *Chanson*', pp. 200-203), the Count of Foix (whose sister was a heretic *perfecta* and who failed to act against the heresy) as much as anyone (cf. *Chanson de la Croisade,* ed. Martin-Chabot, II, pp. 44-56). Note also the sumptuary laws that the Abbot of Cîteaux tried to impose in the

peace conditions (ibid., I, p. 148).

88. This helps to explain the barbarism of the churchmen's methods in the crusade. Cf. the Bishop of Toulouse's treachery (ibid., II, p. 226) during Simon de Montfort's attempts to reduce Toulouse to obedience; the churchmen may not have been directly responsible for the massacre at Béziers (ibid., I, p. 58) or the massacres of non-combatants (ibid., p. 189, note) and prisoners (ibid., p. 244), but we do not hear that they lamented them. While they condemned the use of mercenaries by the South, and massacred and tortured them whenever possible (ibid., pp. 274, 276, 260), they themselves unleashed *arlotz* and adventurers on a defenceless population.

89. Cf. Bagley, '*Paratge* in the Anonymous *Chanson*', pp. 196, 199, for the way in which the Southerners regarded the French not as religious enemies but simply as usurpers. On French law and the prohibition of intermarriage see Dossat, 'Simon de Montfort', pp. 290-293, and *Chanson de la Croisade,* ed. Martin-Chabot, I, p. 280, note. On Simon's difficulties in garrisoning see ibid., pp. 88, 100, 122. French lords accepting lands from Simon had to give unlimited service for twenty years, using only French knights, and could not return to France without permission: Dossat, 'Simon de Montfort', p. 292. The conditions demanded of the Count of Toulouse for peace were those of a repressive occupation: giving up heretics, to be designated by the Church, to the Church's discretion; strict sumptuary laws; demolition of all castles; knights to live outside towns; financial support of the occupiers; submission to the will of the King of France; long penitence by the Count, and restitution of his rights at the Church's discretion (*Chanson de la Croisade,* ed. Martin-Chabot, I, pp. 148-150).

90. Ibid., II, p. 210, and note.

91. The psychology of quasi-Manichaean dualism seems to be manifested in periods of disturbance; according to Jung, the childhood archetypes of total good and total evil are then brought out as messiahs and devils, and we have crusades and witchhunts (cf. e.g. Storr, *Jung,* p. 61). Norman Cohn has clearly linked the messianic movements among the poor in mediaeval Europe—where large groups saw themselves as the Elect in an imminent Apocalypse, and the whole Church-State system as marked with the sign of the Devil: wealth—to the disturbed social conditions in which early urban and rural proletariats were arising in Northern Europe (Cohn, *Millenium,* pp. 57-59). Simple poverty, such as was universal among the peasants of the Middle Ages, was not enough: under normal conditions peasant life was tightly organised into a collectivity, which had a close (if highly unequal) relationship with its lord and where the individual was embedded for mutual help in a group of kin, so that the village was a 'social unit of great cohesiveness' (ibid., pp. 55-56). Social cohesion, not social disturbance, was the norm in Languedoc, and we find that the Languedocian heresy is not grouped by Cohn with mediaeval messianisms, though some of the earlier Northern manifestations commonly called 'Manichaean' quite rightly are (ibid., pp. 44, 46, 48). In Languedoc there was scarcely a sign of radical dissension based on wealth-hatred or of class-friction at all; there were few social disturbances until after the Albigensian Crusade and the Inquisition had done their work. (Cf., however, Guillemain, 'L'Histoire religieuse du Languedoc à la fin du XIIe siècle et au début du XIIIe', p. 104, for certain

signs of dissension; but the oppressed groups were not those that were prominent in abetting the heresy.) Several famous heretics were of the highest positions in the land; knights and barons led their defence; it is only through the sample that fell into the hands of the Inquisition that we receive an impression of the heretics as humble and ignorant (cf. e.g. Niel, *Albigeois*, pp. 83, 85; *Chanson de la Croisade*, ed. Martin-Chabot, II, pp. 200ff., 240ff., 246; Dossat, 'Les Cathares d'après les documents de l'Inquisition', p. 82). When the Crusade attacked, and any section of the population might have made its own safety by compounding with the Church, there was no split along lines of poverty and wealth (cf. *Chanson de la Croisade*, ed. Martin-Chabot, II, p. 210, and the eighty knights who supported the heretics to the death at Lavaur—ibid., p. 166, and note).

92. Guillemain, 'L'Histoire religieuse du Languedoc à la fin du XIIe siècle et au début du XIIIe', p. 104; *Chanson de la Croisade*, ed. Martin-Chabot, I, pp. 58, 60, 62.

93. See Bagley, '*Paratge* in the Anonymous *Chanson*', pp. 195, 200; *Chanson de la Croisade*, ed. Martin-Chabot, II, p. 96. It should be noted that Denis de Rougemont and René Nelli have both made of the troubadour ethic something which they feel fits with the accepted idea of the Albigensian doctrines. Rougemont, in *L'Amour et l'Occident*, traces the West's tradition of glamourising unattainable love to the troubadours. Nelli's *L'Erotique des Troubadours*, based on a much more extensive knowledge of their works, puts behind their classic 'joy' a test of the lover's worth called the *asag*, whereby he lay naked with the lady and proved his chastity. It goes without saying that Nelli thinks the *asag* was a well-kept secret (pp. 177, 197). The tone of Bernart de Ventadorn and that of the many minor poets whom Nelli cites may be close to such an idea, but it is not representative of the great troubadours in general, and in any case is hardly a Manichaean negation of the beauties of this world.

94. For the attitudes of the clergy see especially Dossat, 'Les Cathares d'après les documents de l'Inquisition', pp. 93-97.

95. *Chanson de la Croisade*, ed. Martin-Chabot, I, pp. ix, xiii-xiv, II, pp. xii, xviii-xxiii.

96. This was in 1204; Nelli, *Cathares*, p. 288. In 1215 Raymond-Roger of Foix protested in Rome that he had no connection with the place: *Chanson de la Croisade*, ed. Martin-Chabot, II, p. 52; the *Chanson de la Croisade*, however, unfortunately stops when it reaches the year 1219 (ibid., p. xiv). The Inquisition records a deposition that Montségur became the headquarters of the heresy in about 1222 (Guiraud, *Inquisition*, I, p. 147).

97. Cf. Dossat, 'Le massacre d'Avignonet', pp. 350, 349-351, 353-354. This was while Raymond was attempting an alliance with John Lackland's widow and Henry III of England, to rebel against the hegemony of France; it quickly failed.

98. Cf. Nelli, *Cathares*, pp. 314, 339, 351, and Dossat, 'Le "Bûcher de Montségur" et les Bûchers de l'Inquisition', pp. 361-369.

99. Niel, *Albigeois*, p. 117; contra Runciman, *Manichee*, p. 187: 'The Cathars certainly gave Montségur, as their one physical place of refuge, high-sounding names—as, for instance, Mount Tabor, but such names should never be taken literally. The castle had no spiritual significance to them.' Runciman may be confus-

ing Montségur with the nearby Massif de Tabe, or with the Pic de St. Barthélemy, which was sometimes called 'Mount Tabor'; cf. Nelli, *Cathares,* p. 306, Niel, *Montségur, temple,* pp. 45-51.

100. Cf. Niel, *Le Pog de Montségur,* 'Avant-propos'.

101. Cf. excellent photographs in Nelli, *Le Musée du Catharisme,* passim; also Kenner, *Pound Era,* pp. 333-334.

102. These points are summarised in Nelli, *Cathares,* pp. 289-377.

103. See e.g. Niel, *Montségur, temple,* pp. 103-104.

104. Nelli, *Cathares,* p. 386.

105. Ibid., p. 387.

106. *Essays,* p. 181, where Pound is referring specifically to Frederick II and to Cavalcanti.

107. Cf. *Visiting Card,* p. 36, on 'possibly small, but gristly and resilient' facts as components of the ideogram.

108. This wisdom is the 'il sait vivre' that must be sayable of Pound's hypothetical neophytes; hence it is 'foolproof', since it depends on a man's whole understanding of the 'process' (see above, text before n. 6). For the difference between such an esotericism and a code-book see Mullins, *This Difficult Individual,* pp. 307-308 (Edith Hamilton talking to Pound):

> EH: A Chinese friend of mine was told in the examination halls at Nanking of a great Confucian scholar, such a scholar that he wrote a letter, and there was only one man in all China who could understand it. That is not very democratic, I'm afraid. That is aristocratic, like you, Mr Pound. EP: But it is democratic as long as it provides that anyone may have the opportunity to learn enough to read that letter.

109. 'Interesting French Publications', in the *Philadelphia Book News Monthly,* XXV.I (Sept 1906), quoted in Stock, *Life,* p. 31.

110. Péladan, *Le Secret des Troubadours,* p. 59, makes the Renart of the *Roman de Renart* into the evil Church ('re in art, roi en artifice'), and sets it in combat against 'Cortoise, the wife of Belin (the innocent lamb)'— *bêler* is French for 'to bleat'. On the story of Peire Vidal, Péladan (p. 66) says that '...the parish of Pénautier belongs to the orthodox fold. Vidal disguises himself as a Catholic; the heretics think he has apostatised, and mistreat him until he makes known who he is.' But Péladan also makes the following remarks about mediaeval artists:

> ...they put their self-respect into perfecting procedures....the sculptor of 1300 is not the manipulator of wet earth that we know; with hammer and chisel in his hand, he faced the stone block [p. 13].
> ...those who conceived the choir at Beauvais...considered themselves far superior to their curates [p. 24].
> Each man gave to the Virgin Mother the features dearest to his heart, and I can see no sin in using even one's mistress's beauty for sacred effigies [p. 26].

Though Pound would later have agreed about the 'imperial dream' of the Papacy (p. 52), he would not have accepted Péladan's thesis that the source of the troubadour heresy was Gnostic (p. 21, etc.).

For Zielinski's phrase see *La Sibylle,* p. 14.

111. The essay was delivered as a lecture at Mead's Quest Society, and printed in *Quest*, IV.I (Oct 1912).

112. Moore, *Unicorn*, p. 106; Starkie, *From Gautier to Eliot*, p. 122; Moore, *Unicorn*, p. 113. Note however that Levi is unlikely to have 'revived the sect of Rosicrucians, and . . . given Péladan an important position in its hierarchy' in 1889 (Starkie, *From Gautier to Eliot*, p. 122), since he died in 1875. For the relations between all these spiritualists, and also with Pound and Yeats, see especially Duncan, 'The H. D. Book: Part I. Chapter 5', pp. 4-19; 'The H. D. Book: Part II. Nights and Days. Chapter 4', pp. 27-60; Moore, *Unicorn*, pp. 105-112.

113. 'Psychology', pp. 37-41, 44 (*Spirit*, pp. 87-89, 92). Pound (ibid.) picks out the 'castle' in the third stanza of the same poem as part of the passage that may have 'visionary significance'. The relevant parts of the poem (Arnaut, *Canzoni*, no. XII, *Doutz brais e critz*) may be translated thus (cf. also Pound's translation, *Essays*, pp. 135-136):

> I was not lost
> nor did I take side-tracks
> when I first entered the castle, within the outer walls,
> where my lady is, for whom I have a great hunger. . . .
>
> I was well approved of
> and my words accepted,
> because in the choice [of her] I was not at all stupid,
> but preferred to take fine gold rather than copper,
> the day that I and my lady kissed each other
> and she made me a shield of her beautiful indigo cloak
> so that false flatterers, snake-tongues,
> should not see it, from whom such evil talk escapes.

When he published 'Arnaut Daniel (Razo)' in the spring of 1920, Pound was having doubts about his idea: 'I had once thought of the mantle of indigo as of a thing seen in a vision, but I have now only fancy to support this' ('Arnaut Daniel', p. 46 [*Essays*, p. 111]); but obviously the idea stayed with him. Rita Lejeune, trying to explain William IX of Aquitaine's 'God let me live so long yet / that I have my hands in her cloak' (see Chapter 5, text before n. 76), offers some interesting parallels:

> . . . it is true that the idea of the 'cloak' is an idea of protection. Let us add that this explains the *senhal* [poetic name] that the troubadour Raimon de Miraval gives around 1200 to one of his great muses: Mantel. It explains the iconographic theme of the Virgin with the Cloak, which only arises later, in the thirteenth century. The origin of this belief is not certain; let it suffice to note here that William IX of Aquitaine must already have known of the cloak as a symbol of protection in certain legal and religious rites, and that he had the idea of applying it to his beloved.

She adds the footnote:

> Cf. [Paul] PERDRIZET [*La Vierge de Miséricorde*, Paris 1908], p. 23: 'Jacob Grimm asserts that for the ancient Germans the cloak of kings and queens, lords and ladies was a sign of protection . . . Marriage ceremonies offer some-

thing analogous . . .' (Germany, Russian Jews). ' "Please extend the spread of your cloak over your servant" says Ruth to Booz when she invokes their blood relationship so that he will marry her'. 'The role of the cloak in matrimonial rites perhaps explains the role of the cloak in the rites of adoption and legitimisation. In the Middle Ages, among the peoples of the North (Germany, France, England), a man who adopted or legitimised a child covered it solemnly with his cloak' . . . .

She refers to the placing of the hands on or under the cloak of the lord by the vassal in offering homage ('Formules féodales', p. 245, and note).

114. 'Psychology', pp. 44-48 (*Spirit*, pp. 92-95).

115. Ibid., pp. 41-43 (*Spirit*, pp. 90-91).

116. Ibid., pp. 41, 47 (text changed in *Spirit*, p. 90, to 'Provencal song is never wholly disjunct from. . . .'; ibid., p. 95).

117. Cf. Fauriel, *History of Provencal Poetry*, pp. 35-117; Paris, *Mélanges*, pp. 539-615. Pound had already connected ' "The April-like Queen," or songs of like character' with pagan spring dances in honour of Flora and Venus in *The Spirit of Romance* (p. 39, referring to *A l'entrade del tens clar*, Appel, *Chrestomathie*, no. 48). The Kalenda Maya noted in 'Terra Italica', p. 58, is a May dance by Raimbaut de Vaqueras (*Poems* no. XV). Gaston Paris traced the celebratory May dance, found in Homer but apparently lacking in the Roman world, from our first glimpses of it in the Middle Ages (*Mélanges*, pp. 589-597). The atmosphere of these dances was always that of a 'fictitious "woman's Saturnalia" ' (Spitzer, 'Mozarabic Lyric', p. 17; cf. Paris, *Mélanges*, pp. 601, 607), and this was converted by the Provencal aristocracy into the form of the *pastourelle*, the song of the knight's encounter with a shepherdess, via the song where the shepherdess is imagined singing of her love (ibid., p. 560). The troubadour lyric, with its *joy*, its *amors*, its obligatory spring-opening and its bypassing of marriage and the 'jealous one', grew from these songs of the May dances (ibid., pp. 609-612). James J. Wilhelm has attempted to show that the spring-element in the Provençal lyric simply grew out of the clerical Latin lyric, but the handful of Latin examples (Wilhelm, *The Cruelest Month*, pp. 97-99, 105-107) do not convince one of a continuity of feeling.

118. See 'Cavalcanti', in *Essays*, pp. 149-200, passim.

119. Pound's description, ibid., p. 173.

120. Valli, *Linguaggio*, pp. 16-17.

121. Ibid.; Péladan, *Le Secret des Troubadours*, p. 68; Gourmont, *Dante, Béatrice*, p. 55, and note.

122. *Visiting Card*, p. 22: 'In his *After Strange Gods* Eliot loses all the threads of Arachne, and a new edition of Gabriele Rossetti's *Mistero dell'Amor Platonico* (1840) would be useful'; Valli, *Linguaggio*, p. 16, note.

123. Aroux, *Clef de la Comédie*, s.v. *Albigéisme*.

124. Cf. Valli, *Linguaggio*, p. 18, and Aroux, *Dante, hérétique*, dedication to Pius IX; the report of Aroux given by Valli (*Linguaggio*, pp. 18-19) is extremely unfavourable, and would suggest to Pound that Aroux had the same faults as Valli himself, but worse; and Valli makes it clear that Aroux was the source of most of Péladan's ideas, which Pound had seen; so that Pound might well feel he need not bother with Aroux.

125. *Essays,* pp. 173ff.

126. Ibid., pp. 173, 177.

127. Ibid., pp. 178-181.

128. Ibid., p. 180.

129. Ibid.

130. See above, n. 113 and preceding text, Chapter 8, text before nn. 52, 91.

131. *Selected Prose,* p. 55.

132. Modern interpretations, e.g. by Mylonas and by Kerényi, are much less clear cut than those of the post-Frazer generation; Mylonas (*Eleusis and the Eleusinian Mysteries,* pp. 312ff.) pours scorn on the idea of the enacted holy marriage, and Kerényi (*Eleusis,* pp. 146-148) sets it aside in favour of an enactment of Demeter's search for Persephone.

133. Jane Harrison held that Demeter and Persephone, the two goddesses of Eleusis, were a Corn-goddess represented at two stages of her life, and that Dionysos was Demeter's offspring at the ritual (*Prolegomena,* pp. 263, 240-249); Cornford held that 'the sacred marriage of Kore and Pluto at Eleusis is to be explained as the descent of the Corn-maiden into the underground storehouse after harvest, in order that she may be fertilised by the God of the grain-store and re-emerge as seed for the new sowing in autumn' (*Comedy,* pp. 26-27).

134. *Kulchur,* p. 263. Scotus Erigena was one of the few Western scholars in the ninth century who could read Greek; his translation of Dionysius the Areopagite was very influential in 'Platonising' Christianity. 'Scotus Erigena in Provence' may mean that Erigena had stayed in that area, and either helped to pick up or propagated Hellenist influences, which is possible; or it may refer to the idea of the Church that the Albigensians read Erigena, which appears likely to have been mere gossip (see Makin, 'Ezra Pound and Scotus Erigena', pp. 61-64). In 'Mediaeval Music and Yves Tinayre' (1936), p. 187, Pound said that out of 'dance tunes' like '*La Regine Avrillouse* ['the April-like Queen' — see above, n. 117] came the grace of European civilisation right up to Botticelli', and implied that Erigena was a factor in this. For Avicenna and Grosseteste see *Essays,* pp. 158-161, 173-191.

135. Latreille, Delaruelle, and Palanque, *Histoire du Catholicisme en France,* 1, pp. 47, 112.

136. Ibid., p. 82, and Mâle, *L'Art religieux du XIIᵉ s. en France,* p. 194. In 1912 Pound noted that 'At Marseilles the Greek settlement was very ancient': 'Psychology', p. 49 (*Spirit,* p. 96); Benoit, *Recherches sur l'hellénisation du Midi de la Gaule,* pp. 217-220, says that Marseilles was an important Greek centre from the middle of the seventh century BC. Provençal visual art shows strong resemblances with that of Byzantium; cf. *Essays,* p. 151, and Mâle, *L'Art religieux du XIIᵉ s. en France,* ch. 1, passim. Finally, there seems to have been a particularly hardy survival of learning in classical letters in Provence proper during the 'Dark Ages'; cf. Cappuyns, *Erigène,* p. 17.

The question is whether a specifically pagan Hellenic cult could have survived in Southern Gaul. But Pound probably believed that pagan elements could have moved in and out of the contemporary Church. The 'few clear pages in Davidsohn' that Pound refers to (see above, text before n. 2) are probably those which describe how pagan rituals were taken into Christian worship (e.g. *Storia di Firenze,* I, pp.

1065, 51, IV.II, p. 124, recalling the mourning of Demeter). Pound would also have been interested in the Christian assimilation of Christ to the Sun, and the Virgin to the Moon (cf. Rahner, *Myths*, pp. 106, 165, etc., and Bainton, *Early and Medieval Christianity*, pp. 31, etc.).

137. Cf. above, text before nn. 6, 134, and 'Psychology', pp. 47-48 (*Spirit*, p. 95); cf. Pound's comment on the size of the 'keep' at Montségur: *Cantos*, 101/725: 752:

> The hills here are blue-green with juniper,
> the stream, as Achilöos there below us,
> here one man can hold the whole pass
> over this mountain, at Mont Ségur the chief's cell
>
> you can enter it sideways only, TSO is here named
>
> from the rope bridge, hemp rope? a reed rope?
> and they pay the land tax in buckwheat.
> Food was in Tolosa, not chemical

138. *Selected Prose*, pp. 56, 59.
139. Ibid., p. 55.
140. Ibid.
141. *Cantos*, 74/435:462.
142. *Selected Prose*, p. 56.
143. Cf. Mylonas, *Eleusis and the Eleusinian Mysteries*, p. 294:

Scholars refused to admit the phallus in the cult of Demeter and so Körte maintained that not a phallus but the female pudenda, the *kteis*, suggested by the story of Baubo, was contained in the kiste [a reliquary]. According to Körte, by sliding the *kteis* over his body, the initiate believed that he was reborn, that he became an initiate of Demeter. Kern, an admirer of Körte's, going a step farther, maintained that the initiate actually came into a symbolic union with the Goddess by manipulating his own genital organ in the *kteis*.

Pound did not necessarily have these scholarly fantasies in mind, but was clearly thinking of the female pudenda in some ritual sense. *Pecten* and *kteis* are, respectively, Latin and Greek words, apparently cognate, both meaning 'hair', 'comb', 'pubic hair'; Callimachus and others use *kteis* for the female pudenda: cf. Callimachus, [*Works*], no. 343, etc.

144. *Selected Prose*, p. 59.
145. See Chapter 8, text before n. 63.
146. *Selected Prose*, p. 59.
147. *Confucius to Cummings*, p. 69.
148. Dronke, *European Love-Lyric*, I, pp. 70-71.
149. Ibid., p. 73.
150. Ibid., p. 89; see further examples of sexual metaphor: ibid.
151. *Cantos*, 23/109:113. The protagonists here are Peire and Austors de Maen-

sac and Bernart de Tierci, whose story is in Boutiere and Schutz, *Biographies*, p. 300, and is recounted in 'Troubadours', p. 429 (*Essays*, pp. 96-97). In the 'Troubadours' passage Pound compares Bernart de Tierci to Menelaus, in that Peire had abducted Bernart's wife and Bernart pursued them to the castle of their protector, the Dauphin d'Auvergne. The Dauphin's castle is therefore Troy. In *Cantos*, 5/18: 22, Pound says, 'Troy in Auvergnat / While Menelaus piled up the church at port / He kept Tyndarida.' But here in *Cantos*, 23/109:113, Montségur is Troy; the two stories seem to blend.

In this passage Pound has Bernart going 'past Chaise Dieu, / And he went after it all to Mont Segur.' Rachewiltz, 'Pagan and Magic Elements', p. 184, calls La Chaise-Dieu, an abbey founded in 1046, a 'main Albigensian site', and (p. 192) refers to 'Mt Ségur which, with its Abbey of Chaise Dieu, was the stronghold of the Albigensian heretics'; I know of no evidence for these ideas, but Rachewiltz may have had them from Pound himself. See above, n. 1.

Another part of Pound's myth linking the troubadour *vidas* to the Albigensians is in *Cantos*, 48/243:253 (first published in 1937):

> and the stair there still broken
> the flat stones of the road, Mt Segur.
> From Val Cabrere, were two miles of roofs to San Bertrand
> so that a cat need not set foot in the road
> where now is an inn, and bare rafters [. . .]
> Savairic; hither Gaubertz;
> > Said they wd. not be under Paris.

This is developed from the *vida* of Gausbert de Poicibot (Boutière and Schutz, *Biographies*, pp. 229-230) which is recounted in 'Troubadours', pp. 427-428 (*Essays*, pp. 95-96) and used in *Cantos*, 5/18:22, with the Maensac *vida*. The story of the *vida*, where Gausbert de Poicibot is knighted by Savaric, goes off, and comes back to find his wife has turned whore, is the only obvious connection between Gausbert and Savaric; however, a close look at the *Chanson de la Croisade* shows the probable reason why Pound has both coming to St. Bertrand.

The full name of the place is St. Bertrand-de-Comminges. As Kenner has mentioned in *Pound Era*, p. 338, it was an important city of Roman Gaul. It also saw the first church known in France, built in the fourth century (cf. Latreille, Delaruelle, and Palanque, *Histoire du Catholicisme en France*, 1, p. 82, and Mâle, *L'Art religieux du XIIes. en France*, p. 194). Pound might well therefore have used its present comparative desolation as an emblem of vanished civilisation.

Savaric de Mauléon was a very important Poitevin lord who later became King John's seneschal in the South, and who was himself a troubadour — addressing at least one song to the wife of Raymond of Toulouse (see Chaytor, *Savaric de Mauléon*, pp. 42ff., 65ff., and *Chanson de la Croisade*, ed. Martin-Chabot, I, p. 153). At one point in the Albigensian Crusade he appeared to be the saviour of the South; but his intervention was not decisive, and after he had left the service of Raymond he did great damage to the South's cause. Raymond had not paid him for his help, and so he held Raymond's son to ransom; and Raymond was absent negotiating with him when he was needed at Moissac. See ibid., pp. 152, and note, 204-208, etc., 274, and note.

These passages in the *Chanson* give a clue to Pound's 'San Bertrand / . . . / Savairic; hither Gaubertz; / Said they wd. not be under Paris.' The Abbot of Cîteaux has given Raymond a list of conditions (see above, n. 89), including the demand that they should 'in everything go by the will of the King of France' (*Chanson de la Croisade,* ed. Martin-Chabot, I, p. 150); Raymond's vassals refuse, and the citizens of Moissac and Agen say 'they would sooner flee to the Bordeaux country by river / than that men of Bar or France should be their lords' (ibid., p. 152). Thus Pound: 'Said they wd. not be under Paris.' Immediately after this we read that Raymond wrote to all his friends, including the Count of Comminges (of whose territory St. Bertrand-de-Comminges was of course the chief place) and Savaric de Mauléon, for help. The names of the Count of Comminges and of Savaric then recur together as they help the Crusade, e.g. ibid., pp. 204-208.

152. *Cantos,* 76/452-453:480-481. Ussel is near Ventadour; though this rain and wind is of desolation, it was also the weather in the summer of 1919 when Pound visited these places; see Kenner, *Pound Era,* p. 335. For the 1919 decision about Montségur, see Chapter 4, n. 66.

153. Cf. for *periplous* e.g. Baumann, *Rose,* pp. 60-62; Brooke-Rose, *A ZBC of Ezra Pound,* p. 114; Pearlman, *Barb of Time,* pp. 165-166. As against 'Aquinas-map', cf. *Letters,* to Hubert Creekmore, Feb 1939.

154. *Cantos,* 101/725:752 (quoted above, n. 137).

155. *Cantos,* 192/618-619:651-652. For Anubis see also Rachewiltz, 'Pagan and Magic Elements', p. 178. For 'And if I see her not', see Chapter 7, text before n. 83.

156. *Era in penser d'amor,* Cavalcanti, *Rime,* no. XXX; *Cantos,* 4/16:20. Cavalcanti sends a 'river' to Pinella (see Chapter 8, text before n. 110) both here and in *Cantos,* 91/616:650; see also the image of 'this light / as a river', in *Cantos,* 107/762:787 (cf. Makin, 'Ezra Pound and Scotus Erigena', pp. 76, 81). The river is 'crystal' in *Cantos,* 91/616-617:650, and is also the 'wave-in-the-stone' image from Excideuil that recalls the spiritual life before Montségur, in *Cantos,* 29/145:150:

> So Arnaut turned there
> Above him the wave pattern cut in the stone
> Spire-top alevel the well-curb

80/510:544:

> and the wave pattern runs in the stone
> on the high parapet (Excideuil)
> Mt Segur and the city of Dioce

107/758:783:

> wave pattern at Excideuil
> A spire level the well-curb

and 90/607:641:

> Taking form now,
>   the rilievi,
>   the curled stone at the marge

Cf. perhaps *Cantos,* 110/777:7. Professor Kenner informs me that he identifies Arnaut in *Cantos,* 29/145:150, with T. S. Eliot on the authority of Dorothy Pound, and that the only significance of Excideuil is that it was Giraut de Borneil's birthplace. However, the second quotation above clearly associates Excideuil with Montségur. Boris de Rachewiltz, who was of course close to Pound, baldly asserts, in 'Pagan and Magic Elements', p. 192, that Excideuil was a 'main Albigensian site', but I have come across nothing to substantiate this. For the dialogue between Pound and Eliot at Excideuil in August 1919, see Kenner, *Pound Era,* pp. 336-337.

Canto XCI is full of imagery associated with illuminating love, and begins with a line from Bernart's poem where he sees the lark rising against the sunlight and falling in ecstasy (cf. Chapter 7, text before n. 58). Another passage, in *Cantos,* 74/430-431:456-457, links Bernart's poem (with the line '*Che sublia es laissa cader*') to a sacred mountain (Taishan), woman, and the sun 'in periplum'.

157. The previous Canto ends with a reference to 'Queen Cytherea' and to her sphere, the third sphere of heaven.

158. *Cantos,* 76/452-453:480-481; see above, text before n. 152.

159. ' "In questa lumera appresso" ' is adapted from the lines about the 'whore of Jericho', Rahab, who is described by Folquet de Marseille in Dante, *Paradiso,* 9.112ff. Just before Folquet, Cunizza has been speaking; their positions as 'sinners' redeemed by sensual love are linked by Pound (see Chapter 9, text before n. 59). In *Cantos,* 92/620:653, Pound quotes directly from Cunizza with ' "fui chiamat'/e qui refulgo" ' (Dante, *Paradiso,* 9.32; cf. Chapter 9, text before n. 56).

160. *Essays,* p. 151; cf. 'Psychology', p. 42 (*Spirit,* p. 90), on 'a cult stricter, or more subtle, than that of the celibate ascetics, a cult for the purgation of the soul by a refinement of, and lordship over, the senses.'

For Pound the chain of awareness did not end with Montségur; the Templars were a later link. The Order of the Knights Templars, originally founded as a permanent crusading order in the Holy Land, had become increasingly rich and powerful; as a kind of international bank, it numbered kings among its clients (cf. Parker, *Templars in England,* pp. 59ff.). This drew avaricious attention, and Philip the Fair eventually succeeded in having the Order abolished by the Pope; in France he proceeded as if it had been condemned. The burning of its Grand Master, Jacques de Molay, took place in 1314 (cf. Melville, *Templiers,* pp. 246ff.). Pound suggests that Molay was directing anti-usurious financial dealings which aroused the wrath of the usurers:

> Was De Molay making loans without interest?
> (*Cantos,* 87/576:612)

He suggests that Molay and his Order, which had connections with the mediaeval church-builders and with the later Freemasons, preserved something of the Greek knowledge of the 'golden section':

> Builders had kept the proportion,
> did Jacques de Molay
> know these proportions?
> and was Erigena ours?
> (*Cantos,* 90/605:639; cf. especially ibid., 87/573:609, and Gimpel,
> *Cathedral Builders,* pp. 93, 107ff.)

He links the former palace of the Dukes of Aquitaine, the Hall of Justice in Poitiers
— a town with which Molay had connections — with a tower at San Ku in China. In
the Hall of Justice one can stand without casting a shadow (cf. Kenner, *Pound Era,*
p. 326, and especially *Kulchur,* p. 109), and the Chinese held that 'in the capital,
the gnomon standing on the exact meridian does not cast any shadow on the day of
the summer solstice' (Rachewiltz, 'Pagan and Magic Elements', p. 190). *Cantos,*
90/605:639, links all these together, and concludes with Scotus Erigena, for Pound
a kingpin of the Hellenic awareness.

161. 'Psychology', p. 50 (*Spirit,* p. 97).

162. Cf. Chapter 9, text before n. 75, Chapter 8, text before n. 124.

163. *Kulchur,* p. 261 (quoted in Chapter 1, text before n. 96).

164. See Chapter 4, text before n. 13.

165. *Confucius/Digest,* p. 47 ('Tseng's Comment', VI.1).

166. See Chapter 8, text before n. 41.

167. *Cantos,* 7/24:28 (of Henry James); by contrast, Pound was afraid of the jar-
gonising effect of the universities in his own time.

168. Cf. Stock, *Life,* p. 76.

169. Cf. *Letters,* to John Drummond, 18 Feb 1932.

170. *Cantos,* 107/758:783.

171. Cf. Dick, *Writers at Work,* p. 111.

172. At least it seems to me that, as lawyers always do, Coke rejected precedents
if they did not follow the ancient principles of English law; but he buttressed the
antiquity of his choice of these principles with semi-fictional sources, for which see
Pocock, *The Ancient Constitution and the Feudal Law,* pp. 42ff.

173. Cf. Dick, *Writers at Work,* p. 110.

174. Cf. his excellent definition in *Kulchur,* p. 127.

175. Cf. *Spirit,* p. 44, note; *New Review,* Winter 1931-32, quoted in Stock,
Exile, p. 23; cf. Stock, *Life,* p. 287; *Cantos,* 23/107:111; *ABC of Reading,* p. 14;
cf. Stock, *Life,* p. 300.

176. Makin, 'Pound's Provence and the Mediaeval Paideuma', p. 53.

177. I think it is a symptom of this, that Dante drops out as a live force in this
section: cf. Wilhelm, *Dante and Pound,* pp. 115ff.

178. Makin, 'Pound's Provence and the Mediaeval Paideuma', p. 53.

179. *Cantos,* 48/243:253.

180. *Translations,* p. 23; cf. *Gaudier-Brzeska,* p. 84.

181. *Kulchur,* p. 261.

182. See Chapter 9, text before n. 95.

183. This is a description of the general effect of Jeanroy's *Poésie lyrique des
Troubadours.*

184. See Chapter 5, nn. 56, 54, 81.

APPENDIX 2. ELEANOR, BERNART, BERTRAN, AND ARNAUT.

1. *Essays,* p. 122; Arnaut, *Canzoni,* ed. Toja no. IV.

2. Bertran, *Lieder,* ed. Appel, no. 17; cf. Chapter 8, n. 106.

3. Pound notes that Arnaut says he has the song from someone else; but I think

he would have to have seen the *razo* to infer so much. See below, text before n. 25.

4. Bertran, *Lieder,* no. 28, where Bertran pretends to run out of rhymes:

> Tell Sir Roger and all his kin
> that I can't find any more *omba*'s, *om*'s or *esta*'s.

The form and the rhymes of this song are taken from Arnaut, *Canzoni,* no. XVII (though Toja notes—ibid., p. 10—that Arnaut de Durfort and Uc de Saint-Circ also used this form). That Pound thought of it as a particular test for a poet is shown by the draft Canto III (*Three Cantos of a Poem of Some Length: III,* p. 198):

> I've strained my ear for -*ensa,* -*ombra,* and -*ensa,*
> And cracked my wit on delicate canzoni

and his remarks on its syzygy in *Letters,* to Felix E. Schelling, 8 and 9 July 1922.

5. 'Arnaut Daniel', p. 44 (*Essays,* p. 109).

6. *Cantos,* 6/22:26. Stronski, *Folquet,* p. 43*, takes Bernart to be of the older generation. Dating him by Appel's conjectures about his stay in England, he would be poetically active as early as 1154 (cf. Bernart, *Lieder,* p. lix), though I would point out that Appel gives no reason why the poem written to the 'Queen of the Normans' should not have been written before the 1173 revolt, and the poem about the 'King of the English and the Duke of the Normans' after it. But in any case, since Toja puts Arnaut's birth at around 1150-60, and Appel puts Bernart's birth at around 1120-30, all we know is that Bernart was between twenty and forty years older than Arnaut (Arnaut, *Canzoni,* pp. 9, 11; Bernart, *Lieder,* p. lix). Bertran de Born was probably born in about 1140, and our last information about him is dated 1202 (Clédat, *Bertran,* pp. 22, 92; cf. Appel, *Bertran,* p. 4, note). Chronologically, the three troubadours were in a position to know each other.

7. Cf. Chapter 4, text before n. 25.

8. Bernard, *Chansons,* p. 54.

9. In '*Dompna pois de me no'us cal*', where Bertran just has *N'Audiartz* (cf. *Lieder,* no. 5), Pound translates 'Of Audiart at Malemort'; and he makes considerable play of Malemort both in that translation and in *Near Perigord.* On the identity of Audiart see below, text before n. 16.

10. Bernard, *Chansons,* no. 29.

11. Cf. Ramsay, *Empire,* p. 176.

12. Bernart, *Lieder,* pp. lv-lvii.

13. Bernard, *Chansons,* no. 10; the line 'I shall be well-mannered in court' has been read as 'I shall be present in court': cf. Bernart, *Lieder,* p. 197, note.

14. Text and composite translation, Chapter 4, n. 26, Chapter 7, text before n. 1.

15. Cf. especially Paris, *Melanges,* p. 512.

16. Boutière and Schutz, *Biographies,* p. 170, has 'Audiart' as the friend of Maria de Ventadorn. Maria, according to the *razo,* was sister to the 'Maeut of Montaignac' loved by Bertran de Born—these two with Helis de Montfort making the 'three of Turenne', the daughters of Raimon II of Turenne (ibid., pp. 75, 76-77, and Bertran, *Lieder,* no. 8).

17. Pound has Bernart meeting Eleanor/Audiart when she was 'Turning on

thirty years', which would be around 1152, the year in which Eleanor divorced Louis and married Henry II. As we have seen (above, n. 6), Bertran was probably born in about 1140.

18. Cf. Bertran, *Bertran*, p. 201, but Stronski, *Bertran*, p. 96.

19. Cf. Boutière and Schutz, *Biographies*, p. 319, and Stronski, *Folquet*, p. 160.

20. Boutière and Schutz, *Biographies*, pp. 76-77, cf. p. 24.

21. Arnaut, *Canzoni*, no. XVIII (cf. Chapter 8, text before n. 11); 'Arnaut Daniel', p. 45 (*Essays*, p. 110).

22. *Hesternae Rosae*, II. For a correct translation, see Chapter 8, n. 18.

23. Arnaut, *Canzoni*, p. 166; see Chapter 8, n. 13.

24. See Chapter 8, text before n. 98.

25. Arnaut, *Canzoni*, p. 11; the *razo* is in Boutière and Schutz, *Biographies*, pp. 62-63, and the song in Arnaut, *Canzoni*, no. VII.

26. In fact, Arnaut merely says that he has not forgotten the lady:

> To Miells-de-ben give thanks, song,
> whom [i.e. Miells-de-ben] Arnaut doesn't forget.

Cf. Arnaut, *Canzoni*, no. V:

> and tell her that Arnaut forgets
> every other love for her for whom he makes himself fine.

27. 'Arnaut Daniel', p. 45 (*Essays*, p. 110).

28. Paris, *Mélanges*, p. 511. For Pound on Gaston Paris cf. e.g. *Confucius to Cummings*, p. 79; cf. especially *ABC of Reading*, p. 11, *Impact*, p. 260, and *Gaudier-Brzeska*, p. 115.

29. Cf. especially Stronski, *Folquet*, p. ix. We know that Arnaut attended the coronation of Philippe-Auguste in 1180 (Arnaut, *Canzoni*, note to no. XII, line 51), but given the nature of contemporary war this does not make it unlikely that Arnaut should have been on close terms with Philippe's spasmodic enemy, Richard. For Richard's literary activities see Chapter 6, text before n. 56.

30. See above, n. 2, and Chapter 8, n. 106.

31. See above, text before nn. 1, 25.

32. See above, n. 4.

33. Arnaut's obscurity is mocked also by the Monk of Montaudon, cited in Arnaut, *Canzoni*, p. 8.

34. See above, n. 29.

35. See above, Chapter 3, n. 53; Boutière and Schutz, *Biographies*, p. 59. Stronski, *Folquet*, pp. 3* ff., and Raimbaut, *Works*, pp. 25ff., confirm, respectively, the information in the *vidas* that Folquet de Marseille's father came from Genoa and that Raimbaut d'Orange possessed Courthézon. This information is very specific, and could not be inferred from any general considerations. By contrast, the *romans d'amour* invented by the *vida* writers tend not to include such specific data.

36. See Boutière and Schutz, *Biographies*, p. 24, notes.

37. Bertran, *Lieder*, no. 39. There is a final indication in the gloss by the six-teenth-century Italian Provençalist Giovanni Maria Barbieri, who says that the 'Desirat' named at the end of Arnaut's sestina is Bertran, for they 'were such friends

that they called each other Desirat. . . .' (Arnaut, *Canzoni,* no. XVIII, cf. p. 10, note). This is in keeping with a practice widespread among troubadours and sometimes including their patrons, commented on at length by Stronski (*Folquet,* p. 27*). Stronski also noted that Barbieri's statement seems to be confirmed by a manuscript gloss in MS. H: '[Dezirat] is Sir Bertran de Born with whom he was known as Desirat' (ibid., p. 34*, note). However, these sources may not support each other, since Barbieri may well have seen MS. H; and in any case, as Stronski points out (ibid.), the *razo*ist could well have seen the envoi to *Lancan son passat* (Arnaut, *Canzoni,* no. IV), where Arnaut sends the song to Bertran, and have deduced the rest for himself. Above all it seems to me that the sexual tone of the 'Desirat' lines (see Chapter 8, n. 18) is continuous with the rest of the poem, and the switch to another addressee is sudden and unlikely.

38. Boutière and Schutz, *Biographies,* p. 21; Bertran, *Poésies,* pp. xlvi-xlvii.

BIBLIOGRAPHY

❋❋❋❋❋❋❋❋❋❋

Note: For the publishing history of Pound's works see Gallup, Donald, *A Bibliography of Ezra Pound.*

Adams, Henry, *Mont-Saint-Michel and Chartres,* enl. ed., Boston, 1933.

Adams, John, and Thomas Jefferson, *The Adams-Jefferson Letters,* ed. L. J. Cappon, 2 vols., Chapel Hill, N.C., 1959.

Andrea Capellano, *Trattato d'Amore,* ed. Salvatore Battaglia, Rome, 1947.

Appel, Carl, *Bertran von Born,* Halle, 1931.

——, *Provenzalische Chrestomathie,* Leipzig, 1895.

——, *Provenzalische Chrestomathie,* 6th ed., Leipzig, 1930.

Arnaut Daniel, *Canzoni,* ed. Gianluigi Toja, Florence, 1960.

——, *Les poésies d'Arnaut Daniel,* ed. René Lavaud, Toulouse, 1910.

——, *La vita e le opere del trovatore Arnaldo Daniello,* ed. U. A. Canello, Halle, 1883.

Aroux, Eugène, *Clef de la Comédie anti-catholique de Dante Alighieri,* Paris, 1856.

——, *Dante, hérétique, révolutionnaire et socialiste,* Paris, 1854.

Aston, S. C., 'The Provencal *planh:* I, The lament for a prince', in *Mélanges de philologie romane dédiés à la mémoire de Jean Boutière (1899-1967),* ed. I Cluzel and F. Pirot, 2 vols., Liège, 1971, I, pp. 23-30.

Aucassin et Nicolette: Chantefable du XIIIe siècle, ed. Mario Roques, 2nd ed., Paris, 1936.

Avalle, d'Arco Silvio, *La Letteratura medievale in Lingua d'Oc nella sua Tradizione manoscritta,* Turin, 1961.

Bagley, C. P., '*Paratge* in the Anonymous *Chanson de la Croisade Albigeoise*', in *French Studies,* XXI.3 (July 1967), pp. 195-204.

Bainton, Roland H., *Early and Medieval Christianity,* London, 1965.

Baumann, Walter, *The Rose in the Steel Dust: An Examination of the Cantos of Ezra Pound,* Bern, 1967.

Bec, Pierre, ed., *Petite Anthologie de la lyrique occitane du moyen âge,* Avignon, 1954.

Benedict of Peterborough, *Gesta Regis Henrici Secundi,* ed. William Stubbs, 2 vols., London, 1867.

Benoit, Fernand, *Recherches sur l'hellénisation du Midi de la Gaule,* Aix-en-Provence, 1965.

Benson, Eugene, *Sordello and Cunizza,* London, 1903.

Benton, John F., 'The Court of Champagne as a Literary Center', in *Speculum,* XXXVI.4 (Oct 1961), pp. 551-591.

Bernard, St., of Clairvaux, *The Letters of St. Bernard of Clairvaux,* ed. Bruno Scott-James, London, 1953.

Bernard de Ventadour, *Chansons d'amour,* ed. Moshé Lazar, Paris, 1966.

Bernart de Ventadorn, *Bernart von Ventadorn: Seine Lieder,* ed. Carl Appel, Halle, 1915.

Bertoni, G., *Il Duecento,* Milan, 1911.

———, ed., *Provenza e Italia: Studi,* Florence, 1930.

———, *I trovatori d'Italia,* Modena, 1915.

Bertran de Born, *Bertran von Born,* ed. Albert Stimming, 2nd ed., Halle, 1913.

———, *Die Lieder Bertrans von Born,* ed. Carl Appel, Halle, 1932.

———, *Poésies complètes de Bertran de Born,* ed. Antoine Thomas, Toulouse, 1888.

Bezzola, R. R., *Les Origines et la Formation de la littérature courtoise en Occident (500-1200),* 5 vols., Paris, 1944-63.

Bloch, Marc, *Feudal Society,* tr. L. A. Manyon, London, 1961.

Bloch, Oscar, and Walther von Wartburg, *Dictionnaire étymologique de la langue française,* Paris, 1932.

Boase, T. S. R., 'Fontevrault and the Plantagenets', in *British Architectural Association Journal,* 3rd s., XXXIV (1971), pp. 1-10.

Bondanella, Peter E., 'Arnaut Daniel and Dante's *Rime Petrose:* A Re-Examination', in *Studies in Philology,* LXVIII.4 (Oct 1971), pp. 416-434.

Bordonove, Georges, *La Vie quotidienne des Templiers,* Paris, 1975.

Bouquet, Martin, et al., eds., *Recueil des Historiens des Gaules et de la France,* 24 vols., Paris, 1738-1904.

Boutière, Jean, and A. H. Schutz, eds., *Les Biographies des Troubadours,* 2nd ed., Paris, 1973.

Bowen, Catherine Drinker, *The Lion and the Throne: The Life and Times of Sir Edward Coke,* London, 1957.

Brittain, F., ed., *The Medieval Latin and Romance Lyric to A.D. 1300,* 2nd ed., Cambridge, 1951.

Brooke-Rose, Christine, *A ZBC of Ezra Pound,* London, 1971.

Brown, Norman O., *Life Against Death: The Psychoanalytical Meaning of History,* London, 1959.

Bunting, Basil, *Collected Poems,* 2nd ed., London, 1970.

Bush, Ronald, *The Genesis of Ezra Pound's Cantos,* Princeton, N.J., 1976.

Callimachus, [*Works*], ed. C. A. Trypanis, London and Cambridge, Mass., 1958.

Camproux, Charles, 'Faray un vers *tot* covinen', in *Mélanges de langue et de littérature...Jean Frappier,* 2 vols., Geneva, 1970, I, pp. 159-172.

Cappuyns, Maieul, *Jean Scot Erigène, sa vie, son oeuvre, sa pensée,* Paris and Louvain, 1933.

Carducci, Giosuè, *Opere di Giosuè Carducci,* 30 vols., Bologna, 1944.

Cavalcanti, Guido, *Le Rime,* ed. Guido Favati, Milan, 1957.

Cercamon, *Les Poésies de Cercamon,* ed. Alfred Jeanroy, Paris, 1922.

Chabaneau, Camille, ed., *Les Biographies des Troubadours,* Toulouse, 1885.

Chambers, Frank M., 'Imitation of Form in the Old Provençal Lyric', in *Romance Philology,* VI.2, pp. 104-120.

La Chanson de la Croisade Albigeoise, ed. and tr. Eugène Martin-Chabot, 3 vols.: I, 2nd ed., Paris, 1960; II, Paris, 1957; III, Paris, 1961. Volume III reviewed by Yves Dossat in *Annales du Midi,* LXXIV (1962), pp. 336-337.

La Chanson de la Croisade contre les Albigeois, ed. and tr. Paul Meyer, 3 vols., Paris, 1879.

La Chanson de Roland, ed. and tr. Joseph Bédier, def. ed., Paris, 1964.

Chaplais, Pierre, ed., *Diplomatic Documents Preserved in the Public Record Office,* I: *1101-1271,* London, 1964.

Chaytor, H. J., *From Script to Print: An Introduction to Medieval Vernacular Literature,* Cambridge, 1945.

———, *Savaric de Mauléon: Baron and Troubadour,* Cambridge, 1939.

———, *The Troubadours of Dante: Being Selections from the Works of the Provençal Poets quoted by Dante,* Oxford, 1902.

La Chronique de Rains, ed. Louis Paris, Paris, 1837.

Cipolla, Carlo M., *Money, Prices, and Civilization in the Mediterranean World: Fifth to Seventeenth Century,* Princeton, N.J., 1956.

Clédat, Léon, *Sur le rôle historique de Bertran de Born,* Paris, 1879.

Coghill, N. K., 'Love and "Foul Delight": some contrasted attitudes', in John Lawlor, ed., *Patterns of Love and Courtesy: Essays in Memory of C. S. Lewis,* London, 1966, pp. 141-156.

Cohn, Norman, *The Pursuit of the Millenium,* repr., London, 1970.

Confucius, *Confucian Analects, The Great Learning and The Doctrine of the Mean,* ed. and tr. James Legge, New York, 1971, a photographic reprint of volume I of *The Chinese Classics,* Oxford, 1893, which was the second revised edition.

———, *The Great Digest, The Unwobbling Pivot, The Analects,* tr. Ezra Pound, New York, 1969.

Connolly, Thomas E., 'Ezra Pound's "Near Perigord": The Background of a Poem', in *Comparative Literature,* VIII (Spring 1956), pp. 110-121.

Cornford, F. M., *The Origin of Attic Comedy,* 2nd impr., Cambridge, 1934.

Cumont, Franz, *The Mysteries of Mithra,* London, 1903.

Dando, Marcel, 'The conception of Hell, Purgatory and Paradise in Mediaeval Provençal Literature and in documents relating to the Cathar, Vaudois and other heresies in the South of France,' unpublished Ph.D. dissertation, London University, 1965.

Dante Alighieri, *Dante's Lyric Poetry,* ed. K. Foster and P. Boyde, 2 vols., Oxford, 1967.

———, *La Divina Commedia,* ed. G. A. Scartazzini, 2nd ed., Milan, 1896.

———, *Inferno;* id. *Paradiso;* id. *Purgatorio:* see Dante Alighieri, *La Divina Commedia.*

———, *La Vita Nuova,* ed. T. Casini, 3rd ed., Florence, 1968.

———, *De Vulgari Eloquentia,* ed. A. Meozzi, Milan, 1926.

Davenson, Henri, *Les troubadours,* Paris, 1961.

Davidsohn, Robert, *Firenze ai Tempi di Dante,* tr. E. Dupré-Theseider, Florence, 1929.

———, *Storia di Firenze,* tr. E. Dupré-Theseider, 2nd ed., 9 vols., Florence, 1965.

Davis, G. R. C., *Magna Carta*, 2nd impr. (rev.), London, 1971.

Debenedetti, Santorre, 'Tre secoli di studi provenzali (XVI-XVIII)', in G. Bertoni, ed., *Provenza e Italia: Studi*, Florence, 1930, pp. 143ff.

Dekker, George, *Sailing After Knowledge: The Cantos of Ezra Pound*, London, 1963.

Delaruelle, Etienne, 'L'Etat actuel des études sur le Catharisme', in *Cahiers de Fanjeaux*, 3 (1968), pp. 19-41.

Delisle, Léopold, ed., *Recueil des Actes de Henri II*, 3 vols., Paris, 1909-27.

Del Pra, Mario, *Scoto Eriugena*, 2nd ed., Milan, 1951.

Dembo, L. S., *The Confucian Odes of Ezra Pound: A Critical Appraisal*, London, 1963.

Dick, Kay, ed., *Writers at Work: The Paris Review Interviews*, Harmondsworth, Middx., 1972.

Donaldson, E. Talbot, *Speaking of Chaucer*, London, 1970.

Dondaine, Antoine, 'Les actes du concile albigeois de Saint-Félix-de-Caraman', in *Miscellanea G. Mercati*, 5, Vatican City, 1946 (Studi e Testi, no. 125).

————, ed., *Un traité néo-manichéen du XIIIe siècle: le Liber du duobus principiis, suivi d'un fragment de rituel cathare*, Rome, 1939.

Dossat, Yves, 'A propos du concile cathare de Saint-Félix: les Milingues', in *Cahiers de Fanjeaux*, 3 (1968), pp. 201-214.

————, 'Le "Bûcher de Montségur" et les Bûchers de l'Inquisition', in *Cahiers de Fanjeaux*, 6 (1971), pp. 361-378.

————, 'Les Cathares d'après les documents de l'Inquisition', in *Cahiers de Fanjeaux*, 3 (1968), pp. 71-104.

————, 'La croisade vue par les chroniqueurs', in *Cahiers de Fanjeaux*, 4 (1969), pp. 221-259.

————, 'Le massacre d'Avignonet', in *Cahiers de Fanjeaux*, 6 (1971), pp. 343-359.

————, 'Simon de Montfort', in *Cahiers de Fanjeaux*, 4 (1969), pp. 281-302.

Dragonetti, Roger, '*Aizi* et *aizimen* chez les plus anciens troubadours', in *Mélanges de Linguistique romane et de Philologie médiévale offerts à M. Maurice Delbouille, II: Philologie médiévale*, ed. Madeleine Tyssens, Gembloux, 1964, pp. 127-153.

Dronke, Peter, *Medieval Latin and the Rise of European Love-Lyric*, 2 vols., Oxford, 1965-66.

Dumitrescu, Maria, 'Eble II de Ventadorn et Guillaume IX d'Aquitaine', in *Cahiers de civilisation médiévale*, XI (1968), pp. 379-412.

————, '*L'escola N'Eblon* et ses représentants', in *Mélanges offerts à Rita Lejeune*, 2 vols., Gembloux, 1969, pp. 107-118.

Duncan, Robert, 'The H. D. Book: Part I. Chapter 5', in *Stony Brook*, 1-2 (Fall 1968), pp. 4-19.

————, 'The H. D. Book: Part II. Nights and Days. Chapter 4', in *Caterpillar*, II.2 (Apr 1969), pp. 27-60.

Edwards, J. H., and W. W. Vasse, *Annotated Index to the Cantos of Ezra Pound: Cantos I-LXXXIV*, rev. ed., Berkeley and Los Angeles, 1959.

Eliot, T. S., 'Ezra Pound', in Walter Sutton, ed., *Ezra Pound: A Collection of Critical Essays*, Englewood Cliffs, N.J., 1963.

————, 'Henry James', in Edmund Wilson, ed., *The Shock of Recognition*, rev. ed., New York, 1955, pp. 854-865.

Emery, Clark Mixon, *Ideas Into Action*, Coral Gables, Fla., 1958.

Errante, Guido, *Marcabru e le fonti sacre dell' antica lirica romanza*, Florence, 1948.

Eyton, R. W., *Court, Household and Itinerary of King Henry II*, London, 1878.

Farnell, Ida, *Lives of the Troubadours: translated from the original Provençal*, London, 1896.

Fauriel, C. C., *History of Provençal Poetry*, tr. G. J. Adler, New York, 1860.

Favati, Guido, ed., *Le Biografie trovadoriche*, Bologna, 1961.

Fenollosa, Ernest, *The Chinese Written Character as a Medium for Poetry*, ed. Ezra Pound, repr., San Francisco, n.d.

Fiedler, Leslie A., *Love and Death in the American Novel*, repr., London, 1970.

Frank, Istvan, '"Babariol—babarian" dans Guillaume IX (Notes de philologie pour l'étude des origines lyriques, I)', in *Romania*, LXXIII, pp. 227-234.

————, *Répertoire métrique de la poésie des troubadours*, 2 vols., Paris, 1953-57.

Gallup, Donald, *A Bibliography of Ezra Pound*, 2nd impr. (corr.), London, 1969.

Gaussin, Pierre-Roger, *L'Abbaye de la Chaise-Dieu*, Paris, 1962.

Gennrich, F., *Die altfranzösische Rotruenge*, Halle, 1925.

Gimpel, Jean, *The Cathedral Builders*, tr. Carl F. Barnes, Jr., New York and London, 1961.

Giraldus Cambrensis, *De Principis Instructione*, ed. George F. Warner, in id., *Opera*, ed. J. S. Brewer, 8 vols., London 1861-91, vol. 8.

Girart de Roussillon, Chanson de Geste, ed. W. M. Hackett, 3 vols., Paris, 1953-55.

Girart de Roussillon, Chanson de Geste, tr. Paul Meyer, Paris, 1884.

Giraut de Bornelh, *Sämtliche Lieder des Trobadors Giraut de Bornelh*, ed. A. Kolsen, 2 vols., Halle, 1910-35.

Goldin, Frederick, 'The Array of Perspectives in the Early Courtly Love Lyric', in Joan M. Ferrante and George D. Economou, eds., *In Pursuit of Perfection: Courtly Love in Medieval Literature*, Port Washington, N.Y., 1975, pp. 51-99.

————, ed., *Lyrics of the Troubadours and Trouvères*, Garden City, N.Y., 1973.

————, *The Mirror of Narcissus in the Courtly Love Lyric*, Ithaca, N.Y., 1967.

Gordon, David, 'Thought Built on Sagetrieb', in *Paideuma*, 3.2 (Fall 1974), pp. 169-190 (indexed in *Paideuma* as 'The Sacred Edict').

Gourmont, Remy de, *Les Chevaux de Diomède*, repr., Paris, 1922.

————, *Dante, Béatrice et la Poésie amoureuse*, repr., Paris, 1922.

————, *Le Latin mystique: les poètes de l'antiphonaire et la symbolique au moyen âge*, repr., Paris, 1922.

————, *Lettres à l'Amazone*, repr., Paris, 1922.

————, *Lettres d'un Satyre*, repr., Paris, 1919.

————, *The Natural Philosophy of Love*, tr. Ezra Pound, repr., London, 1957.

————, *Physique de l'Amour*, repr., Paris, 1904.

Griffin, Ernest, '"E. P. Ode Pour L'Election de Son Sépulchre" and Max Plowman's Pamphlet, "The Right to Live"', in *Paideuma*, 5.2 (Fall 1976), pp. 269-273.

Guibert de Nogent, *Self and Society in Medieval France: The Memoirs of Abbot*

Guibert of Nogent (1064?—c. 1125), ed. John F. Benton, New York and Evanston, Ill., 1970.

Guillaume IX Duc d'Aquitaine, *Les chansons de Guillaume IX Duc d'Aquitaine (1071-1127)*, ed. Alfred Jeanroy, Paris, 1913.

Guillaume le Maréchal, *Histoire:* see *L'Histoire de Guillaume le Maréchal.*

Guillemain, Bernard, 'L'Histoire religieuse du Languedoc à la fin du XIIe siècle et au début du XIIIe', in *Annales du Midi,* 83 (1971), pp. 101-117.

Guiraud, Jean, *Histoire de l'Inquisition au Moyen Age,* 2 vols., Paris, 1935-38.

Guiraut von Calanso, *Die Lieder des provenzalischen Trobadors Guiraut von Calanso,* ed. Willy Ernst, Erlangen, 1930.

Hackett, W. M., 'Le problème de "midons"', in I. Cluzel and F. Pirot, eds., *Mélanges de philologie romane dédiés à la mémoire de Jean Boutière (1899-1967),* Liège, 1971, pp. 285-294.

Hankins, John E., [a note on 'E li mestiers ecoutes'], in 'Notes and Queries', in *Paideuma,* 2.1 (Spring 1973), p. 141.

Harrison, Jane E., *Prolegomena to the Study of the Greek Religion,* 3rd ed., Cambridge, 1922.

Hatto, Arthur T., ed., *Eos: An Enquiry into the Theme of Lovers' Meetings and Partings at Dawn in Poetry,* London, The Hague, and Paris, 1965.

Hauvette, H., *La France et la Provence dans l'oeuvre de Dante,* Paris, 1930.

Hesse, Eva, [note on 'e li mestiers ecoutes'], in 'Notes in Answer to Queries', in *Paideuma,* 1.2 (Winter 1972), p. 271.

————, [note on melody in Canto 91], in 'Notes in Answer to Queries', in *Paideuma,* 1.2 (Winter 1972), p. 272.

Higounet, Charles, 'Un grand chapitre de l'histoire du XIIe siècle: la rivalité des maisons de Toulouse et de Barcelone pour la prépondérance méridionale', in *Mélanges d'Histoire du Moyen Age dédiés à la mémoire de Louis Halphen,* Paris, 1951, pp. 313-322.

————, *Histoire de l'Aquitaine,* Toulouse, 1971.

L'Histoire de Guillaume le Maréchal, ed. Paul Meyer, 3 vols., Paris, 1891-94.

Holt, J. C., *Magna Carta,* Cambridge, 1965.

Hugen, D. J., '"...Small Birds of Cyprus"', in *Paideuma,* 3.2 (Fall 1974), pp. 229-238.

Hutchins, Patricia, 'Ezra Pound's "Approach to Paris"', in *Southern Review,* 6 (1970), pp. 340-355.

————, *Ezra Pound's Kensington: An Exploration, 1885-1913,* London, 1965.

Interrogatio Iohannis, in I. von Doellinger, *Beiträge zur Sektengeschichte im Mittelalter,* 2 vols., Munich, 1890, II, pp. 85ff.

James, Henry, *The House of Fiction: Essays on the Novel,* ed. Leon Edel, London, 1957.

Jeanroy, Alfred, *La Poésie lyrique des Troubadours,* 2 vols., Paris, 1934.

Jernigan, Charles, 'The Song of Nail and Uncle: Arnaut Daniel's Sestina "Lo ferm voler q'el cor m'intra"', in *Studies in Philology,* LXXI.2 (Apr 1974), pp. 127-151.

Jones, P. J., *The Malatesta of Rimini and the Papal State: A Political History,* Cambridge, 1974.

Kelly, Amy, *Eleanor of Aquitaine and the Four Kings*, Cambridge, Mass., 1950.

Kennedy, George, 'Fenollosa, Pound, and the Chinese Character', in *Yale Literary Magazine*, CXXVI.5 (Dec 1958, issue entitled *Ezra Pound: A New Montage*), pp. 24-36.

Kenner, Hugh, *A Homemade World: The American Modernist Writers*, New York, 1975.

————, 'The Broken Mirrors and the Mirror of Memory', in Lewis Leary, ed., *Motive and Method in the Cantos of Ezra Pound*, New York, 1961, pp. 3-32.

————, 'D. P. Remembered', in *Paideuma*, 2.3 (Winter 1973), pp. 485-493.

————, *The Pound Era*, Berkeley and Los Angeles, 1971.

Ker, W. P., *Dante, Guido Guinicelli and Arnaut Daniel*, Cambridge, 1909.

Kerényi, K., *Eleusis: Archetypal Image of Mother and Daughter*, tr. R. Mannheim, London, 1967.

Klein, Karen Wilk, *The Partisan Voice: A Study of the Political Lyric in France and Germany 1180-1230*, The Hague, 1971.

————, 'The Political Message of Bertran de Born', in *Studies in Philology*, 65 (1968), pp. 612-630.

Koehler, Erich, 'Observations historiques et sociologiques sur la poésie des troubadours', in *Cahiers de Civilisation médiévale*, VII (1964), pp. 27-51.

Labande, Edmond-René, 'La civilisation de l'Aquitaine à la fin de la période ducale', in *Bulletin du Centre international d'études romanes*, I-II (1964), pp. 15-30.

————, 'Pour une image véridique d'Aliénor d'Aquitaine', in *Bulletin de la Société des antiquaires de l'Ouest*, 4th s., II (1952-54), pp. 175-234.

Lafitte-Houssat, Jacques, *Troubadours et Cours d'Amour*, Paris, 1950.

Lafont, Robert, and Christian Anatole, *Nouvelle Histoire de la Littérature Occitane*, 2 vols., Paris, 1970.

Latreille, A., E. Delaruelle, and J.-R. Palanque, *Histoire du Catholicisme en France*, 3 vols., Paris, 1957.

Lavisse, Ernest, *Histoire de France depuis les Origines à la Révolution*, 9 vols., Paris, 1900-11, III, part I: Achille Luchaire, *Louis VII—Philippe-Auguste— Louis VIII (1137-1226)*, Paris, 1911.

Lawner, Lynne, 'Notes towards an interpretation of the *vers de dreyt nien*', in *Cultura Neolatina*, XXVIII (1968), pp. 147-164.

Lea, Henry Charles, *The Inquisition of the Middle Ages*, London, 1963 (I, chapters VII-XIV of *The History of the Inquisition of the Middle Ages*, 3 vols., London, 1887).

Lefèvre, Yves, 'Bertran de Born et la Littérature française de son temps', in *Mélanges de Langue et de Littérature du moyen âge et de la renaissance offerts à Jean Frappier*, 2 vols., Geneva, 1970, II, pp. 603-609.

Leff, Gordon, *Heresy in the Later Middle Ages: A Study of the Relation of Heterodoxy to Dissent*, London, 1966.

Le Goff, Jacques, ed., *Hérésies et sociétés dans l'Europe pré-industrielle (11e-18e siècles)*, Paris and The Hague, 1968 ('Communications et débats du Colloque de Royaumont').

Lejeune, Rita, 'Formules féodales et style amoureux chez Guillaume IX d'Aquitaine', in *Atti del VIII Congresso internazionale di studi romanzi,* Florence, 1959, 2 vols., Florence, 1960, II, pp. 229-248.

———, 'Rôie littéraire d'Aliénor d'Aquitaine et de sa famille I: Aliénor', in *Cultura Neolatina,* XIV.1 (1954), pp. 5-57.

———, 'Rôle littéraire de la famille d'Aliénor d'Aquitaine', in *Cahiers de Civilisation médiévale,* I (1958), pp. 319-337.

———, and Jacques Stiennon, *La légende de Roland dans l'art du moyen âge,* 2nd ed., 2 vols., Brussels, 1967.

Levy, Emil, *Provenzalisches Supplement-Wörterbuch: Berichtigungen und Ergänzungen zu Raynouards Lexique Roman,* Leipzig, 1894ff.

Liber de Duobus Principiis: see Dondaine, Antoine, ed., *Un traité néo-manichéen du XIIIe siècle: le Liber de duobus principiis, suivi d'un fragment de rituel cathare.*

Lot-Borodine, Myrrha, 'Sur les Origines et les Fins du *Service d'Amour*', in *Mélanges de Linguistique et de Littérature offerts à M. Alfred Jeanroy par ses élèves et ses amis,* Paris, 1928, pp. 223-242.

McDougal, Stuart Y., *Ezra Pound and the Troubadour Tradition,* Princeton, 1972. Reviewed by the present author in *Modern Language Review,* 70.3 (July 1975), pp. 615-617.

Makin, Peter, 'The American Poet Ezra Pound (1885-   ) and Mediaeval provençal Poetry', unpublished Ph.D. dissertation, London University, 1972.

———, 'Ezra Pound and Scotus Erigena', in *Comparative Literature Studies,* X.1 (Mar 1973), pp. 60-83.

———, 'Ezra Pound's Abilities as a Translator of Provençal', in *Poetica* (Tokyo), 4 (Autumn 1975), pp. 111-132.

———, 'Pound's Provence and the Mediaeval Paideuma', in Philip Grover, ed., *Ezra Pound: The London Years, 1908-1920,* New York, 1977, pp. 31-60.

Mâle, Emile, *L'Art religieux du XIIe s. en France: Etude sur les origines de l'iconographie du moyen âge,* 3rd rev. ed., Paris, 1928.

Manselli, Raoul, 'De la "Persuasio" à la "Coercitio"', in *Cahiers de Fanjeaux,* 6 (1971), pp. 175-197.

———, 'Eglises et théologies cathares', in *Cahiers de Fanjeaux,* 3 (1968), pp. 129-176.

Marcabru, *Poésies complètes du troubadour Marcabru,* ed. J.-M.-L. Dejeanne, Toulouse, 1909.

Martindale, Jane P., 'The Origins of the Duchy of Aquitaine', unpublished Ph.D. dissertation, Oxford University, 1965.

Melville, Marion, *La Vie des Templiers,* 3rd ed., Paris, 1951.

Michaud, Joseph François, *Histoire des Croisades,* rev. ed., 4 vols., Paris, 1857.

Molinier, Charles, *Un traité inédit du XIIIe s. contre les hérétiques cathares,* Bordeaux, 1883.

Moore, Olin H., *The Young King, Henry Plantagenet (1155-1183), in History, Literature and Tradition,* Columbus, Ohio, 1925.

Moore, Virginia, *The Unicorn: William Butler Yeats' Search for Reality,* New York, 1954.

Morghen, Raffaello, *Medioevo cristiano,* Bari, 1951.

Mullins, Eustace, *This Difficult Individual, Ezra Pound*, New York, 1961.

Muratori, L. A., *Rerum Italicarum Scriptores: Raccolta degli storici italiani dal cinquecento al millecinquecento*, 2nd ed., Bologna, 1900ff.

Mylonas, George E., *Eleusis and the Eleusinian Mysteries*, Princeton, N.J. and London, [1962].

Nagy, N. Christoph de, *Ezra Pound's Poetics and Literary Tradition: The Critical Decade*, Bern, 1966.

————, *The Poetry of Ezra Pound: The Pre-Imagist Stage*, Bern, 1960.

Nassar, Eugene Paul, *The Cantos of Ezra Pound: The Lyric Mode*, Baltimore and London, 1975.

Nelli, René, ed., *Ecritures cathares: textes cathares et précathares*, Paris, 1959.

————, *L'Erotique des Troubadours*, Toulouse, 1963.

————, *Le Musée du Catharisme*, Paris, 1966.

————, Fernand Niel, J. Duvernoy, and Déodat Roché, *Les Cathares*, Paris, 1965.

Nickson, M. A. E., ed., 'A critical edition of the treatise on heresy ascribed to Pseudo-Reinerius', unpublished Ph.D dissertation, London University, 1962.

Niel, Fernand, *Albigeois et Cathares*, Paris, 1955.

————, *Montségur, temple et forteresse des Cathares d'Occitanie*, Grenoble, 1967.

————, *Le Pog de Montségur*, Toulouse, 1949.

Norgate, Kate, *England Under the Angevin Kings*, 2 vols., London, 1887.

Norman, Charles, *The Case of Ezra Pound*, New York, 1948.

————, *Ezra Pound*, rev. ed., London, 1969.

Noyes, Ella, *The Story of Ferrara*, London, 1904.

Olson, Charles, *Letters for Origin 1950-1956*, ed. Albert Glover, London, 1969.

Oppen, George, *Discrete Series*: see Pound, Ezra, 'Preface: *Discrete Series* by George Oppen'.

Orderic Vitalis, *The Ecclesiastical History of England and Normandy*, tr. Thomas Forester, 4 vols., London, 1854.

————, *The Ecclesiastical History of Orderic Vitalis*, ed. and tr. Marjorie Chibnall, 5 vols., Oxford, 1969ff.

Pacaut, Marcel, *Louis VII et son royaume*, Paris, 1964.

Paden, William D., Jr., et al., 'The Troubadour's Lady: Her Marital Status and Social Rank', in *Studies in Philology*, LXXII.1 (Jan 1975), pp. 28-50.

Paris, Gaston, 'Etudes sur les romans de la table ronde. Lancelot du Lac. II. Le Conte de la Charrette', in *Romania*, XII (1883), pp. 459-534.

————, 'La Légende de Saladin', in *Journal des Savants* (May, June, July, Aug 1893), pp. 284-299, 354-365, 428-438, 486-498.

————, *Mélanges de littérature francaise du moyen âge*, Paris, 1966.

Parker, T. W., *The Knights Templars in England*, Tucson, Ariz., 1963.

Pasero, Nicolo, '*Companho, tant ai agutz d'avols conres* di Guglielmo IX d'Aquitania e il tema dell' amore invincibile', in *Cultura Neolatina*, XXVII (1967), pp. 19-29.

————, '*Devinalh*, "non-senso" e "interiorizzazione testuale": osservazioni sui rapporti fra strutture formali e contenuti ideologici nella poesia provenzale', in *Cultura Neolatina*, XXVIII (1968), pp. 113-146.

Paterson, Linda M., *Troubadours and Eloquence*, Oxford, 1975.

Pearlman, Daniel, *The Barb of Time,* New York, 1970.

Pearsall, Derek A., and Elizabeth Salter, *Landscapes and Seasons of the Medieval World,* London, 1973.

Peck, John, 'Landscape as Ceremony in the Later *Cantos:* From "The Roads of France" to "Rock's World"', in *Agenda,* 9.2-3 (Spring-Summer, 1971), pp. 26-69.

Peire Bremon Ricas Novas, *Les Poésies du troubadour Peire Bremon Ricas Novas,* ed. Jean Boutière, Toulouse and Paris, 1930.

Peire Cardenal, *Poésies complétes du troubadour Peire Cardenal (1180-1278),* ed. Rene Lavaud, Toulouse, 1957.

Peire Vidal, *Poésie,* ed. D'Arco Silvio Avalle, 2 vols., Milan and Naples, 1960.

Péladan, Josephin Aimé [known as] Sâr, *Le Secret des Troubadours,* Paris, 1906.

Perdrizet, Paul, *La Vierge de Misèricorde,* Paris, 1908.

Peters, Edward, ed., *The First Crusade: The Chronicle of Fulcher of Chartres and Other Source Materials,* Philadelphia, 1971.

Pocock, J. G. A., *The Ancient Constitution and the Feudal Law: A Study of English Historical Thought in the Seventeenth Century,* repr., New York, 1967.

Pound, Ezra, *ABC of Reading,* repr., London, 1961.

———, *Antheil and the Treatise on Harmony,* Paris 1924.

———, 'The Approach to Paris...II', in *New Age,* XIII.20 (11 Sept 1913), pp. 577-579.

———, 'Arnaut Daniel (Razo)', in *Art & Letters,* N.S., III.2 (Spring 1920), pp. 44-49. Reprinted as part I of 'Arnaut Daniel', in *Essays,* pp. 109-115.

———, *The Cantos of Ezra Pound,* London, 1964 ('New Collected' ed., Cantos 1-109).

———, *The Cantos of Ezra Pound,* London, 1975 ('Revised Collected' ed., Cantos 1-117).

———, *The Cantos of Ezra Pound,* New York, 1970.

———, 'Cavalcanti', in *Essays,* pp. 149-200. For details of first publication see Gallup, *A Bibliography of Ezra Pound,* A36, etc.

———, *Collected Early Poems of Ezra Pound,* ed. Michael King, intr. Louis L. Martz, London, 1976.

———, *Confucius; Confucius/Analects; Confucius/Digest; Confucius/Pivot:* see Confucius, *The Great Digest, The Unwobbling Pivot, The Analects.*

Pound, Ezra, and Marcella Spann, edd., *Confucius to Cummings: An Anthology of Poetry,* New York 1964.

———, *'Dompna pois de me no'us cal':* see Pound, Ezra, *A Translation from the Provençal of En Bertrans de Born.*

———, *Drafts and Fragments of Cantos CX-CXVII,* London, 1970.

———, *Essays:* see Pound, Ezra, *Literary Essays of Ezra Pound.*

———, *Gaudier-Brzeska: A Memoir,* enl. ed., Hessle, Yorks., 1960.

———, *Gold and Labour,* tr. John Drummond, London, [1952].

———, *Guide to Kulchur,* repr., London, 1966.

———, *Hesternae Rosae:* see Rummel, Walter Morse, *Hesternae Rosae.*

———, *Homage to Sextus Propertius,* in J. P. Sullivan, *Ezra Pound and Sextus Propertius: A Study in Creative Translation,* London, 1965, pp. 115-171.

———, 'How I Began', in *T. P.'s Weekly*, XXI.552 (6 June 1913), p. 707. Reproduced in Noel Stock, ed., *Ezra Pound Perspectives: Essays in Honour of his Eightieth Birthday*, Chicago, 1965, p. 1.

———, 'I Gather the Limbs of Osiris III', in *New Age*, X.7 (14 Dec 1911), pp. 155-156.

———, 'I Gather the Limbs of Osiris IV: A Beginning', in *New Age*, X.8 (21 Dec 1911), pp. 178-180.

———, 'I Gather the Limbs of Osiris V: Four Early Poems of Arnaut Daniel', in *New Age*, X.9 (28 Dec 1911), pp. 201-202.

———, 'I Gather the Limbs of Osiris VI: On Virtue', in *New Age*, X.10 (4 Jan 1912), pp. 224-225.

———, 'I Gather the Limbs of Osiris IX: On Technique', in *New Age*, X.13 (25 Jan 1912), pp. 297-299.

———, 'I Gather the Limbs of Osiris XI', in *New Age*, X.16 (15 Feb 1912), pp. 369-370.

———, *Impact: Essays on Ignorance and the Decline of American Civilization*, ed. Noel Stock, Chicago, 1960.

———, 'Interesting French Publications', in *Philadelphia Book News Monthly*, XXV.1 (Sept 1906), pp. 54-55.

———, *Jefferson and/or Mussolini: L'Idea statale: Fascism As I Have Seen It*, New York, 1936.

———, *Kulchur:* see Pound, Ezra, *Guide to Kulchur.*

———, *Letters:* see Pound, Ezra, *The Selected Letters of Ezra Pound 1907-1941.*

———, *Literary Essays of Ezra Pound*, ed. T. S. Eliot, repr., London, 1960.

———, *Make It New: Essays by Ezra Pound*, London, 1934.

———, 'Mediaeval Music and Yves Tinayre', in *Listener*, XVI.395 (22 July 1936), pp. 187-188.

———, *Near Perigord*, in *Poetry*, VII.3 (Dec 1915), pp. 111-119.

———, 'On "Near Perigord"', in *Poetry*, VII.3 (Dec 1915), pp. 143-146.

———, 'Pastiche. The Regional. VIII', in *New Age*, XXV.18 (28 Aug 1919), p. 300.

———, 'Pastiche. The Regional. IX', in *New Age*, XXV.17 (21 Aug 1919), p. 284.

———, 'Pastiche. The Regional. XVIII', in *New Age*, XXVI.3 (20 Nov 1919), p. 48.

———, *Patria Mia and the Treatise on Harmony*, London, 1962.

———, *Pavannes and Divisions*, New York, 1918.

———, 'Preface: *Discrete Series* by George Oppen', reprinted in *Stony Brook*, 3-4 (1969), p. 21, from George Oppen, *Discrete Series*, New York, 1934, pp. v-vi.

———, 'Psychology and Troubadours', in *Quest*, IV.1 (Oct 1912), pp. 37-53. Reprinted with changes in *Spirit*, pp. 87-100.

———, *The Selected Letters of Ezra Pound 1907-1941*, ed. D. D. Paige, repr., New York, 1971.

———, *Selected Poems*, ed. T. S. Eliot, repr., London, 1959.

———, *Selected Prose 1909-1965*, ed. William Cookson, repr., New York, 1975.

———, *The Sixth Canto*, in *Poems 1918-21, including Three Portraits and Four Cantos*, New York, 1921, pp. 83-86.

————, *Social Credit: An Impact,* London, 1951.

————, *The Spirit of Romance: An Attempt to Define Somewhat the Charm of the Pre-Renaissance Literature of Latin Europe,* London, 1910. This edition is referred to only where so indicated; otherwise reference is to the following.

————, *The Spirit of Romance,* 3rd ed., repr., New York, 1968.

————, tr., *Ta Hio: The Great Learning,* Seattle, 1928.

————, 'Terra Italica', in *New Review,* I.4 (Winter 1931-32), pp. 386-389.

————, *Three Cantos: I,* in *Poetry,* X.3 (June 1917), pp. 113-121.

————, *Three Cantos: II,* in *Poetry,* X.4 (July 1917), pp. 180-188.

————, *Three Cantos: III,* in *Poetry,* X.5 (Aug. 1917), pp. 248-254.

————, *Three Cantos of a Poem of Some Length: I,* in Ezra Pound, *Lustra of Ezra Pound,* New York, 1917, pp. 180-187.

————, *Three Cantos of a Poem of Some Length: III,* in Ezra Pound, *Lustra of Ezra Pound,* New York, 1917, pp. 195-202.

————, *A Translation from the Provencal of En Bertrans de Born,* in *Poetry and Drama,* II.1 (Mar 1914), pp. 22-24.

————, *Translations,* enl. ed., New York, 1963.

————, 'Troubadours: Their Sorts and Conditions', in *Quarterly Review,* CCXIX. 437 (Oct 1913), pp. 426-440. Reprinted with minor changes in *Essays,* pp. 94-108.

————, *A Visiting Card,* London, 1952.

————, 'Vortex. Pound', in *Blast,* I (20 June 1914), pp. 153-154.

————, and Marcella Spann, eds., *Confucius to Cummings: An Anthology of Poetry,* New York, 1964.

Quinn, (Sister) M. Bernetta, 'The Metamorphoses of Ezra Pound', in Lewis Leary, ed., *Motive and Method in the Cantos of Ezra Pound,* New York, 1961.

Rachewiltz, Boris de, 'Pagan and Magical Elements in Ezra Pound's Works', in Eva Hesse, ed., *New Approaches to Ezra Pound: A Co-Ordinated Investigation of Pound's Poetry and Ideas,* London, 1969, pp. 174-197.

Rachewiltz, Mary de, *Discretions: A Memoir by Ezra Pound's Daughter,* London, 1971.

Rahner, Hugo, *Greek Myths and Christian Mystery,* London, 1963.

Raimbaut d'Orange, *The Life and Works of the Troubadour Raimbaut d'Orange,* ed. W. T. Pattison, Minneapolis, 1952.

Raimbaut de Vaqueiras, *The Poems of the Troubadour Raimbaut de Vaqueiras,* ed. J. Linskill, The Hague, 1964.

Raimon de Miraval, *Les Poésies du Troubadour Raimon de Miraval,* ed. L. T. Topsfield, Paris, 1971.

Rajna, Pio, 'Guglielmo conte di Poitiers, trovatore bifronte', in *Mélanges de Linguistique et de Littérature offerts à M. Alfred Jeanroy par ses élèves et ses amis,* Paris, 1928, pp. 349-360.

————, 'Spigolature provenzali. II: La badia di Niort', in *Romania,* VI, pp. 249-360.

Rakosi, Carl, 'A Note on the "Objectivists": Feb 8, 1969', in *Stony Brook,* 3-4 (1969), pp. 36-37.

Ramsay, (Sir) James H., *The Angevin Empire: Or the Three Reigns of Henry II, Richard I, and John (A.D. 1154-1216)*, London, 1903.

———, *The Foundations of England: Or Twelve Centuries of British History (B.C. 55-A.D. 1154)*, 2 vols., London, 1898.

Raynouard, M., *Lexique Roman, ou Dictionnaire de la Langue des Troubadours...*, 6 vols., Paris, 1838-44.

Récits d'un Ménestrel de Reims, ed. N. de Wailly, Paris, 1876.

Richard, Alfred, *Histoire des Comtes de Poitou (778-1204)*, 2 vols., Paris, 1903.

Robert de Torigni, *Chronique de Robert de Torigni, Abbé du Mont-Saint-Michel*, ed. Léopold Delisle, 2 vols., Rouen, 1872-73.

Robertson, D. W., *A Preface to Chaucer: Studies in Medieval Perspectives*, Princeton, N.J. and London, 1963.

Rochester: see Wilmot, John, Earl of Rochester.

Roland, ed. Bédier: see *La Chanson de Roland*.

Roncaglia, Aurelio, 'Obediens', in *Mélanges de Linguistique romane et de Philologie médiévale offerts à M. Maurice Delbouille*, II: *Philologie Médiévale*, ed. Madeleine Tyssens, Gembloux, 1964, pp. 597-614.

Rossetti, Dante Gabriel, *Il mistero dell'amor platonico nel medioevo*, 5 vols., London, 1840.

Rougemont, Denis de, *L'Amour et l'Occident*, Paris, 1939.

Rummel, Walter Morse, *Haesternae [i.e. Hesternae] Rosae. Serta II. Neuf Chansons de Troubadours*, London, 1913.

Runciman, Steven, *The Medieval Manichee*, 2nd ed., Cambridge, 1955.

Russell, Jeffrey Burton, *Dissent and Reform in the Early Middle Ages*, Berkeley and Los Angeles, 1965.

Russell, Peter, ed., *An Examination of Ezra Pound: A Collection of Essays*, rev. ed., New York, 1973.

Ruthven, K. K., *A Guide to Ezra Pound's 'Personae' (1926)*, Berkeley and Los Angeles, 1969.

Santangelo, Salvatore, *Dante e i trovatori provenzali*, 2nd ed., Catania, 1959.

Schon, Donald, 'Dynamic Conservatism' (Reith Lecture), in *Listener*, 84.2174 (26 Nov 1970), pp. 724-728.

Schmidt, Charles G. A., *Histoire et doctrine de la secte des Cathares ou Albigeois*, 2 vols., Paris, 1848-49.

Schrötter, Wilibald, *Ovid und die Troubadours*, Halle, 1908.

Schultz-Gora, O., *Altprovenzalisches Elementarbuch*, Heidelberg, 1906.

Schutz, A. H., 'Pound as Provençalist', in *Romance Notes*, III.2 (1962), pp. 58-63.

The Seafarer, ed. I. L. Gordon, London, 1960.

Setton, Kenneth M., editor-in-chief, *A History of the Crusades*, I: *The First Hundred Years*, ed. Marshall W. Baldwin, Philadelphia, 1955.

Slatin, Myles, 'A History of Pound's *Cantos* I-XVI, 1915-1925', in *American Literature*, 35 (May 1963), pp. 183-195.

Smith, Justin H., *The Troubadours at Home*, New York and London, 1899.

Sophocles, *Women of Trachis*, tr. Ezra Pound, repr., London, 1969.

Sordello, *Le Poesie*, ed. Marco Boni, Bologna, 1954.

————, *Vita e Poesie di Sordello di Goito,* ed. Cesare de Lollis, Halle, 1896.

Spitzer, Leo, 'The Mozarabic Lyric and Theodor Frings' Theories', in *Comparative Literature,* IV.1 (Winter 1952), pp. 1-22.

Starkie, Enid, *From Gautier to Eliot: The Influence of France on English Literature 1851-1939,* London, 1960.

Stock, Noel, ed., *Ezra Pound Perspectives: Essays in Honour of his Eightieth Birthday,* Chicago, 1965.

————, *The Life of Ezra Pound,* London, 1970.

————, *Poet in Exile: Ezra Pound,* Manchester, 1964.

————, *Reading the Cantos: A Study of Meaning in Ezra Pound,* repr., New York, 1968.

Storr, Anthony, *Jung,* London, 1973.

Stronski, Stanislaw, *La légende amoureuse de Bertran de Born,* Paris, 1914.

————, *Le troubadour Folquet de Marseille, édition critique,* Cracow, 1910.

Terrell, Carroll F., 'The Sacred Edict of K'ang-Hsi', in *Paideuma,* 2.1 (Spring 1973), pp. 69-112.

Thouzellier, Christine, *Catharisme et Valdéisme en Languedoc à la fin du XIIe et au début du XIIIe s.,* Paris, 1966.

Topsfield, L. T., *Troubadours and Love,* Cambridge, 1975.

Uc de Saint-Circ, *Poésies de Uc de Saint-Circ,* ed. Alfred Jeanroy and J.-J. Salverda de Grave, Toulouse, 1913.

Valli, Luigi, *Il Linguaggio Segreto di Dante e dei 'Fedeli d'Amore',* 2 vols., Rome, 1928-30.

[Vanel], *Intrigues galantes de la Cour de France,* 2 vols., Cologne [a fictitious imprint], 1694.

Vicaire, Marie-Humbert, 'Les Cathares albigeois vus par les polémistes', in *Cahiers de Fanjeaux,* 3 (1968), pp. 105-128.

Veith, David M., *Attribution in Restoration Poetry: A Study of Rochester's 'Poems' of 1680,* New Haven, Conn. and London, 1963.

Villon, Francois, *Oeuvres,* ed. A. Longnon, Paris, 1932.

Viscardi, Antonio, *Storia delle Letterature d'Oc e d'Oil,* 3rd ed., repr., Milan, 1962.

Walker, Curtis Howe, *Eleanor of Aquitaine,* Chapel Hill, N.C., 1950.

Warren, W. L., *Henry II,* London, 1974.

————, *King John,* repr., Harmondsworth, Middx., 1966.

Widengren, Geo, *Mani and Manichaeism,* tr. Charles Kessler, London, 1965.

Wilhelm, James J., *The Cruelest Month: Spring, Nature and Love in Classical and Medieval Lyrics,* New Haven, Conn. and London, 1965.

————, *Dante and Pound: The Epic of Judgement,* Orono, Maine, 1974.

————, [note on melody in Canto 91], in 'Notes and Queries', in *Paideuma,* 2.2 (Fall 1973), pp. 333-335.

Wilmot, John, Earl of Rochester, *The Complete Poems of John Wilmot, Earl of Rochester,* ed. David M. Vieth, New Haven, Conn. and London, 1968.

————, *The Gyldenstolpe Manuscript Miscellany of Poems by John Wilmot, Earl of Rochester, and other Restoration Authors,* ed. Bror Danielsson and David M. Vieth, Stockholm, 1967.

Wolff, Philippe, ed., *Documents de l'Histoire du Languedoc,* Toulouse, 1969.

Zaehner, R. C., *The Dawn and Twilight of Zoroastrianism,* London, 1961.

Zamboni, Filippo, *Gli Ezzelini, Dante e gli schiavi,* Florence, 1902.

Zeller, Berthold, and Achille Luchaire, *Philippe Auguste et Louis VIII: la royauté conquérante,* Paris, 1884.

Zielinski, Tadeusz, *La Sibylle,* Paris, 1925.

Zukofsky, Louis, *Prepositions: The Collected Critical Essays of Louis Zukofsky,* London, 1967.

———, 'Sincerity and Objectification', in *Poetry,* XXXVII.5 (Feb 1931), pp. 272-285.

Zumthor, Paul, *Langue et techniques poétiques à l'époque romane (XIe-XIIIe siècles),* Paris, 1963.

INDEX

❧❧❧❧❧❧❧❧❧❧

409